William Sanday, Walter R. Cassels

The Gospels in the Second Century

an examination of the critical part of a work entitled Supernatural religion

William Sanday, Walter R. Cassels

The Gospels in the Second Century
an examination of the critical part of a work entitled Supernatural religion

ISBN/EAN: 9783337285319

Printed in Europe, USA, Canada, Australia, Japan

Cover: Foto ©Lupo / pixelio.de

More available books at **www.hansebooks.com**

THE GOSPELS

IN THE SECOND CENTURY

IN THE

SECOND CENTURY

AN EXAMINATION OF THE CRITICAL PART OF A WORK

ENTITLED 'SUPERNATURAL RELIGION'

BY

W. SANDAY, M.A.

Rector of Barton-on-the-Heath, Warwickshire; and late Fellow of Trinity College, Oxford
Author of a Work on the Fourth Gospel

London

MACMILLAN AND CO.

1876

OXFORD:
Printed by E. Pickard Hall and J. H. Stacy.
PRINTERS TO THE UNIVERSITY.

I HAD HOPED TO INSCRIBE IN THIS BOOK THE REVERED AND CHERISHED NAME OF MY OLD HEAD MASTER, DR. PEARS OF REPTON. HIS CONSENT HAD BEEN VERY KINDLY AND WARMLY GIVEN, AND I WAS JUST ON THE POINT OF SENDING THE DEDICATION TO THE PRINTERS WHEN I RECEIVED A TELEGRAM NAMING THE DAY AND HOUR OF HIS FUNERAL. HIS HEALTH HAD FOR SOME TIME SINCE HIS RESIGNATION OF REPTON BEEN SERIOUSLY FAILING, BUT I HAD NOT ANTICIPATED THAT THE END WAS SO NEAR. ALL WHO KNEW HIM WILL DEPLORE HIS TOO EARLY LOSS, AND THEIR REGRET WILL BE SHARED BY THE WIDER CIRCLE OF THOSE WHO CAN APPRECIATE A LIFE IN WHICH THERE WAS NOTHING IGNOBLE, NOTHING UNGENEROUS, NOTHING UNREAL. I HAD LONG WISHED THAT HE SHOULD RECEIVE SOME TRIBUTE OF REGARD FROM ONE WHOM HE HAD DONE HIS BEST BY PRECEPT, AND STILL MORE BY EXAMPLE, TO FIT AND TRAIN FOR HIS PLACE AND DUTY IN THE WORLD. THIS PLEASURE AND THIS HONOUR HAVE BEEN DENIED ME. I CANNOT PLACE MY BOOK, AS I HAD HOPED, IN HIS HAND, BUT I MAY STILL LAY IT REVERENTLY UPON HIS TOMB.

CONTENTS.

CHAP.		AGE
I.	INTRODUCTORY	1
II.	ON QUOTATIONS GENERALLY IN THE EARLY CHRISTIAN WRITERS	15
III.	THE APOSTOLIC FATHERS	58
IV.	JUSTIN MARTYR	88
V.	HEGESIPPUS—PAPIAS	138
VI.	THE CLEMENTINE HOMILIES	161
VII.	BASILIDES AND VALENTINUS	188
VIII.	MARCION	204
IX.	TATIAN - DIONYSIUS OF CORINTH	238
X.	MELITO—APOLLINARIS—ATHENAGORAS THE EPISTLE OF VIENNE AND LYONS	244
XI.	PTOLEMAEUS AND HERACLEON CELSUS—THE MURATORIAN FRAGMENT	254
XII.	THE EXTERNAL EVIDENCE FOR THE FOURTH GOSPEL	269
XIII.	ON THE STATE OF THE CANON IN THE LAST QUARTER OF THE SECOND CENTURY	310
XIV.	CONCLUSION	350
APPENDIX.	SUPPLEMENTAL NOTE ON THE RECONSTRUCTION OF MARCION'S GOSPEL	362
INDICES		373

PREFACE.

It will be well to explain at once that the following work has been written at the request and is published at the cost of the Christian Evidence Society, and that it may therefore be classed under the head of Apologetics. I am aware that this will be a drawback to it in the eyes of some, and I confess that it is not altogether a recommendation in my own.

Ideally speaking, Apologetics ought to have no existence distinct from the general and unanimous search for truth, and in so far as they tend to put any other consideration, no matter how high or pure in itself, in the place of truth, they must needs stand aside from the path of science.

But, on the other hand, the question of true belief itself is immensely wide. It is impossible to approach what is merely a branch of a vast subject without some general conclusions already formed as to the whole. The mind cannot, if it would, become a sheet of blank paper on which the writing is inscribed by an external process alone. It must needs have its *praejudicia*—i.e. judgments formed on grounds extrinsic to the special matter of enquiry—of one sort or another. Accordingly we find that an absolutely and strictly impartial temper never has existed and never will. If it did, its verdict would still be false, because it would represent an incomplete or half-suppressed humanity. There is no question that touches, directly or indirectly, on the moral and spiritual nature of man that can be settled by the bare reason. A certain amount of sympathy is necessary in order to estimate the weight of the forces that are to be analysed: yet that very sympathy itself becomes an extraneous influence, and the perfect balance and adjustment of the reason is disturbed.

But though impartiality, in the strict sense, is not to be had, there is another condition that may be rightly demanded—resolute honesty. This I hope may be attained as well from one point of view as from another, at least that there is no very great antecedent reason to the contrary. In past generations indeed there was such a reason. Strongly negative views could only be expressed at considerable personal risk and loss. But now, public opinion is so tolerant, especially among the reading and thinking classes, that both parties are practically upon much the same footing. Indeed for bold and strong and less sensitive minds negative views will have an attraction and will find support that will go far to neutralise any counterbalancing disadvantage.

On either side the remedy for the effects of bias must be found in a rigorous and searching criticism. If misleading statements and unsound arguments are allowed to pass unchallenged the fault will not lie only with their author.

It will be hardly necessary for me to say that the Christian Evidence Society is not responsible for the contents of this work, except in so far as may be involved in the original request that I should write it. I undertook the task at first with some hesitation, and I could not have undertaken it at all without stipulating for entire freedom. The Society very kindly and liberally granted me this, and I am conscious of having to some extent availed myself of it. I have not always stayed to consider whether the opinions expressed were in exact accordance with those of the majority of Christians. It will be enough if they should find points of contact in some minds, and the tentative element in them will perhaps be the more indulgently judged now that the reconciliation of the different branches of knowledge and belief is being so anxiously sought for.

The instrument of the enquiry had to be fashioned as the enquiry itself went on, and I suspect that the consequences of this will be apparent in some inequality and incompleteness in the earlier portions. For instance, I am afraid that the textual analysis of the quotations in Justin may seem somewhat less satisfactory than that of those in the Clementine Homilies, though Justin's quotations are the more important of the two. Still I hope that the treatment of the first may be, for the scale of the book, sufficiently adequate. There seemed to be a certain advantage in presenting the results of the enquiry in the order in which it was conducted. If time and strength are allowed me, I hope to be able to carry several of the investigations that are begun in this book some stages further.

I ought perhaps to explain that I was prevented by other engagements from beginning seriously to work upon the subject until the latter end of December in last year. The first of Dr. Lightfoot's articles in the Contemporary Review had then appeared. The next two articles (on the Silence of Eusebius and the Ignatian Epistles) were also in advance of my own treatment of the same topics. From this point onwards I was usually the first to finish, and I have been compelled merely to allude to the progress of the controversy in notes. Seeing the turn that Dr. Lightfoot's review was taking, and knowing how utterly vain it would be for any one else to go over the same ground, I felt myself more at liberty to follow a natural bent in confining myself pretty closely to the internal aspect of the enquiry. My object has been chiefly to test in detail the alleged quotations from our Gospels, while Dr. Lightfoot has taken a wider sweep in collecting and bringing to bear the collateral matter of which his unrivalled knowledge of the early Christian literature gave him such command. It will be seen that in some cases, as notably in regard to the evidence of Papias, the external and the internal methods have led to an opposite result; and I shall look forward with much interest to the further discussion of this subject.

I should be sorry to ignore the debt I am under to the author of 'Supernatural Religion' for the copious materials he has supplied to criticism. I have also to thank him for his courtesy in sending me a copy of the sixth edition of his work. My obligations to other writers I hope will be found duly acknowledged. If I were to single out the one book to which I owed most, it would probably be Credner's 'Beiträge zur Einleitung in die Biblischen Schriften,' of which I have spoken somewhat fully in an early chapter. I have used a certain amount of discretion and economy in avoiding as a rule the works of previous apologists (such as Semisch, Riggenbach, Norton, Hofstede de Groot) and consulting rather those of an opposite school in such representatives as Hilgenfeld and Volkmar. In this way, though I may very possibly have omitted some arguments which may be sound, I hope I shall have put forward few that have been already tried and found wanting.

As I have made rather large use of the argument supplied by text-criticism, I should perhaps say that to the best of my belief my attention was first drawn to its importance by a note in Dr. Lightfoot's work on Revision. The evidence adduced under this head will be found, I believe, to be independent of any particular theory of text-criticism. The idea of the Analytical Index is taken, with some change of plan, from Volkmar. It may serve to give a sort of *coup d'œil* of the subject.

It is a pleasure to be able to mention another form of assistance from which it is one of the misfortunes of an anonymous writer to find himself cut off. The proofs of this book have been seen in their passage through the press by my friend the Rev. A. J. Mason, Fellow of Trinity College, Cambridge, whose exact scholarship has been particularly valuable to me. On another side than that of scholarship I have derived the greatest benefit from the advice of my friend James Beddard, M.B., of Nottingham, who was among the first to help me to realise, and now does not suffer me to forget, what a book ought to be. The Index of References to the Gospels has also been made for me.

The chapter on Marcion has already appeared, substantially in its present form, as a contribution to the Fortnightly Review.

BARTON-ON-THE-HEATH,
SHIPSTON-ON-STOUR,
November, 1875.

τὰ δὲ πάντα ἐλεγχόμενα ὑπὸ τοῦ φωτὸς φανεροῦται·
πᾶν γὰρ τὸ φανερούμενον φῶς ἐστιν.

ERRATA.

P. 70, l. 21, *for* 'fourth' *read* 'first.'
P. 197, l. 1, *for* 'Mark viii. 34' *read* 'Luke xiv. 27.'

CHAPTER I.

INTRODUCTORY.

It would be natural in a work of this kind, which is a direct review of a particular book, to begin with an account of that book, and with some attempt to characterise it. Such had been my own intention, but there seems to be sufficient reason for pursuing a different course. On the one hand, an account of a book which has so recently appeared, which has been so fully reviewed, and which has excited so much attention, would appear to be superfluous; and, on the other hand, as the character of it has become the subject of somewhat sharp controversy, and as controversy—or at least the controversial temper—is the one thing that I wish to avoid, I have thought it well on the whole to abandon my first intention, and to confine myself as much as possible to a criticism of the argument and subject-matter, with a view to ascertain the real facts as to the formation of the Canon of the four Gospels.

I shall correct, where I am able to do so, such mistakes as may happen to come under my notice and have not already been pointed out by other reviewers, only dilating upon them where what seem to be false principles of criticism are involved. On the general subject of these mistakes—misleading references and the like—I think that enough has been said[1]. Much is perhaps charged upon the individual which is rather due to the system of theological training and the habits of research that are common in England at the present day. Inaccuracies no doubt have been found, not a few. But, unfortunately, there is only one of our seats of learning where—in theology at least—the study of accuracy has quite the place that it deserves. Our best scholars and ablest men—with one or two conspicuous exceptions—do not write, and the work is left to be done by *littérateurs* and clergymen or laymen who have never undergone the severe preliminary discipline which scientific investigation requires. Thus a low standard is set; there are but few sound examples to follow, and it is a chance whether the student's attention is directed to these at the time when his habits of mind are being formed.

Again, it was claimed for 'Supernatural Religion' on its first appearance that it was impartial. The

---

[1] With regard to the references in vol. i. p. 259, n. 1, I had already observed, before the appearance of the preface to the sixth edition, that they were really intended to apply to the first part of the sentence annotated rather than the second. Still, as there is only one reference out of nine that really supports the proposition in immediate connection with which the references are made, the reader would be very apt to carry away a mistaken impression. The same must be said of the set of references defended on p. xl. sqq. of the new preface. The expressions used do not accurately represent the state of the facts. It is not careful writing, and I am afraid it must be said that the prejudice of the author has determined the side to which the expression leans. But how difficult is it to make words express all the due shades and qualifications of meaning—how difficult especially for a mind that seems to be naturally distinguished by force rather than by exactness and delicacy of observation! We have all 'les défauts de nos qualités.'

claim has been indignantly denied, and, I am afraid I must say, with justice. Any one conversant with the subject (I speak of the critical portion of the book) will see that it is deeply coloured by the author's prepossessions from beginning to end. Here again he has only imbibed the temper of the nation. Perhaps it is due to our political activity and the system of party-government that the spirit of party seems to have taken such a deep root in the English mind. An Englishman's political opinions are determined for him mainly (though sometimes in the way of reaction) by his antecedents and education, and his opinions on other subjects follow in their train. He takes them up with more of practical vigour and energy than breadth of reflection. There is a contagion of party-spirit in the air. And thus advocacy on one side is simply met by advocacy on the other. Such has at least been hitherto the history of English thought upon most great subjects. We may hope that at last this state of things is coming to an end. But until now, and even now, it has been difficult to find that quiet atmosphere in which alone true criticism can flourish.

Let it not be thought that these few remarks are made in a spirit of censoriousness. They are made by one who is only too conscious of being subject to the very same conditions, and who knows not how far he may need indulgence on the same score himself. How far his own work is tainted with the spirit of advocacy it is not for him to say. He knows well that the author whom he has set himself to criticise is at least a writer of remarkable vigour and ability, and that he cannot lay claim to these qualities; but he has confidence in the power of truth—whatever that truth may be—to assert itself in the end. An open and fair field and full and free criticism are all that is needed to eliminate the effects of individual strength or weakness. 'The opinions of good men are but knowledge in the making'—especially where they are based upon a survey of the original facts. Mistakes will be made and have currency for a time. But little by little truth emerges; it receives the suffrages of those who are competent to judge; gradually the controversy narrows; parts of it are closed up entirely, and a solid and permanent advance is made.

The author of 'Supernatural Religion' starts from a rigid and somewhat antiquated view of Revelation—Revelation is a direct and external communication by God to man of truths undiscoverable by human reason. The divine origin of this communication is proved by miracles. Miracles are proved by the record of Scripture, which, in its turn, is attested by the history of the Canon.—This is certainly the kind of theory which was in favour at the end of the last century, and found expression in works like Paley's Evidences. It belongs to a time of vigorous and clear but mechanical and narrow culture, when the philosophy of religion was made up of abrupt and violent contrasts; when Christianity (including under that name the Old Testament as well as the New) was thought to be simply true and all other religions simply false; when the revelation of divine truth was thought to be as sudden and complete as the act of creation; and when the presence of any local and temporary elements in the Christian documents or society was ignored.

The world has undergone a great change since then.

A new and far-reaching philosophy is gradually displacing the old. The Christian sees that evolution is as much a law of religion as of nature. The Ethnic, or non-Christian, religions are no longer treated as outside the pale of the Divine government. Each falls into its place as part of a vast divinely appointed scheme, of the character of which we are beginning to have some faint glimmerings. Other religions are seen to be correlated to Christianity much as the other tentative efforts of nature are correlated to man. A divine operation, and what from our limited human point of view we should call a *special* divine operation, is not excluded but rather implied in the physical process by which man has been planted on the earth, and it is still more evidently implied in the corresponding process of his spiritual enlightenment. The deeper and more comprehensive view that we have been led to take as to the dealings of Providence has not by any means been followed by a depreciation of Christianity. Rather it appears on a loftier height than ever. The spiritual movements of recent times have opened men's eyes more and more to its supreme spiritual excellence. It is no longer possible to resolve it into a mere 'code of morals.' The Christian ethics grow organically out of the relations which Christianity assumes between God and man, and in their fulness are inseparable from those relations. The author of 'Supernatural Religion' speaks as if they were separable, as if a man could assume all the Christian graces merely by wishing to assume them. But he forgets the root of the whole Christian system, 'Except ye be converted and become as little children, ye shall in no case enter into the kingdom of heaven.'

The old idea of the *Aufklärung* that Christianity was nothing more than a code of morals, has now long ago been given up, and the self-complacency which characterised that movement has for the most part, though not entirely, passed away. The nineteenth century is not in very many quarters regarded as the goal of things. And it will hardly now be maintained that Christianity is adequately represented by any of the many sects and parties embraced under the name. When we turn from even the best of these, in its best and highest embodiment, to the picture that is put before us in the Gospels, how small does it seem! We feel that they all fall short of their ideal, and that there is a greater promise and potentiality of perfection in the root than has ever yet appeared in branch or flower.

No doubt theology follows philosophy. The special conception of the relation of man to God naturally takes its colour from the wider conception as to the nature of all knowledge and the relation of God to the universe. It has been so in every age, and it must needs be so now. Some readjustment, perhaps a considerable readjustment, of theological and scientific beliefs may be necessary. But there is, I think, a strong presumption that the changes involved in theology will be less radical than often seems to be supposed. When we look back upon history, the world has gone through many similar crises before. The discoveries of Darwin and the philosophies of Mill or Hegel do not mark a greater relative advance than the discoveries of Newton and the philosophies of Descartes and Locke. These latter certainly had an effect upon theology. At one time they seemed to shake it to its base; so much so that Bishop Butler wrote in the Advertisement to the first edition of his Analogy that 'it is come to be taken for granted that Christianity is not so much as a subject of inquiry; but that it is now at length discovered to be fictitious.' Yet what do we see after a lapse of a hundred and forty years? It cannot be said that there is less religious life and activity now than there was then, or that there has been so far any serious breach in the continuity of Christian belief. An eye that has learnt to watch the larger movements of mankind will not allow itself to be disturbed by local oscillations. It is natural enough that some of our thinkers and writers should imagine that the last word has been spoken, and that they should be tempted to use the word 'Truth' as if it were their own peculiar possession. But Truth is really a much vaster and more unattainable thing. One man sees a fragment of it here and another there; but, as a whole, even in any of its smallest subdivisions, it exists not in the brain of any one individual, but in the gradual, and ever incomplete but ever self-completing, onward movement of the whole. 'If any man think that he knoweth anything, he knoweth nothing yet as he ought to know.' The forms of Christianity change, but Christianity itself endures. And it would seem as if we might well be content to wait until it was realised a little less imperfectly before we attempt to go farther afield.

Yet the work of adaptation must be done. The present generation has a task of its own to perform. It is needful for it to revise its opinions in view of the advances that have been made both in general knowledge and in special theological criticism. In so far as 'Supernatural Religion' has helped to do this, it has served the cause of true progress; but its main plan and design I cannot but regard as out of date and aimed in the air.

The Christian miracles, or what in our ignorance we call miracles, will not bear to be torn away from their context. If they are facts we must look at them in strict connection with that Ideal Life to which they seem to form the almost natural accompaniment. The Life itself is the great miracle. When we come to see it as it really is, and to enter, if even in some dim and groping way, into its inner recesses, we feel ourselves abashed and dumb. Yet this self-evidential character is found in portions of the narrative that are quite unmiraculous. These, perhaps, are in reality the most marvellous, though the miracles themselves will seem in place when their spiritual significance is understood and they are ranged in order round their common centre. Doubtless some elements of superstition may be mixed up in the record as it has come down to us. There is a manifest gap between the reality and the story of it. The Evangelists were for the most part 'Jews who sought after a sign.' Something of this wonder-seeking curiosity may very well have given a colour to their account of events in which the really transcendental element was less visible and tangible. We cannot now distinguish with any degree of accuracy between the subjective and the objective in the report. But that miracles, or what we call such, did in some shape take place, is, I believe, simply a matter of attested fact. When we consider it in its relation to the rest of the narrative, to tear out the miraculous bodily from the Gospels seems to me in the first instance a violation of history and criticism rather than of faith.

Still the author of 'Supernatural Religion' is, no

doubt, justified in raising the question, Did miracles really happen? I only wish to protest against the idea that such a question can be adequately discussed as something isolated and distinct, in which all that is necessary is to produce and substantiate the documents as in a forensic process. Such a 'world-historical' event (if I may for the moment borrow an expressive Germanism) as the founding of Christianity cannot be thrown into a merely forensic form. Considerations of this kind may indeed enter in, but to suppose that they can be justly estimated by themselves alone is an error. And it is still more an error to suppose that the riddle of the universe, or rather that part of the riddle which to us is most important, the religious nature of man and the objective facts and relations that correspond to it, can all be reduced to some four or five simple propositions which admit of being proved or disproved by a short and easy Q. E. D.

It would have been a far more profitable enquiry if the author had asked himself, What is Revelation? The time has come when this should be asked and an attempt to obtain a more scientific definition should be made. The comparative study of religions has gone far enough to admit of a comparison between the Ethnic religions and that which had its birth in Palestine—the religion of the Jews and Christians. Obviously, at the first blush, there is a difference: and that difference constitutes what we mean by Revelation. Let us have this as yet very imperfectly known quantity scientifically ascertained, without any attempt either to minimise or to exaggerate. I mean, let the field which Mr. Matthew Arnold has lately been traversing with much of his usual insight but in a light and popular manner, be seriously mapped out and explored. Pioneers have been at work, such as Dr. Kuenen, but not perhaps quite without a bias: let the same enquiry be taken up so widely as that the effects of bias may be eliminated; and instead of at once accepting the first crude results, let us wait until they are matured by time. This would be really fruitful and productive, and a positive addition to knowledge; but reasoning such as that in 'Supernatural Religion' is vitiated at the outset, because it starts with the assumption that we know perfectly well the meaning of a term of which our actual conception is vague and indeterminate in the extreme—Divine Revelation [1].

With these reservations as to the main drift and bearing of the argument, we may however meet the author of 'Supernatural Religion' on his own ground. It is a part of the question—though a more subordinate part apparently than he seems to suppose—to decide whether miracles did or did not really happen. Even of this part too it is but quite a minor subdivision that is included in the two volumes of his work that have hitherto appeared. In the first place, merely as a matter of historical attestation, the Gospels are not the strongest evidence for the Christian miracles. Only one of the four, in its present shape, is claimed as the

---

[1] Much harm has been done by rashly pressing human metaphors and analogies; such as, that Revelation is a *message* from God and therefore must be infallible, &c. This is just the sort of argument that the Deists used in the last century, insisting that a revelation, properly so called, *must* be presented with conclusive proofs, *must* be universal, *must* be complete, and drawing the conclusion that Christianity is not such a revelation. This kind of reasoning has received its sentence once for all from Bishop Butler. We have nothing to do with what *must* be (of which we are, by the nature of the case, incompetent judges), but simply with what *is*.

work of an Apostle, and of that the genuineness is disputed. The Acts of the Apostles stand upon very much the same footing with the Synoptic Gospels, and of this book we are promised a further examination. But we possess at least some undoubted writings of one who was himself a chief actor in the events which followed immediately upon those recorded in the Gospels; and in these undoubted writings St. Paul certainly shows by incidental allusions, the good faith of which cannot be questioned, that he believed himself to be endowed with the power of working miracles, and that miracles, or what were thought to be such, were actually wrought both by him and by his contemporaries. He reminds the Corinthians that 'the signs of an Apostle were wrought among them .. in signs, and wonders, and mighty deeds' (ἐν σημείοις καὶ τέρασι καὶ δυνάμεσι—the usual words for the higher forms of miracle—2 Cor. xii. 12). He tells the Romans that 'he will not dare to speak of any of those things which Christ hath not wrought in him, to make the Gentiles obedient, by word and deed, through mighty signs and wonders, by the power of the Spirit of God' (ἐν δυνάμει σημείων καὶ τεράτων, ἐν δυνάμει πνεύματος Θεοῦ, Rom. xv. 18, 19). He asks the Galatians whether 'he that ministereth to them the Spirit, and worketh miracles (ὁ ἐνεργῶν δυνάμεις) among them, doeth it by the works of the law, or by the hearing of faith?' (Gal. iii. 5). In the first Epistle to the Corinthians, he goes somewhat elaborately into the exact place in the Christian economy that is to be assigned to the working of miracles and gifts of healing (1 Cor. xii. 10, 28, 29). Besides these allusions, St. Paul repeatedly refers to the cardinal miracles of the Resurrection and Ascension; he refers to them as notorious and unquestionable facts at a time when such an assertion might have been easily refuted. On one occasion he gives a very circumstantial account of the testimony on which the belief in the Resurrection rested (1 Cor. xv. 4-8). And, not only does he assert the Resurrection as a fact, but he builds upon it a whole scheme of doctrine: 'If Christ be not risen,' he says, 'then is our preaching vain, and your faith is also vain.' We do not stay now to consider the exact philosophical weight of this evidence. It will be time enough to do this when it has received the critical discussion that may be presumed to be in store for it. But as external evidence, in the legal sense, it is probably the best that can be produced, and it has been entirely untouched so far.

Again, in considering the evidence for the age of the Synoptic Gospels, that which is derived from external sources is only a part, and not perhaps the more important part, of the whole. It points backwards indeed, and we shall see with what amount of force and range. But there is still an interval within which only approximate conclusions are possible. These conclusions need to be supplemented from the phenomena of the documents themselves. In the relation of the Gospels to the growth of the Christian society and the development of Christian doctrine, and especially to the great turning-point in the history, the taking of Jerusalem, there is very considerable internal evidence for determining the date within which they must have been composed. It is well known that many critics, without any apologetic object, have found a more or less exact criterion in the eschatological discourses (Matt. xxiv, Mark xiii, Luke xxi. 5-36), and to this large additions may be made. As I hope some day to have an opportunity of discussing the whole question of the origin and composition of the Synoptic Gospels, I shall not go into this at present: but in the mean time it should be remembered that all these further questions lie in the background, and that in tracing the formation of the Canon of the Gospels the whole of the evidence for miracles—even from this *ab extra* point of view—is very far from being exhausted.

There is yet another remaining reason which makes the present enquiry of less importance than might be supposed, derived from the particular way in which the author has dealt with this external evidence. In order to explain the *primâ facie* evidence for our canonical Gospels, he has been compelled to assume the existence of other documents containing, so far as appears, the same or very similar matter. In other words, instead of four Gospels he would give us five or six or seven. I do not know that, merely as a matter of policy, and for apologetic purposes only, the best way to refute his conclusion would not be to admit his premisses and to insist upon the multiplication of the evidence for the facts of the Gospel history which his argument would seem to involve. I mention this however, not with any such object, but rather to show that the truth of Christianity is not intimately affected, and that there are no such great reasons for partiality on one side or on the other.

I confess that it was a relief to me when I found that this must be the case. I do not think the time has come when the central question can be approached with any safety. Rough and ready methods (such as I am afraid I must call the first part of 'Supernatural Religion') may indeed cut the Gordian knot, but they do not untie it. A number of preliminary questions will have to be determined with a greater degree of accuracy and with more general consent than has been done hitherto. The Jewish and Christian literature of the century before and of the two centuries after the birth of Christ must undergo a more searching examination, by minds of different nationality and training, both as to the date, text, and character of the several books. The whole balance of an argument may frequently be changed by some apparently minute and unimportant discovery; while, at present, from the mere want of consent as to the data, the state of many a question is necessarily chaotic. It is far better that all these points should be discussed as disinterestedly as possible. No work is so good as that which is done without sight of the object to which it is tending and where the workman has only his measure and rule to trust to. I am glad to think that the investigation which is to follow may be almost, if not quite, classed in this category; and I hope I may be able to conduct it with sufficient impartiality. Unconscious bias no man can escape, but from conscious bias I trust I shall be free.

CHAPTER II.

ON QUOTATIONS GENERALLY IN THE EARLY CHRISTIAN WRITERS.

THE subject then proposed for our investigation is the extent to which the canonical Gospels are attested by the early Christian writers, or, in other words, the history of the process by which they became canonical. This will involve an enquiry into two things; first, the proof of the existence of the Gospels, and, secondly, the degree of authority attributed to them. Practically this second enquiry must be very subordinate to the first, because the data are much fewer; but it too shall be dealt with, cursorily, as the occasion arises, and we shall be in a position to speak upon it definitely before we conclude.

It will be convenient to follow the example that is set us in 'Supernatural Religion,' and to take the first three, or Synoptic, Gospels separately from the fourth.

At the outset the question will occur to us, On what principle is the enquiry to be conducted? What sort of rule or standard are we to assume? In order to prove either the existence or the authority of the Gospels, it is necessary that we should examine the quotations from them, or what are alleged to be quotations from them, in the early writers. Now these quotations are notoriously lax. It will be necessary then to have some means of judging, what degree and kind of laxity is admissible; what does, and what does not, prevent the reference of a quotation to a given source.

The author of 'Supernatural Religion,' indeed, has not felt the necessity for this preliminary step. He has taken up, as it were, at haphazard, the first standard that came to his hand; and, not unnaturally, this is found to be very much the standard of the present literary age, when both the mechanical and psychological conditions are quite different from those that prevailed at the beginning of the Christian era. He has thus been led to make a number of assertions which will require a great deal of qualification. The only sound and scientific method is to make an induction (if only a rough one) respecting the habit of early quotation generally, and then to apply it to the particular cases.

Here there will be three classes of quotation more or less directly in point: (1) the quotations from the Old Testament in the New; (2) the quotations from the Old Testament in the same early writers whose quotations from the New Testament are the point in question; (3) quotations from the New Testament, and more particularly from the Gospels, in the writers subsequent to these, at a time when the Canon of the Gospels was fixed and we can be quite sure that our present Gospels are being quoted.

This method of procedure however is not by any means so plain and straightforward as it might seem. The whole subject of Old Testament quotations is highly perplexing. Most of the quotations that we meet with are taken from the LXX version; and the text of that version was at this particular time especially uncertain and fluctuating. There is evidence to show that it must have existed in several forms which differed more or less from that of the extant MSS. It would be rash therefore to conclude at once, because we find a quotation differing from the present text of the LXX, that it differed from that which was used by the writer making the quotation. In some cases this can be proved from the same writer making the same quotation more than once and differently each time, or from another writer making it in agreement with our present text. But in other cases it seems probable that the writer had really a different text before him, because he quotes it more than once, or another writer quotes it, with the same variation. This however is again an uncertain criterion; for the second writer may be copying the first, or he may be influenced by an unconscious reminiscence of what the first had written. The early Christian writers copied each other to an extent that we should hardly be prepared for. Thus, for instance, there is a string of quotations in the first Epistle of Clement of Rome (cc. xiv, xv)—Ps. xxxvii. 36-38; Is. xxix. 13; Ps. lxii. 4, lxxviii. 36, 37, xxxi, 19, xii. 3-6; and these very quotations in the same order reappear in the Alexandrine Clement (Strom. iv. 6). Clement of Alexandria is indeed fond of copying his Roman namesake, and does so without acknowledgment. Tertullian and Epiphanius in like manner drew largely from the works of Irenaeus. But this confuses evidence that would otherwise be clear. For instance, in Eph. iv. 8 St. Paul quotes Ps. lxviii. 19, but with a marked variation from all the extant texts of the LXX. Thus:—

Ps. lxviii. 18 (19).

Ἀναβὰς εἰς ὕψος ᾐχμαλώτευσας αἰχμαλωσίαν, ἔλαβες δόματα ἐν ἀνθρώπῳ.

ᾐχμαλώτευσεν ... ἐν ἀνθρώποις ℵ, perhaps from assimilation to N. T.

Eph. iv. 8.

Ἀναβὰς εἰς ὕψος ᾐχμαλώτευσεν αἰχμαλωσίαν, καὶ ἔδωκε δόματα τοῖς ἀνθρώποις.

καί om. ℵ¹ A C² D¹, &c. It. Vulg. Memph. &c.; ins. B C³ D³ ℵ¹, &c.

Now we should naturally think that this was a very free quotation—so free that it substitutes 'giving' for 'receiving.' A free quotation perhaps it may be, but at any rate the very same variation is found in Justin (Dial. 39). And, strange to say, in five other passages which are quoted variantly by St. Paul, Justin also agrees with him[1], though cases on the other hand occur where Justin differs from St. Paul or holds a position midway between him and the LXX (e. g. 1 Cor. i. 19 compared with Just. Dial. cc. 123, 32, 78, where will be found some curious variations, agreement with LXX, partial agreement with LXX, partial agreement with St. Paul). Now what are we to say to these phenomena? Have St. Paul and Justin both a variant text of the LXX, or is Justin quoting mediately through St. Paul? Probability indeed seems to be on the side of the latter of these two alternatives, because in one place (Dial. cc. 95, 96) Justin quotes the two passages Deut. xxvii. 26 and Deut. xxi. 23 consecutively, and applies them just as they are applied in Gal. iii. 10, 13[2]. On the other hand, it is somewhat strange that Justin nowhere refers to the Epistles of St. Paul by name, and that the allusions to them in the genuine writings, except for these

---

[1] Cf. Westcott, *Canon*, p. 152, n. 2 (3rd ed. 1870).

[2] See Lightfoot, *Galatians*, p. 60; also Credner, *Beiträge*, ii. 66 ('certainly' from St. Paul).

marked resemblances in the Old Testament quotations, are few and uncertain. The same relation is observed between the Pauline Epistles and that of Clement of Rome. In two places at least Clement agrees, or nearly agrees, with St. Paul, where both differ from the LXX; in c. xiii (ὁ καυχώμενος ἐν Κυρίῳ καυχάσθω; compare 1 Cor. i. 31, 2 Cor. x. 16), and in c. xxxiv (ὀφθαλμὸς οὐκ εἶδεν κ.τ.λ.; compare 1 Cor. ii. 9). Again, in c. xxxvi Clement has the πυρὸς φλόγα of Heb. i. 7 for πῦρ φλέγον of the LXX. The rest of the parallelisms in Clement's Epistle are for the most part with Clement of Alexandria, who had evidently made a careful study of his predecessor. In one place, c. liii, there is a remarkable coincidence with Barnabas (Μωϋσῆ Μωϋσῆ κατάβηθι τὸ τάχος κ.τ.λ.; compare Barn. cc. iv and xiv). In the Epistle of Barnabas itself there is a combined quotation from Gen. xv. 6, xvii. 5, which has evidently and certainly been affected by Rom. iv. 11. On the whole we may lean somewhat decidedly to the hypothesis of a mutual study of each other by the Christian writers, though the other hypothesis of the existence of different versions (whether oral and traditional or in any shape written) cannot be excluded. Probably both will have to be taken into account to explain all the facts.

Another disturbing influence, which will affect especially the quotations in the Gospels, is the possibility, perhaps even probability, that many of these are made, not directly from either Hebrew or LXX, but from or through Targums. This would seem to be the case especially with the remarkable applications of prophecy in St. Matthew. It must be admitted as possible that the Evangelist has followed some Jewish interpretation that seemed to bear a Christian construction. The quotation in Matt. ii. 6, with its curious insertion of the negative (οὐδαμῶς ἐλαχίστη for ὀλιγοστός), reappears identically in Justin (Dial. c. 78). We shall probably have to touch upon this quotation when we come to consider Justin's relations to the canonical Gospels. It certainly seems upon the face of it the more probable supposition that he has here been influenced by the form of the text in St. Matthew, but he may be quoting from a Targum or from a peculiar text.

Any induction, then, in regard to the quotations from the LXX version will have to be used with caution and reserve. And yet I think it will be well to make such an induction roughly, especially in regard to the Apostolic Fathers whose writings we are to examine.

The quotations from the Old Testament in the New have, as it is well known, been made the subject of a volume by Mr. McCalman Turpie[1], which, though perhaps not quite reaching a high level of scholarship, has yet evidently been put together with much care and pains, and will be sufficient for our purpose. The summary result of Mr. Turpie's investigation is this. Out of two hundred and seventy-five in all which may be considered to be quotations from the Old Testament, fifty-three agree literally both with the LXX and the Hebrew, ten with the Hebrew and not with the LXX, and thirty-seven with the LXX and not with the Hebrew, making in all just a hundred that are in literal (or nearly literal, for slight variations of order are not taken into account) agreement with some still extant authority. On the other hand, seventy-six passages differ both from the Hebrew and LXX where

[1] *The Old Testament in the New* (London and Edinburgh, 1868).

the two are together, ninety-nine differ from them where they diverge, and besides these, three, though introduced with marks of quotation, have no assignable original in the Old Testament at all. Leaving them for the present out of the question, we have a hundred instances of agreement against a hundred and seventy-five of difference; or, in other words, the proportion of difference to agreement is as seven to four.

This however must be taken with the caution given above; that is to say, it must not at once be inferred that because the quotation differs from extant authority therefore it necessarily differs from all non-extant authority as well. It should be added that the standard of agreement adopted by Mr. Turpie is somewhat higher than would be naturally held to be sufficient to refer a passage to a given source. His lists must therefore be used with these limitations.

Turning to them, we find that most of the possible forms of variation are exemplified within the bounds of the Canon itself. I proceed to give a few classified instances of these.

(*a*) *Paraphrase.* Many of the quotations from the Old Testament in the New are highly paraphrastic. We may take the following as somewhat marked examples: Matt. ii. 6, xii. 18-21, xiii. 35, xxvii. 9, 10; John viii. 17, xii. 40, xiii. 18; 1 Cor. xiv. 21; 2 Cor. ix. 7. Matt. xxvii. 9, 10 would perhaps mark an extreme point in freedom of quotation[1], as will be seen when it is compared with the original:—

[1] Mr. M'Clellan (*The New Testament*, &c., vol. i. p. 606, n. c) makes the suggestion, which from his point of view is necessary, that 'S. Matthew has cited a prophecy spoken by Jeremiah, but nowhere written in the Old Testament, and of which the passage in Zechariah is only a partial reproduction.' Cf. Credner, *Beiträge*, ii. 152.

Matt. xxvii. 9, 10.

[Τότε ἐπληρώθη τὸ ῥηθὲν διὰ τοῦ προφήτου Ἱερεμίου λέγοντος] Καὶ ἔλαβον τὰ τριάκοντα ἀργύρια, τὴν τιμὴν τοῦ τετιμημένου ὃν ἐτιμήσαντο ἀπὸ υἱῶν Ἰσραήλ· καὶ ἔδωκαν αὐτὰ εἰς τὸν ἀγρὸν τοῦ κεραμέως, καθὰ συνέταξέν μοι Κύριος.

Zech. xi. 13.

Κάθες αὐτοὺς εἰς τὸ χωνευτήριον, καὶ σκέψομαι εἰ δόκιμόν ἐστιν, ὃν τρόπον ἐδοκιμάσθην ὑπὲρ αὐτῶν. Καὶ ἔλαβον τοὺς τριάκοντα ἀργυροῦς καὶ ἐνέβαλον αὐτοὺς εἰς οἶκον Κυρίου εἰς τὸ χωνευτήριον.

It can hardly be possible that the Evangelist has here been influenced by any Targum or version. The form of his text has apparently been determined by the historical event to which the prophecy is applied. The sense of the original has been entirely altered. There the prophet obeys the command to put the thirty pieces of silver, which he had received as his shepherd's hire, into the treasury (χωνευτήριον). Here the hierarchical party refuse to put them into the treasury. The word 'potter' seems to be introduced from the Hebrew.

(β) *Quotations from Memory.* Among the numerous paraphrastic quotations, there are some that have specially the appearance of having been made from memory, such as Acts vii. 37; Rom. ix. 9, 17, 25, 33, x. 6–8, xi. 3, xii. 19, xiv. 11; 1 Cor. i. 19, ii. 9; Rev. ii. 27. Of course it must always be a matter of guess-work what is quoted from memory and what is not, but in these quotations (and in others which are ranged under different heads) there is just that general identity of sense along with variety of expression which usually characterises such quotations. A simple instance would be—

Rom. ix. 25.

[ὡς καὶ ἐν τῷ Ὡσηὲ λέγει] Καλέσω τὸν οὐ λαόν μου λαόν μου καὶ τὴν οὐκ ἠγαπημένην ἠγαπημένην.

Hosea ii. 23.

Καὶ ἀγαπήσω τὴν οὐκ ἠγαπημένην, καὶ ἐρῶ τῷ οὐ λαῷ μου Λαός μου εἶ σύ.

(γ) *Paraphrase with Compression.* There are many marked examples of this; such as Matt. xxii. 24 (par.); Mark iv. 12; John xii. 14, 15; Rom. iii. 15–17, x. 15; Heb. xii. 20. Take the first:—

Matt. xxii. 24.

[Μωυσῆς εἶπεν] Ἐάν τις ἀποθάνῃ μὴ ἔχων τέκνα, ἐπιγαμβρεύσει ὁ ἀδελφὸς αὐτοῦ τὴν γυναῖκα αὐτοῦ καὶ ἀναστήσει σπέρμα τῷ ἀδελφῷ αὐτοῦ.

Deut. xxv. 5.

Ἐὰν δὲ κατοικῶσιν ἀδελφοὶ ἐπὶ τὸ αὐτό, καὶ ἀποθάνῃ εἷς ἐξ αὐτῶν, σπέρμα δὲ μὴ ᾖ αὐτῷ, οὐκ ἔσται ἡ γυνὴ τοῦ τεθνηκότος ἔξω ἀνδρὶ μὴ ἐγγίζοντι· ὁ ἀδελφὸς τοῦ ἀνδρὸς αὐτῆς εἰσελεύσεται πρὸς αὐτὴν καὶ λήψεται αὐτὴν ἑαυτῷ γυναῖκα καὶ συνοικήσει αὐτῇ.

It is highly probable that all the examples given under this head are really quotations from memory.

(δ) *Paraphrase with Combination of Passages.* This again is common; e. g. Luke iv. 19; John xv. 25, xix. 36; Acts xiii. 22; Rom. iii. 11–18, ix. 33, xi. 8; 1 Pet. ii. 24. The passage Rom. iii. 11–18 is highly composite, and reminds us of long strings of quotations that are found in some of the Fathers; it is made up of Ps. xiv. 1, 2, v. 9, cxl. 3, x. 7, Is. lix. 7, 8, Ps. xxxvi. 1. A shorter example is—

Rom. ix. 33.

[Καθὼς γέγραπται] Ἰδοὺ τίθημι ἐν Σιὼν λίθον προσκόμματος καὶ πέτραν σκανδάλου, καὶ ὁ πιστεύων ἐπ' αὐτῷ οὐ καταισχυνθήσεται.

Is. viii. 14.

καὶ οὐχ ὡς λίθου προσκόμματι συναντήσεσθε, οὐδὲ ὡς πέτρας πτώματι.

Is. xxviii. 16.

Ἰδοὺ ἐγὼ ἐμβάλλω εἰς τὰ θεμέλια Σιὼν λίθον . . . , καὶ ὁ πιστεύων οὐ μὴ καταισχυνθῇ.

This fusion of passages is generally an act of 'unconscious cerebration.' If we were to apply the standard assumed in 'Supernatural Religion,' it would be pronounced impossible that this and most of the passages above could have the originals to which they are certainly to be referred.

(ε) *Addition.* A few cases of addition may be quoted, e.g. μὴ ἀποστερήσῃς inserted in Mark x. 19, καὶ εἰς θήραν in Rom. xi. 9.

(ζ) *Change of Sense and Context.* But little regard— or what according to our modern habits would be considered little regard—is paid to the sense and original context of the passage quoted; e.g. in Matt. viii. 17 the idea of healing disease is substituted for that of vicarious suffering, in Matt. xi. 10 the persons are altered (σου for μου), in Acts vii. 43 we find Βαβυλῶνος for Δαμασκοῦ, in 2 Cor. vi. 17 'I will receive you' is put for 'I will go before you,' in Heb. i. 7 'He maketh His angels spirits' for 'He maketh the winds His messengers.' This constant neglect of the context is a point that should be borne in mind.

(η) *Inversion.* Sometimes the sense of the original is so far departed from that a seemingly opposite sense is substituted for it. Thus in Matt. ii. 6 οὐδαμῶς ἐλαχίστη = ὀλιγοστός of Mic. v. 2, in Rom. xi. 26 ἐκ Σιών = ἕνεκεν Σιών LXX = '*to* Sion' Heb. of Is. lix. 20, in Eph. iv. 8 ἔδωκεν δόματα = ἔλαβες δόματα of Ps. lxvii. 19.

(θ) *Different Form of Sentence.* The grammatical form of the sentence is altered in Matt. xxvi. 31 (from aorist to future), in Luke viii. 10 (from oratio recta to oratio obliqua), and in 1 Pet. iii. 10–12 (from the second person to the third). This is a kind of variation that we should naturally look for.

(ι) *Mistaken Ascriptions or Nomenclature.* The following passages are wrongly assigned:—Mal. iii. 1 to

Isaiah according to the correct reading of Mark i. 2, and Zech. xi. 13 to Jeremiah in Matt. xxvii. 9, 10; Abiathar is apparently put for Abimelech in Mark ii. 26; in Acts vii. 16 there seems to be a confusion between the purchase of Machpelah near Hebron by Abraham and Jacob's purchase of land from Hamor the father of Shechem. These are obviously lapses of memory.

(κ) *Quotations of Doubtful Origin.* There are a certain number of quotations, introduced as such, which can be assigned directly to no Old Testament original; Matt. ii. 23 (Ναζωραῖος κληθήσεται), 1 Tim. v. 18 ('the labourer is worthy of his hire'), John vii. 38 ('out of his belly shall flow rivers of living water'), 42 (Christ should be born of Bethlehem where David was), Eph. v. 14 ('Awake thou that sleepest [1]').

It will be seen that, in spite of the reservations that we felt compelled to make at the outset, the greater number of the deviations noticed above can only be explained on a theory of free quotation, and remembering the extent to which the Jews relied upon memory and the mechanical difficulties of exact reference and verification, this is just what before the fact we should have expected.

The Old Testament quotations in the canonical books afford us a certain parallel to the object of our enquiry, but one still nearer will of course be presented by the Old Testament quotations in those books the New Testament quotations in which we are to investigate. I have thought it best to draw up tables of these in order to give an idea of the extent and character of the variation. In so tentative an enquiry as this, the standard through-

---

[1] We do not stay to discuss the real origin of these quotations: the last is probably not from the Old Testament at all.

out will hardly be so fixed and accurate as might be desirable; the tabular statement therefore must be taken to be approximate, but still I think it will be found sufficient for our purpose; certain points come out with considerable clearness, and there is always an advantage in drawing data from a wide enough area. The quotations are ranged under heads according to the degree of approximation to the text of the LXX. In cases where the classification has seemed doubtful an indicatory mark (†) has been used, showing by the side of the column on which it occurs to which of the other two classes the instance leans. All cases in which this sign is used to the left of the middle column may be considered as for practical purposes literal quotations. It may be assumed, where the contrary is not stated, that the quotations are direct and not of the nature of allusions; the marks of quotation are generally quite unmistakeable (γέγραπται, λέγει, εἶπεν, &c.). Brief notes are added in the margin to call attention to the more remarkable points, especially to the repetition of the same quotation in different writers and to the apparent bearing of the passage upon the general habit of quotation.

Taking the Apostolic Fathers in order, we come first to—

Clement of Rome (1 *Ep. ad Cor.*).

Exact.	Slightly variant.	Variant.	Remarks.
		3. Deut. 32.14,15. Is. 3. 5, al. Is. 59. 14, al.	also in Justin, differently.
3. Wisd. 2. 24.			
	† 4. Gen. 4. 3–8. Ex. 2. 14 †.		
6. Gen. 2. 23.			Acts 7. 27, more exactly.
		8. Ezek. 33. 11. Ezek. 18. 30. Ps. 103.10,11. Jer. 3. 19, 22. Is. 1. 18.	from Apocryphal or interpolated Ezekiel?

Exact.	Slightly variant.	Variant.	Remarks.
	†8. Is. 1. 16-20.		
	10. Gen. 12. 1-3.		
	†Gen. 13. 14-16.		
	Gen. 15. 5, 6.		
		12. Josh. 2. 3-19.	compression and paraphrase.
		13. 1 Sam. 2. 10. Jer. 9. 23, 24.	similarly St. Paul, 1 Cor. 1. 31, 2 Cor. 10. 17.
	13. Is. 46. 2.		
		14. Prov. 2. 21, 22, v. l. (Ps. 37. 39.)	from memory?
	14. Ps. 37. 35-38.		
		15. Is. 29. 13.[1]	Matt. 15. 8, Mark 7. 6, with partial similarity, Clem. Alex. following Clem. Rom.
15. Ps. 78. 36, 37.[1] Ps. 31. 19.[1] Ps. 12. 3-6.[1]	15. Ps. 62. 4.[1]		
	†16. Is. liii. 1-12.		quoted in full by Justin, also by other writers with text slightly different from Clement.
16. Ps. 22. 6-8.			
17. Gen. 18. 27.			
		17. Job 1. 1, v. l. Job 14. 4, 5, v.l.	Clem. Alex. similarly.
	17. Num. 12. 7. Ex. 3. 11; 4. 10.		
		17. ἐγὼ δέ εἰμι ἀτμὶς ἀπὸ κύθρας.	Assumptio Mosis, Hilg., Eldad and Modad, Lft.
		18. Ps. 89. 21, v.l. 1 Sam. 13. 14.	Clem. Alex. as LXX.
18. Ps. 51. 1-17.			
		20. Job 38. 11.	
		21. Prov. 15. 27.	Clem. Alex. similarly; from memory? (λέγει γάρ που).
22. Ps. 34. 11-17.			
		23. ταλαίπωροί εἰσιν οἱ δίψυχοι κ.τ.λ.	from an Apocryphal book, Ass. Mos. or Eld. and Mod.
		23. Is. 13. 22. Mal. 3. 1.	composition and compression.

[1] The quotations in this chapter are continuous, and are also found in Clement of Alexandria.

Exact.	Slightly variant.	Variant.	Remarks.
		26. Ps. 28. 7. Ps. 3. 5.	composition from memory? (λέγει γάρ που).
		27. Wisd. 12. 12. Wisd. 11. 22.	from memory? cp. Eph. 1. 19.
27. Ps. 19. 1–3.			
		28. Ps. 139. 7–10.	from memory? (λέγει γάρ που).
29. Deut. 32. 8, 9.			
		29. Deut. 4. 34. Deut. 14. 2. Num. 18. 27. 2 Chron. 31. 14. Exek. 48. 12.	from memory? or from an Apocryphal Book?
	30. Prov. 3. 34.		
30. Job 11. 2, 3.			LXX, not Heb.
		32. Gen. 15. 5. (Gen. 22. 17. Gen. 26. 4.)	
	33. Gen. 1. 26–28.	(omissions).	
		34. Is. 40. 10. Is. 62. 11. Prov. 24. 12.	composition from memory? Clem. Alex., after Clem. Rom.
	34. Dan. 7. 10. Is. 6. 3†.		curiously repeated transposition; see Lightfoot, *ad. loc.*
		34. Is. 64. 4.	so in 1 Cor. 2. 9.
	35. Ps. 50. 16–23.		
	36. Ps. 104. 4, v.l.		Heb. 1. 7.
36. Ps. 2. 7, 8. Ps. 110. 1.			Heb. 1. 5. Acts 13. 33.
	39. Job 4.16–5.5. (Job 15. 15.)		
		42. Is. 60. 17.	from memory? (λέγει γάρ που).
		46. Κολλᾶσθε τοῖς ἁγίοις ὅτι οἱ κολλώμενοι αὐτοῖς ἁγιασθήσονται.	from Apocryphal book, or Ecclus. vi. 34? Clem. Alex.
46. Ps. 18. 26, 27.			context ignored.
48. Ps. 118. 19, 20.			Clem. Alex. loosely.
		50. Is. 26. 20. Ezek. 37. 12.	from memory?
50. Ps. 32. 1, 2.			

Exact.	Slightly variant.	Variant.	Remarks.
		52. Ps. 69. 31, 32.	
52. Ps. 50.14,15.† Ps. 51. 17.	}		
	53. Deut. 9. 12-14. Ex. 32. 7, 8, 11, 31, 32. }		Barnabas similarly. Compression.
54. Ps. 24. 1.			
56. Ps. 118. 18. Prov. 3. 12. Ps. 141. 5.			
	†56. Job 5. 17-26, v. l.		
	†57. Prov. 1. 23-31.		

It will be observed that the longest passages are among those that are quoted with the greatest accuracy (e. g. Gen. xiii. 14-16; Job v. 17-26; Ps. xix. 1-3, xxii. 6-8, xxxiv. 11-17, li. 1-17; Prov. i. 23-31; Is. i. 16-20, liii. 1-12). Others, such as Gen. xii. 1-3, Deut. ix. 12-14, Job iv. 16-v. 5, Ps. xxxvii. 35-38, l. 16-23, have only slight variations. There are only two passages of more than three consecutive verses in length that present wide divergences. These are, Ps. cxxxix. 7-10, which is introduced by a vague reference (λέγει γάρ που) and is evidently quoted from memory, and the historical narration Josh. ii. 3-19. This is perhaps what we should expect: in longer quotations it would be better worth the writer's while to refer to his cumbrous manuscript. These purely mechanical conditions are too much lost sight of. We must remember that the ancient writer had not a small compact reference Bible at his side, but, when he wished to verify a reference, would have to take an unwieldy roll out of its case, and then would not find it divided into chapter and verse like our modern books, but would have only the columns, and those perhaps not numbered, to guide him. We must remember too that the memory was much more practised and relied upon in ancient times, especially among the Jews.

The composition of two or more passages is frequent, and the fusion remarkably complete. Of all the cases in which two passages are compounded, always from different chapters and most commonly from different books, there is not, I believe, one in which there is any mark of division or an indication of any kind that a different source is being quoted from. The same would hold good (with only a slight and apparent exception) of the longer strings of quotations in cc. viii, xxix, and (from ἠγάπησαν to ἐν αὐτῷ) in c. xv. But here the question is complicated by the possibility, and in the first place at least perhaps probability, that the writer is quoting from some apocryphal work no longer extant. It may be interesting to give one or two short examples of the completeness with which the process of welding has been carried out. Thus in c. xvii, the following reply is put into the mouth of Moses when he receives his commission at the burning bush, τίς εἰμι ἐγώ, ὅτι με πέμπεις; ἐγὼ δέ εἰμι ἰσχνόφωνος καὶ βραδύγλωσσος. The text of Exod. iii. 11 is τίς εἰμι ἐγώ, ὅτι πορεύσομαι; the rest of the quotation is taken from Exod. iv. 10. In c. xxxiv Clement introduces 'the Scripture' as saying, Μύριαι μυριάδες παρειστήκεισαν αὐτῷ καὶ χίλιαι χιλιάδες ἐλειτούργουν αὐτῷ· καὶ ἐκέκραγον· ἅγιος, ἅγιος, ἅγιος, Κύριος Σαβαώθ, πλήρης πᾶσα ἡ κτίσις τῆς δόξης αὐτοῦ. The first part of this quotation comes from Dan. vii. 10; the second, from καὶ ἐκέκραγον, which is part of the quotation, from Is. vi. 3. These examples have been taken almost at random; the others are blended quite as thoroughly.

Some of the cases of combination and some of the

divergences of text may be accounted for by the assumption of lost apocryphal books or texts; but it would be wholly impossible, and in fact no one would think of so attempting to account for all. There can be little doubt that Clement quotes from memory, and none that he quotes at times very freely.

We come next to the so-called Epistle of Barnabas, the quotations in which I proceed to tabulate in the same way:—

Barnabas.

Exact.	Slightly variant.	Variant.	Remarks.
	†2. Is. 1. 11–14.		note for exactness.
		2. Jer. 7. 22, 23.	} combination
		Zech. 8. 17.	} from memory?
		Ps. 51. 19.	strange addition.
	3. Is. 58. 4, 5.		
	— Is. 58. 6–10.		
		4. Dan. 7. 24.	} very divergent.
		Dan. 7. 7, 8.	
		Ex. 34. 28.	} combination
		Ex. 31. 18.	} from memory?
	4. Deut. 9. 12		see below.
	(Ex. 32. 7).		
	†Is. 5. 21.		
	†5. Is. 53. 5, 7		text of Cod. A.
	(omissions).		
5. Prov. 1. 17.			
Gen. 1. 26†.			
		5. Zech. 13. 7.	text of A. (Hilg.) Matt. 26. 3.
		Ps. 22. 21.	from memory?
	5. Ps. 119. 120.		paraphrastic combination from memory?
		Ps. 22. 17.	
	Is. 50. 6, 7		ditto.
	(omissions).	6. Is. 50. 8, 9.	ditto.
	6. Is. 28. 16.		first clause exact, second variant; in N. T. quotations, first variant, second exact.
	Is. 50. 7.		note repetition, nearer to LXX.
6. Ps. 118. 22.			so Matt. 21. 42; 1 Pet. 11. 7.

Exact.	Slightly variant.	Variant.	Remarks.
		6. Ps. 118. 24.	from memory?
6. Ps. 22. 17 †(order).			note repetition, nearer to LXX.
Ps. 118. 12.			
Ps. 22. 19.			
Is. 3. 9, 10.			
		Ex. 33. 1.	from memory? note repetition, further from LXX.
	Gen. 1. 26†.		
Gen. 1. 28.			
		Ezek. 11. 19; 36. 26.	paraphrastic.
		Ps. 41. 3.	
		Ps. 22. 23.	different version?
		Gen. 1. 26, 28.	paraphrastic fusion.
		7. Lev. 23. 29.	paraphrastic.
		Lev. 16. 7, sqq.	with apocryphal addition; cp. Just. and Tert.
	9. Ps. 18. 44.		
9. Is. 33. 13†.			
		9. Jer. 4. 4.	
		Jer. 7. 2.	
		Ps. 34. 13.	
Is. 1. 2.			but with additions.
	Is. 1. 10†.		from memory? ἄρχοντες τοῦ λαοῦ τούτου for a. Σοδόμων.
		Is. 40. 3.	addition.
		Jer. 4. 3, 4.	} repetition, nearer to LXX.
		Jer. 7. 26.	
		Jer. 9. 26.	
		Gen. 17, 26, 27; cf. 14. 14.	inferred sense merely, but with marks of quotation.
		10. Lev. 11, Deut. 14.	selected examples, but with marks of quotation.
		Deut. 4. 1.	
10. Ps. 1. 1.			
		Lev. 11. 3.	
		11. Jer. 2. 12, 13.	
		†Is. 16. 1, 2.	Σινᾶ for Σιών. γνώσῃ Α. (γνῶσιν Barn.), but in other points more divergent.
	11. Is. 45. 2, 3.		

Exact.	Slightly variant.	Variant.	Remarks.
	†Is. 33. 16-18.		omissions.
11. Ps. 1. 3-6.			note for exactness.
		11. Zeph. 3. 19.	markedly diverse.
		Ezek. 47. 12.	ditto.
	12. Is. 65. 2.		
		12. Num. 21. 9, sqq.	apparently a quotation.
		Deut. 27. 15.	from memory?
		Ex. 17. 14.	
12. Ps. 110. 1.			
	12. Is. 45. 1.		Κυρίῳ for Κύρῳ.
	13. Gen. 25. 21, 23.		
		13. Gen. 48. 11-19.	very paraphrastic.
		Gen. 15. 6; 17. 5.	combination; cf. Rom. 4. 11.
		14. Ex. 24. 18.	note addition of νηστεύων.
		Ex. 31. 18.	note also for additions.
	14. Deut. 9. 12-17†. (Ex. 32. 7.)		repetition with similar variation.
14. Is. 42. 6, 7.			note reading of A. πεπεδημένους for δεδεμένους (καί om. A.).
	Is. 49. 6, 7.		
Is. 61. 1, 2.			Luke 4. 18, 19 diverges.
		15. Ex. 20. 8; Deut. 5. 12.	paraphrastic, with addition.
		Jer. 17. 24, 25.	very paraphrastic.
		Gen. 2. 2.	
		Ps. 90. 4.	σήμερον for ἐχθές.
15. Is. 1. 13.			
	16. Is. 40. 12.		omissions.
	Is. 66. 1.		
		16. Is. 49. 17.	completely paraphrastic.
		Dan. 9. 24, 25, 27.	ditto.

The same remarks that were made upon Clement will hold also for Barnabas, except that he permits himself still greater licence. The marginal notes will have called attention to his eccentricities. He is carried away by slight resemblances of sound; e.g. he puts ἱμάτια for ἰάματα[1], Σινᾶ for Σιών, Κυρίῳ for Κύρῳ. He not only omits clauses, but also adds to the text freely; e.g. in Ps. li 19 he makes the strange insertion which is given in brackets, Θυσία τῷ Θεῷ καρδία συντετριμμένη, [ὀσμὴ εὐωδίας τῷ κυρίῳ καρδία δοξάζουσα τὸν πεπλακότα αὐτήν]. He has also added words and clauses in several other places. There can be no question that he quotes largely from memory; several of his quotations are repeated more than once (Deut. ix. 12; Is. l. 7; Ps. xxii. 17; Gen. i. 28; Jer. iv. 4); and of these only one, Deut. ix. 12, reappears in the same form. Often he gives only the sense of a passage; sometimes he interprets, as in Is. i. 10, where he paraphrases ἄρχοντες Σοδόμων by the simpler ἄρχοντες τοῦ λαοῦ τούτου. He has curiously combined the sense of Gen. xvii. 26, 27 with Gen. xiv. 14—in the pursuit of the four kings, it is said that Abraham armed his servants three hundred and eighteen men; Barnabas says that he circumcised his household, in all three hundred and eighteen men. In several cases a resemblance may be noticed between Barnabas and the text of Cod. A, but this does not appear consistently throughout.

It may be well to give a few examples of the extent to which Barnabas can carry his freedom of quotation. Instances from the Book of Daniel should perhaps not be given, as the text of that book is known to have been in a peculiarly corrupt and unsettled state; so much so that, when the translation of Theodotion was made towards the end of the second century, it was adopted as the standard text. Barnabas also combines passages, though not quite to such an extent or so elaborately as Clement,

---

[1] It should be noticed, however, that the same reading is found in Justin and other writers.

and he too inserts no mark of division. We will give an example of this, and at the same time of his paraphrastic method of quotation :—

Barnabas c. ix.	Jer. iv. 3, 4 *and* vii. 26.
[καὶ τί λέγει ;] Περιτμήθητε τὸ σκληρὸν τῆς καρδίας ὑμῶν, καὶ τὸν τράχηλον ὑμῶν οὐ μὴ σκληρύνητε.	Περιτμήθητε τῷ Θεῷ ὑμῶν, καὶ περιτέμεσθε τὴν σκληροκαρδίαν ὑμῶν ... καὶ ἐσκλήρυναν τὸν τράχηλον αὐτῶν ...

A similar case of paraphrase and combination, with nothing to mark the transition from one passage to the other, would be in c. xi, Jer. ii. 12, 13 and Is. xvi. 1, 2. For paraphrase we may take this, from the same chapter :—

Barnabas c. xi.	Zeph. iii. 19.
[καὶ πάλιν ἕτερος προφήτης λέγει] Καὶ ἦν ἡ γῆ Ἰακὼβ ἐπαινουμένη παρὰ πᾶσαν τὴν γῆν.	καὶ θήσομαι αὐτοὺς εἰς καύχημα καὶ ὀνομαστοὺς ἐν πάσῃ τῇ γῇ.

Barnabas c. xv.	Ps. xc. 4.
[αὐτὸς δέ μοι μαρτυρεῖ λέγων] Ἰδοὺ σήμερον ἡμέρα ἔσται ὡς χίλια ἔτη.	ὅτι χίλια ἔτη ἐν ὀφθαλμοῖς σου ὡς ἡ ἡμέρα ἡ ἐχθὲς ἥτις διῆλθε.

A very curious instance of freedom is the long narrative of Jacob blessing the two sons of Joseph in c. xiii (compare Gen. xlviii. 11–19). We note here (and elsewhere) a kind of dramatic tendency, a fondness for throwing statements into the form of dialogue rather than narrative. As a narrative this passage may be compared with the history of Rahab and the spies in Clement.

And yet, in spite of all this licence in quotation, there are some rather marked instances of exactness; e.g. Is. i. 11–14 in c. ii, the combined passages from Ps. xxii. 17, cxvii. 12, xxii. 19 in c. vi, and Ps. i. 3–6 in

c. xi. It should also be remembered that in one case, Deut. ix. 12 in cc. iv and xiv, the same variation is repeated and is also found in Justin.

It tallies with what we should expect, supposing the writings attributed to Ignatius (the seven Epistles) to be genuine, that the quotations from the Old as well as from the New Testament in them are few and brief. A prisoner, travelling in custody to the place of execution, would naturally not fill his letters with long and elaborate references. The quotations from the Old Testament are as follows:—

Exact.	Slightly variant.	Variant.	Remarks.
Ad Eph.	5. Prov. 3. 34.		James 4. 6, 1 Pet. 5. 5, as Ignatius.
Ad Magn.	12. Prov. 18. 17.		
Ad Trall.		8. Is. 52. 5.	

The Epistle to the Ephesians is found also in the Syriac version. The last quotation from Isaiah, which is however not introduced with any express marks of reference, is very freely given. The original is, τάδε λέγει κύριος, Δι' ὑμᾶς διὰ παντὸς τὸ ὄνομά μου βλασφημεῖται ἐν τοῖς ἔθνεσι, for which Ignatius has, Οὐαὶ γὰρ δι' οὗ ἐπὶ ματαιότητι τὸ ὄνομά μου ἐπί τινων βλασφημεῖται.

The Epistle of Polycarp to the Philippians and the Martyrium S. Ignatii contain the following quotations:—

Exact.	Slightly variant.	Variant.	Remarks.
Polycarp, Ad Phil.	2. Ps. 2. 11.		
10. Tob. 4. 11.			
12. Ps. 4. 4; but through Eph. 4. 26.			in Latin version only.
Mart. S. Ign.			
6. Prov. 10. 24.		2. Lev. 26. 12.	

The quotation from Leviticus differs widely from the original, Καὶ ἐμπεριπατήσω ἐν ὑμῖν καὶ ἔσομαι ὑμῶν θεὸς καὶ ὑμεῖς ἔσεσθέ μοι λαός, for which we read, [γέγραπται γὰρ] Ἐνοικήσω ἐν αὐτοῖς καὶ ἐμπεριπατήσω.

The quotations from the Clementine Homilies may be thus presented:—

Exact.	Slightly variant.	Variant.	Remarks.
Hom. 3.		18. Deut. 32. 7.	
	39. †Gen. 18. 21.		
	Gen. 3. 22.		
39. Gen. 6. 6.			
	Gen. 8. 21.		omission.
	Gen. 22. 1.		
		42. Gen. 3. 3.	
43. Gen. 6. 6.			
	43. Gen. 22. 1.		not quite as above.
	†Gen. 18. 21.		as above.
Gen. 15. 13–16.			v. l. comp. text of A; note for exactness.
44. Gen. 18. 21.			as LXX.
		45. Num. 11. 34 (al.)	βουνὸν ἐπιθυμιῶν for μνήματα τῆς ἐπιθυμίας.
	47. Deut. 34. 4, 5.		
	49. Gen. 49. 10.		cf. Credner, Beit. 2. 53.
Hom. 11.			
22. Gen. 1. 1.			
Hom. 16.			
6. Gen. 3. 22.			twice with slightly different order.
Gen. 3. 5.			
	6. Ex. 22. 28.		
		6. Deut. 4. 34.	?mem. (ἀλλοθί που γέγραπται).
Jer. 10. 11.			
		Deut. 13. 6.	?mem. (ἄλλῃ που).
		Josh. 23. 7.	
	Deut. 10. 17.		
Ps. 35. 10.			
Ps. 50. 1.			
Ps. 82. 1.			
	Deut. 10. 14.		
	Deut. 4. 39.		
	Deut. 10. 17.		repeated as above.
		Deut. 10. 17.	very paraphrastic.

Exact.	Slightly variant.	Variant.	Remarks.
Hom. 16.		6. Deut. 4. 39.	
7. Deut. 6. 13.			
Deut. 6. 4.			
		8. Josh. 23. 7.	as above.
8. Exod. 22. 28†.			
Jer. 10. 11.			
Gen. 1. 1.			
Ps. 19. 2.			
	8. Ps. 102. 26.		
Gen. 1. 26.			
		13. Deut. 13. 1–3,	very free.
		9, 5, 3.	
Hom. 17.		18. Num. 12. 6.	} paraphrastic
		Ex. 33. 11.	} combination.
Hom. 18.		17. Is. 40. 26, 27.	free quotation.
		Deut. 30. 15.	ditto.
18. Is. 1. 3.			
Is. 1. 4.			

The example of the Clementine Homilies shows conspicuously the extremely deceptive character of the argument from silence. All the quotations from the Old Testament found in them are taken from five Homilies (iii, xi, xvi, xvii, xviii) out of nineteen, although the Homilies are lengthy compositions, filling, with the translation and various readings, four hundred and fourteen large octavo pages of Dressel's edition [1]. Of the whole number of quotations all but seven are taken from two Homilies, iii and xvi. If Hom. xvi and Hom. xviii had been lost, there would have been no evidence that the author was acquainted with any book of the Old Testament besides the Pentateuch; and, if the five Homilies had been lost, there would have been nothing to show that he was acquainted with the Old Testament at all. Yet the loss of the two Homilies would have left a volume of three hundred and seventy-seven pages, and that of the five a volume

[1] *Clementis Romani quae feruntur Homiliae Viginti* (Gottingae, 1853).

of three hundred and fifteen pages. In other words, it is possible to read three hundred and fifteen pages of the Homilies with five breaks and come to no quotation from the Old Testament at all, or three hundred and fifteen pages with only two breaks and come to none outside the Pentateuch. But the reduced volume that we have supposed, containing the fourteen Homilies, would probably exceed in bulk the whole of the extant Christian literature of the second century up to the time of Irenaeus, with the single exception of the works of Justin; it will therefore be seen how precarious must needs be any inference from the silence, not of all these writings, but merely of a portion of them.

For the rest, the quotations in the Homilies may be said to observe a fair standard of exactness, one apparently higher than that in the genuine Epistle of Clement to the Corinthians; at the same time it should be remembered that the quotations in the Homilies are much shorter, only two reaching a length of three verses, while the longest quotations in the Epistle are precisely those that are most exact. The most striking instance of accuracy of quotation is perhaps Gen. xv. 13-16 in Hom. iii. 43. On the other hand, there is marked freedom in the quotations from Deut. iv. 34, x. 17, xiii. 1-3, xiii. 6. xxx. 15, Is. xl. 26, 27, and the combined passage, Num. xii. 6 and Ex. xxiii. 11. There are several repetitions, but these occur too near to each other to permit of any inference.

Our examination of the Old Testament quotations in Justin is greatly facilitated by the collection and discussion of them in Credner's Beiträge[1], a noble

---

[1] *Beiträge zur Einleitung in die biblischen Schriften* (Halle, 1832).

example of that true patient work which is indeed the reverse of showy, but forms the solid and well-laid foundation on which alone genuine knowledge can be built. Credner has collected and compared in the most elaborate manner the whole of Justin's quotations with the various readings in the MSS. of the LXX; so that we may state our results with a much greater confidence than in any other case (except perhaps Clement of Rome, where we have the equally accurate and scholarly guidance of Dr. Lightfoot[1]) that we are not led astray by imperfect materials. I have availed myself freely of Credner's collection of variants, indicating the cases where the existence of documentary (or, in some places, inferential) evidence for Justin's readings has led to the quotation being placed in a different class from that to which it would at first sight seem to belong. I have also, as hitherto, not assumed an absolutely strict standard for admission to the first class of 'exact' quotations. Many of Justin's quotations are very long, and it seemed only right that in these the standard should be somewhat, though very slightly, relaxed. The chief point that we have to determine is the extent to which the writers of the first century were in the habit of freely paraphrasing or quoting from memory, and it may as a rule be assumed that all the instances in the first class and most (not quite all) of those in the second do not admit of such an explanation. I have been glad in every case where a truly scientific and most impartial writer like Credner gives his opinion, to make use of it instead of my own. I have the satisfaction to think that whatever may be the value of the other

---

[1] *The Epistles of S. Clement of Rome* (London and Cambridge, 1869).

sections of this enquiry, this at least is thoroughly sound, and based upon a really exhaustive sifting of the data.

The quotations given below are from the undoubted works of Justin, the Dialogue against Tryphon and the First Apology; the Second Apology does not appear to contain any quotations either from the Old or New Testament.

Exact.	Slightly variant.	Variant.	Remarks.
	Apol. 1. 59, Gen. 1. 1–3.		
Dial. 62, Gen. 1. 26–28.			
	Dial. 102, Gen. 3. 15.		free quotation (Credner).
D. 62, Gen. 3. 22.			
	D. 127, Gen. 7. 16.		
	D. 139, Gen. 9. 24–27.		
	D. 127, Gen. 11. 5.		free quotation (Cr.)
D. 102, Gen. 11. 6.			
	D. 92, Gen. 15. 6.		free quotation (Cr.)
		Dial. 10, †Gen. 17. 14.	
D. 127, Gen. 17. 22.			
	D. 56, †Gen. 18. 1, 2.		ver. 2 repeated similarly.
	†Gen. 18. 13, 14.		repeated, slightly more divergent.
	†Gen. 18. 16–23, 33.		
	Gen. 19. 1, 10, 16–28 (om. 26).		marked exactness in the whole passage.
D. 56, Gen. 21. 9–12.			
D. 120, Gen. 26. 4.			
D. 58, Gen. 28. 10–12.			
	D. 58, †(v. l.) Gen. 28. 13–19.		
	†(v. l.) Gen. 31. 10–13.		
D. 58, Gen. 32. 22–30.			note for exactness.
		D. 59, Gen. 35. 1.	free quotation (Cr.)
D. 58, Gen. 35. 6–10 (v. l.).			

Exact.	Slightly variant.	Variant.	Remarks.
D. 52, Gen. 49. 8–12.			repeated similarly.
D. 59, Ex. 2. 23.			
D. 60, Ex. 3. 2–4†.	D. 59, Ex. 3. 16.	A. 1. 62, Ex. 3. 5.	from memory (Cr.)
		A. 1. 63, Ex. 3. 16 (ter), 17.	ver. 16 freely quoted (Cr.) εἴρηταί που.
	D. 126, Ex. 6. 2–4.		
		D. 49, Ex. 17. 16.	free quotation (Cr.)
		D. 94, Ex. 20. 4.	ditto (Cr.).
	D. 75, Ex. 23. 20, 21.		from Lectionary (Cr.)
D. 16, Lev. 26. 40, 41 (v. l.)		D. 20, Ex. 32. 6.	free (Cr.)
	D. 126, Num. 11. 23.		
		A. 1. 60 (or. obl.), D. 94, Num. 21. 8, 9.	free (Cr.)
	D. 106, Num. 24. 17.		through Targum (Cr.)
		D. 16, Deut. 10. 16, 17.	from memory (Cr.)
		D. 96, Deut. 21. 23 Deut. 27. 26.	both precisely as St. Paul in Galatians, and quoted thence (Cr.)
D. 126, Deut. 31. 2, 3 (v. l.)			
D. 74, Deut. 31. 16–18 (v. l.)			
D. 131, Deut. 32. 7–9 (tr.)			
	D. 20, Deut. 32. 15.		
D. 119, Deut. 32. 16–23.			Targum (Cr.)
D. 130, Deut. 32. 43 (v. l.)			
	D. 91, †Deut. 33. 13–17.		
A. 1. 40, Ps. 1 and 2 entire.			parts repeated.
	D. 97, Ps. 3. 5, 6.		repeated, more freely.
D. 114, Ps. 8. 4.			
D. 27, Ps. 14. 3.			
D. 28, Ps. 18. 44, 45.			

Exact.	Slightly variant.	Variant.	Remarks.
D. 64, Ps. 19. 1-6 (A.1.40, vv.1-5).			perhaps from different MSS., see Credner.
D. 97 ff., Ps. 22. 1-23.			quoted as *whole* Psalm (bis).
D. 133 ff., Ps. 24 entire.			
	D. 141, Ps. 32. 2.		
D. 38, Ps. 45. 1-17.			parts repeated.
D. 37, Ps. 47. 6-9.			
D. 22, Ps. 49 entire.			
		D. 34 } Ps. 68. 18. D. 37 }	from Eph. 4. 8, Targum.
D. 34, Ps. 72 entire.			
D. 124, Ps. 82 entire.			
D. 73, Ps. 96 entire.			note Christian interpolation in ver. 10.
D. 37, Ps. 99 entire.			
D. 32, Ps. 110 entire.		D. 83, Ps. 110. 1-4.	from memory (Cr.)
		D. 110, Ps. 128. 3.	from memory (Cr.)
D. 85, Ps. 148. 1, 2.			
A. 1. 37, Is. 1. 3, 4.			
		A. 1. 47, Is. 1. 7 (Jer. 2. 15).	sense only (Cr.)
		D. 140 (A. 1. 53), Is. 1. 9.	
		A. 1. 37, Is. 1. 11-14.	from memory (Cr.)
	A. 1. 44 (61), Is. 1. 16-30.		omissions.
		D. 82, Is. 1. 23.	from memory (Cr.)
A. 1. 39, Is. 2. 3, 4.			
	D. 135, Is. 2. 5, 6.		Targum (Cr.)
D. 133, Is. 3. 9-15 (v. l.)			
		D. 27, Is. 3. 16.	free quotation (Cr.)
	D. 133, Is. 5. 18-25 (v. l.)		repeated.
	D. 43 (66), Is. 7. 10-17 (v. l.)		repeated, with slight variation.
		A. 1. 35, Is. 9. 6.	free (Cr.)
D. 87, Is. 11. 1-3.		[A. 1. 32, Is. 11. 1; Num. 24. 17.	free combination (Cr.)]
	D. 123, Is. 14. 1.		
D. 123, Is. 19. 24, 25†.			

Exact.	Slightly variant.	Variant.	Remarks.
	D. 78, Is. 29.13, 14.		repeated (v. l.), partly from memory.
D. 79, Is. 30. 1-5.			
	D. 70, Is. 33.13-19.		
	D. 69, Is. 35. 1-7.	A. 1. 48, Is. 35. 5, 6.	free; cf. Matt. 11. 5 (var.)
D. 50, Is. 39. 8, 40. 1-17.			
		D. 125 } Is. 42.1-4. D. 135 }	{ cf. Mat. 12. 17-21, Targum (Cr.)
D. 65, Is. 42. 6-13 (v. l.)			
		D. 122, Is. 42. 16.	free (Cr.)
	D. 123, Is. 42. 19, 20.		
D. 122, Is. 43. 10.			
		A. 1. 52, Is. 45. 24 (v. l.)	cf. Rom. 14. 11.
D. 121, Is. 49. 6 (v. l.)			
D. 122, Is. 49. 8 (v. l.)			
	D. 102, Is. 50. 4.		
A. 1. 38, Is. 50. 6-8.			Barn., Tert., Cypr.
D. 11, Is. 51. 4, 5.			
D. 17, Is. 52. 5 (v. l.)			
D. 12, Is. 52, 10-15, 53. 1-12, 54. 1-6.			
	A. 1. 50, Is. 52. 13-53. 12.		
		D. 138, Is. 54. 9.	very free.
D. 14, Is. 55. 3-13.		[D. 12, Is. 55. 3-5.	from memory (Cr.)]
D. 16, Is. 57. 1-4.			repeated.
D. 15, Is. 58. 1-11 (v. l.)			ἱμάτια for ἰάματα; so Barn., Tert., Cyp., Amb., Aug.
D. 27, Is. 58. 13, 14.			
	D. 26, †Is. 62. 10-63. 6.		συσσεισμόν for σύσσημον.
D. 25, Is. 63. 15-19, 64. 1-12.			
D. 24, Is. 65. 1-3.		[A. 1. 49, Is. 65. 1-3.	from memory (Cr.)]
D. 136, Is. 65. 8.			
D. 135, Is. 65. 9-12.			
D. 81, Is. 65. 17-25.			

Exact.	Slightly variant.	Variant.	Remarks.
		D. 22, Is. 66. 1.	from memory (Cr.)
D. 85, Is. 66. 5–11.			
		D. 44, Is. 66. 24 (ter).	from memory (Cr.)
		D. 114, Jer. 2. 13; Is. 16. 1; Jer. 3. 8.	as from Jeremiah, traditional combination; cf. Barn. 2.
	D. 28, Jer. 4. 3, 4 (v. l.)		
		D. 23, Jer. 7. 21, 22.	free quotation (Cr.)
	D. 28, Jer. 9. 25, 26.	[A. 1. 53, Jer. 9. 26.	quoted freely (Cr.) as from Isaiah.]
	D. 72, Jer. 11. 19.		omissions.
		D. 78, Jer. 31. 15 (38. 15, LXX).	so Matt. 2. 18 through Targum (Cr.)
		D. 123, Jer. 31. 27 (38. 27).	free quotation (Cr.)
	D. 11, Jer. 31. 31, 32 (38. 31, 32).		
		D. 72.	a passage quoted as from Jeremiah, which is not recognisable in our present texts.
		D. 82, Ezek. 3. 17–19.	free quotation (Cr.)
		D. 45, 44, 140 Ezek. 14. 20; cf. 14, 16, 18.	repeated similarly and equally divergent from LXX.
D. 77, Ezek. 16. 3.			
D. 21, Ezek. 20. 19–26.			
D. 123, Ezek. 36. 12.			
		A. 1. 52, Ezek. 37. 7.	very free (Cr.)

[Justin has in Dial. 31 (also in Apol. 1. 51, ver. 13, from memory) a long quotation from Daniel, Dan. 7. 9–28; his text can only be compared with a single MS. of the LXX, Codex Chisianus; from this it differs considerably, but many of the differences reappear in the version of Theodotion; 7. 10, 13 are also similarly quoted in Rev., Mark, Clem. Rom.]

Exact.	Slightly variant.	Variant.	Remarks.
		D. 19, Hos. 1. 9.	
		D. 102, Hos. 10.6.	referred to trial before Herod (Cr.)
		D. 87, Joel 2. 28.	from memory (Cr.)
	D. 22, †Amos 5. 18-6. 7 (v. l.)		
	D. 107, Jonah 4. 10,11 (v.l. Heb.)		
	D. 109, Micah 4. 1-7 (Heb.?)		divergent from LXX.
		A. 1. 34 } Micah 5. D. 78 . } 2.	precisely as Matt. 2. 6.
		A. 1.52, Zech. 2.6. D. 137, Zech. 2. 8.	free quotations (Cr.)
	D. 115, Zach. 2. 10-3. 2 (Heb.?)	[D. 79, Zech. 3. 1, 2.	freely (Cr.)]
D. 106, Zach. 6.12.			
		A. 1. 52, Zech. 12. 11, 12, 10.	repeated diversely [note reading of Christian origin (Cr.) in ver. 10: so John 19. 37; cp. Rev. 1. 7].
		D. 43, Zech. 13. 7.	diversely in Matt. 26. 31, proof that Justin is not dependent on Matthew (Cr.)
	D. 28, 41, Mal. 1. 10-12 (v. l.)	D. 117, Mal. 1. 10-12.	
	D. 62, †Joshua 5. 13-15; 6. 1, 2 (v. l.)		omissions.
		D. 118, 2 Sam. 7. 14-16.	from memory (Cr.)
		D. 39, 1 Kings 19. 14, 15, 18.	freely (Cr.); cf. Rom. 11. 3.
A. 1. 55, Lam. 4. 20 (v. l.)			
		D. 79, Job 1. 6.	sense only (Cr.) coincidence with Irenaeus.
	D. 61, †Prov. 8. 21-36.		

[D. 72 a passage ostensibly from Ezra, but probably an apocryphal addition, perhaps from Preaching of Peter; same quotation in Lactantius.]

It is impossible not to be struck with the amount of matter that Justin has transferred to his pages bodily. He has quoted nine Psalms entire, and a tenth with the statement (twice repeated) that it is given entire, though really he has only quoted twenty-three verses. The later chapters of Isaiah are also given with extraordinary fulness. These longer passages are generally quoted accurately. If Justin's text differs from the received text of the LXX, it is frequently found that he has some extant authority for his reading. The way in which Credner has drawn out these varieties of reading, and the results which he obtained as to the relations and comparative value of the different MSS., form perhaps the most interesting feature of his work. The more marked divergences in Justin may be referred to two causes; (1) quotation from memory, in which he indulges freely, especially in the shorter passages, and more in the Apology than in the Dialogue with Tryphon; (2) in Messianic passages the use of a Targum, not immediately by Justin himself but in some previous document from which he quotes, in order to introduce a more distinctly Christian interpretation; the coincidences between Justin and other Christian writers show that the text of the LXX had been thus modified in a Christian sense, generally through a closer comparison with and nearer return to the Hebrew, before his time. The instances of free quotation are not perhaps quite fully given in the above list, but it will be seen that though they form a marked phenomenon, still more marked is the amount of exactness. Any long, not Messianic, passage, it appears to be the rule with Justin to quote exactly. Among the passages quoted freely there seem to be none of greater length than four verses.

The exactness is especially remarkable in the plain historical narratives of the Pentateuch and the Psalms, though it is also evident that Justin had the MS. before him, and referred to it frequently throughout the quotations from the latter part of Isaiah. Through following the arrangement of Credner we have failed to notice the cases of combination; these however are collected by Dr. Westcott (On the Canon, p. 156). The most remarkable instance is in Apol. i. 52, where six different passages from three separate writers are interwoven together and assigned bodily to Zechariah. There are several more examples of mistaken ascription.

The great advantage of collecting the quotations from the Old Testament is that we are enabled to do so in regard to the very same writers among whom our enquiry is to lie. We can thus form a general idea of their idiosyncracies, and we know what to expect when we come to examine a different class of quotations. There is, however, the element of uncertainty of which I have spoken above. We cannot be quite clear what text the writer had before him. This difficulty also exists, though to a less degree, when we come to consider quotations from the New Testament in writers of an early date whom we know to have used our present Gospels as canonical. The text of these Gospels is so comparatively fixed, and we have such abundant materials for its reconstruction, that we can generally say at once whether the writer is quoting from it freely or not. We have thus a certain gain, though at the cost of the drawback that we can no longer draw an inference as to the practice of individuals, but merely attain to a general conclusion as to the habits of mind current in the age. This too will be subject to a deduction for the individual bent and peculiarities of the writer. We must therefore, on the whole, attach less importance to the examples under this section than under that preceding.

I chose two writers to be the subject of this examination almost, I may say, at random, and chiefly because I had more convenient access to their works at the time. The first of these is Irenaeus, that is to say the portions still extant in the Greek of his Treatise against Heresies[1], and the second Epiphanius.

Irenaeus is described by Dr. Tregelles 'as a close and careful quoter in general from the New Testament[2].' He may therefore be taken to represent a comparatively high standard of accuracy. In the following table the quotations which are merely allusive are included in brackets:—

Exact.	Slightly variant.	Variant.	Remarks.
I. Praef. Matt. 10. 26.			
I. 3. 2, Matt. 5. 18.			quoted from Gnostics.
I. 3. 3, Mark 5. 31.			Gnostics.
		I. 3. 5, Luke 14. 27.	Valentinians.
	I. 3. 5, Mark 10. 21 (v. l.).		the same.
I. 3. 5, Matt. 10. 34.			the same.
I. 3. 5, Luke 3. 17.			the same.
I. 4. 3, Matt. 10. 8.			
[I. 6. 1, Matt. 5. 13, 14, al.]			
		I. 7. 4, Matt. 8. 9. Luke 7. 8.	the same.

[1] The Latin translation is not in most cases a sufficient guarantee for the original text. The Greek has been preserved in the shape of long extracts by Epiphanius and others. The edition used is that of Stieren, Lipsiae, 1853.

[2] Horne's *Introduction* (ed. 1856), p. 333.

Exact.	Slightly variant.	Variant.	Remarks.
		I. 8. 2, Matt. 27. 46.	Valentinians.
I. 8. 2, Matt. 26. 38.			the same.
	I. 8. 2, Matt. 26. 39.		the same.
		I. 8. 2, John 12. 27.	the same.
		I. 8. 3, Luke 9. 57, 58.	the same.
		I. 8. 3, Luke 9. 61, 62.	the same.
	I. 8. 3, Luke 9. 60.		the same.
	I. 8. 3, Luke 19. 5.		the same.
		I. 8. 4, Luke 15. 4.	the same.
	[I. 8. 4, Luke 15. 8, al.]		the same.
	I. 8. 4, Luke 2. 28.		the same.
[I. 8. 4, Luke 6. 36, al.]			the same.
I. 8. 4, Luke 7. 35 (v. l.)			the same.
I. 8. 5, John 1. 1, 2.			the same.
I. 8. 5, John 1. 3 (v. l.)			the same.
I. 8. 5, John 1. 4.			the same.
		I. 8. 5, John 1. 5.	the same.
I. 8. 5, John 1. 14.		I. 8. 5, John 1. 14.	[the same verse repeated differently.]
		[I. 14. 1, Matt. 18. 10, al.]	Marcus.
	[I. 16. 1, Luke 15. 8, al.]		Marcosians.
		[I. 16. 3, Matt. 12. 43, al.]	the same.
	I. 20. 2, Luke 2. 49.		the same.
		I. 20. 2, Mark 10. 18.	['memoriter' Stieren; but comp. Clem. Hom. and Justin.]
	I. 20. 2, Matt. 21. 23.		Marcosians.
		I. 20. 2, Luke 19. 42.	the same.
I. 20. 2, Matt. 11. 28 (? om.).			the same.
		I. 20. 3, Luke 10. 21. (Matt. 11. 25.)	the same; [v. l., comp. Marcion, Clem. Hom., Justin, &c.]
		I. 21. 2, Luke 12. 50.	Marcosians.

Exact.	Slightly variant.	Variant.	Remarks.
	I. 21. 2, Mark 10. 36.		Marcosians.
III. 11. 8, John 1. 1–3 (?).			
III. 11. 8, Matt. 1. 1, 18 (v. l.)			
	III. 11. 8, Mark 1. 1, 2.		omissions.
III. 22. 2, John 4. 6.			
III. 22. 2, Matt. 26. 38.			
	IV. 26. 1, } Matt. IV. 40. 3, } 13. 38.		
	IV. 40. 3, Matt. 13. 25.		
V. 17. 4, Matt. 3. 10.			
		V. 36. 2, John 14. 2 (or. obl.)	
		Fragm. 14, Matt. 15. 17.	

On the whole these quotations of Irenaeus seem fairly to deserve the praise given to them by Dr. Tregelles. Most of the free quotations, it will be seen, belong not so much to Irenaeus himself, as to the writers he is criticising. In some places (e. g. iv. 6. 1, which is found in the Latin only) he expressly notes a difference of text. In this very place, however, he shows that he is quoting from memory, as he speaks of a parallel passage in St. Mark which does not exist. Elsewhere there can be little doubt that either he or the writer before him quoted loosely from memory. Thus Luke xii. 50 is given as ἄλλο βάπτισμα ἔχω βαπτισθῆναι καὶ πάνυ ἐπείγομαι εἰς αὐτό for βάπτισμα δὲ ἔχω βαπτισθῆναι καὶ πῶς συνέχομαι ἕως ὅτου τελεσθῇ. The quotation from Matt. viii. 9 is represented as καὶ γὰρ ἐγὼ ὑπὸ τὴν ἐμαυτοῦ ἐξουσίαν ἔχω στρατιώτας καὶ δούλους καὶ ὃ ἐὰν προστάξω ποιοῦσι, which is evidently free; those from Matt. xviii. 10, xxvii. 46, Luke ix. 57, 58, 61, 62, xiv. 27, xix. 42,

John i. 5, 14 (where however there appears to be some confusion in the text of Irenaeus), xiv. 2, also seem to be best explained as made from memory.

The list given below, of quotations from the Gospels in the Panarium or 'Treatise against Heresies' of Epiphanius[1], is not intended to be exhaustive. It has been made from the shorter index of Petavius, and being confined to the 'praecipui loci' consists chiefly of passages of substantial length and entirely (I believe) of express quotations. It has been again necessary to distinguish between the quotations made directly by Epiphanius himself and those made by the heretical writers whose works he is reviewing.

Exact.	Slightly variant.	Variant.	Remarks.
426 A, Matt. 1. 1; Matt. 1. 18 (v. l.)			
	426 B C, Matt. 1. 18–25†.		abridged, divergent in middle.
		430 B, Matt. 2. 13.	Porphyry&Celsus.
		44 C, Matt. 5. 34, 37.	
	59 C, Matt. 5. 17, 18.		
180 B, Matt. 5. 18†.			Valentinians.
		226 A, Matt. 5. 45.	
	72 A, Matt. 7. 6.		Basilidians.
404 C, Matt. 7. 15.			
		67 C, Matt. 8. 11.	
		650 B, Matt. 8. 28–34 (par.)	
	303 A, Matt. 9. 17, 16.		Marcion.
	71 D, Matt. 10. 33.		Basilidians.
	274 B, Matt. 10. 16.		
88 A, Matt. 11. 7.	143 B, Matt. 11. 18.		Gnostics.
	254 B, Matt. 11. 28.		Marcosians.
		139 A B, Matt. 12. 48 sqq. (v. l.)	Ebionites.
174 C, Matt. 10. 26.			

[1] Ed. Dindorf, Lipsiae, 1859. [The index given in vol. iii. p. 893 sqq. contains many inaccuracies, and is, indeed, of little use for identifying the passages of Scripture.]

IN THE EARLY CHRISTIAN WRITERS. 53

Exact.	Slightly variant.	Variant.	Remarks.
		464 B, Matt. 12. 31, 32.	Theodotus.
	33 A, Matt. 23. 5.	218 D, Matt. 15. 4-6 (or. obl.)	Ptolemaeus.
		490 C, Matt. 15. 20. Mark 7. 21, 22.	
		490 A, Matt. 18. 8. Mark 9. 43.	} compression.
		679 B C, Matt. 13. 24-30, 37-39.	Manes.
		152 B, Matt. 5. 17.	
	59 C D, Matt. 19. 10-12.		
	59 D, Matt. 19. 6.		
		81 A, Matt. 19. 12.	
		97 D, Matt. 22. 30.	
		36 B C, Matt. 23. 23, 25; 23. 18-20 (5. 35); Mark 7. 11-13; Matt. 23. 15.	remarkable composition, probably from memory.
		226 A. Matt. 23. 29; Luke 11. 47.	composition.
		281 A, Matt. 23. 35.	
		508 C, Matt. 25. 34.	
		146 A B, Matt. 26. 17, 18; Mark 14. 12-14; Luke 22. 9-11.	narrative.
		279 D, Matt. 26. 24.	
		390 B, Matt. 21. 33, par.	
	50 A, Matt. 28. 19.		
	427 B, Mark 1. 1, 2 (v. l.)		
	428 C, Mark 1. 4.		
		457 D, Mark 3. 29; Matt. 12. 31; Luke 12. 10.	singular composition.
	400 D, Matt. 19. 6; Mark 10. 9.		
		650 C, Matt. 8. 28-34; Mark 5. 1-20; Luke 8. 26-39.	narrative.

Exact.	Slightly variant.	Variant.	Remarks.
		218 D, Matt. 15. 4-9; Mark 7. 6-13.	
		224 C, Mark 7. 13.	Ptolemaeans.
		1045 C, Mark 14. 51, 52.	
144 D, Luke 1. 34, 35 (v. l.)	115 B, Luke 1. 34, 35.		
154 D, Luke 2. 14.			
		95 A, Luke 1. 76, 17.	strange composition.
322 D, Luke 5. 14 (v. l.)			Marcion.
	155 A B, Luke 2. 48, 49.		
	155 C, Luke 3. 23.		
		154 D, Luke 2. 11.	
	181 C, Luke 3. 17.		Valentinians.
		428 D, Luke 1. 1-4.	
		205 D, Luke 8. 10; Mark 4. 11; Matt. 13. 11.	
	325 A, Luke 7. 27.		Marcion.
	325 B, Luke 7. 36-38.		the same.
	326 D, Luke 8. 23; Matt. 8. 26.		the same (and Epiphanius?).
		194 D, Luke 9. 61.	Valentinians.
	194 D, Luke 9. 58.		the same.
		194 D, Luke 9. 62.	the same.
		254 C, Luke 10. 21, 22; Matt. 11. 25-27.	Marcosians.
		255 B, Luke 12. 50.	the same.

[These last five quotations have already been given under Irenaeus, whom Epiphanius is transcribing.]

	464 D, Luke 12. 9; Matt. 10. 33.		composition.
	181 B, Luke 14. 27.		Valentinians.
	401 A, Luke 21. 34.		
	143 C, Luke 24. 42 (v. l.)		
	349 C, Luke 24. 38, 39.		Marcion.

Exact.	Slightly variant.	Variant.	Remarks.
384 B, John 1. 1–3.			
148 A, John 1. 23.			
	148 B, John 2. 16, 17.		
	89 C, John 3. 12.		Gnostics.
	274 A, John 3. 14.		
59 C, John 5. 46.			
66 C. John 5. 17.		162 B, John 5. 8.	
	919 A, John 5. 18.		
		117 D, John 6. 15.	the same.
	89 D, John 6. 53.		
	279 D, John 6. 70.		
		279 B, John 8. 44.	Theodotus.
	463 D, John 8. 40.		
		148 B, John 12.41.	
		153 A, John 12.22.	
	75 C, John 14. 6.		
919 C, John 14.10.			
921 D, John 17. 3.			
		279 D, John 17. 11, 12.	
	119 D, John 18.36.		

It is impossible here not to notice the very large amount of freedom in the quotations. The exact quotations number only fifteen, the slightly variant thirty-seven, and the markedly variant forty. By far the larger portion of this last class and several instances in the second it seems most reasonable to refer to the habit of quoting from memory. This is strikingly illustrated by the passage 117 D, where the retreat of Jesus and His disciples to Ephraim is treated as a consequence of the attempt 'to make Him king' (John vi. 15), though in reality it did not take place till after the raising of Lazarus and just before the Last Passover (see John xi. 54). A very remarkable case of combination is found in 36 B C, where a single quotation is made up of a cento of no less than six separate passages taken from all three Synoptic Gospels and in the most broken order. Fusions so complete as this are usually the result of unconscious acts of the mind, i.e. of memory. A curious instance of the way in which the Synoptic parallels are blended together in a compound which differs from each and all of them is presented in 437 D (τῷ βλασφημοῦντι εἰς τὸ πνεῦμα τὸ ἅγιον οὐκ ἀφεθήσεται αὐτῷ οὔτε ἐν τῷ νῦν αἰῶνι οὔτε ἐν τῷ μέλλοντι). Another example of Epiphanius' manner in skipping backwards and forwards from one Synoptic to another may be seen in 218 D, which is made up of Matt. xv. 4–9 and Mark vii. 6–13. A strange mistake is made in 428 D, where παρηκολουθηκότι is taken with τοῖς αὐτόπταις καὶ ὑπηρέταις τοῦ λόγου. Many kinds of variation find examples in these quotations of Epiphanius, to some of which we may have occasion to allude more particularly later on.

It should be remembered that these are not by any means selected examples. Neither Irenaeus nor Epiphanius are notorious for free quotation — Irenaeus indeed is rather the reverse. Probably a much more plentiful harvest of variations would have been obtained e.g. from Clement of Alexandria, from whose writings numerous instances of quotation following the sense only, of false ascription, of the blending of passages, of quotations from memory, are given in the treatise of Bp. Kaye[1]. Dr. Westcott has recently collected[2] the quotations from Chrysostom *On the Priesthood*, with the result that about one half present variations from the Apostolic texts, and some of these variations,

---

[1] *Some Account of the Writings and Opinions of Clement of Alexandria*, p. 407 sqq.

[2] In the new Preface to his work on the Canon (4th edition, 1875), p. xxxii.

which he gives at length, are certainly very much to the point.

I fear we shall have seemed to delay too long upon this first preliminary stage of the enquiry, but it is highly desirable that we should start with a good broad inductive basis to go upon. We have now an instrument in our hands by which to test the alleged quotations in the early writers; and, rough and approximate as that instrument must still be admitted to be, it is at least much better than none at all.

CHAPTER III.

THE APOSTOLIC FATHERS.

To go at all thoroughly into all the questions that may be raised as to the date and character of the Christian writings in the early part of the second century would need a series of somewhat elaborate monographs, and, important as it is that the data should be fixed with the utmost attainable precision, the scaffolding thus raised would, in a work like the present, be out of proportion to the superstructure erected upon it. These are matters that must be decided by the authority of those who have made the provinces to which they belong a subject of special study: all we can do will be to test the value of the several authorities in passing.

In regard to Clement of Rome, whose First (genuine) Epistle to the Corinthians is the first writing that meets us, the author of 'Supernatural Religion' is quite right in saying that 'the great mass of critics ... assign the composition of the Epistle to the end of the first century (A.D. 95–100)[1].' There is as usual a right and a left wing in the array of critics. The right includes several of the older writers; among the moderns the

---

[1] *S. R.* i. p. 221, and note.

most conspicuous figure is the Roman Catholic Bishop Hefele. Tischendorf also, though as it is pointed out somewhat inconsistently, leans to this side. According to their opinion the Epistle would be written shortly before A.D. 70. On the left, the names quoted are Volkmar, Baur, Scholten, Stap, and Schwegler[1]. Baur contents himself with the remark that the Epistle to the Corinthians, 'as one of the oldest documents of Christian antiquity, might have passed without question as a writing of the Roman Clement,' had not this Clement become a legendary person and had so many spurious works palmed off upon him[2]. But it is surely no argument to say that because a certain number of extravagant and spurious writings are attributed to Clement, therefore one so sober and consistent with his position, and one so well attested as this, is not likely to have been written by him. The contrary inference would be the more reasonable, for if Clement had not been an important person, and if he had left no known and acknowledged writings, divergent parties in the Church would have had no reason for making use of his name. But arguments of this kind cannot have much weight. Probably not one half of the writings attributed to Justin Martyr are genuine; but no one on that account doubts the Apologies and the Dialogue with Tryphon.

Schwegler[3], as is his wont, has developed the opinion of Baur, adding some reasons of his own. Such as, that the letter shows Pauline tendencies, while 'according to the most certain traditions' Clement was a follower of

---

[1] *S. R.* i. p. 222, n. 3.
[2] *Lehrb. chr. Dogmengesch.* p. 74 (p. 82 *S. R.*?).
[3] *Das nachapost. Zeitalter*, p. 126 sq.

St. Peter; but the evidence for the Epistle (Polycarp, Dionysius of Corinth, A.D. 165–175, Hegesippus, and Irenaeus in the most express terms) is much older and better than these 'most certain traditions' (Tertullian and Origen), even if they proved anything: 'in the Epistle of Clement use is made of the Epistle to the Hebrews;' but surely, according to any sober canons of criticism, the only light in which this argument can be regarded is as so much evidence for the Epistle to the Hebrews: the Epistle implies a development of the episcopate which 'demonstrably' (nachweislich) did not take place until during the course of the second century; what the 'demonstration' is does not appear, and indeed it is only part of the great fabric of hypothesis that makes up the Tübingen theory.

Volkmar strikes into a new vein[1]. The Epistle of Clement presupposes the Book of Judith; but the Book of Judith must be dated A.D. 117–118; and therefore the Epistle of Clement will fall about A.D. 125. What is the ground for this reasoning? It consists in a theory, which Volkmar adopted and developed from Hitzig, as to the origin of the Book of Judith. That book is an allegorical or symbolical representation of events in the early part of the rising of the Jews under Barcochba; Judith is Judaea, Nebuchadnezzar Trajan; Assyria stands for Syria, Nineveh for Antioch, Arphaxad for a Parthian king Arsaces, Ecbatana for Nisibis or perhaps Batnae; Bagoas is the eunuch-service in general; Holofernes is the Moor Lucius Quietus. Out of these elements an elaborate historical theory is constructed, which Ewald and Fritzsche have taken the trouble to

---

[1] *Der Ursprung unserer Evangelien*, p. 64; compare Fritzsche, art. 'Judith' in Schenkel's *Bibel-Lexicon*.

refute on historical grounds. To us it is very much as if Ivanhoe were made out to be an allegory of incidents in the French Revolution; or as if the 'tale of Troy divine' were, not a nature-myth or Euemeristic legend of long past ages, but a symbolical representation of events under the Pisistratidae.

Examples such as this are apt to draw from the English reader a sweeping condemnation of German criticism, and yet they are really only the sports or freaks of an exuberant activity. The long list given in 'Supernatural Religion'[1] of those who maintain the middle date of Clement's Epistle (A.D. 95–100) includes apparently all the English writers, and among a number of Germans the weighty names of Bleek, Ewald, Gieseler, Hilgenfeld, Köstlin, Lipsius, Laurent, Reuss, and Ritschl. From the point of view either of authority or of argument there can be little doubt which is the soundest and most judicious decision.

Now what is the bearing of the Epistle of Clement upon the question of the currency and authority of the Synoptic Gospels? There are two passages of some length which are without doubt evangelical quotations, though whether they are derived from the Canonical Gospels or not may be doubted.

The first passage occurs in c. xiii. It will be necessary to give it in full with the Synoptic parallels, in order to appreciate the exact amount of difference and resemblance which it presents.

---

[1] Vol. i. p. 221, n. I feel it due to the author to say that I have found his long lists of references, though not seldom faulty, very useful. I willingly acknowledge the justice of his claim to have 'fully laid before readers the actual means of judging of the accuracy of every statement which has been made' (Preface to sixth edition, p. lxxx).

Matt. v. 7, vi. 14, vii. 12, 2.	Clem. ad Cor. c. xiii.	Luke vi. 36, 37, 31, vi. 38, 37, 38.
	[Especially remembering the word of the Lord Jesus which he spake. . . . For thus he said:]	
v. 7. Blessed are the pitiful, for they shall be pitied. vi. 14. For if ye forgive men their trespasses, etc. vii. 12. All things therefore whatsoever ye would that men should do unto you, even so do ye unto them. vii. 2. For with what judgment ye judge, ye shall be judged: and with what measure ye mete, it shall be measured unto you.	Pity ye, that ye may be pitied: forgive, that it may be forgiven unto you. As ye do, so shall it be done unto you: as ye give, so shall it be given unto you: as ye judge, so shall it be judged unto you: as ye are kind, so shall kindness be shown unto you: with what measure ye mete, with it shall it be measured unto you.	vi. 36. Be ye merciful, etc. vi. 37. Acquit, and ye shall be acquitted. vi. 31. And as ye would that they should do unto you, do ye also unto them likewise. vi. 38. Give, and it shall be given unto you. vi. 37. And judge not, and ye shall not be judged. For with what measure ye mete, it shall be measured unto you again.

Matt. v. 7, vi. 14, vii. 12, 2.	Clem. ad Cor. c. xiii.	Luke vi. 36, 37, 31, 38, 37.
v. 7. μακάριοι οἱ ἐλεήμονες ὅτι αὐτοὶ ἐλεηθήσονται.	ἐλεεῖτε ἵνα ἐλεηθῆτε.	vi. 36. γίνεσθε οἰκτίρμονες, κ.τ.λ.
vi. 14. ἐὰν γὰρ ἀφῆτε τοῖς ἀνθ. τὰ παραπτώματα αὐτῶν.	ἀφίετε ἵνα ἀφεθῇ ὑμῖν.	vi. 37. ἀπολύετε καὶ ἀπολυθήσεσθε.
vii. 12. πάντα οὖν ὅσα ἐὰν θέλητε ἵνα ποιῶσιν ὑμῖν οἱ ἄνθ.	ὡς ποιεῖτε οὕτω ποιηθήσεται ὑμῖν.	vi. 31. καὶ καθὼς θέλετε ἵνα ποιῶσιν ὑμῖν οἱ ἄνθρωποι καὶ

Matt. v. 7, vi. 14, vii. 12, 2.	*Clem. ad Cor.* c. xiii.	*Luke* vi. 36, 37, 31, 38, 37.
οὕτως καὶ ὑμεῖς ποιεῖτε αὐτοῖς.		ὑμεῖς ποιεῖτε αὐτοῖς ὁμοίως.
	ὡς δίδοτε οὕτως δοθήσεται ὑμῖν.	vi. 38. δίδοτε, καὶ δοθήσεται ὑμῖν.
vii. 2. ἐν ᾧ γὰρ κρίματι κρίνετε κριθήσεσθε.	ὡς κρίνετε οὕτως κριθήσεται ὑμῖν.	vi. 37. καὶ μὴ κρίνετε καὶ οὐ μὴ κριθῆτε.
	ὡς χρηστεύεσθε οὕτως χρηστευθήσεται ὑμῖν.	
καὶ ἐν ᾧ μέτρῳ μετρεῖτε μετρηθήσεται ὑμῖν.	ᾧ μέτρῳ μετρεῖτε ἐν αὐτῷ μετρηθήσεται ὑμῖν.	vi. 38. τῷ γὰρ αὐτῷ μέτρῳ ᾧ μετρεῖτε ἀντιμετρηθήσεται ὑμῖν.

We are to determine whether this quotation was taken from the Canonical Gospels. Let us try to balance the arguments on both sides as fairly as possible. Dr. Lightfoot writes in his note upon the passage as follows: 'As Clement's quotations are often very loose, we need not go beyond the Canonical Gospels for the source of this passage. The resemblance to the original is much closer here, than it is for instance in his account of Rahab above, § 12. The hypothesis therefore that Clement derived the saying from oral tradition, or from some lost Gospel, is not needed.' (1) No doubt it is true that Clement does often quote loosely. The difference of language, taking the parallel clauses one by one, is not greater than would be found in many of his quotations from the Old Testament. (2) Supposing that the order of St. Luke is followed, there will be no greater dislocation than e. g. in the quotation from Deut. ix. 12-14 and Exod. xxxii. (7, 8), 11, 31, 32 in c. liii, and the backward order of the quotation would have a parallel in Clem. Hom. xvi. 13, where the verses Deut. xiii. 1-3, 5, 9 are quoted in the order Deut. xiii. 1–3, 9, 5, 3, and elsewhere. The composition of a passage from different places in the same book, or more often from places in different books, such as would be the case if Clement was following Matthew, frequently occurs in his quotations from the Old Testament. (3) We have no positive evidence of the presence of this passage in any non-extant Gospel. (4) Arguments from the manner of quoting the Old Testament to the manner of quoting the New must always be to a certain extent *a fortiori*, for it is undeniable that the New Testament did not as yet stand upon the same footing of respect and authority as the Old, and the scarcity of MSS. must have made it less accessible. In the case of converts from Judaism, the Old Testament would have been largely committed to memory in youth, while the knowledge of the New would be only recently acquired. These considerations seem to favour the hypothesis that Clement is quoting from our Gospels.

But on the other hand it may be urged, (1) that the parallel adduced by Dr. Lightfoot, the story of Rahab, is not quite in point, because it is narrative, and narrative both in Clement and the other writers of his time is dealt with more freely than discourse. (2) The passage before us is also of greater length than is usual in Clement's free quotations. I doubt whether as long a piece of discourse can be found treated with equal freedom, unless it is the two doubtful cases in c. viii and c. xxix. (3) It will not fail to be noticed that the passage as it stands in Clement has a roundness, a compactness, a balance of style, which give it an individual and independent appearance. Fusions effected by an unconscious process of thought are, it is true, sometimes marked by this completeness; still there is a difficulty in supposing the terse antitheses of the Clementine version to be derived from the fuller, but more lax and disconnected, sayings in our Gospels. (4) It is noticed in 'Supernatural Religion [1]' that the particular phrase χρηστεύεσθε has at least a partial parallel in Justin (γίνεσθε χρηστοὶ καὶ οἰκτίρμονες), though it has none in the Canonical Gospels. This may seem to point to a documentary source no longer extant.

Doubtless light would be thrown upon the question if we only knew what was the common original of the two Synoptic texts. How do they come to be so like and yet so different as they are? How do they come to be so strangely broken up? The triple synopsis, which has to do more with narrative, presents less difficulty, but the problem raised by these fragmentary parallelisms in discourse is dark and complex in the extreme; yet if it were only solved it would in all probability give us the key to a wide class of phenomena. The differences in these extra-canonical quotations do not exceed the differences between the Synoptic Gospels themselves; yet by far the larger proportion of critics regard the resemblances in the Synoptics as due to a common written source used either by all three or by two of them. The critics have not however, I believe, given any satisfactory explanation of the state of dispersion in which the fragments of this latter class are found. All that can be at present done is to point out that the solution of this problem and that of such quotations as the one discussed in Clement hang together, and that while the one remains open the other must also.

[1] i. p. 226.

Looking at the arguments on both sides, so far as we can give them, I incline on the whole to the opinion that Clement is not quoting directly from our Gospels, but I am quite aware of the insecure ground on which this opinion rests. It is a nice balance of probabilities, and the element of ignorance is so large that the conclusion, whatever it is, must be purely provisional. Anything like confident dogmatism on the subject seems to me entirely out of place.

Very much the same is to be said of the second passage in c. xlvi compared with Matt. xxvi. 24, xviii. 6, or Luke xvii. 1, 2. It hardly seems necessary to give the passage in full, as this is already done in 'Supernatural Religion,' and it does not differ materially from that first quoted, except that it is less complicated and the supposition of a quotation from memory somewhat easier. The critic indeed dismisses the question summarily enough. He says that 'the slightest comparison of the passage with our Gospels is sufficient to convince any unprejudiced mind that it is neither a combination of texts nor a quotation from memory[1].' But this very confident assertion is only the result of the hasty and superficial examination that the author has given to the facts. He has set down the impression that a modern might receive, at the first blush, without having given any more extended study to the method of the patristic quotations. I do not wish to impute blame to him for this, because we are all sure to take up some points superficially; but the misfortune is that he has spent his labour in the wrong place. He has, in a manner, revived the old ecclesiastical argument from authority by heaping together references, not always quite di-

[1] i. p. 228.

gested and sifted, upon points that often do not need them, and he has neglected that consecutive study of the originals which alone could imbue his mind with their spirit and place him at the proper point of view for his enquiry.

The hypothesis that Clement's quotation is made *memoriter* from our Gospel is very far from being inadmissible. Were it not that the other passage seems to lean the other way, I should be inclined to regard it as quite the most probable solution. Such a fusion is precisely what *would* and frequently *does* take place in quoting from memory. It is important to notice the key phrases in the quotation. The opening phrases οὐαὶ τῷ ἀνθρώπῳ ἐκείνῳ· καλὸν ἦν αὐτῷ εἰ οὐκ ἐγεννήθη are found *exactly* (though with omissions) in Matt. xxvi. 24. Clement has in common with the Synoptists all the more marked expressions but two, σκανδαλίσαι (-σῃ Synoptics), the unusual word μύλος (Matt., Mark), καταποντισθῆναι (-θῇ Matt.), εἰς τὴν θάλασσαν (Mark, Luke), ἕνα τῶν μικρῶν (μου Clement, τούτων Synoptics). He differs from them, so far as phraseology is concerned, only in writing *once* (the second time he agrees with the Synoptics) τῶν ἐκλεκτῶν μου for τῶν μικρῶν τούτων, by an easy paraphrase, and περιτεθῆναι where Mark and Luke have περίκειται and Matthew κρεμασθῇ. But on the other hand, it should be noticed that Matthew has, besides this variation, ἐν τῷ πελάγει τῆς θαλάσσης, where the two companion Gospels have εἰς τὴν θάλασσαν; where he has καταποντισθῇ, Mark has βέβληται and Luke ἔρριπται; and in the important phrase for 'it were better' all the three Gospels differ, Matthew having συμφέρει, Mark καλόν ἐστιν, and Luke λυσιτελεῖ; so that it seems not at all too much to say that Clement does not differ from the Synoptics more than they differ from each other. The remarks that the author makes, in a general way, upon these differences lead us to ask whether he has ever definitely put to himself the question, How did they arise? He must be aware that the mass of German authorities he is so fond of quoting admit of only two alternatives, that the Synoptic writers copied either from the same original or from each other, and that the idea of a merely oral tradition is scouted in Germany. But if this is the case, if so great a freedom has been exercised in transcription, is it strange that Clement (or any other writer) should be equally free in quotation?

The author rightly notices—though he does not seem quite to appreciate its bearing—the fact that Marcion and some codices (of the Old Latin translation) insert, as Clement does, the phrase εἰ οὐκ ἐγεννήθη ἤ in the text of St. Luke. Supposing that this were the text of St. Luke's Gospel which Clement had before him, it would surely be so much easier to regard his quotation as directly taken from the Gospel; but the truer view perhaps would be that we have here an instance (and the number of such instances in the older MSS. is legion) of the tendency to interpolate by the insertion of parallel passages from the same or from the other Synoptic Gospels. Clement and Marcion (with the Old Latin) will then confirm each other, as showing that even at this early date the two passages, Matt. xxvi. 24 and Matt. xviii. 6 (Luke xvii. 2), had already begun to be combined.

There is one point more to be noticed before we leave the Epistle of Clement. There is a quotation from Isaiah in this Epistle which is common to it with the first two Synoptics. Of this Volkmar writes as follows, giving the words of Clement, c. xv, 'The Scripture says somewhere, This people honoureth me with their lips, but their heart is far from me,' (οὗτος ὁ λαὸς τοῖς χείλεσίν με τιμᾷ ἡ δὲ καρδία αὐτῶν πόρρω ἄπεστιν ἀπ' ἐμοῦ). 'This "Scripture" the writer found in Mark vii. 6 (followed in Matt. xv. 8), and in that shape he could not at once remember where it stood in the Old Testament. It is indeed Mark's peculiar reproduction of Is. xxix. 13, in opposition to the original and the LXX. A further proof that the Roman Christian has here our Synoptic text in his mind, may be taken from c. xiii, where he quotes Jer. ix. 24 with equal divergence from the LXX, after the precedent of the Apostle (1 Cor. i. 31, 2 Cor. x. 17) whose letters he expressly refers to (c. xlvii)[1].' It is difficult here to avoid the conclusion that Clement is quoting the Old Testament through the medium of our Gospels. The text of the LXX is this, ἐγγίζει μοι ὁ λαὸς οὗτος ἐν τῷ στόματι αὐτοῦ καὶ ἐν τοῖς χείλεσιν αὐτῶν τιμῶσίν με. Clement has the passage exactly as it is given in Mark (ὁ λαὸς οὗτος Matt.), except that he writes ἄπεστιν where both of the Gospels have ἀπέχει with the LXX. The passage is not Messianic, so that the variation cannot be referred to a Targum; and though A. and six other MSS. in Holmes and Parsons omit ἐν τῷ στόματι αὐτοῦ (through wrong punctuation—Credner), still there is no MS. authority whatever, and naturally could not be, for the omission of ἐγγίζει μοι .. καὶ and for the change of τιμῶσιν to τιμᾷ. There can be little doubt that this was a free quotation in the original of the Synoptic Gospels, and it is in a high degree probable that it has passed through them into Clement

[1] *Der Ursprung*, p. 138.

of Rome. It might perhaps be suggested that Clement was possibly quoting the earlier document, the original of our Synoptics, but this suggestion seems to be excluded both by his further deviation from the LXX in ἄπεστιν, and also by the phenomena of the last quotation we have been discussing, which are certainly of a secondary character. Altogether I cannot but regard this passage as the strongest evidence we possess for the use of the Synoptic Gospels by Clement; it seems to carry the presumption that he did use them up to a considerable degree of probability.

It is rather singular that Volkmar, whose speculations about the Book of Judith we have seen above, should be so emphatic as he is in asserting the use of all three Synoptics by Clement. We might almost, though not quite, apply with a single change to this critic a sentence originally levelled at Tischendorf, to the intent that 'he systematically adopts the latest (earliest) possible or impossible dates for all the writings of the first two centuries,' but he is able to admit the use of the third and fourth Synoptics (the publication of which he places respectively in 100 and 110 A.D.) by throwing forward the date of Clement's Epistle, through the Judith-hypothesis, to A.D. 125. We may however accept the assertion for what it is worth, as coming from a mind something less than impartial, while we reject the concomitant theories. For my own part I do not feel able to speak with quite the same confidence, and yet upon the whole the evidence, which on a single instance might seem to incline the other way, does appear to favour the conclusion that Clement used our present Canonical Gospels.

2.

There is not, so far as I am aware, any reason to complain of the statement of opinion in 'Supernatural Religion' as to the date of the so-called Epistle of Barnabas. Arguing then entirely from authority, we may put the *terminus ad quem* at about 130 A.D. The only writer who is quoted as placing it later is Dr. Donaldson, who has perhaps altered his mind in the later edition of his work, as he now writes: 'Most (critics) have been inclined to place it not later than the first quarter of the second century, and all the indications of a date, though very slight, point to this period[1].'

The most important issue is raised on a quotation in c. iv, 'Many are called but few chosen,' in the Greek of the Codex Sinaiticus [προσέχωμεν, μήποτε, ὡς γέγραπται], πολλοὶ κλητοί, ὀλίγοι δὲ ἐκλεκτοὶ εὑρεθῶμεν. This corresponds exactly with Matt. xxii. 14, πολλοὶ γάρ εἰσιν κλητοί, ὀλίγοι δὲ ἐκλεκτοί. The passage occurs twice in our present received text of St. Matthew, but in xx. 16 it is probably an interpolation. There also occurs in 4 Ezra (2 Esdras) viii. 3 the sentence, 'Many were created but few shall be saved[2].' Our author spends several pages in the attempt to prove that this is the original of the quotation in Barnabas and not the saying in St. Matthew. We have the usual positiveness of statement: 'There can be no doubt that the sense of the reading in 4 Ezra is exactly that of the Epistle.' 'It is impossible to imagine a saying more irrelevant

---

[1] *The Apostolical Fathers* (London, 1874), p. 273.

[2] The original Greek of this work is lost, but in the text as reconstructed by Hilgenfeld from five still extant versions (Latin, Syriac, Æthiopic, Arabic, Armenian) the verse runs thus, πολλοὶ μὲν ἐκτίσθησαν, ὀλίγοι δὲ σωθήσονται (*Messias Judaeorum*, p. 69).

to its context than "Many are called but few chosen" in Matt. xx. 16,' where it is indeed spurious, though the relevancy of it might very well be maintained. In Matt. xxii. 14, where the saying is genuine, 'it is clear that the facts distinctly contradict the moral that "few are chosen."' When we come to a passage with a fixed idea it is always easy to get out of it what we wish to find. As to the relevancy or irrelevancy of the clause in Matt. xxii. 14 I shall say nothing, because it is in either case undoubtedly genuine. But it is surely a strange paradox to maintain that the words 'Many were created but few shall be saved' are nearer in meaning to 'Many are called but few chosen' than the repetition of those very words themselves. Our author has forgotten to notice that Barnabas has used the precise word κλητοί just before; indeed it is the very point on which his argument turns, 'because we are called do not let us therefore rest idly upon our oars; Israel was called to great privileges, yet they were abandoned by God as we see them; let us therefore also take heed, for, as it is written, many are called but few chosen.' I confess I find it difficult to conceive anything more relevant, and equally so to see any special relevancy, in the vague general statement 'Many were created but few shall be saved.'

But even if it were not so, if it were really a question between similarity of context on the one hand and identity of language on the other, there ought to be no hesitation in declaring that to be the original of the quotation in which the language was identical though the context might be somewhat different. Any one who has studied patristic quotations will know that context counts for very little indeed. What could be more to all appearance remote from the context than the quotation in Heb. i. 7, 'Who maketh his angels spirits and his ministers a flaming fire'? where the original is certainly referring to the powers of nature, and means 'who maketh the winds his messengers and a flame of fire his minister;' with the very same sounds we have a complete inversion of the sense. This is one of the most frequent phenomena, as our author cannot but know [1].

Hilgenfeld, in his edition of the Epistle of Barnabas, repels somewhat testily the imputation of Tischendorf, who criticises him as if he supposed that the saying in St. Matthew was not directly referred to [2]. This Hilgenfeld denies to be the case. In regard to the use of the word γέγραπται introducing the quotation, the same writer urges reasonably enough that it cannot surprise us at a time when we learn from Justin Martyr that the Gospels were read regularly at public worship; it ought not however to be pressed too far as involving a claim to special divine inspiration, as the same word is used in the Epistle in regard to the apocryphal book of Enoch, and it is clear also from Justin that the Canon of the Gospels was not yet formed but only forming.

The clause, 'Give to every one that asketh of thee' (παντὶ τῷ αἰτοῦντί σε δίδου), though admitted into the text of c. xix by Hilgenfeld and Weizsäcker, is wanting in the Sinaitic MS., and the comparison with Luke vi. 30 or Matt. v. 42 therefore cannot be insisted upon.

The passage '[in order that He might show that] He came not to call the righteous but sinners' (ἵνα δείξῃ ὅτι

---

[1] A curious instance of disregard of context is to be seen in Tertullian's reading of John i. 13, which he referred to *Christ*, accusing the Valentinians of falsification because they had the ordinary reading (cf. Rönsch, *Das Neue Testament Tertullian's*, pp. 252, 654). Compare also p. 24 above.

[2] *Novum Testamentum extra Canonem Receptum*, Fasc. ii. p. 69.

οὐκ ἦλθεν καλέσαι δικαίους ἀλλὰ ἁμαρτωλούς[1]) is removed by the hypothesis of an interpolation which is supported by a precarious argument from Origen, and also by the fact that εἰς μετάνοιαν has been added (clearly from Luke v. 32) by later hands both to the text of Barnabas and in Matt. ix. 13[2]. This theory of an interpolation is easily advanced, and it is drawn so entirely from our ignorance that it can seldom be positively disproved, but it ought surely to be alleged with more convincing reasons than any that are put forward here. We now possess six MSS. of the Epistle of Barnabas, including the famous Codex Sinaiticus, the accuracy of which in the Biblical portions can be amply tested, and all of these six MSS., without exception, contain the passage. The addition of the words εἰς μετάνοιαν represents much more the kind of interpolations that were at all habitual. The interpolation hypothesis, as I said, is easily advanced, but the *onus probandi* must needs lie heavily against it. In accepting the text as it stands we simply obey the Baconian maxim *hypotheses non fingimus*, but it is strange, and must be surprising to a philosophic mind, to what an extent the more extreme representatives of the negative criticism have gone back to the most condemned parts of the scholastic method; inconvenient facts are explained away by hypotheses as imaginary and unverifiable as the 'cycles and epicycles' by which the schoolmen used to explain the motions of the heavenly bodies.

'If however,' the author continues, the passage 'originally formed part of the text, it is absurd to affirm that it is any proof of the use or existence of the first Gospel.' 'Absurd' is under the circumstances a rather strong

---

[1] c. v. [2] *S. R.* i. p. 250 sqq.

word to use; but, granting that it would have been even 'absurd' to allege this passage, if it had stood alone, as a sufficient proof of the use of the Gospel, it does not follow that there can be any objection to the more guarded statement that it invests the use of the Gospel with a certain antecedent probability. No doubt the quotation *may* have been made from a lost Gospel, but here again εἰς ἀφανὲς τὸν μῦθον ἀνενέγκας οὐκ ἔχει ἔλεγχον—there is no verifying that about which we know nothing. The critic may multiply Gospels as much as he pleases and an apologist at least will not quarrel with him, but it would be more to the point if he could prove the existence in these lost writings of matter *conflicting* with that contained in the extant Gospels. As it is, the only result of these unverifiable hypotheses is to raise up confirmatory documents in a quarter where apologists have not hitherto claimed them.

We are delaying, however, too long upon points of quite secondary importance. Two more passages are adduced; one, an application of Ps. cx (The Lord said unto my Lord) precisely as in Matt. xxii. 44, and the other a saying assigned to our Lord, 'They who wish to see me and lay hold on my kingdom must receive me through affliction and suffering.' Of neither of these can we speak positively. There is perhaps a slight probability that the first was suggested by our Gospel, and considering the character of the verifiable quotations in Barnabas, which often follow the sense only and not the words, the second may be 'a free reminiscence of Matt. xvi. 24 compared with Acts xiv. 22,' but it is also possible that it may be a saying quoted from an apocryphal Gospel.

It should perhaps be added that Lardner and Dr.

Westcott both refer to a quotation of Zech. xiii. 7 which appears in the common text of the Epistle in a form closely resembling that in which the quotation is given in Matt. xxvi. 31 and diverging from the LXX, but here again the Sinaitic Codex varies, and the text is too uncertain to lay stress upon, though perhaps the addition $τῆs$ $ποίμνης$ may incline the balance to the view that the text of the Gospel has influenced the form of the quotation [1].

The general result of our examination of the Epistle of Barnabas may perhaps be stated thus, that while not supplying by itself certain and conclusive proof of the use of our Gospels, still the phenomena accord better with the hypothesis of such a use. This Epistle stands in the second line of the evidence, and as a witness is rather confirmatory than principal.

3.

After Dr. Lightfoot's masterly exposition there is probably nothing more to be said about the genuineness, date, and origin of the Ignatian Epistles. Dr. Lightfoot has done in the most lucid and admirable manner just that which is so difficult to do, and which 'Supernatural Religion' has so signally failed in doing; he has succeeded in conveying to the reader a true and just sense of the exact weight and proportion of the different parts of the evidence. He has avoided such phrases as 'absurd,' 'impossible,' 'preposterous,' that his opponent has dealt in so freely, but he has weighed and balanced the evidence piece by piece; he has carefully guarded his language so as never to let the positiveness of his

---

[1] Lardner, *Credibility, &c.*, ii. p. 23; Westcott, *On the Canon*, p. 50, n. 5.

conclusion exceed what the premises will warrant; he has dealt with the subject judicially and with a full consciousness of the responsibility of his position[1].

We cannot therefore, I think, do better than adopt Dr. Lightfoot's conclusion as the basis of our investigation, and treat the Curetonian (i. e. the three short Syriac) letters as (probably) 'the work of the genuine Ignatius, while the Vossian letters (i. e. the shorter Greek recension of seven Epistles) are accepted as valid testimony at all events for the middle of the second century—the question of the genuineness of the letters being waived.'

The Curetonian Epistles will then be dated either in 107 or in 115 A.D., the two alternative years assigned to the martyrdom of Ignatius. In the Epistle to Polycarp which is given in this version there is a parallel to Matt. x. 16, 'Be ye therefore wise as serpents and harmless as doves.' The two passages may be compared thus:—

Ign. ad Pol. ii.	*Matt.* x. 16.
Φρόνιμος γίνου ὡς ὄφις ἐν ἅπασιν καὶ ἀκέραιος ὡσεὶ περιστερά.	Γίνεσθε οὖν φρόνιμοι ὡς οἱ ὄφεις καὶ ἀκέραιοι ὡς αἱ περιστεραί.

We should naturally place this quotation in the second column of our classified arrangement, as pre-

[1] Since this was written the author of 'Supernatural Religion' has replied in the preface to his sixth edition. He has stated his case in the ablest possible manner: still I do not think that there is anything to retract in what has been written above. There *would* have been something to retract if Dr. Lightfoot had maintained positively the genuineness of the Vossian Epistles. As to the Syriac, the question seems to me to stand thus. On the one side are certain improbabilities—I admit, improbabilities, though not of the weightiest kind—which are met about half way by the parallel cases quoted. On the other hand, there is the express testimony of the Epistle of Polycarp quoted in its turn by Irenaeus. Now I cannot think that there is any improbability so great (considering our ignorance) as not to be outweighed by this external evidence.

senting a slight variation. At the same time we should have little hesitation in referring it to the passage in our Canonical Gospel. All the marked expressions are identical, especially the precise and selected words φρόνιμος and ἀκέραιος. It is however possible that Ignatius may be quoting, not directly from our Gospel, but from one of the original documents (such as Ewald's hypothetical 'Spruch-sammlung') out of which our Gospel was composed—though it is somewhat remarkable that this particular sentence is wanting in the parallel passage in St. Luke (cf. Luke x. 3). This may be so or not; we have no means of judging. But it should at any rate be remembered that this original document, supposing it to have had a substantive existence, most probably contained repeated references to miracles. The critics who refer Matt. x. 16 to the document in question, also agree in referring to it Matt. vii. 22, x. 8, xi. 5, xii. 24 foll., &c., which speak distinctly of miracles, and precisely in that indirect manner which is the best kind of evidence. Therefore if we accept the hypothesis suggested in 'Supernatural Religion'—and it is a mere hypothesis, quite unverifiable —the evidence for miracles would not be materially weakened. The author would, I suppose, admit that it is at least equally probable that the saying was quoted from our present Gospel.

This probability would be considerably heightened if the allusion to 'the star' in the Syriac of Eph. xix has, as it appears to have, reference to the narrative of Matt. ii. In the Greek or Vossian version of the Epistle it is expanded, 'How then was He manifested to the ages? A star shone in heaven above all the stars, and the light thereof was unspeakable, and the strangeness thereof caused astonishment' (Πῶς οὖν ἐφανερώθη τοῖς αἰῶσιν; Ἀστὴρ ἐν οὐρανῷ ἔλαμψεν ὑπὲρ πάντας τοὺς ἀστέρας, καὶ τὸ φῶς αὐτοῦ ἀνεκλάλητον ἦν, καὶ ξενισμὸν παρεῖχεν ἡ καινότης αὐτοῦ). This is precisely, one would suppose, the kind of passage that might be taken as internal evidence of the genuineness of the Curetonian and later character of the Vossian version. The Syriac (ἅτινα ἐν ἡσυχίᾳ Θεοῦ τῷ ἀστέρι [or ἀπὸ τοῦ ἀστέρος] ἐπράχθη), abrupt and difficult as it is, does not look like an epitome of the Greek, and the Greek has exactly that exaggerated and apocryphal character which would seem to point to a later date. It corresponds indeed somewhat nearly to the language of the Protevangelium of James, § 21, εἴδομεν ἀστέρα παμμεγέθη λάμψαντα ἐν τοῖς ἄστροις τοῦ οὐρανοῦ καὶ ἀμβλύνοντα τοὺς ἄλλους ἀστέρας ὥστε μὴ φαίνεσθαι αὐτούς. Both in the Protevangelium and in the Vossian Ignatius we see what is clearly a developement of the narrative in St. Matthew. If the Vossian Epistles are genuine, then by showing the existence of such a developement at so early a date they will tend to throw back still further the composition of the Canonical Gospel. If the Syriac version, on the other hand, is the genuine one, it will be probable that Ignatius is directly alluding to the narrative which is peculiar to the first Evangelist.

These are (so far as I am aware) the only coincidences that are found in the Curetonian version. Their paucity cannot surprise us, as in the same Curetonian text there is not a single quotation from the Old Testament. One Old Testament quotation and two Evangelical allusions occur in the Epistle to the Ephesians, which is one of the three contained in Cureton's MS.; the fifth and sixth chapters, however, in which they are found, are wanting in the Syriac. The allusions are, in Eph. v,

'For if the prayer of one or two have such power, how much more that of the bishop and of the whole Church,' which appears to have some relation to Matt. xviii. 19 ('If two of you shall agree' &c.), and in Eph. vi, 'For all whom the master of the house sends to be over his own household we ought to receive as we should him that sent him,' which may be compared with Matt. x. 40 ('He that receiveth you' &c.). Both these allusions have some probability, though neither can be regarded as at all certain. The Epistle to the Trallians has one coincidence in c. xi, 'These are not plants of the Father' (φυτεία Πατρός), which recalls the striking expression of Matt. xv. 13, 'Every plant (πᾶσα φυτεία) that my heavenly Father hath not planted shall be rooted up.' This is a marked metaphor, and it is not found in the other Synoptics; it is therefore at least more probable that it is taken from St. Matthew. The same must be said of another remarkable phrase in the Epistle to the Smyrnaeans, c. vi, ὁ χωρῶν χωρείτω (ὁ δυνάμενος χωρεῖν χωρείτω, Matt. xix. 12), and also of the statement in c. i. of the same Epistle that Jesus was baptized by John 'that He might fulfil all righteousness' (ἵνα πληρωθῇ πᾶσα δικαιοσύνη ὑπ' αὐτοῦ). This corresponds with the language of Matt. iii. 15 (οὕτως γὰρ πρέπον ἐστὶν ἡμῖν πληρῶσαι πᾶσαν δικαιοσύνην), which also has no parallel in the other Gospels. The use of the phrase πληρῶσαι πᾶσαν δικαιοσύνην is so peculiar, and falls in so entirely with the characteristic Christian Judaizing of our first Evangelist, that it seems especially unreasonable to refer it to any one else. There is not the smallest particle of evidence to connect it with the Gospel according to the Hebrews to which our author seems to hint that it may belong; indeed all that we know of that Gospel may be said almost positively to exclude it. In this Gospel our Lord is represented as saying, when His mother and His brethren urge that He should accept baptism from John, 'What have I sinned that I should go and be baptized by him?' and it is almost by compulsion that He is at last induced to accompany them. It will be seen that this is really an *opposite* version of the event to that of Ignatius and the first Gospel, where the objection comes from *John* and is overruled by our Lord Himself[1].

There is however one quotation, introduced as such, in this same Epistle, the source of which Eusebius did not know, but which Origen refers to the 'Preaching of Peter' and Jerome seems to have found in the Nazarene version of the 'Gospel according to the Hebrews.' This phrase is attributed to our Lord when He appeared 'to those about Peter and said to them, Handle Me and see that I am not an incorporeal spirit' (ψηλαφήσατέ με, καὶ ἴδετε, ὅτι οὐκ εἰμὶ δαιμόνιον ἀσώματον). But for the statement of Origen that these words occurred in the 'Preaching of Peter' they might have been referred without much difficulty to Luke xxiv. 39. The Preaching of Peter seems to have begun with the Resurrection, and to have been an offshoot rather in the direction of the Acts than the Gospels[2]. It would not therefore follow from the use of it by Ignatius here, that the other quotations could also be referred to it. And, supposing it to be taken from the 'Gospel according to the Hebrews,' this would not annul what has been said above as to the reason for thinking that Ignatius (or

---

[1] Cf. Hilgenfeld, *Nov. Test. ext. Can. Rec.*, Fasc. iv. p. 15.
[2] Cf. *ibid.*, pp. 56, 62, also p. 29.

the writer who bears his name) cannot have used that Gospel systematically and alone.

4.

Is the Epistle which purports to have been written by Polycarp to the Philippians to be accepted as genuine? It is mentioned in the most express terms by Irenaeus, who declares himself to have been a disciple of Polycarp in his early youth, and speaks enthusiastically of the teaching which he then received. Irenaeus was writing between the years 180–190 A.D., and Polycarp is generally allowed to have suffered martyrdom about 167 or 168[1]. But the way in which Irenaeus speaks of the Epistle is such as to imply, not only that it had been for some time in existence, but also that it had been copied and disseminated and had attained a somewhat wide circulation. He is appealing to the Catholic tradition in opposition to heretical teaching such as that of Valentinus and Marcion, and he says, 'There is an Epistle written by Polycarp to the Philippians of great excellence (ἱκανωτάτη), from which those who wish to do so and who care for their own salvation may learn both the character of his faith and the preaching of the truth[2].' He would hardly have used such language if he had not had reason to think that the Epistle was at least fairly accessible to the Christians for whom he is writing. But allowing for the somewhat slow (not too slow)

---

[1] But see *Contemporary Review*, 1875, p. 838, from which it appears that M. Waddington has recently proved the date to be rather 155 or 156. Compare Hilgenfeld, *Einleitung*, p. 72, where reference is made to an essay by Lipsius, *Der Märtyrertod Polycarp's* in *Z. f. w. T.* 1874, ii. p. 180 f.

[2] *Adv. Haer.* iii. 3, 4.

multiplication and dissemination of writings among the Christians, this will throw back the composition of the letter well into the lifetime of Polycarp himself. In any case it must have been current in circles immediately connected with Polycarp's person.

Against external evidence such as this the objections that are brought are really of very slight weight. That which is reproduced in 'Supernatural Religion' from an apparent contradiction between c. ix and c. xiii, is dismissed even by writers such as Ritschl who believe that one or both chapters are interpolated. In c. ix the martyrdom of Ignatius is upheld as an example, in c. xiii Polycarp asks for information about Ignatius 'et de his qui cum eo sunt,' apparently as if he were still living. But, apart from the easy and obvious solution which is accepted by Ritschl, following Hefele and others[1], that the sentence is extant only in the Latin translation and that the phrase 'qui cum eo sunt' is merely a paraphrase for τῶν μετ' αὐτοῦ; apart from this, even supposing the objection were valid, it would prove nothing against the genuineness of the Epistle. It might be taken to prove that the second passage is an interpolation; but a contradiction between two passages in the same writing in no way tends to show that that writing is not by its ostensible author. But surely either interpolator or forger must have had more sense than to place two such gross and absurd contradictions within about sixty lines of each other.

An argument brought by Dr. Hilgenfeld against the date dissolves away entirely on examination. He thinks that the exhortation Orate pro regibus (et potestatibus

---

[1] Ritschl, *Entstehung der alt-katholischen Kirche*, p. 586; Hefele, *Patrum Apostolicorum Opera*, p. lxxx.

et principibus) in c. xii must needs refer to the double rule of Antoninus Pius (147 A. D.) or Marcus Aurelius and Lucius Verus (161 A. D.). But the writer of the Epistle is only reproducing the words of St. Paul in 1 Tim. ii. 2 (παρακαλῶ .. ποιεῖσθαι δεήσεις .. ὑπὲρ βασιλέων καὶ πάντων τῶν ἐν ὑπεροχῇ ὄντων). The passage is wrongly referred in 'Supernatural Religion' to 1 Pet. ii. 17[1]. It is very clear that the language of Polycarp, like that of St. Paul, is quite general. In order to limit it to the two Caesars we should have had to read ὑπὲρ τῶν βασιλέων.

The allusions which Schwegler finds to the Gnostic heresies are explained when that critic at the end of his argument objects to the Epistle that it makes use of a number of writings 'the origin of which must be placed in the second century, such as the Acts, 1 Peter, the Epistles to the Philippians and to the Ephesians, and 1 Timothy.' The objection belongs to the gigantic confusion of fact and hypothesis which makes up the so-called Tübingen theory, and falls to the ground with it.

It should be noticed that those who regard the Epistle as interpolated yet maintain the genuineness of those portions which are thought to contain allusions to the Gospels. Ritschl states this[2]; Dr. Donaldson confines the interpolation to c. xiii[3]; and Volkmar not only affirms with his usual energy the genuineness of these portions of the Epistle, but he also asserts that the allusions are really to our Gospels[4].

The first that meets us is in c. ii, 'Remembering what the Lord said teaching, Judge not that ye be not judged;

[1] Cf. *S. R.* i. p. 278.
[2] *Ent. d. a. K.* pp. 593, 599.
[3] *Apostolical Fathers*, p. 227 sq.
[4] *Ursprung*, pp. 43, 131.

forgive and it shall be forgiven unto you; pity that ye may be pitied; with what measure ye mete it shall be measured unto you again; and that blessed are the poor and those who are persecuted for righteousness' sake, for theirs is the kingdom of God[1].' This passage (if taken from our Gospels) is not a continuous quotation, but is made up from Luke vi. 36-38, 20, Matt. v. 10, or of still more *disjecta membra* of St. Matthew. It will be seen that it covers very similar ground with the quotation in Clement, and there is also a somewhat striking point of similarity with that writer in the phrase ἐλεεῖτε ἵνα ἐλεηθῆτε. There is moreover a closer resemblance than to our Gospels in the clause ἀφίετε καὶ ἀφεθήσεται ὑμῖν. But the order of the clauses is entirely different from that in Clement, and the first clause μὴ κρίνετε ἵνα μὴ κριθῆτε is identical with St. Matthew and more nearly resembles the parallel in St. Luke than in Clement. These are perplexing phenomena, and seem to forbid a positive judgment. It would be natural to suppose, and all that we know of the type of doctrine in the early Church would lead us to believe, that the Sermon on the Mount would be one of the most familiar parts of Christian teaching, that it would be largely committed to memory and quoted from memory. There would be no difficulty in employing that hypothesis here if the passage stood alone. The breaking up of the order too would not surprise us when we compare the way in which the same discourse appears in St. Luke and in St. Matthew. But then comes in the

---

[1] μνημονεύοντες δὲ ὧν εἶπεν ὁ κύριος διδάσκων· μὴ κρίνετε ἵνα μὴ κριθῆτε· ἀφίετε καὶ ἀφεθήσεται ὑμῖν· ἐλεεῖτε ἵνα ἐλεηθῆτε· ἐν ᾧ μέτρῳ μετρεῖτε, ἀντιμετρηθήσεται ὑμῖν· καὶ ὅτι μακάριοι οἱ πτωχοὶ καὶ οἱ διωκόμενοι ἕνεκεν δικαιοσύνης, ὅτι αὐτῶν ἐστὶν ἡ βασιλεία τοῦ Θεοῦ.

strange coincidence in the single clause with Clement; and there is also another curious phenomenon, the phrase ἀφίετε καὶ ἀφεθήσεται ὑμῖν compared with Luke's ἀπολύετε καὶ ἀπολυθήσεσθε has very much the appearance of a parallel translation from the same Aramaic original, which may perhaps be the famous 'Spruch-sammlung.' This might however be explained as the substitution of synonymous terms by the memory. There is I believe nothing in the shape of direct evidence to show the presence of a different version of the Sermon on the Mount in any of the lost Gospels, and, on the other hand, there are considerable traces of disturbance in the Canonical text (compare e.g. the various readings on Matt. v. 44). It seems on the whole difficult to construct a theory that shall meet all the facts. Perhaps a mixed hypothesis would be best. It is probable that memory has been to some extent at work (the form of the quotation naturally suggests this) and is to account for some of Polycarp's variations; at the same time I cannot but think that there has been somewhere a written version different from our Gospels to which he and Clement have had access.

There are several other sayings which seem to belong to the Sermon on the Mount; thus in c. vi, 'If we pray the Lord to forgive us we also ought to forgive' (cf. Matt. vi. 14 sq.); in c. viii, 'And if we suffer for His name let us glorify Him' (cf. Matt. v. 11 sq.); in c. xii, 'Pray for them that persecute you and hate you, and for the enemies of the cross; that your fruit may be manifest in all things, that ye may be therein perfect' (cf. Matt. v. 44, 48). All these passages give the sense, but only the sense, of the first (and partly also of the third) Gospel. There is however one quotation which coincides verbally with two of the Synoptics [Praying the all-seeing God not to lead us into temptation, as the Lord said], The spirit indeed is willing but the flesh is weak (τὸ μὲν πνεῦμα πρόθυμον, ἡ δὲ σὰρξ ἀσθενής, Matt., Mark, Polycarp; with the introductory clause compare, not Matt. vi. 13, but xxvi. 41). In the cases where the sense alone is given there is no reason to think that the writer intends to give more. At the same time it will be observed that all the quotations refer either to the double or triple synopsis where we have already proof of the existence of the saying in question in more than a single form, and not to those portions that are peculiar to the individual Evangelists. The author of 'Supernatural Religion' is therefore not without reason when he says that they may be derived from other collections than our actual Gospels. The possibility cannot be excluded. It ought however to be borne in mind that if such collections did exist, and if Polycarp's allusions or quotations are to be referred to them, they are to the same extent evidence that these hypothetical collections did not materially differ from our present Gospels, but rather bore to them very much the same relation that they bear to each other. And I do not know that we can better sum up the case in regard to the Apostolic Fathers than thus; we have two alternatives to choose between, either they made use of our present Gospels, or else of writings so closely resembling our Gospels and so nearly akin to them that their existence only proves the essential unity and homogeneity of the evangelical tradition.

CHAPTER IV.

JUSTIN MARTYR.

HITHERTO the extant remains of Christian literature have been scanty and the stream of evangelical quotation has been equally so, but as we approach the middle of the second century it becomes much more abundant. We have copious quotations from a Gospel used about the year 140 by Marcion; the Clementine Homilies, the date of which however is more uncertain, also contain numerous quotations; and there are still more in the undoubted works of Justin Martyr. When I speak of quotations, I do not wish to beg the question by implying that they are necessarily taken from our present Gospels, I merely mean quotations from an evangelical document of some sort. This reservation has to be made especially in regard to Justin.

Strictly according to the chronological order we should not have to deal with Justin until somewhat later, but it will perhaps be best to follow the order of 'Supernatural Religion,' the principle of which appears to be to discuss the orthodox writers first and heretical writings afterwards. Modern critics seem pretty generally to place the two Apologies in the years 147–150 A. D. and the Dialogue against Tryphon a little later. Dr. Keim indeed would throw forward the date of Justin's writings as far as from 155–160 on account of the mention of Marcion[1], but this is decided by both Hilgenfeld[2] and Lipsius to be too late. I see that Mr. Hort, whose opinion on such matters deserves high respect, comes to the conclusion 'that we may without fear of considerable error set down Justin's First Apology to 145, or better still to 146, and his death to 148. The Second Apology, if really separate from the First, will then fall in 146 or 147, and the Dialogue with Tryphon about the same time[3].'

No definite conclusion can be drawn from the title given by Justin to the work or works he used, that of the 'Memoirs' or 'Recollections' of the Apostles, and it will be best to leave our further enquiry quite unfettered by any assumption in respect to them. The title certainly does not of necessity imply a single work composed by the Apostles collectively[4], any more than the parallel phrase 'the writings of the Prophets[5]' (τὰ συγγράμματα τῶν προφητῶν), which Justin couples with the 'Memoirs' as read together in the public services of the Church, implies a single and joint production on the part of the Prophets. This hypothesis too is

---

[1] *Geschichte Jesu von Nazara*, i. p. 138, n. 2.
[2] *Einleitung in das N. T.* p. 66, where Lipsius' view is also quoted.
[3] Cf. Westcott, *On the Canon*, p. 88, n. 4.
[4] As appears to be suggested in *S. R.* i. p. 292. The reference in the note to Bleek, *Einl.* p. 637 (and Ewald?), does not seem to be exactly to the point.
[5] *Apol.* i. 67.

open to the very great objection that so authoritative a work, if it existed, should have left absolutely no other trace behind it. So far as the title is concerned, the 'Memoirs of the Apostles' may be either a single work or an almost indefinite number. In one place Justin says that the Memoirs were composed 'by His Apostles and their followers[1],' which seems to agree remarkably, though not exactly, with the statement in the prologue to St. Luke. In another he says expressly that the Memoirs are called Gospels (ἃ καλεῖται εὐαγγέλια)[2]. This clause has met with the usual fate of parenthetic statements which do not quite fall in with preconceived opinions, and is dismissed as a 'manifest interpolation,' a gloss having crept into the text from the margin. It would be difficult to estimate the exact amount of probability for or against this theory, but possible at any rate it must be allowed to be; and though the *primâ facie* view of the genuineness of the words is supported by another place in which a quotation is referred directly 'to the Gospel,' still too much ought not perhaps to be built on this clause alone.

A convenient distinction may be drawn between the material and formal use of the Gospels; and the most satisfactory method perhaps will be, to run rapidly through Justin's quotations, first with a view to ascertain their relation to the Canonical Gospels in respect to their general historical tenor, and secondly to examine the amount of verbal agreement. I will try to bring out as clearly as possible the double phenomena both of agreement and difference; the former (in regard to which condensation will be necessary) will be indicated

[1] *Dial. c. Tryph.* 103.   [2] *Apol.* i. 66; cf. *S. R.* i. p. 294.

both by touching in the briefest manner the salient points and by the references in the margin; the latter, which I have endeavoured to give as exhaustively as possible, are brought out by italics in the text. The thread of the narrative then, so far as it can be extracted from the genuine writings of Justin, will be much as follows[1].

According to Justin the Messiah was born, without sin, of a virgin *who* was descended from Matt. 1. 2-6. David, Jesse, Phares, Judah, Luke 3. 31-34. Jacob, Isaac, and Abraham, if not (the reading here is doubtful) from Adam himself. [Justin therefore, it may be inferred, had before him a genealogy, though not apparently, as the Canonical Gospels, that of Joseph but of Mary.] To Mary it was announced by the angel Gabriel Luke 1. 26. that, while yet a virgin, the power of God, or of the Highest, Luke 1. 35. should overshadow her and she should conceive and bear a Son Luke 1. 31. Matt. 1. 21. whose name she should call Jesus, because He should save His people from their sins. Joseph observing that Mary, his espoused, was with child was Matt. 1. 18-25. warned in a dream not to put

---

[1] The evangelical references and allusions in Justin have been carefully collected by Credner and Hilgenfeld, and are here thrown together in a sort of running narrative.

her away, because that which was in her womb was of the Holy Ghost. Thus the prophecy, Is. vii. 14 (Behold the virgin &c.), was fulfilled. The mother of John the Baptist was Elizabeth. The birth-place of the Messiah had been indicated by the prophecy of Micah (v. 2, Bethlehem not the least among the princes of Judah). There He was born, as the Romans might learn from the census taken by Cyrenius the first *procurator* (ἐπιτρόπου) *of Judaea*. His life extended from Cyrenius to Pontius Pilate. So, in consequence of this the first census in Judaea, Joseph went up from Nazareth where he dwelt to Bethlehem *whence he was*, as a member of the tribe of Judah. The parents of Jesus could find no lodging in Bethlehem, so it came to pass that He was born *in a cave near the village* and laid in a manger. At His birth there came Magi *from Arabia*, who knew by a star that had appeared in the *heaven* that a king had been born in Judaea. Having paid Him their homage and offered gifts of gold, frank-

	incense and myrrh, they were
Matt. 2. 12.	warned not to return to Herod
Matt. 2. 1–7.	whom they had consulted on the way. He however not willing that the Child should escape,
Matt. 2. 16.	ordered a massacre of *all* the children in Bethlehem, fulfilling
Matt. 2. 17, 18.	the prophecy of Jer. xxxi. 15 (Rachel weeping for her children &c.). Joseph and his wife mean-
Matt. 2. 13–15.	while with the Babe had fled to Egypt, for the Father resolved that He to whom He had given birth should not die before He had preached His word as a man. There they stayed
Matt. 2. 22.	until Archelaus succeeded Herod, and then returned.

By process of nature He grew to the age of thirty years or more, *not comely of aspect (as had been prophesied)*, practising the trade of a carpenter, *making ploughs and yokes, emblems of righteousness*. He remained hidden till John, the herald of his coming, came forward, the spirit of Elias being in him, and as he *sat* by the river Jordan cried to men to repent. As he preached in his wild garb he declared that he was not the Christ, but that One stronger

Luke 3. 23.

Matt. 17. 12, 13.
Matt. 3. 2.   Luke 3. 3.
Matt. 3. 4.
(John 1. 19 ff.)

Matt. 3. 11, 12.	than he was coming after him	Luke 3. 16, 17.
	whose shoes he was not worthy to bear, &c. The later history of John Justin also mentions,	
Matt. 14. 3.	how, having been put in prison,	Luke 3. 20.
	at a feast on Herod's birthday	
Matt. 14. 6 ff.	he was beheaded at the instance of his sister's daughter. This	
Matt. 17. 11–13.	John was Elias who was to come before the Christ.	
	At the baptism of Jesus *a fire was kindled on the Jordan*, and, as He went up out of the water,	
Matt. 3. 16.	the Holy Ghost alighted upon Him, and a voice was heard from heaven *saying in the words of David*, 'Thou art My Son, *this day have I begotten Thee.*' After	Luke 3. 21, 22.
Matt. 4. 1, 9.	His baptism He was tempted by the devil, who ended by claiming homage from Him. To this Christ replied, 'Get thee behind	
Matt 4. 11.	Me, Satan,' &c. So the devil departed from Him at that time worsted and convicted.	Luke 4. 13.
	Justin knew that the words of Jesus were short and concise, not like those of a Sophist. That He wrought miracles *might be learnt from the Acts of Pontius Pilate, fulfilling Is. xxxv.* 4–6.	
Matt. 9. 29–31, 32, 33, 1–8.	Those who from their *birth* were blind, dumb, lame, He healed—	Luke 18. 35–43. Luke 11. 14 ff. Luke 5. 17–26.

Matt. 4. 23.	indeed He healed all sickness and
Matt. 9. 18 ff.	disease—and He raised the dead. *The Jews ascribed these miracles to magic.*

Luke 8. 41 ff.
Luke 7. 11-18.

Jesus, too (like John, *whose mission ceased when He appeared in public*), began His ministry by proclaiming that the kingdom of heaven was at hand. Many precepts of the Sermon on the Mount Justin has preserved, the righteousness of the Scribes and Pharisees, the adultery of the heart, the offending eye, divorce, oaths, returning good for evil, loving and praying for enemies, giving to those that need, placing the treasure in heaven, not caring for bodily wants, but copying the mercy and goodness of God, not acting from worldly motives—above all, deeds not words.

Justin quotes sayings from the narrative of the centurion of Capernaum and of the feast in the house of Matthew. He has, the choosing of the twelve Apostles, with the name given to the sons of Zebedee, Boanerges or 'sons of thunder,' the commission of the Apostles, the discourse after the departure of

Margin references (left):
Matt. 4. 17.
Matt. 5. 20.
Matt. 5. 28.
Matt. 5. 29-32.
Matt. 5. 34, 37, 39.
Matt. 5. 44.
Matt. 5. 42.
Matt. 6. 19, 20.
Matt. 6. 25-27.
Matt. 5. 45.
Matt. 6. 21, &c.
Matt. 7. 22, 23.
Matt. 8. 11, 12.
Matt. 9. 13.
Matt. 10. 1 ff.
Mark 3. 17.
Matt. 11. 12-15.

Margin references (right):
Luke 6. 30.
Luke 12. 22-24.
Luke 13. 26, 27.
Luke 13. 28, 29.
Luke 5. 32.
Luke 6. 13.
Luke 10. 19.
Luke 16. 16.

	the messengers of John, the	
Matt. 16. 4.	sign of the prophet Jonas, the	
Matt. 13. 3 ff.	parable of the sower, Peter's	Luke 8. 5 ff.
Matt. 16. 15–18.	confession, the announcement of	Luke 9. 22.
Matt. 16. 21.	the Passion.	

From the account of the last journey and the closing scenes of our Lord's life, Justin has,

Matt.19.16,17.	the history of the rich young	Luke 18.18,19.
Matt. 21. 1 ff.	man, the entry into Jerusalem,	Luke 19. 29 ff.
	the cleansing of the Temple, the	Luke 19. 46.
Matt. 22. 11.	wedding garment, the controversial discourses about the	Luke 20.22–25.
Matt. 22. 21.	tribute money, the resurrection,	Luke 20.35,36.
Matt.22.37,38.	and the greatest commandment,	
Matt. 23. 2 ff.	those directed against the Pharisees, and the eschatological discourse, the parable of the talents. Justin's account of the	Luke 11.42,52.
Matt.25.34,41.		
Matt. 25. 14–30.		
	institution of the Lord's Supper	Luke 22.19,20.
	agrees with that of Luke. After	
Matt. 26. 30.	it Jesus sang a hymn, and taking	
Matt.26.36,37.	with Him three of His disciples to the Mount of Olives He was in an agony, His sweat falling in	Luke 22.42–44.
	drops (not necessarily of blood) to the ground. His captors surrounded Him *like the 'horned bulls' of Ps. xxii.* 11–14; there	
Matt. 26. 56.	was none to help, for His followers *to a man* forsook Him.	
Matt. 26. 57 ff.	He was led both before the Scribes and Pharisees and before	Luke 22. 66 ff.

Matt. 27. 11 ff.	Pilate. In the trial before Pilate	Luke 23. 1 ff.
Matt. 27. 14.	He kept silence, *as Ps. xxii.* 15. Pilate sent Him bound to Herod.	Luke 23. 7.
	Justin relates most of the incidents of the Crucifixion in detail, for confirmation of which he refers to the *Acts of Pilate*. He marks especially the fulfilment in various places of Ps. xxii. He has the piercing with nails, the casting	Luke 24. 40.
Matt. 27. 35.	of lots and dividing of the gar-	Luke 23. 34.
Matt. 27. 39 ff.	ments, the *sneers* of the crowd	Luke 23. 35.
Matt. 27. 42.	(somewhat expanded from the Synoptics), and their taunt, *He who raised the dead* let Him save	
Matt. 27. 46.	Himself; also the cry of despair, 'My God, My God, why hast Thou forsaken Me?' and the last words, 'Father, into Thy hands I commend My Spirit.'	Luke 23. 46.
Matt. 27. 57–60.	The burial took place in the evening, the disciples being all	
Matt. 26. 31, 56.	scattered in accordance with Zech. xiii. 7. On the third day,	Luke 24. 21.
Matt. 28. 1 ff.	the day of the sun or the first (or eighth) day of the week, Jesus rose from the dead. He then convinced His disciples that	Luke 24. 1 ff.
	His sufferings had been prophe-	Luke 24. 26, 46.
	tically foretold and they repented	Luke 24. 32.
	of having deserted Him. Having given them His last commission they saw Him ascend up into	Luke 24. 50.

H

heaven. Thus believing and having first waited to receive power from Him they went forth into all the world and preached the word of God. To this day Christians baptize in the name of the Father of all, and of our Saviour Jesus Christ, and of the Holy Ghost.

Matt. 28. 19.

The Jews spread a story that the disciples stole the body of Jesus from the grave and so deceived men by asserting that He was risen from the dead and ascended into heaven.

Matt. 28. 12–15.

There is nothing in Justin (as in Luke xxiv, but cp. Acts i. 3) to show that the Ascension did not take place *on the same day* as the Resurrection.

I have taken especial pains in the above summary to bring out the points in which Justin may seem to differ from or add to the canonical narratives. But, without stopping at present to consider the bearing of these upon Justin's relation to the Gospels, I will at once proceed to make some general remarks which the summary seems to suggest.

(1) If such is the outline of Justin's Gospel, it appears to be really a question of comparatively small importance whether or not he made use of our present Gospels in their present form. If he did not use these Gospels he used other documents which contained substantially the same matter. The question of the reality of miracles

clearly is not affected. Justin's documents, whatever they were, not only contained repeated notices of the miracles in general, the healing of the lame and the paralytic, of the maimed and the dumb, and the raising of the dead — not only did they include several discourses, such as the reply to the messengers of John and the saying to the Centurion whose servant was healed, which have direct reference to miracles, but they also give marked prominence to the chief and cardinal miracles of the Gospel history, the Incarnation and the Resurrection. It is antecedently quite possible that the narrative of these events may have been derived from a document other than our Gospels; but, if so, that is only proof of the existence of further and independent evidence to the truth of the history. This document, supposing it to exist, is a surprising instance of the homogeneity of the evangelical tradition; it differs from the three Synoptic Gospels, nay, we may say even from the four Gospels, *less* than they differ from each other.

(2) But we may go further than this. If Justin really used a separate substantive document now lost, that document, to judge from its contents, must have represented a secondary, or rather a tertiary, stage of the evangelical literature; it must have implied the previous existence of our present Gospels. I do not now allude to the presence in it of added traits, such as the cave of the Nativity and the fire on Jordan, which are of the nature of those mythical details that we find more fully developed in the Apocryphal Gospels. I do not so much refer to these — though, for instance, in the case of the fire on Jordan it is highly probable that Justin's statement is a translation into literal fact of the canonical

(and Justinian) saying, 'He shall baptize with the Holy Ghost and with fire'—but, on general grounds, the relation which this supposed document bears to the extant Gospels shows that it must have been in point of time posterior to them.

The earlier stages of evangelical composition present a nucleus, with a more or less defined circumference, of unity, and outside of this a margin of variety. There was a certain body of narrative, which, in whatever form it was handed down—whether as oral or written—at a very early date obtained a sort of general recognition, and seems to have been as a matter of course incorporated in the evangelical works as they appeared.

Besides this there was also other matter which, without such general recognition, had yet a considerable circulation, and, though not found in all, was embodied in more than one of the current compilations. But, as we should naturally expect, these two classes did not exhaust the whole of the evangelical matter. Each successive historian found himself able by special researches to add something new and as yet unpublished to the common stock. Thus, the first of our present Evangelists has thirty-five sections or incidents besides the whole of the first two chapters peculiar to himself. The third Evangelist has also two long chapters of preliminary history, and as many as fifty-six sections or incidents which have no parallel in the other Gospels. Much of this peculiar matter in each case bears an individual and characteristic stamp. The opening chapters of the first and third Synoptics evidently contain two distinct and independent traditions. So independent indeed are they, that the negative school of critics maintain them to be irreconcilable, and the attempts to harmonise them have certainly not been completely successful. These differences, however, show what rich quarries of tradition were open to the enquirer in the first age of Christianity, and how readily he might add to the stores already accumulated by his predecessors. But this state of things did not last long. As in most cases of the kind the productive period soon ceased, and the later writers had a choice of two things, either to harmonise the conflicting records of previous historians, or to develope their details in the manner that we find in the Apocryphal Gospels.

But if Justin used a single and separate document or any set of documents independent of the canonical, then we may say with confidence that that document or set of documents belonged entirely to this secondary stage. It possesses both the marks of secondary formation. Such details as are added to the previous evangelical tradition are just of that character which we find in the Apocryphal Gospels. But these details are comparatively slight and insignificant; the main tendency of Justin's Gospel (supposing it to be a separate composition) was harmonistic. The writer can hardly have been ignorant of our Canonical Gospels: he certainly had access, if not to them, yet to the sources both general and special, from which they are taken. He not only drew from the main body of the evangelical tradition, but also from those particular and individual strains which appear in the first and third Synoptics. He has done this in the spirit of a true *harmoniser*, passing backwards and forwards first to one and then to the

¹ This was written before the appearance of Mr M'Clellan's important work on the Four Gospels *The New Testament*, vol. i. London, 1875, to which I have not yet had time to give the study that it deserves.

other, inventing no middle links, but merely piecing together the two accounts as best he could. Indeed the preliminary portions of Justin's Gospel read very much like the sort of rough *primâ facie* harmony which, without any more profound study, most people make for themselves. But the harmonising process necessarily implies matter to harmonise, and that matter must have had the closest possible resemblance to the contents of our Gospels.

If, then, Justin made use either of a single document or set of documents distinct from those which have become canonical, we conclude that it or they belonged to a later and more advanced stage of formation. But it should be remembered that the case is a hypothetical one. The author of 'Supernatural Religion' seems inclined to maintain that Justin did use such a document or documents, and not our Gospels. If he did, then the consequence above stated seems to follow. But I do not at all care to press this inference; it is no more secure than the premiss upon which it is founded. Only it seems to me that the choice lies between two alternatives and no more; either Justin used our Gospels, or else he used a document later than our Gospels and presupposing them. The reader may take which side of the alternative he pleases.

The question is, which hypothesis best covers and explains the facts. It is not impossible that Justin may have had a special Gospel such as has just been described. There is a tendency among those critics who assign Justin's quotations to an uncanonical source to find that source in the so-called Gospel according to the Hebrews or some of its allied forms. But a large majority of critics regard the Gospel according to the

Hebrews as holding precisely this secondary relation to
the canonical Matthew. Justin's document can hardly
have been the Gospel according to the Hebrews, at least
alone, as that Gospel omitted the section Matt. i. 18–
ii. 23[1], which Justin certainly retained. But it is within
the bounds of possibility—it would be hazardous to say
more—that he may have had another Gospel so modified
and compiled as to meet all the conditions of the case.
For my own part, I think it decidedly the more probable
hypothesis that he used our present Gospels with some
peculiar document, such as this Gospel according to the
Hebrews, or perhaps, as Dr. Hilgenfeld thinks, the ground
document of the Gospel according to Peter (a work of
which we know next to nothing except that it favoured
Docetism and was not very unlike the Canonical Gospels)
and the Protevangelium of James (or some older document on which that work was founded) in addition.

It will be well to try to establish this position a little
more in detail; and therefore I will proceed to collect
first, the evidence for the use, either mediate or direct, of
the Synoptic Gospels, and secondly, that for the use of
one or more Apocryphal Gospels. We still keep to the
substance of Justin's Gospel, and reserve the question of
its form.

Of those portions of the first Synoptic which appear
to be derived from a peculiar source, and for the presence
of which we have no evidence in any other Gospel of the
same degree of originality, Justin has the following:
Joseph's suspicions of his wife, the special statement of
the significance of the name Jesus ('for He shall save

---

[1] Unless indeed it was found in one of the many forms of the Gospel
(cf. *S. R.* i. p. 436, and p. 141 below). The section appears in none of the
forms reproduced by Dr. Hilgenfeld (*N. T. extra Can. Recept.* Fasc. iv).

His people from their sins,' Matt. i. 21, verbally identical), the note upon the fulfilment of the prophecy Is. vii. 14 ('Behold a virgin,' &c.), the visit of the Magi guided by a star, their peculiar gifts, their consultation of Herod and the warning given them not to return to him, the massacre of the children at Bethlehem, fulfilling Jer. xxxi. 15, the descent into Egypt, the return of the Holy Family at the succession of Archelaus. The Temptations Justin gives in the order of Matthew. From the Sermon on the Mount he has the verses v. 14. 20, 28, vi. 1, vii. 15, 21, and from the controversial discourse against the Pharisees, xxiii. 15, 24, which are without parallels. The prophecy, Is. xlii. 1–4, is applied as by Matthew alone. There is an apparent allusion to the parable of the wedding garment. The comment of the disciples upon the identification of the Baptist with Elias (Matt. xvii. 13), the sign of the prophet Jonas (Matt. xvi. 1, 4), and the triumphal entry (the ass *with the colt*), show a special affinity to St. Matthew. And, lastly, in concert with the same Evangelist, Justin has the calumnious report of the Jews (Matt. xxviii. 12–15) and the baptismal formula (Matt. xxviii. 19).

Of the very few details that are peculiar to St. Mark, Justin has the somewhat remarkable one of the bestowing of the surname Boanerges on the sons of Zebedee. Mark also appears to approach most nearly to Justin in the statements that Jesus practised the trade of a carpenter (cf. Mark vi. 3) and that He healed those who were diseased *from their birth* (cf. Mark ix. 21), and perhaps in the emphasis upon the oneness of God in the reply respecting the greatest commandment.

In common with St. Luke, Justin has the mission of the angel Gabriel to Mary, the statement that Elizabeth was the mother of John, that the census was taken under Cyrenius, that Joseph went up from Nazareth to Bethlehem ὅθεν ἦν, that no room was found in the inn, that Jesus was thirty years old when He began His ministry, that He was sent from Pilate to Herod, with the account of His last words. There are also special affinities in the phrase quoted from the charge to the Seventy (Luke x. 19), in the verse Luke xi. 52, in the account of the answer to the rich young man, of the institution of the Lord's Supper, of the Agony in the Garden, and of the Resurrection and Ascension.

These coincidences are of various force. Some of the single verses quoted, though possessing salient features in common, have also, as we shall see, more or less marked differences. Too much stress should not be laid on the allegation of the same prophecies, because there may have been a certain understanding among the Christians as to the prophecies to be quoted as well as the versions in which they were to be quoted. But there are other points of high importance. Just in proportion as an event is from a historical point of view suspicious, it is significant as a proof of the use of the Gospel in which it is contained; such would be the adoration of the Magi, the slaughter of the innocents, the flight into Egypt, the conjunction of the foal with the ass in the entry into Jerusalem. All these are strong evidence for the use of the first Gospel, which is confirmed in the highest degree by the occurrence of a reflection peculiar to the Evangelist, 'Then the disciples understood that He spake unto them of John the Baptist' (Matt. xvii. 13, compare Dial. 49). Of the same nature are the allusions to the census of Cyrenius (there is no material discrepancy between Luke and Justin), and the statement of the age at which the ministry of Jesus began. These are almost certainly remarks by the third Evangelist himself, and not found in any previously existing source. The remand to Herod in all probability belonged to a source that was quite peculiar to him. The same may be said with only a little less confidence of the sections of the preliminary history.

Taking these salient points together with the mass of the coincidences each in its place, and with the due weight assigned to it, the conviction seems forced upon us that Justin did either mediately or immediately, and most probably immediately and directly, make use of our Canonical Gospels.

On the other hand, the argument that he used, whether in addition to these or exclusively, a Gospel now lost, rests upon the following data. Justin apparently differs from the Synoptics in giving the genealogy of Mary, not of Joseph. In Apol. i. 34 he says that Cyrenius was the first governor (procurator) of Judaea, instead of saying that the census first took place under Cyrenius. [It should be remarked, however, that in another place, Dial. 78, he speaks of 'the census which then took place for the first time (οὔσης τότε πρώτης) under Cyrenius.'] He states that Mary brought forth her Son in a cave near the village of Bethlehem. He ten times over speaks of the Magi as coming from Arabia, and not merely from the East. He says emphatically that all the children (πάντας ἁπλῶς τοὺς παῖδας) in Bethlehem were slain without mentioning the limitation of age given in St. Matthew. He alludes to details in the humble occupation of Jesus who practised the trade of a carpenter. Speaking of the ministry of John, he three times repeats the phrase 'as he sat' by the river Jordan. At the baptism of Jesus he says that 'fire was kindled on' or rather 'in the Jordan,' and that a voice was heard saying, 'Thou art My Son, this day have I begotten Thee.' He adds to the notice of the miracles that the Jews thought they were the effect of magic. Twice he refers, as evidence for what he is saying, to the Acts of Pontius Pilate. In two places Justin sees a fulfilment of Ps. xxii, where none is pointed out by the Synoptics. He says that *all* the disciples forsook their Master, which seems to overlook Peter's attack on the high priest's servant. In the account of the Crucifixion he somewhat amplifies the Synoptic version of the mocking gestures of the crowd. And besides these matters of fact he has two sayings, 'In whatsoever I find you, therein will I also judge you,' and 'There shall be schisms and heresies,' which are without parallel, or have no exact parallel, in our Gospels.

Some of these points are not of any great importance. The reference to the Acts of Pilate should in all probability be taken along with the parallel reference to the census of Cyrenius, in which Justin asserts that the birth of Jesus would be found registered. Both appear to be based, not upon any actual document that Justin had seen, but upon the bold assumption that the official documents must contain a record of facts which he knew from other sources[1]. In regard to Cyrenius he evidently has the Lucan version in his mind, though he seems to have confused this with his knowledge that Cyrenius was the first to exercise the Roman

---

[1] In like manner Tertullian refers his readers to the 'autograph copies' of St. Paul's Epistles, and the very 'chairs of the Apostles,' preserved at Corinth and elsewhere (*De Praescript. Haeret.* c. 36). Tertullian also refers to the census of Augustus, 'quem testem fidelissimum dominicae nativitatis Romana archiva custodiunt' (*Adv. Marc.* iv. 7).

sovereignty in Judaea, which was matter of history. Justin seems to be mistaken in regarding Cyrenius as 'procurator' (ἐπιτρόπου) of Judaea. He instituted the census not in this capacity, but as proconsul of Syria. The first procurator of Judaea was Coponius. Some of Justin's peculiarities may quite fairly be explained as unintentional. General statements without the due qualifications, such as those in regard to the massacre of the children and the conduct of the disciples in Gethsemane, are met with frequently enough to this day, and in works of a more professedly critical character than Justin's. The description of the carpenter's trade and of the crowd at the Crucifixion may be merely rhetorical amplifications in the one case of the general Synoptic statement, in the other of the special statement in St. Mark. A certain fulness of style is characteristic of Justin. That he attributes the genealogy to Mary may be a natural instance of reflection; the inconsistency in the Synoptic Gospels would not be at first perceived, and the simplest way of removing it would be that which Justin has adopted. It should be noticed however that he too distinctly says that Joseph was of the tribe of Judah (Dial. 78) and that his family came from Bethlehem, which looks very much like an unobliterated trace of the same inconsistency. It is also noticeable that in the narrative of the Baptism one of the best MSS. of the Old Latin (a, Codex Vercellensis) has, in the form of an addition to Matt. iii. 15, 'et cum baptizaretur lumen ingens circumfulsit de aqua ita ut timerent omnes qui advenerant,' and there is a very similar addition in g^1 (Codex San-Germanensis). Again, in Luke iii. 22 the reading ἐγὼ σήμερον γεγέννηκά σε for ἐν σοὶ εὐδόκησα is shared with

Justin by the most important Græco-Latin MS. D (Codex Bezae) and a, b, c, ff, 1 of the Old Version; Augustine expressly states that the reading was found 'in several respectable copies (aliquibus fide dignis exemplaribus), though not in the older Greek Codices.'

There will then remain the specifying of Arabia as the home of the Magi, the phrase καθεζόμενος used of John on the banks of the Jordan, the two unparallelled sentences, and the cave of the Nativity. Of these the phrase καθεζόμενος, which occurs in three places, Dial. 49, 51, 88, but always in Justin's own narrative and not in quotation, *may* be an accidental recurrence; and it is not impossible that the other items may be derived from an unwritten tradition.

Still, on the whole, I incline to think that though there is not conclusive proof that Justin used a lost Gospel besides the present Canonical Gospels, it is the more probable hypothesis of the two that he did. The explanations given above seem to me reasonable and possible; they are enough, I think, to remove the *necessity* for assuming a lost document, but perhaps not quite enough to destroy the greater probability. This conclusion, we shall find, will be confirmed when we pass from considering the substance of Justin's Gospel to its form.

But now if we ask ourselves *what* was this hypothetical lost document, all we can say is, I believe, that the suggestions hitherto offered are insufficient. The Gospels according to the Hebrews or according to Peter and the Protevangelium of James have been most in favour. The Gospel according to the Hebrews in the form in which it was used by the Nazarenes contained the fire upon Jordan, and as used by the

Ebionites it had also the voice, 'This day have I begotten Thee.' Credner[1], and after him Hilgenfeld[2], thought that the Gospel according to Peter was used. But we know next to nothing about this Gospel, except that it was nearly related to the Gospel according to the Hebrews, that it made the 'brethren of the Lord' sons of Joseph by a former wife, that it was found by Serapion in the churches of his diocese, Rhossus in Cilicia, that its use was at first permitted but afterwards forbidden, as it was found to favour Docetism, and that its contents were in the main orthodox though in some respects perverted[3]. Obviously these facts and the name (which falls in with the theory—itself also somewhat unsubstantial—that Justin's Gospel must have a 'Petrine' character) are quite insufficient to build upon. The Protevangelium of James, which it is thought might have been used in an earlier form than that which has come down to us, contains the legend of the cave, and has apparently a similar view to the Gospel last mentioned as to the perpetual virginity of Mary. The kindred Evangelium Thomae has the 'ploughs and yokes.' And there are some similarities of language between the Protevangelium and Justin's Gospel, which will come under review later[4].

It does not, however, appear to have been noticed that these Gospels satisfy most imperfectly the conditions of the problem. We know that the Gospel according to the Hebrews in its Nazarene form omitted the whole section Matt. i. 18 – ii. 23, containing the

---

[1] *Beiträge*, i. p. 261 sqq.
[2] *Evangelien Justin's u. s. w.*, p. 270 sqq.
[3] The chief authority is Eus. *H. E.* vi. 12.
[4] Cf. Hilgenfeld, *Ev. Justin's*, p. 157.

conception, the nativity, the visit of the Magi, and the flight into Egypt, all of which were found in Justin's Gospel; while in its Ebionite form it left out the first two chapters altogether. There is not a tittle of evidence to show that the Gospel according to Peter was any more complete; in proportion as it resembled the Gospel according to the Hebrews the presumption is that it was not. And the Protevangelium of James makes no mention of Arabia, while it expressly says that the star appeared 'in the East' (instead of 'in the heaven' as Justin); it also omits, and rather seems to exclude, the flight into Egypt.

It is therefore clear that whether Justin used these Gospels or not, he cannot in any case have confined himself to them; unless indeed this is possible in regard to the Gospel that bears the name of Peter, though the possibility is drawn so entirely from our ignorance that it can hardly be taken account of. We thus seem to be reduced to the conclusion that Justin's Gospel or Gospels was an unknown entity of which no historical evidence survives, and this would almost be enough, according to the logical Law of Parsimony, to drive us back upon the assumption that our present Gospels only had been used. This assumption however still does not appear to me wholly satisfactory, for reasons which will come out more clearly when from considering the matter of the documents which Justin used we pass to their form.

The reader already has before him a collection of Justin's quotations from the Old Testament, the results of which may be stated thus. From the Pentateuch eighteen passages are quoted exactly, nineteen with slight variations, and eleven with marked divergence. From the Psalms sixteen exactly, including nine (or ten) whole Psalms, two with slight and three with decided variation. From Isaiah twenty-five exactly, twelve slightly variant, and sixteen decidedly. From the other Major Prophets Justin has only three exact quotations, four slightly divergent, and eleven diverging more widely. From the Minor Prophets and other books he has two exact quotations, seven in which the variation is slight, and thirteen in which it is marked. Of the distinctly free quotations in the Pentateuch (eleven in all), three may be thought to have a Messianic character (the burning bush, the brazen serpent, the curse of the cross), but in none of these does the variation appear to be due to this. Of the three free quotations from the Psalms two are Messianic, and one of these has probably been influenced by the Messianic application. In the free quotations from Isaiah it is not quite easy to say what are Messianic and what are not; but the only clear case in which the Messianic application seems to have caused a marked divergence is xlii. 1–4. Other passages, such as ii. 5, 6, vii. 10–17, lii. 13–liii. 12 (as quoted in A. i. 50), appear under the head of slight variation. The long quotation lii. 10–liv. 6, in Dial. 12, is given with substantial exactness. Turning to the other Major Prophets, one passage, Jer. xxxi. 15, has probably derived its shape from the Messianic application. And in the Minor Prophets three passages (Hos. x. 6, Zech. xii. 10–12, and Micah v. 2) appear to have been thus affected. The rest of the free quotations and some of the variations in those which are less free may be set down to defect of memory or similar accidental causes.

Let us now draw up a table of Justin's quotations from the Gospels arranged as nearly as may be on the same standard and scale as that of the quotations from the Old Testament. Such a table will stand thus. [Those only which appear to be direct quotations are given.]

Exact.	Slightly variant.	Variant.	Remarks.
	†D. 49, Matt. 3. 11. 12 (v. l.)		repeated in part similarly.
	D. 51, Matt. 11. 12–15; Luke 16. 16†.		compounded with omissions but striking resemblances.
D. 49, Matt. 17. 11–13.			
	A. 1. 15, Matt. 5. 28.		
		A. 1. 15, Matt. 5. 29; Mark 9. 47.	from memory?
	A. 1. 15, Matt. 5. 32.		confusion of readings.
		†A. 1. 15, Matt. 19. 12.	from memory?
		A. 1. 15, Matt. 5. 42; Luke 6. 30, 34.	compounded.
Continuous. {	A. 1. 15, Matt. 6. 19, 20; 16. 26; 6. 20.		
	Continuous. {	A. 1. 15 (D. 96), Luke 6. 36; Matt. 5. 45; 6. 25–27; Luke 12. 22–24; Matt. 6. 32, 33; 6. 21.	from memory (Cr.), but prob. different document; rather marked identity in phrase.
	A. 1. 15, Matt. 6. 1.		
A. 1. 15, Matt. 9. 13 (?).			do the last words belong to the quotation?
		Continuous. { A. 1. 15, Luke 6. 32; Matt. 5. 46.	
		A. 1. 15 (D. 128), Luke 6. 27, 28; Matt. 5. 44.	repeated in part similarly, in part diversely; confusion in MSS.

I

Exact.	Slightly variant.	Variant.	Remarks.
Continuous {	A. 1. 16, Luke 6. 29 (Matt. 5. 39, 40).		
		A. 1. 16, Matt. 5. 22 (v. l.)	
		A. 1. 16, Matt. 5. 41.	ἀγγαρεύσει.
	A. 1. 16, Matt. 5. 16.		
		D. 93, A. 1. 16, Matt. 22. 40, 37, 38.	
		A. 1. 16, D. 101, Matt. 19. 16, 17 (v. l.); Luke 18. 18, 19 (v. l.).	repeated diversely.
	A. 1. 16, Matt. 5. 34, 37.		
A. 1. 16, Matt. 7. 21.	A. 1. 16 (A. 1. 62). Luke 10. 16 (v. l.).		repeated in part similarly, in part diversely.
Continuous {		†A. 1. 16 (D. 76), Matt. 7. 22, 23 (v. l.); Luke 13. 26, 27 (v. l.)	
	A. 1. 16, Matt. 13. 42, 43 (v. l.)		addition.
		A. 1. 16 (D. 35), Matt. 7. 15.	
	A. 1. 16, Matt. 7. 16, 19.		
D 76, Matt. 8. 11. 12†.			
		D. 35, ἔσονται σχίσματα καὶ αἱρέσεις.	
	D. 76, Matt. 25. 41 (v. l.)		
	D. 35, Matt. 7. 15.		repeated with nearer approach to Matthew, perh. v. l.
		D. 35, 82, Matt. 24. 24 (Mark 13. 22).	repeated with similarity and divergence.
		D. 82, Matt. 10. 22, par.	freely.

Exact.	Slightly variant.	Variant.	Remarks.
A. 1. 19, Luke 18. 27†.			
		A. 1. 19, Luke 12. 4, 5; Matt. 10. 28.	compounded.
		A. 1. 17, Luke 12. 48 (v. l.)	
	D. 76, Luke 10. 19†.		ins. σκολοπενδρῶν.
D. 105, Matt. 5. 20.			
		D. 125. Matt. 13. 3 sqq.	condensed narrative.
		†D. 17, Luke 11. 52.	
	D. 17, Matt. 23. 23; Luke 11. 42.		compounded.
	D. 17, 112, Matt. 23. 27; 23. 24.		repeated similarly.
		D. 47, ἐν οἷς ἂν ὑμᾶς καταλάβω ἐν τούτοις καὶ κρινῶ.	
	D. 81, Luke 20. 35, 36.		marked resemblance with difference.
D. 107, Matt. 16. 4.			
	D. 122, Matt. 23. 15.		
	†D. 17, Matt. 21. 13, 12.		
		†A. 1. 17, Luke 20. 22–25 (v. l.)	narrative portion free.
	D. 100, A. 1. 63, Matt. 11. 27 (v. l.)		repeated not identically.
	D. 76, 100, Luke 9. 22.		repeated diversely; free (Credner).
A. 1. 35, Matt. 21. 5 (addition).		D. 53, Matt. 21. 5.	(Zech. 9. 9).
		A. 1. 66, Luke 22. 19, 20.	
	D. 99, Matt. 26. 39 (v. l.)		
		D. 103, Luke 22. 42–44.	
		D. 101, Matt. 27. 43.	

Exact.	Slightly variant.	Variant.	Remarks.
		A. 1. 38, ὁ νεκροὺς ἀνεγείρας ῥυσά- σθω ἑαυτόν.	
D 99, Matt. 27. 46; Mark 15. 34. D. 105, Luke 23. 46.			compounded.

The total result may be taken to be that ten passages are substantially exact, while twenty-five present slight and thirty-two marked variations[1]. This is only rough and approximate, because of the passages that are put down as exact two, or possibly three, can only be said to be so with a qualification; though, on the other hand, there are passages entered under the second class as 'slightly variant' which have a leaning towards the first, and passages entered under the third which have a perceptible leaning towards the second. We can therefore afford to disregard these doubtful cases and accept the classification very much as it stands. Comparing it then with the parallel classification that has been made of the quotations from the Old Testament, we find that in the latter sixty-four were ranked as exact, forty-four as slightly variant, and fifty-four as decidedly variant. If we reduce these roughly to a common standard of comparison the proportion of variation may be represented thus:—

	Exact.	Slightly variant.	Variant.
Quotations from the Old Testament	10	7	9
Quotations from the Synoptic Gospels	10	25	32

It will be seen from this at once how largely the pro-

[1] A somewhat similar classification has been made by De Wette, *Einleitung in das N. T.*, pp. 104-110, in which however the standard seems to be somewhat lower than that which I have assumed; several instances of variation which I had classed as decided, De Wette considers to be only slight. I hope I may consider this a proof that the classification above given has not been influenced by bias.

portion of variation rises; it is indeed more than three times as high for the quotations from the Gospels as for those from the Old Testament. The amount of combination too is decidedly in excess of that which is found in the Old Testament quotations.

There is, it is true, something to be said on the other side. Justin quotes the Old Testament rather as Scripture, the New Testament rather as history. I think it will be felt that he has permitted his own style a freer play in regard to the latter than the former. The New Testament record had not yet acquired the same degree of fixity as the Old. The 'many' compositions of which St. Luke speaks in his preface were still in circulation, and were only gradually dying out. One important step had been taken in the regular reading of the 'Memoirs of the Apostles' at the Christian assemblies. We have not indeed proof that these were confined to the Canonical Gospels. Probably as yet they were not. But it should be remembered that Irenaeus was now a boy, and that by the time he had reached manhood the Canon of the Gospels had received its definite form.

Taking all these points into consideration I think we shall find the various indications converge upon very much the same conclusion as that at which we have already arrived. The *a priori* probabilities of the case, as well as the actual phenomena of Justin's Gospel, alike tend to show that he did make use either mediately or immediately of our Gospels, but that he did not assign to them an exclusive authority, and that he probably made use along with them of other documents no longer extant.

The proof that Justin made use of each of our three

Synoptics individually is perhaps more striking from the point of view of substance than of form, because his direct quotations are mostly taken from the discourses rather than from the narrative, and these discourses are usually found in more than a single Gospel, while in proportion as they bear the stamp of originality and authenticity it is difficult to assign them to any particular reporter. There is however some strong and remarkable evidence of this kind.

At least one case of parallelism seems to prove almost decisively the use of the first Gospel. It is necessary to give the quotation and the original with the parallel from St. Mark side by side.

Justin, Dial. c. 49.

Ἠλίας μὲν ἐλεύσεται καὶ ἀποκαταστήσει πάντα· λέγω δὲ ὑμῖν, ὅτι Ἠλίας ἤδη ἦλθε καὶ οὐκ ἐπέγνωσαν αὐτὸν ἀλλ' ἐποίησαν αὐτῷ ὅσα ἠθέλησαν. Καὶ γέγραπται ὅτι τότε συνῆκαν οἱ μαθηταί, ὅτι περὶ Ἰωάννου τοῦ βαπτιστοῦ εἶπεν αὐτοῖς.

Matt. xvii. 11–13.

Ἠλίας μὲν ἔρχεται καὶ ἀποκαταστήσει πάντα· λέγω δὲ ὑμῖν ὅτι Ἠλίας ἤδη ἦλθεν καὶ οὐκ ἐπέγνωσαν αὐτόν, ἀλλὰ ἐποίησαν αὐτῷ ὅσα ἠθέλησαν· [οὕτως καὶ ὁ υἱὸς τοῦ ἀνθρώπου μέλλει πάσχειν ὑπ' αὐτῶν.] τότε συνῆκαν οἱ μαθηταὶ ὅτι περὶ Ἰωάννου τοῦ βαπτιστοῦ εἶπεν αὐτοῖς. The clause in brackets is placed at the end of ver. 13 by D. and the Old Latin.

Mark ix. 12, 13.

Ὁ δὲ ἔφη αὐτοῖς· Ἠλίας [μὲν] ἐλθὼν πρῶτον ἀποκαθιστάνει πάντα· καὶ πῶς γέγραπται ἐπὶ τὸν υἱὸν τοῦ ἀνθρώπου, ἵνα πολλὰ πάθῃ καὶ ἐξουδενηθῇ. ἀλλὰ λέγω ὑμῖν ὅτι καὶ Ἠλίας ἐλήλυθεν καὶ ἐποίησαν αὐτῷ ὅσα ἤθελον, καθὼς γέγραπται ἐπ' αὐτόν.

We notice here, first, an important point, that Justin reproduces at the end of his quotation what appears to be not so much a part of the object-matter of the narrative as a *comment or reflection of the Evangelist* ('Then the disciples understood that He spake unto them of John the Baptist'). This was thought by Credner, who as a rule is inclined to press the use of an apocryphal Gospel by Justin, to be sufficient proof that the quotation is taken from our present Matthew[1]. On this point, however, there is an able and on the whole a sound argument in 'Supernatural Religion[2].' There are certainly cases in which a similar comment or reflection is found either in all three Synoptic Gospels or in two of them (e. g. Matt. vii. 28, 29 = Mark i. 22 = Luke iv. 32; Matt. xiii. 34 = Mark iv. 33, 34; Matt. xxvi. 43 = Mark xiv. 40; Matt. xix. 22 = Mark x. 22). The author consequently maintains that these were found in the original document from which all three, or two Synoptics at least, borrowed; and he notes that this very passage is assigned by Ewald to the 'oldest Gospel.'

The observation in itself is a fine and true one, and has an important bearing upon the question as to the way in which our Synoptic Gospels were composed. We may indeed remark in passing that the author seems to have overlooked the fact that, when once this principle of a common written basis or bases for the Synoptic Gospels is accepted, nine-tenths of his own argument is overthrown; for there are no divergences in the text of the patristic quotations from the Gospels that may not be amply paralleled by the differences which exist in the text of the several Gospels themselves, showing that the Evangelists took liberties with their ground documents to an extent that is really greater than that of

---

[1] *Beiträge*, i. p. 237.   [2] *S. R.* i. p. 396 sqq.

any subsequent misquotation. But putting aside for the present this *argumentum ad hominem* which seems to follow from the admission here made, there is, I think, the strongest reason to conclude that in the present case the first Evangelist is not merely reproducing his ground document. There is one element in the question which the author has omitted to notice; that is, the *parallel passage in St. Mark*. This differs so widely from the text of St. Matthew as to show that that text cannot accurately represent the original; it also wants the reflective comment altogether. Accordingly, if the author will turn to p. 275 of Ewald's book[1] he will find that that writer, though roughly assigning the passage as it appears in both Synoptics to the 'oldest Gospel,' yet in reconstructing the text of this Gospel does so, not by taking that of either of the Synoptics pure and simple, but by mixing the two. All the other critics who have dealt with this point, so far as I am aware, have done the same. Holtzmann[2] follows Ewald, and Weiss[3] accepts Mark's as more nearly the original text.

The very extent of the divergence in St. Mark throws out into striking relief the close agreement of Justin's quotation with St. Matthew. Here we have three verses word for word the same, even to the finest shades of expression. To the single exception ἐλεύσεται for ἔρχεται I cannot, as Credner does[4], attach any importance. The present tense in the Gospel has undoubtedly a future signification[5], and Justin was very naturally led to give

---

[1] *Die drei ersten Evangelien*, Göttingen, 1850. [A second, revised, edition of this work has recently appeared.]

[2] *Die Synoptischen Evangelien*, Leipzig, 1863, p. 88.

[3] *Das Marcus-evangelium*, Berlin, 1872, p. 299.   [4] *Beiträge*, i. p. 219.

[5] Dr. Westcott well calls this 'the *prophetic* sense of the present' (*On the Canon*, p. 128).

it also a future form by ἀποκαταστήσει which follows. For the rest, the order, particles, tenses are so absolutely identical, where the text of St. Mark shows how inevitably they must have differed in another Gospel or even in the original, that I can see no alternative but to refer the quotation directly to our present St. Matthew.

If this passage had stood alone, taken in connection with the coincidence of matter between Justin and the first Gospel, great weight must have attached to it. But it does not by any means stand alone. There is an exact verbal agreement in the verses Matt. v. 20 ('Except your righteousness' &c.) and Matt. vii. 21 ('Not every one that saith unto me,' &c.) which are peculiar to the first Gospel. There is a close agreement, if not always with the best, yet with some very old, text of St. Matthew in v. 22 (note especially the striking phrase and construction ἔνοχος εἰς), v. 28 (note βλεπ. πρὸς τὸ ἐπιθυμ.), v. 41 (note the remarkable word ἀγγαρεύσει), xxv. 41, and not too great a divergence in v. 16, vi. 1 (πρὸς τὸ θεαθῆναι, εἰ δὲ μή γε μισθὸν οὐκ ἔχετε), and xix. 12, all of which passages are without parallel in any extant Gospel. There are also marked resemblances to the Matthaean text in synoptic passages such as Matt. iii. 11, 12 (εἰς μετάνοιαν, τὰ ὑποδήματα βαστάσαι), Matt. vi. 19, 20 (ὅπου σὴς καὶ βρῶσις ἀφανίζει, where Luke has simply σὴς διαφθείρει, and διορύσσουσι where Luke has ἐγγίζει), Matt. vii. 22, 23 (ἐκείνῃ τῇ ἡμέρᾳ Κύριε, Κύριε, κ. τ. λ.), Matt. xvi. 26 (δώσει Matt. only, ἀντάλλαγμα Matt., Mark), Matt. xvi. 1, 4 (the last verse exactly). As these passages are all from the discourses I do not wish to say that they may not be taken from other Gospels than the canonical, but we have absolutely no evidence that they were so taken, and every additional instance increases the probability that they were taken directly from St. Matthew, which by this time, I think, has reached a very high degree of presumption.

I have reserved for a separate discussion a single instance which I shall venture to add to those already quoted, although I am aware that it is alleged on the opposite side. Justin has the saying, 'Let your yea be yea and your nay nay, for whatsoever is more than these cometh of the Evil One' (Μὴ ὀμόσητε ὅλως· Ἔστω δὲ ὑμῶν τὸ ναὶ ναί, καὶ τὸ οὒ οὔ· τὸ δὲ περισσὸν τούτων ἐκ τοῦ πονηροῦ), which is set against the first Evangelist's 'Let your conversation be Yea yea, Nay nay, for whatsoever is more than these cometh of the Evil One' (ἐγὼ δὲ λέγω ὑμῖν μὴ ὀμόσαι ὅλως . . . Ἔστω δὲ ὁ λόγος ὑμῶν ναὶ ναί, οὒ οὔ· τὸ δὲ περισσόν, κ. τ. λ.). Now it is perfectly true that as early as the Canonical Epistle of James (v. 12) we find the reading ἤτω δὲ ὑμῶν τὸ ναὶ ναί, καὶ τὸ οὒ οὔ, and that in the Clementine Homilies twice over we read ἔστω ὑμῶν τὸ ναὶ ναί, (καὶ) τὸ οὒ οὔ, καὶ being inserted in one instance and not in the other. Justin's reading is found also exactly in Clement of Alexandria, and a similar reading (though with the ἤτω of James) in Epiphanius. These last two examples show that the misquotation was an easy one to fall into, because there can be little doubt that Clement and Ephiphanius supposed themselves to be quoting the canonical text. There remains however the fact that the Justinian form is supported by the pseudo-Clementines; and at the first blush it might seem that 'Let your yea be yea' (stand to your word) made better, at least a complete and more obvious, sense than 'Let your conversation be' (let it not go beyond) 'Yea yea' &c.[1]. There is, however, what seems to be

[1] 'This is meaningless,' writes Mr. Baring-Gould of the canonical text,

a decisive proof that the original form both of Justin's and the Clementine quotation is that which is given in the first Gospel. Both Justin and the writer who passes under the name of Clement add the clause 'Whatsoever is more than these cometh of evil' (or 'of the Evil One'). But this, while it tallies perfectly with the canonical reading, evidently excludes any other. It is consequent and good sense to say, 'Do not go beyond a plain yes or no, because whatever is in excess of this must have an evil motive,' but the connection is entirely lost when we substitute 'Keep your word, for whatever is more than this has an evil motive'— more than what?

The most important points that can be taken to imply a use of St. Mark's Gospel have been already discussed as falling under the head of matter rather than of form.

The coincidences with Luke are striking but complicated. In his earlier work, the 'Beiträge[1],' Credner regarded as a decided reference to the Prologue of this Gospel the statement of Justin that his Memoirs were composed ὑπὸ τῶν ἀποστόλων αὐτοῦ καὶ τῶν ἐκείνοις παρακολουθησάντων: but, in the posthumous History of the Canon[2], he retracts this view, having come to recognise a greater frequency in the use of the word παρακολουθεῖν in this sense. It will also of course be noticed that Justin has παρ. τοῖς ἀπ. and not παρ. τοῖς πράγμασιν, as Luke. It is doubtless true that the use of the word can

---

rather hastily, and forgetting, as it would appear, the concluding clause (*Lost and Hostile Gospels*, p. 166); cp. *S. R.* i. p. 354, ii. p. 28.

[1] i. pp. 196, 227, 258.
[2] *Geschichte des Neutestamentlichen Kanon* (ed. Volkmar, Berlin, 1860), p. 16.

be paralleled to such an extent as to make it not a matter of certainty that the Gospel is being quoted: still I think there will be a certain probability that it has been suggested by a reminiscence of this passage, and, strangely enough, there is a parallel for the substitution of the historians for the subject-matter of their history in Epiphanius, who reads παρ. τοῖς αὐτόπταις καὶ ὑπηρέταις τοῦ λόγου[1], where he is explicitly and unquestionably quoting St. Luke.

There are some marked coincidences of phrase in the account of the Annunciation—ἐπέρχεσθαι, ἐπισκιάζειν, δύναμις ὑψίστου (a specially Lucan phrase), τὸ γεννώμενον (also a form characteristic of St. Luke), ἰδού, συλλήψῃ ἐν γαστρὶ καὶ τέξῃ υἱόν. Of the other peculiarities of St. Luke Justin has in exact accordance the last words upon the cross (Πάτερ, εἰς χεῖράς σου παρατίθεμαι τὸ πνεῦμά μου). In the Agony in the Garden Justin has the feature of the Bloody Sweat; but it is right to notice—

(1) That he has θρόμβοι alone, without αἵματος. Luke, ἐγένετο ὁ ἱδρὼς αὐτοῦ ὡσεὶ θρόμβοι αἵματος καταβαίνοντες. Justin, ἱδρὼς ὡσεὶ θρόμβοι κατεχεῖτο.

(2) That this is regarded as a fulfilment of Ps. xxii. 14 ('All my tears are poured out' &c.).

(3) That in continuing the quotation Justin follows Matthew rather than Luke. These considerations may be held to qualify, though I do not think that they suffice to remove, the conclusion that St. Luke's Gospel is being quoted. It seems to be sufficiently clear that θρόμβοι might be used in this signification without αἵματος[2],

---

[1] *Adv. Haer.* 428 D.

[2] I am not quite clear that more is meant (as Meyer, Ellicott *Huls. Lect.* p. 339, n. 2, and others maintain) in the evangelical language than that the drops of sweat 'resembled blood;' ὡσεί seems to qualify αἵματος as much

and it appears from the whole manner of Justin's narrative that he intends to give merely the sense and not the words, with the exception of the single saying 'Let this cup pass from Me,' which is taken from St. Matthew. We cannot say positively that this feature did not occur in any other Gospel, but there is absolutely no reason apart from this passage to suppose that it did. The construction with ὡσεί is in some degree characteristic of St. Luke, as it occurs more often in the works of that writer than in all the rest of the New Testament put together.

In narrating the institution of the Lord's Supper Justin has the clause which is found only in St. Luke and St. Paul, 'This do in remembrance of Me' (μου for ἐμήν). The giving of the cup he quotes rather after the first two Synoptics, and adds 'that He gave it to them (the Apostles) alone.' This last does not seem to be more than an inference of Justin's own.

Two other sayings Justin has which are without parallel except in St. Luke. One is from the mission of the seventy.

Justin, Dial. 76.	*Luke* x. 19.
Δίδωμι ὑμῖν ἐξουσίαν καταπατεῖν ἐπάνω ὄφεων, καὶ σκορπίων, καὶ σκολοπενδρῶν, καὶ ἐπάνω πάσης δυνάμεως τοῦ ἐχθροῦ.	Ἰδού, δίδωμι ὑμῖν τὴν ἐξουσίαν τοῦ πατεῖν ἐπάνω ὄφεων, καὶ σκορπίων, καὶ ἐπὶ πᾶσαν τὴν δύναμιν τοῦ ἐχθροῦ.

The insertion of σκολοπενδρῶν here is curious. It may be perhaps to some extent paralleled by the insertion of καὶ εἰς θήραν in Rom. xi. 9: we have also seen a strange addition in the quotation of Ps. li. 19 in the

as θρόμβοι. Compare especially the interesting parallels from medical writers quoted by M'Clellan *ad loc.*

Epistle of Barnabas (c. ii). Otherwise the resemblance of Justin to the Gospel is striking. The second saying, 'To whom God has given more, of him shall more be required' (Apol. i. 17), if quoted from the Gospel at all, is only a paraphrase of Luke xii. 48.

Besides these there are other passages, which are perhaps stronger as separate items of evidence, where, in quoting synoptic matter, Justin makes use of phrases which are found only in St. Luke and are discountenanced by the other Evangelists. Thus in the account of the rich young man, the three synoptical versions of the saying that impossibilities with men are possible with God, run thus:—

Luke xviii. 27.	*Mark* x. 27.	*Matt.* xix. 26.
Τὰ ἀδύνατα παρὰ ἀνθρώποις δυνατὰ παρὰ τῷ Θεῷ ἐστίν.	Παρὰ ἀνθρώποις ἀδύνατον, ἀλλ' οὐ παρὰ Θεῷ· πάντα γὰρ δυνατὰ παρὰ τῷ Θεῷ.	Παρὰ ἀνθρώποις τοῦτο ἀδύνατόν ἐστιν, παρὰ δὲ Θεῷ δυνατὰ πάντα.

Here it will be observed that Matthew and Mark (as frequently happens) are nearer to each other than either of them is to Luke. This would lead us to infer that, as they are two to one, they more nearly represent the common original, which has been somewhat modified in the hands of St. Luke. But now Justin has the words precisely as they stand in St. Luke, with the omission of ἐστίν, the order of which varies in the MSS. of the Gospel. This must be taken as a strong proof that Justin has used the peculiar text of the third Gospel. Again, it is to be noticed that in another section of the triple synopsis (Mark xii. 20 = Matt. xxii. 30 = Luke xx. 35, 36) he has, in common with Luke and diverging from the other Gospels which are in near agreement, the remarkable compound ἰσάγγελοι and the equally remarkable phrase υἱοὶ τῆς ἀναστάσεως (τέκνα τοῦ Θεοῦ τῆς ἀναστάσεως Justin). This also I must regard as supplying a strong argument for the direct use of the Gospel. Many similar instances may be adduced; ἔρχεται (ἥξει Justin) ὁ ἰσχυρότερος (Luke iii. 16), ὁ νόμος καὶ οἱ προφῆται ἕως (μέχρι Justin) 'Ιωάννου (Luke xvi. 16), παντὶ τῷ αἰτοῦντι (Luke vi. 30), τῷ τύπτοντί σε ἐπὶ (σου Justin) τὴν σιαγόνα πάρεχε καὶ τὴν ἄλλην κ. τ. λ. (Luke vi. 29; compare Matt. v. 39, 40), τί με λέγεις ἀγαθόν and οὐδεὶς ἀγαθὸς εἰ μή (Luke xviii. 19; compare Matt. xix. 17), μετὰ ταῦτα μὴ ἐχόντων (δυνάμενους Justin) περισσότερόν (om. Justin) τι ποιῆσαι κ. τ. λ. (Luke xii. 4, 5; compare Matt. x. 28), πήγανον and ἀγάπην τοῦ Θεοῦ (Luke xi. 42). In the parallel passage to Luke ix. 22 (= Matt xvi. 21 = Mark viii. 31) Justin has the striking word ἀποδοκιμασθῆναι, with Mark and Luke against Matthew, and ὑπό with Mark against the ἀπό of the two other Synoptics. This last coincidence can perhaps hardly be pressed, as ὑπό would be the more natural word to use.

In the cases where we have only the double synopsis to compare with Justin, we have no certain test to distinguish between the primary and secondary features in the text of the Gospels. We cannot say with confidence what belonged to the original document and what to the later editor who reduced it to its present form. In these cases therefore it is possible that when Justin has a detail that is found in St. Matthew and wanting in St. Luke, or found in St. Luke and wanting in St. Matthew, he is still not quoting directly from either of those Gospels, but from the common document on which they are based. The triple synopsis however furnishes such a criterion. It enables us to see what was the original text and how any single Evangelist has diverged from it. Thus in the two instances quoted at the beginning of the last paragraph it is evident that the Lucan text represents a deviation from the original, and *that deviation Justin has reproduced*. The word ἰσάγγελοι may be taken as a crucial case. Both the other Synoptics have simply ὡς ἄγγελοι, and this may be set down as undoubtedly the reading of the original; the form ἰσάγγελοι, which occurs nowhere else in the New Testament, and I believe, so far as we know, nowhere else in Greek before this passage[1], has clearly been coined by the third Evangelist and has been adopted from him by Justin. So that in a quotation which otherwise presents considerable variation we have what I think must be called the strongest evidence that Justin really had St. Luke's narrative, either in itself or in some secondary shape, before him.

We are thus brought once more to the old result. If Justin did not use our Gospels in their present shape as they have come down to us, he used them in a later shape, not in an earlier. His resemblances to them cannot be accounted for by the supposition that he had access to the materials out of which they were composed, because he reproduces features which by the nature of the case cannot have been present in those originals, but of which we are still able to trace the authorship and the exact point of their insertion. Our Gospels form a secondary stage in the history of the text, Justin's quotations a tertiary. In order to reach the state in which it is found in Justin, the road lies *through* our Gospels, and not outside them.

---

[1] The only parallel that I can find quoted is a reference by Mr. M'Clellan to Philo i. 164 (ed. Mangey), where the phrase is however ἴσος ἀγγέλοις (γεγονώς).

This however does not exclude the possibility that Justin may at times quote from uncanonical Gospels as well. We have already seen reason to think that he did so from the substance of the Evangelical narrative, as it appears in his works, and this conclusion too is not otherwise than confirmed by its form. The degree and extent of the variations incline us to introduce such an additional factor to account for them. Either Justin has used a lost Gospel or Gospels, besides those that are still extant, or else he has used a recension of these Gospels with some slight changes of language and with some apocryphal additions. We have seen that he has two short sayings and several minute details that are not found in our present Gospels. A remarkable coincidence is noticed in 'Supernatural Religion' with the Protevangelium of James[1]. As in that work so also in Justin, the explanation of the name Jesus occurs in the address of the angel to Mary, not to Joseph, 'Behold thou shalt conceive of the Holy Ghost and bear a Son and He shall be called the Son of the Highest, and thou shalt call His name Jesus, for He shall save His people from their sins.' Again the Protevangelium has the phrase 'Thou shalt conceive of His Word,' which, though not directly quoted, appears to receive countenance from Justin. The author adds that 'Justin's divergences from the Protevangelium prevent our supposing that in its present form it could have been the actual source of his quotations,' though he thinks that he had before him a still earlier work to which both the Protevangelium and the third Gospel were indebted. So far as the Protevangelium is con-

[1] *S. R.* i. p. 304 sqq.

cerned this may very probably have been the case; but what reason there is for assuming that the same document was also anterior to the third Gospel I am not aware. On the contrary, this very passage seems to suggest an opposite conclusion. The quotation in Justin and the address in the Protevangelium both present a combination of narratives that are kept separate in the first and third Gospels. But this very fact supplies a strong presumption that the version of those Gospels is the earliest. It is unlikely that the first Evangelist, if he had found his text already existing, as part of the speech of the angel to Mary, would have transferred it to an address to Joseph; and it is little less unlikely that the third Evangelist, finding the fuller version of Justin and the Protevangelium, should have omitted from it one of its most important features. If a further link is necessary to connect Justin with the Protevangelium, that link comes into the chain after our Gospels and not before. Dr. Hilgenfeld has also noticed the phrase χαρὰν δὲ λαβοῦσα Μαριάμ as common to Justin and the Protevangelium [1]. This, too, may belong to the older original of the latter work.

The other verbal coincidences with the Gospel according to the Hebrews in the account of the Baptism, and with that of Thomas in the 'ploughs and yokes,' have been already mentioned, and are, I believe, along with those just discussed, all that can be directly referred to an apocryphal source.

Besides these there are some coincidences in form between quotations as they appear in Justin and in other writers, such as especially the Clementine Homi-

---

[1] *Ev. Justin's*, p. 157.

lies. These are thought to point to the existence of a common Gospel (now lost) from which they may have been extracted. It is unnecessary to repeat what has been said about one of these passages ('Let your yea be yea,' &c.). Another corresponds roughly to the verse Matt. xxv. 41, where both Justin and the Clementine Homilies read ὑπάγετε εἰς τὸ σκότος τὸ ἐξώτερον ὃ ἡτοίμασεν ὁ πατὴρ τῷ σατανᾷ (τῷ διαβόλῳ Clem. Hom.) καὶ τοῖς ἀγγέλοις αὐτοῦ for the canonical πορεύεσθε ἀπ' ἐμοῦ εἰς τὸ πῦρ τὸ αἰώνιον τὸ ἡτοιμασμένον κ. τ. λ. It is true that there is a considerable approximation to the reading of Justin and the Clementines, found especially in MSS. and authorities of a Western character (D. Latt. Iren. Cypr. Hil.), but there still remains the coincidence in regard to ἐξώτερον (?) for αἰώνιον and σκότος for πῦρ, which seems to be due to something more than merely a variant text of the Gospel. A third meeting-point between Justin and the Clementines is afforded by a text which we shall have to touch upon when we come to speak of the fourth Gospel. Of the other quotations common to the Clementines and Justin there is a partial but not complete coincidence in regard to Matt. vii. 15, xi. 27, xix. 16, and Luke vi. 36. In Matt. vii. 15 the Clementines have πολλοὶ ἐλεύσονται where Justin has once πολλοὶ ἐλεύσονται, once πολλοὶ ἥξουσιν, and once the Matthaean version προσέχετε ἀπὸ τῶν ψευδοπροφητῶν οἵτινες ἔρχονται κ. τ. λ. There is however a difference in regard to the reading ἐν ἐνδύμασι, where the Clementines have ἐν ἐνδύματι, and Justin twice over ἐνδεδυμένοι. In Matt. xi. 27, Justin and the Clementines agree as to the order of the clauses, and twice in the use of the aorist ἔγνω (Justin has once γινώσκω), but in the concluding clause (ᾧ [οἷς Clem.] ἐὰν βούληται ὁ υἱὸς ἀποκαλύψαι)

Justin has uniformly in the three places where the verse is quoted οἷς ἂν ὁ υἱὸς ἀποκαλύψῃ. In Matt. xix. 16, 17 (Luke xviii. 18, 19) the Clementines and Justin alternately adhere to the Canonical text while differing from each other, but in the concluding phrase Justin has on one occasion the Clementine reading, ὁ πατήρ μου ὁ ἐν τοῖς οὐρανοῖς. In Luke vi. 36 the Clementines have γίνεσθε ἀγαθοὶ καὶ οἰκτίρμονες, where Justin has γίνεσθε χρηστοὶ καὶ οἰκτίρμονες against the Canonical γίνεσθε οἰκτίρμονες. On the other hand, it should be said that the remaining quotations common to the Clementines and Justin have to all appearance no relation to each other. This applies to Matt. iv. 10, v. 39, 40, vi. 8, viii. 11, x. 28; Luke xi. 52. Speaking generally we seem to observe in comparing Justin and the Clementines phenomena not dissimilar to those which appear on a comparison with the Canonical Gospels. There is perhaps about the same degree at once of resemblance and divergence.

The principal textual coincidence with other writers is that with the Gospel used by the Marcosians as quoted by Irenaeus (Adv. Haer. i. 20. 3). Here the reading of Matt. xi. 27 is given in a form very similar to that of Justin, οὐδεὶς ἔγνω τὸν πατέρα εἰ μὴ ὁ υἱός, καὶ (οὐδέ Justin) τὸν υἱόν, εἰ μὴ ὁ πατὴρ καὶ ᾧ (οἷς Justin) ἂν ὁ υἱὸς ἀποκαλύψῃ. This verse however is quoted by the early writers, orthodox as well as heretical, in almost every possible way, and it is not clear from the account in Irenaeus whether the Marcosians used an extra-canonical Gospel or merely a different text of the Canonical. Irenaeus himself seems to hold the latter view, and in favour of it may be urged the fact that they quote passages peculiar both to the first and the third Gospel; on the other hand, one of their quotations, πολλάκις ἐπεθύμησα ἀκοῦσαι ἕνα τῶν λόγων τούτων, does not appear to have a canonical original.

On reviewing these results we find them present a chequered appearance. There are no traces of coincidence so definite and consistent as to justify us in laying the finger upon any particular extra-canonical Gospel as that used by Justin. But upon the whole it seems best to assume that some such Gospel was used, certainly not to the exclusion of the Canonical Gospels, but probably in addition to them.

A confusing element in the whole question is that to which we have just alluded in regard to the Gospel of the Marcosians. It is often difficult to decide whether a writer has really before him an unknown document or merely a variant text of one with which we are familiar. In the case of Justin it is to be noticed that there is often a very considerable approximation to his readings, not in the best text, but in some very early attested text, of the Canonical Gospels. It will be well to collect some of the most prominent instances of this.

Matt. iii. 15 ad fin. καὶ πῦρ ἀνήφθη ἐν τῷ Ἰορδάνῃ Justin. So a. (Codex Vercellensis of the Old Latin translation) adds 'et cum baptizaretur lumen ingens circumfulsit de aqua ita ut timerent omnes qui advenerant;' g¹. (Codex Sangermanensis of the same) 'lumen magnum fulgebat de aqua,' &c. See above.

Luke iii. 22. Justin reads υἱός μου εἶ σύ, ἐγὼ σήμερον γεγέννηκά σε. So D, a, b, c, ff, l, Latin Fathers ('nonnulli codices' Augustine). See above.

Matt. v. 28. ὃς ἂν ἐμβλέψῃ for πᾶς ὁ βλέπων. Origen five times as Justin, only once the accepted text.

Matt. v. 29. Justin and Clement of Alexandria read here ἔκκοψον for ἔξελε, probably from the next verse or from Matt. xviii. 8.

Matt. vi. 20. οὐρανοῖς Clem. Alex. with Justin; οὐρανῷ the accepted reading.

Matt. xvi. 26. ὠφελεῖται Justin with most MSS. both of the Old Latin and of the Vulgate, the Curetonian Syriac (Crowfoot), Clement,

Hilary, and Lucifer, against ὠφεληθήσεται of the best Alexandrine authorities.

Matt. vi. 21. There is a striking coincidence here with Clement of Alexandria, who reads, like Justin, νοῦς for καρδία; it would seem that Clement had probably derived his reading from Justin.

Matt. v. 22. ὅστις ἂν ὀργισθῇ Syr. Crt. (Crowfoot); so Justin (ὅς).

Matt. v. 16. Clement of Alexandria (with Tertullian and several Latin Fathers) has λαμψάτω τὰ ἔργα and τὰ ἀγαθὰ ἔργα, where Justin has λαμψάτω τὰ καλὰ ἔργα, for λαμψάτω τὸ φῶς. Both readings would seem to be a gloss on the original.

Matt. v. 37. καί is inserted, as in Justin, by a, b, g, h, Syr. Crt. and Pst.

Luke x. 16. Justin has the reading ὁ ἐμοῦ ἀκούων ἀκούει τοῦ ἀποστείλαντός με: so D, i, l (of the Old Latin) in place of ὁ ἐμὲ ἀθετῶν κ.τ.λ.; in addition to it, E, a, b, Syr. Crt. and Hcl. &c.

Matt. vii. 22. οὐ τῷ σῷ ὀνόματι ἐφάγομεν καὶ ἐπίομεν Justin; similarly Origen, four times, and Syr. Crt.

Luke xiii. 27. ἀνομίας for ἀδικίας, D and Justin.

Matt. xiii. 43. λάμψωσιν for ἐκλάμψωσιν, with Justin, D, and Origen (twice).

Matt. xxv. 41. Of Justin's readings in this verse ὑπάγετε for πορεύεσθε is found also in א and Hippolytus, ἐξώτερον for αἰώνιον in the cursive manuscript numbered 40 (Credner; I am unable to verify this), ὃ ἡτοίμασεν ὁ πατήρ μου for τὸ ἡτοιμασμένον D. 1, most Codd. of the Old Latin, Iren. Tert. Cypr. Hil. Hipp. and Origen in the Latin translation.

Luke xii. 48. D, like Justin, has here πλέον for περισσότερον and also the compound form ἀπαιτήσουσιν.

Luke xx. 24. Though in the main following (but loosely) the text of Luke, Justin has here τὸ νόμισμα, as Matt., instead of δηνάριον; so D.

Though it will be seen that Justin has thus much in common with D and the Old Latin version, it should be noticed that he has the verse, Luke xxii. 19, and especially the clause τοῦτο ποιεῖτε εἰς τὴν ἐμὴν ἀνάμνησιν which is wanting in these authorities. On the other hand, he appears to have with them and other authorities, including Syr. Crt., the Agony in the Garden as given in Luke xxii. 43, 44, which verses are omitted in MSS. of the best Alexandrine type. Luke xxiii. 34, Justin also has, with the divided support of the majority of Greek MSS. Vulgate, c, e, f, ff of the Old Latin, Syr. Crt. and Pst. &c. against B, D (prima manu), a, b, Memph. (MSS.) Theb.

These readings represent in the main a text which was undoubtedly current and widely diffused in the second century. 'Though no surviving manuscript of the Old Latin version dates before the fourth century and most of them belong to a still later age, yet the general correspondence of their text with that of the first Latin Fathers is a sufficient voucher for its high antiquity. The connexion subsisting between this Latin version, the Curetonian Syriac and Codex Bezae, proves that the text of these documents is considerably older than the vellum on which they are written.' Such is Dr. Scrivener's verdict upon the class of authorities with which Justin shows the strongest affinity, and he goes on to add; 'Now it may be said without extravagance that no set of Scriptural records affords a text less probable in itself, less sustained by any rational principles of external evidence, than that of Cod. D, of the Latin codices, and (so far as it accords with them) of Cureton's Syriac. Interpolations as insipid in themselves as un-supported by other evidence abound in them all .... It is no less true to fact than paradoxical in sound, that the worst corruptions to which the New Testament has ever been subjected originated within a hundred years after it was composed[1].' This is a point on which text critics of all schools are substantially agreed. However much they may differ in other respects, no one of them has ever thought of taking

---

[1] Scrivener, *Introduction to the Criticism of the N. T.* p. 452 (2nd edition, 1874).

the text of the Old Syriac and Old Latin translations as the basis of an edition. There can be no question that this text belongs to an advanced, though early, stage of corruption.

At the same stage of corruption, then, Justin's quotations from the Gospels are found, and this very fact is a proof of the antiquity of originals so corrupted. The coincidences are too many and too great all to be the result of accident or to be accounted for by the parallel influence of the lost Gospels. The presence, for instance, of the reading ὁ ἡτοίμασεν ὁ πατήρ for τὸ ἡτοιμασμένον in Irenaeus and Tertullian (who has both 'quem praeparavit deus' and 'praeparatum') is a proof that it was found in the canonical text at a date little later than Justin's. And facts such as this, taken together with the arguments which make it little less than certain that Justin had either mediately or immediately access to our Gospels, render it highly probable that he had a form of the canonical text before him.

And yet large as is the approximation to Justin's text that may be made without stirring beyond the bounds of attested readings within the Canon, I still retain the opinion previously expressed that he did also make use of some extra-canonical book or books, though what the precise document was the data are far too insufficient to enable us to determine. So far as the history of our present Gospels is concerned, I have only to insist upon the alternative that Justin either used those Gospels themselves or else a later work, of the nature of a harmony based upon them[1]. The theory (if it

---

[1] [On reviewing this chapter I am inclined to lean more than I did to the hypothesis that Justin used a Harmony. The phenomena of variation

is really held) that he was ignorant of our Gospels in any shape, seems to me, in view of the facts, wholly untenable.

seem to be too persistent and too evenly distributed to allow of the supposition of alternate quoting from different Gospels. But the data will need a closer weighing before this can be determined.]

CHAPTER V.

HEGESIPPUS—PAPIAS.

DR. LIGHTFOOT has rendered a great service to criticism by his masterly exposure of the fallacies in the argument which has been drawn from the silence of Eusebius in respect to the use of the Canonical Gospels by the early writers[1]. The author of 'Supernatural Religion' is not to be blamed for using this argument. In doing so he has only followed in the wake of the Germans who have handed it on from one to the other without putting it to a test so thorough and conclusive as that which has now been applied[2]. For the future, I imagine, the question has been set at rest and will not need to be reopened[3].

---

[1] *Contemporary Review*, 1875, p. 169 sqq.

[2] Tischendorf, however, devotes several pages to an argument which follows in the same line as Dr. Lightfoot's, and is, I believe, in the main sound (*Wann wurden unsere Evangelien verfasst?* p. 113 sqq., 4th edition, 1866).

[3] I gather from the sixth edition of *S. R.* that the argument from silence is practically waived. If the silence of Eusebius is not pressed as proving that the authors about whom he is silent were ignorant of or did not acknowledge particular Gospels, we on our side may be content not to press it as proving that the Gospels in question *were* acknowledged. The

Dr. Lightfoot has shown, with admirable fulness and precision, that the object of Eusebius was only to note quotations in the case of books the admission of which into the Canon had been or was disputed. In the case of works, such as the four Gospels, that were universally acknowledged, he only records what seem to him interesting anecdotes or traditions respecting their authors or the circumstances under which they were composed. This distinction Dr. Lightfoot has established, not only by a careful examination of the language of Eusebius, but also by comparing his statements with the actual facts in regard to writings that are still extant, and where we are able to verify his procedure. After thus testing the references in Eusebius to Clement of Rome, the Ignatian Epistles, Polycarp, Justin, Theophilus of Antioch, and Irenaeus, Dr. Lightfoot arrives, by a strict and ample induction, at the conclusion that the silence of Eusebius in respect to quotations from any canonical book is so far an argument *in its favour* that it shows the book in question to have been generally acknowledged by the early Church. Instead of being a proof that the writer did not know the work in reference to which Eusebius is silent, the

matter may well be allowed to rest thus: that, so far as the silence of Eusebius is concerned, Hegesippus, Papias, and Dionysius of Corinth are not alleged either for the Gospels or against them. I agree with the author of 'Supernatural Religion' that the point is not one of paramount importance, though it has been made more of by other writers, e. g. Strauss and Renan. [The author has missed Dr. Lightfoot's point on p. xxiii. What Eusebius bears testimony to is, *not* his own belief in the canonicity of the fourth Gospel, but its *undisputed* canonicity, i. e. a historical fact which includes within its range Hegesippus, Papias, &c. If I say that *Hamlet* is an undisputed play of Shakspeare's, I mean, not that I believe it to be Shakspeare's myself, but that all the critics from Shakspeare's time downwards have believed it to be his.]

presumption is rather that he did, like the rest of the Church, receive it. Eusebius only records what seems to him specially memorable, except where the place of the work in or out of the Canon has itself to be vindicated.

But if this holds good, then most of what is said against the use of the Gospels by Hegesippus falls to the ground. Eusebius expressly says[1] that Hegesippus made occasional use of the Gospel according to the Hebrews (ἔκ τε τοῦ καθ' Ἑβραίους εὐαγγελίου ... τινὰ τίθησιν). But apart from the conclusion referred to above, the very language of Eusebius (τίθησίν τινα ἐκ) is enough to suggest that the use of the Gospel according to the Hebrews was subordinate and subsidiary. Eusebius can hardly have spoken in this way of '*the* Gospel of which Hegesippus made use' in all the five books of his 'Memoirs.' The expression tallies exactly with what we should expect of a work used *in addition to* but not *to the exclusion* of our Gospels. The fact that Eusebius says nothing about these shows that his readers would take it for granted that Hegesippus, as an orthodox Christian, received them.

With this conclusion the fragments of the work of Hegesippus that have come down to us agree. The quotations made in them are explained most simply and naturally, on the assumption that our Gospels have been used. The first to which we come is merely an allusion to the narrative of Matt. ii; 'For Domitian feared the coming of the Christ as much as Herod.' Those therefore who take the statement of Eusebius to mean that Hegesippus used only the Gospel according to the Hebrews are compelled to seek for the account of the

[1] *H. E.* iv. 22.

Massacre of the Innocents in that Gospel. It appears however from Epiphanius that precisely this very portion of the first Gospel was wanting in the Gospel according to the Hebrews as used both by the Ebionites and by the Nazarenes. 'But if it be doubtful whether some forms of that Gospel contained the two opening chapters of Matthew, it is certain that Jerome found them in the version which he translated[1].' I am afraid that here, as in so many other cases, the words 'doubtful' and 'certain' are used with very little regard to their meanings. In support of the inference from Jerome, the author refers to De Wette, Schwegler, and an article in a periodical publication by Ewald. De Wette expressly says that the inference does *not* follow ('Aus Comm. ad Matt. ii. 6 ... lässt sich *nicht* schliessen dass er hierbei das Evang. der Hebr. verglichen habe.... Nicht viel besser beweisen die St. ad Jes. xi. 1; ad Abac. iii. 3[2]'). He thinks that the presence of these chapters in Jerome's copy cannot be satisfactorily proved, but is probable just from this allusion in Hegesippus— in regard to which De Wette simply follows the traditional, but, as we have seen, erroneous assumption that Hegesippus used only the Gospel according to the Hebrews. Schwegler[3] gives no reasons, but refers to the passages quoted from Jerome in Credner. Credner, after examining these passages, comes to the conclusion that 'the Gospel of the Nazarenes did *not* contain the chapters[4].' Ewald's periodical I cannot refer to, but Hilgenfeld, after an elaborate review of the question, decides that the chapters were omitted[5]. This is the

---

[1] *S. R.* i. p. 436.
[2] *Einleitung*, p. 103.
[3] *Das Nachapost. Zeit.* i. p. 238.
[4] *Beiträge*, i. p. 401.
[5] *Nov. Test. extra Can. Recept.* Fasc. iv. pp. 19, 20.

only authority I can find for the 'certainty that Jerome found them' in his version.

On the whole, then, it seems decidedly more probable (certainties we cannot deal in) that the incident referred to by Hegesippus was missing from the Gospel according to the Hebrews. That Gospel therefore was not quoted by him, but, on the contrary, there is a presumption that he is quoting from the Canonical Gospel. The narrative of the parallel Gospel of St. Luke seems, if not to exclude the Massacre of the Innocents, yet to imply an ignorance of it.

The next passage that appears to be quotation occurs in the account of the death of James the Just; 'Why do ye ask me concerning Jesus the Son of Man? He too sits in heaven on the right hand of the great Power and will come on the clouds of heaven' (Τί με ἐπερωτᾶτε περὶ Ἰησοῦ τοῦ υἱοῦ τοῦ ἀνθρώπου; καὶ αὐτὸς κάθηται ἐν τῷ οὐρανῷ ἐκ δεξιῶν τῆς μεγάλης δυνάμεως, καὶ μέλλει ἔρχεσθαι ἐπὶ τῶν νεφελῶν τοῦ οὐρανοῦ). It seems natural to suppose that this is an allusion to Matt. xxvi. 64, ἀπ' ἄρτι ὄψεσθε τὸν υἱὸν τοῦ ἀνθρώπου καθήμενον ἐκ δεξιῶν τῆς δυνάμεως, καὶ ἐρχόμενον ἐπὶ τῶν νεφελῶν τοῦ οὐρανοῦ. The passage is one that belongs to the triple synopsis, and the form in which it appears in Hegesippus shows a preponderating resemblance to the version of St. Matthew. Mark inserts καθήμενον between ἐκ δεξιῶν and τῆς δυνάμεως, while Luke thinks it necessary to add τοῦ θεοῦ. The third Evangelist omits the phrase ἐπὶ τῶν νεφελῶν τοῦ οὐρανοῦ altogether, and the second substitutes μετά for ἐπί. In fact the phrase ἐπὶ τῶν νεφελῶν occurs in the New Testament only in St. Matthew; the Apocalypse, like St. Mark, has μετά and ἐπί only with the singular.

In like manner, when we find Hegesippus using the

phrase πρόσωπον οὐ λαμβάνεις, this seems to be a reminiscence of Luke xx. 21, where the synoptic parallels have βλέπεις.

A more decided reference to the third Gospel occurs in the dying prayer of St. James; παρακαλῶ, κύριε θεὲ πάτερ, ἄφες αὐτοῖς· οὐ γὰρ οἴδασιτί ποιοῦσιν, which corresponds to Luke xxiii. 34, πάτερ, ἄφες αὐτοῖς· οὐ γὰρ οἴδασιν τί ποιοῦσιν. There is the more reason to believe that Hegesippus' quotation is derived from this source that it reproduces the peculiar use of ἀφιέναι in the sense of 'forgive' without an expressed object. Though the word is of very frequent occurrence, I find no other instance of this in the New Testament[1], and the Clementine Homilies, in making the same quotation, insert τὰς ἁμαρτίας αὐτῶν. The saying is well known to be peculiar to St. Luke. There is perhaps a balance of evidence against its genuineness, but this is of little importance, as it undoubtedly formed part of the Gospel as early as Irenaeus, who wrote much about the same time as Hegesippus.

The remaining passage occurs in a fragment preserved from Stephanus Gobarus, a writer of the sixth century, by Photius, writing in the ninth. Referring to the saying 'Eye hath not seen,' &c., Gobarus says 'that Hegesippus, an ancient and apostolical man, asserts — he knows not why — that these words are vainly spoken, and that those who use them give the lie to the sacred writings and to our Lord Himself who said, "Blessed are your eyes that see and your ears that

---

[1] We have, however, had occasion to note a somewhat parallel, though not quite parallel, instance in the quotation of Clement of Rome and Polycarp, ἀφίετε, ἵνα ἀφεθῇ ὑμῖν [καὶ ἀφεθήσεται ὑμῖν].

hear,"' &c. 'Those who use these words' are, we can hardly doubt, as Dr. Lightfoot after Routh has shown[1], the Gnostics, though Hegesippus would seem to have forgotten 1 Cor. ii. 9. The anti-Pauline position assigned to Hegesippus on the strength of this is, we must say, untenable. But for the present we are concerned rather with the second quotation, which agrees closely with Matt. xiii. 26 (ὑμῶν δὲ μακάριοι οἱ ὀφθαλμοὶ ὅτι βλέπουσιν, καὶ τὰ ὦτα ὑμῶν ὅτι ἀκούουσιν). The form of the quotation has a slightly nearer resemblance to Luke x. 23 (μακάριοι οἱ ὀφθαλμοὶ οἱ βλέποντες ἃ βλέπετε κ.τ.λ.), but the marked difference in the remainder of the Lucan passage increases the presumption that Hegesippus is quoting from the first Gospel[2].

The use of the phrase τῶν θείων γραφῶν is important and remarkable. There is not, so far as I am aware, any instance of so definite an expression being applied to an apocryphal Gospel. It would tend to prepare us for the strong assertion of the Canon of the Gospels in Irenaeus; it would in fact mark the gradually culminating process which went on in the interval which separated Irenaeus from Justin. To this interval the evidence of Hegesippus must be taken to apply, because though writing like Irenaeus under Eleutherus (from 177 A.D.) he was his elder contemporary, and had been received with high respect in Rome as early as the episcopate of Anicetus (157–168 A.D.).

The relations in which Hegesippus describes himself

---

[1] *Contemporary Review*, Dec. 1874, p. 8; cf. Routh, *Reliquiae Sacrae*, i. p. 281 *ad fin*.

[2] Tregelles, writing on the 'Ancient Syriac Versions' in Smith's Dictionary, iii. p. 1635 a, says that 'these words might be a Greek rendering of Matt. xiii. 16 as they stand' in the Curetonian text.

as standing to the Churches and bishops of Corinth and Rome seem to be decisive as to his substantial orthodoxy. This would give reason to think that he made use of our present Gospels, and the few quotations that have come down to us confirm that view not inconsiderably, though by themselves they might not be quite sufficient to prove it.

There is one passage that may be thought to point to an apocryphal Gospel, 'From these arose false Christs, false prophets, false apostles;' which recalls a sentence in the Clementines, 'For there shall be, as the Lord said, false apostles, false prophets, heresies, ambitions.' It is not, however, nearer to this than to the canonical parallel, Matt. xxiv. 24 ('There shall arise false Christs and false prophets').

2.

In turning from Hegesippus to Papias we come at last to what seems to be a definite and satisfactory statement as to the origin of two at least of the Synoptic Gospels, and to what is really the most enigmatic and tantalizing of all the patristic utterances.

Like Hegesippus, Papias may be described as 'an ancient and apostolic man,' and appears to have better deserved the title. He is said to have suffered martyrdom under M. Aurelius about the same time as Polycarp, 165–167 A.D.[1] He wrote a commentary on the Discourses or more properly Oracles of the Lord, from which Eusebius extracted what seemed to him 'memorable' statements respecting the origin of the first and second

[1] Or rather perhaps 155, 156; see p. 82 above.

Gospels. 'Matthew,' Papias said[1], 'wrote the oracles (τὰ λόγια) in the Hebrew tongue, and every one interpreted them as he was able.' 'Mark, as the interpreter of Peter, wrote down accurately, though not in order, all that he remembered that was said or done by Christ. For he neither heard the Lord nor attended upon Him, but later, as I said, upon Peter, who taught according to the occasion and not as composing a connected narrative of the Lord's discourses; so that Mark made no mistake in writing down some things as he remembered them. For he took care of one thing, not to omit any of the particulars that he heard or to falsify any part of them.'

Let us take the second of these statements first. According to it the Gospel of St. Mark consisted of notes taken down, or rather recollected, from the teaching of Peter. It was not written 'in order,' but it was an original work in the sense that it was first put in writing by Mark himself, having previously existed only in an oral form.

Does this agree with the facts of the Gospel as it appears to us now? There is a certain ambiguity as to the phrase 'in order.' We cannot be quite sure what Papias meant by it, but the most natural conclusion seems to be that it meant chronological order. If so, the statement of Papias seems to be so far borne out that none of the Synoptic Gospels is really in exact chronological order; but, strange to say, if there is any in which an approach to such an order is made, it is precisely this of St. Mark. This appears from a com-

---

[1] *H. E.* iii. 39.

parison of the three Synoptics. From the point at which the second Gospel begins, or, in other words, from the Baptism to the Crucifixion, it seems to give the outline that the other two Gospels follow[1]. If either of them diverges from it for a time it is only to return. The early part of St. Matthew is broken up by the intrusion of the so-called Sermon on the Mount, but all this time St. Mark is in approximate agreement with St. Luke. For a short space the three Gospels go together. Then comes a second break, where Luke introduces his version of the Sermon on the Mount. Then the three rejoin and proceed together, Matthew being thrown out by the way in which he has collected the parables into a single chapter, and Luke later by the place which he has assigned to the incident at Nazareth. After this Matthew and Mark proceed side by side, Luke dropping out of the ranks. At the confession of Peter he takes his place again, and there is a close agreement in the order of the three narratives. The incident of the miracle-worker is omitted by Matthew, and then comes the insertion of a mass of extraneous matter by Luke. When he resumes the thread

[1] In Mr. M'Clellan's recent *Harmony* I notice only two deviations from the order in St. Mark, ii. 15-22, vi. 17-29. In Mr. Fuller's *Harmony* (the Harmony itself and not the Table of Contents, in which there are several oversights) there seem to be two, Mark vi. 17-20, xiv. 3-9; in Dr. Robinson's English *Harmony* three, ii. 15-22, vi. 17-20, xiv. 22-72 (considerable variation). Of these passages vi. 17-20 (the imprisonment of the Baptist) is the only one the place of which all three writers agree in changing. [Dr. Lightfoot, in *Cont. Rev.*, Aug. 1875, p. 394, appeals to Anger and Tischendorf in proof of the contrary proposition, that the order of Mark cannot be maintained. But Tischendorf's Harmony is based on the assumption that St. Luke's use of καθεξῆς pledges him to a chronological order, and Anger adopts Griesbach's hypothesis that Mark is a compilation from Matthew and Luke. The remarks in the text turn, not upon precarious harmonistic results, but upon a simple comparison of the three Gospels.]

of the common narrative again all three are together. The insertion of a single parable on the part of Matthew, and omissions on the part of Luke, are the only interruptions. There is an approximate agreement of all three, we may say, for the rest of the narrative. We observe throughout that, in by far the preponderating number of instances, where Matthew differs from the order of Mark, Luke and Mark agree, and where Luke differs from the order of Mark, Matthew and Mark agree. Thus, for instance, in the account of the healings in Peter's house and of the paralytic, in the relation of the parables of Mark iv. 1–34 to the storm at sea which follows, of the healing of Jairus' daughter to that of the Gadarene demoniac and to the mission of the Twelve in the place of Herod's reflections (Mark vi. 14–16), in the warning against the Scribes and the widow's mite (Mark xii. 38–44), the second and third Synoptics are allied against the first. On the other hand, in the call of the four chief Apostles, the death of the Baptist, the walking on the sea, the miracles in the land of Gennesareth, the washing of hands, the Canaanitish woman, the feeding of the four thousand and the discourses which follow, the ambition of the sons of Zebedee, the anointing at Bethany, and several insertions of the third Evangelist in regard to the last events, the first two are allied against him. While Mark thus receives such alternating support from one or other of his fellow Evangelists, I am not aware of any clear case in which, as to the order of the narratives, they are united and he is alone, unless we are to reckon as such his insertion of the incident of the fugitive between Matt. xxvi. 56, 57, Luke xxii. 53, 54.

It appears then that, so far as there is an order in

the Synoptic Gospels, the normal type of that order is to be found precisely in St. Mark, whom Papias alleges to have written not in order.

But again there seems to be evidence that the Gospel, in the form in which it has come down to us, is not original but based upon another document previously existing. When we come to examine closely its verbal relations to the other two Synoptics, its normal character is in the main borne out, but still not quite completely. The number of particulars in which Matthew and Mark agree together against Luke, or Mark and Luke agree together against Matthew, is far in excess of that in which Matthew and Luke are agreed against Mark. Mark is in most cases the middle term which unites the other two. But still there remains a not inconsiderable residuum of cases in which Matthew and Luke are in combination and Mark at variance. The figures obtained by a not quite exact and yet somewhat elaborate computation[1] are these; Matthew and Mark agree together against Luke in 1684 particulars, Luke and Mark against Matthew in 944, but Matthew and Luke against Mark in only 334. These 334 instances are distributed pretty evenly over the whole of the narrative. Thus (to take a case at random) in the parallel narratives Matt. xii. 1–8, Mark ii. 23–28, Luke vi. 1–5 (the plucking of the ears on the Sabbath day), there are fifty-one points (words or parts of words) common to all three Evangelists, twenty-three are common only to Mark and Luke, ten to Mark and Matthew, and eight to Matthew and Luke. In the next section, the healing of

---

[1] Perhaps I should explain that this was made by underlining the points of resemblance between the Gospels in different coloured pencil and reckoning up the results at the end of each section.

the withered hand, twenty points are found alike in all three Gospels, twenty-seven in Mark and Luke, twenty-one in Mark and Matthew, and five in Matthew and Luke. Many of these coincidences between the first and third Synoptics are insignificant in the extreme. Thus, in the last section referred to (Mark iii. 1–6= Matt. xii. 9–14=Luke vi. 6–11), one is the insertion of the article τὴν (συναγωγήν), one the insertion of σου (τὴν χεῖρά σου), two the use of δέ for καί, and one that of εἶπεν for λέγει. In the paragraph before, the eight points of coincidence between Matthew and Luke are made up thus, two καὶ ἤσθιον (=καὶ ἐσθίειν), εἶπον (=εἶπαν), ποιεῖν, εἶπεν, μετ' αὐτοῦ (=σὺν αὐτῷ), μόνους (=μόνοις). But though such points as these, if they had been few in number, might have been passed without notice, still, on the whole, they reach a considerable aggregate and all are not equally unimportant. Thus, in the account of the healing of the paralytic, such phrases as ἐπὶ κλίνης, ἀπῆλθεν εἰς τὸν οἶκον αὐτοῦ, can hardly have come into the first and third Gospels and be absent from the second by accident; so again the clause ἀλλὰ βάλλουσιν (βλητέον) οἶνον νέον εἰς ἀσκοὺς καινούς. In the account of the healing of the bloody flux the important word τοῦ κρασπέδου is inserted in Matthew and Luke but not in Mark; in that of the mission of the twelve Apostles, the two Evangelists have, and the single one has not, the phrase καὶ θεραπεύειν νόσον (νόσους), and the still more important clause λέγω ὑμῖν ἀνεκτότερον ἔσται (γῇ) Σοδόμων ... ἐν ἡμέρᾳ ... ἢ τῇ πόλει ἐκείνῃ: in Luke ix. 7 (=Matt. xiv. 1) Herod's title is τετράρχης, in Mark vi. 14 βασιλεύς; in the succeeding paragraph οἱ ὄχλοι ἠκολούθησαν and the important τὸ περισσεῦον (-σαν) are wanting in the intermediate Gospel; in the first prophecy of the Passion it has ἀπό where the other two have ὑπό, and μετὰ τρεῖς ἡμέρας where they have τῇ τρίτῃ ἡμέρᾳ: in the healing of the lunatic boy it omits the noticeable καὶ διεστραμμένη: in the second prophecy of the Passion it omits μέλλει, in the paragraph about offences, ἐλθεῖν τὰ σκάνδαλα ... οὐαὶ ... δι' οὗ ἔρχεται. These points might be easily multiplied as we go on; suffice it to say that in the aggregate they seem to prove that the second Gospel, in spite of its superior originality and adhesion to the normal type, still does not entirely adhere to it or maintain its primary character throughout. The theory that we have in the second Gospel one of the primitive Synoptic documents is not tenable.

No doubt this is an embarrassing result. The question is easy to ask and difficult to answer—If our St. Mark does not represent the original form of the document, what does represent it? The original document, if not quite like our Mark, must have been very nearly like it; but how did any writer come to reproduce a previous work with so little variation? If he had simply copied or reproduced it without change, that would have been intelligible; if he had added freely to it, that also would have been intelligible: but, as it is, he seems to have put in a touch here and made an erasure there on principles that it is difficult for us now to follow. We are indeed here at the very *crux* of Synoptic criticism.

For our present purpose however it is not necessary that the question should be solved. We have already obtained an answer on the two points raised by Papias. The second Gospel *is* written in order; it is *not* an original document. These two characteristics make it improbable that it is in its present shape the document to which Papias alludes.

Does his statement accord any better with the phenomena of the first Gospel? He asserts that it was originally written in Hebrew, and that the large majority of modern critics deny to have been the case with our present Gospel. Many of the quotations in it from the Old Testament are made directly from the Septuagint and not from the Hebrew. There are turns of language which have the stamp of an original Greek idiom and could not have come in through translation. But, without going into this question as to the original language of the first Gospel, a shorter method will be to ask whether it can have been an original document at all? The work to which Papias referred clearly was such, but the very same investigation which shows that our present St. Mark was not original, tells with increased force against St. Matthew. When a document exists dealing with the same subject-matter as two other documents, and those two other documents agree together and differ from it on as many as 944 separate points, there can be little doubt that in the great majority of those points it has deviated from the original, and that it is therefore secondary in character. It is both secondary and secondary on a lower stage than St. Mark: it has preserved the features of the original with a less amount of accuracy. The points of the triple synopsis on which Matthew fails to receive verification are in all 944; those on which Mark fails to receive verification 334; or, in other words, the inaccuracies of Matthew are to those of Mark nearly as three to one. In the case of Luke the proportion is still greater—as much as five to one.

This is but a tithe of the arguments which show that the first Gospel is a secondary composition. An original composition would be homogeneous; it is markedly heterogeneous. The first two chapters clearly belong to a different stock of materials from the rest of the Gospel. A broad division is seen in regard to the Old Testament quotations. Those which are common to the other two Synoptists are almost if not quite uniformly taken from the Septuagint; those, on the other hand, which seem to belong to the reflection of the Evangelist betray more or less distinctly the influence of the Hebrew[1]. Our Gospel is thus seen to be a recension of another original document or documents and not an original document itself.

Again, if our St. Matthew had been an original composition and had appeared from the first in its present full and complete form, it would be highly difficult to account for the omissions and variations in Mark and Luke. We should be driven back, indeed, upon all the impossibilities of the 'Benutzungs-hypothese.' On the one hand, the close resemblance between the three compels us to assume that the authors have either used each other's works or common documents; but the differences practically preclude the supposition that the later writer had before him the whole work of his predecessor. If Luke had had before him the first two chapters of Matthew, he could not have written his own first two chapters as he has done.

Again, the character of the narrative is such as to be inconsistent with the view that it proceeds from an eye-witness of the events. Those graphic touches, which are so conspicuous in the fourth Gospel, and come out from time to time in the second, are entirely wanting in

[1] This subject has been carefully worked out since Credner by Bleek and De Wette. The results will be found in Holtzmann, *Synopt. Ev.* p. 259 sqq.

the first. If parallel narratives, such as the healing of the paralytic, the cleansing of the Temple, or the feeding of the five thousand, are compared, this will be very clearly seen. More; there are features in the first Gospel that are to all appearance unhistorical and due to the peculiar method of the writer. He has a way of reduplicating, so to speak, the personages of one narrative in order to make up for the omission of another[1]. For instance, he is silent as to the healing of the demoniac at Capernaum, but, instead of this, he gives us two Gadarene demoniacs, at the same time modifying the language in which he describes this latter incident after the pattern of the former; in like manner he speaks of the healing of two blind men at Jericho, but only because he had passed over the healing of the blind man at Bethsaida. Of a somewhat similar nature is the adding of the ass's colt to the ass in the account of the Triumphal Entry. There are also fragmentary sayings repeated in the Gospel in a way that would be natural in a later editor piecing together different documents and finding the same saying in each, but unnatural in an eye- and ear-witness drawing upon his own recollections. Some clear cases of this kind would be Matt. v. 29, 30 (= Matt. xviii. 8, 9) the offending member, Matt. v. 32 (= Matt. xix. 9) divorce, Matt. x. 38, 39 (= Matt. xvi. 24, 25) bearing the cross, loss and gain; and there are various others.

These characteristics of the first Gospel forbid us to suppose that it came fresh from the hands of the Apostle

---

[1] Cf. Holtzmann, *Die Synoptischen Evangelien*, p. 255 sq.; Ebrard, *The Gospel History* (Engl. trans.), p. 247; Bleek, *Synoptische Erklärung der drei ersten Evangelien*, i. p. 367. The theory rests upon an acute observation, and has much plausibility.

in the shape in which we now have it ; they also forbid us to identify it with the work alluded to by Papias. Neither of the two first Gospels, as we have them, complies with the conditions of Papias' description to such an extent that we can claim Papias as a witness to them.

But now a further enquiry opens out upon us. The language of Papias does not apply to our present Gospels; will it apply to some earlier and more primary state of those Gospels, to documents *incorporated in* the works that have come down to us but not co-extensive with them? German critics, it is well known, distinguish between 'Matthäus'— the present Gospel that bears the name of St. Matthew—and 'Ur-Matthäus,' or the original work of that Apostle, 'Marcus'—our present St. Mark— and 'Ur-Marcus,' an older and more original document, the real production of the companion of St. Peter. Is it to these that Papias alludes?

Here we have a much more tenable and probable hypothesis. Papias says that Matthew composed 'the oracles' (τὰ λόγια) in the Hebrew tongue. The meaning of the word λόγια has been much debated. Perhaps the strictest translation of it is that which has been given, 'oracles'—short but weighty and solemn or sacred sayings. I should be sorry to say that the word would not bear the sense assigned to it by Dr. Westcott, who paraphrases it felicitously (from his point of view) by our word 'Gospel[1].' It is, however, difficult to help feeling that the *natural* sense of the word has to be

---

[1] *On the Canon*, p. 181, n. 2. [That the word will bear this sense appears still more decidedly from Dr. Lightfoot's recent investigations, in view of which the two sentences that follow should perhaps be cancelled; see *Cont. Rev.*, Aug. 1875, p. 399 sqq.]

somewhat strained in order to make it cover the whole of our present Gospel, and to bring under it the record of facts to as great an extent as discourse. It seems at least the simplest and most obvious interpretation to confine the word strictly or mainly to discourse. 'Matthew composed the discourses (those brief yet authoritative discourses) in Hebrew.'

At this point we are met by a further coincidence. The common matter in the first three Gospels is divided into a triple synopsis and a double synopsis—the first of course running through all three Gospels, the second found only in St. Matthew and St. Luke. But this double synopsis is nearly, though not quite, confined to discourse; where it contains narration proper, as in the account of John the Baptist and the Centurion of Capernaum, discourse is largely mingled with it. But, if the matter common to Matthew and Luke consists of discourse, may it not be these very λόγια that Papias speaks of? Is it not possible that the two Evangelists had access to the original work of St. Matthew and incorporated its material into their own Gospels in different ways? It would thus be easy to understand how the name that belonged to a special and important part of the first Gospel gradually came to be extended over the whole. Bulk would not unnaturally be a great consideration with the early Christians. The larger work would quickly displace the smaller; it would contain all that the smaller contained with additions no less valuable, and would therefore be eagerly sought by the converts, whose object would be rather fulness of information than the best historical attestation. The original work would be simply lost, absorbed, in the larger works that grew out of it.

This is the kind of presumption that we have for identifying the Logia of Papias with the second ground document of the first Gospel—the document, that is, which forms the basis of the double synopsis between the first Gospel and the third. As a hypothesis the identification of these two documents seems to clear up several points. It gives a 'local habitation and a name' to a document, the separate and independent existence of which there is strong reason to suspect, and it explains how the name of St. Matthew came to be placed at the head of the Gospel without involving too great a breach in the continuity of the tradition. It should be remembered that Papias is not giving his own statement but that of the Presbyter John, which dates back to a time contemporary with the composition of the Gospel. On the other hand, by the time of Irenaeus, whose early life ran parallel with the closing years of Papias, the title was undoubtedly given to the Gospel in its present form. It is therefore as difficult to think that the Gospel had no connection with the Apostle whose name it bears, as it is impossible to regard it as entirely his work. The Logia hypothesis seems to suggest precisely such an intermediate relation as will satisfy both sides of the problem.

There are, however, still difficulties in the way. When we attempt to reconstruct the 'collection of discourses' the task is very far from being an easy one. We do indeed find certain groups of discourse in the first Gospel—such as the Sermon on the Mount ch. v–vii, the commission of the Apostles ch. x, a series of parables ch. xiii, of instructions in ch. xviii, invectives against the Pharisees in ch. xxvi, and long eschatological discourses in ch. xxiv and xxv, which seem at once to give a handle to the theory that the Evangelist has incorporated a work consisting specially of discourses into the main body of the Synoptic narrative. But the appearance of roundness and completeness which these discourses present is deceptive. If we are to suppose that the form in which the discourses appear in St. Matthew at all nearly represents their original structure, then how is it that the same discourses are found in the third Gospel in such a state of dispersion? How is it, for instance, that the parallel passages to the Sermon on the Mount are found in St. Luke scattered over chapters vi, xi, xii, xiii, xiv, xvi, with almost every possible inversion and variety of order? Again, if the Matthaean sections represent a substantive work, how are we to account for the strange intrusion of the triple synopsis into the double? What are we to say to the elaborately broken structure of ch. x? On the other hand, if we are to take the Lucan form as nearer to the original, that original must have been a singular agglomeration of fragments which it is difficult to piece together. It is easy to state a theory that shall look plausible so long as it is confined to general terms, but when it comes to be worked out in detail it will seem to be more and more difficult and involved at every step. The Logia hypothesis in fact carries us at once into the very nodus of Synoptic criticism, and, in the present state of the question, must be regarded as still some way from being established.

The problem in regard to St. Mark and the triple synopsis is considerably simpler. Here the difficulty arises from the necessity of assuming a distinction between our present second Gospel and the original document on which that Gospel is based. I have already touched upon this point. The synoptical analysis seems to conduct us to a ground document greatly resembling our present St. Mark, which cannot however be quite identical with it, as the Canonical Gospel is found to contain secondary features. But apart from the fact that these secondary features are so comparatively few that it is difficult to realise the existence of a work in which they, and they only, should be absent, there is this further obstacle to the identification even of the ground document with the Mark of Papias, that even in that original shape the Gospel still presented the normal type of the Synoptic order, though 'order' is precisely the characteristic that Papias says was, in this Gospel, wanting.

Everywhere we meet with difficulties and complexities. The testimony of Papias remains an enigma that can only be solved—if ever it is solved—by close and detailed investigations. I am bound in candour to say that, so far as I can see myself at present, I am inclined to agree with the author of 'Supernatural Religion' against his critics[1], that the works to which Papias alludes cannot be our present Gospels in their present form.

What amount of significance this may have for the enquiry before us is a further question. Papias is repeating what he had heard from the Presbyter John, which would seem to take us up to the very fountain-

[1] [It will be seen that the arguments above hardly touch those of Dr. Lightfoot in the *Contemporary Review* for August and October: neither do Dr. Lightfoot's arguments seem very much to affect them. The method of the one is chiefly external, that of the other almost entirely internal. I can only for the present leave what I had written; but I do not for a moment suppose that the subject is fathomed even from the particular standpoint that I have taken.]

head of evangelical composition. But such a statement does not preclude the possibility of subsequent changes in the documents to which it refers. The difficulties and restrictions of local communication must have made it hard for an individual to trace all the phases of literary activity in a society so widely spread as the Christian, even if it had come within the purpose of the writer or his informant to state the whole, and not merely the essential part, of what he knew.

CHAPTER VI.

THE CLEMENTINE HOMILIES.

IT is unfortunate that there are not sufficient materials for determining the date of the Clementine Homilies. Once given the date and a conclusion of considerable certainty could be drawn from them; but the date is uncertain, and with it the extent to which they can be used as evidence either on one side or on the other.

Some time in the second century there sprang up a crop of heretical writings in the Ebionite sect which were falsely attributed to Clement of Rome. The two principal forms in which these have come down to us are the so-called Homilies and Recognitions. The Recognitions however are only extant in a Latin translation by Rufinus, in which the quotations from the Gospels have evidently been assimilated to the Canonical text which Rufinus himself used. They are not, therefore, in any case available for our purpose. Whether the Recognitions or the Homilies came first in order of time is a question much debated among critics, and the even way in which the best opinions seem to be divided is a proof of the uncertainty of the data.

On the one side are ranged Credner, Ewald, Reuss, Schwegler, Schliemann, Uhlhorn, Dorner, and Lücke, who assign the priority to the Homilies: on the other, Hilgenfeld, Köstlin, Ritschl (doubtfully), and Volkmar, who give the first place to the Recognitions[1]. On the ground of authority perhaps the preference should be given to the first of these, as representing more varied parties and as carrying with them the greater weight of sound judgment, but it is impossible to say that the evidence on either side is decisive.

The majority of critics assign the Clementines, in one form or the other, to the middle of the second century. Credner, Schliemann, Scholten, and Renan give this date to the Homilies; Volkmar and Hilgenfeld to the Recognitions; Ritschl to both recensions alike[2]. We shall assume hypothetically that the Homilies are rightly thus dated. I incline myself to think that this is more probable, but, speaking objectively, the probability could not have a higher value put upon it than, say, two in three.

One reason for assigning the Homilies to the middle of the second century is presented by the phenomena

---

[1] The lists given in *Supernatural Religion* (ii. p. 2) seem to be correct so far as I am able to check them. In the second edition of his work on the Origin of the Old Catholic Church, Ritschl modified his previous opinion so far as to admit that the indications were divided. sometimes on the one side, sometimes on the other (p. 451, n. 1). There is a seasonable warning in Reuss (*Gesch. h. S. N. T.* p. 254) that the Tübingen critics here, as elsewhere, are apt to exaggerate the polemical aspect of the writing.

[2] It should be noticed that Hilgenfeld and Volkmar, though assigning the second place to the Homilies, both take the *terminus ad quem* for this work no later than 180 A.D. It seems that a Syriac version, partly of the Homilies, partly of the Recognitions, exists in a MS. which itself was written in the year 411, and bears at that date marks of transcription from a still earlier copy (cf. Lightfoot, *Galatians*, p. 341, n. 1).

of the quotations from the Gospels which correspond generally to those that are found in writings of this date, and especially, as has been frequently noticed, to those which we meet with in Justin. I proceed to give a tabulated list of the quotations. In order to bring out a point of importance I have indicated by a letter in the left margin the presence in the Clementine quotations of some of the *peculiarities* of our present Gospels. When this letter is unbracketed, it denotes that the passage is *only* found in the Gospel so indicated; when the letter is enclosed in brackets, it is implied that the passage is synoptical, but that the Clementines reproduce expressions peculiar to that particular Gospel. The direct quotations are marked by the letter Q. Many of the references are merely allusive, and in more it is sufficiently evident that the writer has allowed himself considerable freedom [1].

	Exact.	*Slightly variant.*	*Variant.*	*Remarks.*
(M.)			8. 21, Luke 4. 6–8 (=Matt. 4. 8–10), Q.	narrative.
			3. 55, ὁ πονηρός ἐστιν ὁ πειράζων, Q.	
			15. 10, Matt. 5. 3; Luke 6. 20.	
M.		17. 7, Matt. 5. 8.		
(M.)		3. 51 } Matt. 5. Ep. Pet. 2 } 17, 18.		repeated identically.
			11. 32, Matt. 5. 21–48.	highly condensed paraphrase, οἱ ἐν πλάνῃ.
			12. 32 { Matt. 5. 44, 45 (=Luke 6. 27, 28, 35). 3. 19	allusive merely.

[1] This table is made, as in the case of Justin, with the help of the collection of passages in the works of Credner and Hilgenfeld.

Exact.	Slightly variant.	Variant.	Remarks.
M.	3. 56, Matt. 5. 34, 35, Q.		
M.	3. 55 ⎫ Matt. 5. 37, 19. 2 ⎭ Q.		repeated identically; so Justin.
(M.)		3.57, Matt. 5.45, Q.	
		12. 26 ⎫ 18. 2 ⎬ 11. 12 ⎭	oblique and allusive, repeated in part similarly; φέρει τὸν ὑετόν.
M.	3. 55, Matt. 6. 6, Q.		
19. 2, Matt. 6. 13, Q.			
(M.)	3. 55, Matt. 6. 32; 6. 8 (= Luke 12. 30).		combination.
		18. 16, Matt. 7. 2 (12).	oblique and allusive.
	3. 52, Matt. 7. 7 (= Luke 11. 9).		εὑρίσκετε for εὑρήσετε in both.
(L. M.)	3. 56, Matt. 7. 9–11 (= Luke 11. 11–13).		striking division of peculiarities of both Gospels.
		12. 32 ⎫ Matt. 7. 12 7. 4 ⎬ (= Luke 11. 4 ⎭ 6. 31.	repeated diversely, allusive.
(M.)	18. 17, Matt. 7. 13, 14.	(omissions), Q.	
		7. 7, Matt. 7. 13, 14.	allusive paraphrase.
(L.)	8. 7, Luke 6. 46.		
	11. 35, Matt. 7. 15.		Justin, in part similarly, in part diversely.
(M.)	8. 4, Matt. 8. 11, 12 (Luke 13. 29).	(addition), Q.	Justin diversely.
	9. 21, Matt. 8. 9 (Luke 7. 8).		allusive merely.
M.	3. 56, Matt. 9. 13 (12. 7).	(addition), Q.	from LXX.
(L. M.)		13. 30, 31 ⎧ Matt. 10. 13, 15 = Luke 10, 5, 6, 10–12 (9. 5) = Mark 6. 11. ⎫	mixed peculiarities, oblique and allusive.
(L. M.)	17. 5, Matt. 10. 28 (= Luke 12, 4, 5), Q.		mixed peculiarities; Justin diversely.

THE CLEMENTINE HOMILIES.

Exact.	Slightly variant.	Variant.	Remarks.
		12. 31, Matt. 10. 29, 30 (= Luke 12. 6, 7).	allusive merely.
	3. 17 {Matt. 11. 11. / Luke 7. 28.		allusive.
	8. 6, Matt. 11. 25 (= Luke x. 21).	(addition)† .	perhaps from Matt. 21. 16.
(M.)		17. 4 18. 4 } Matt. 11. 27 18. 7 } (= Luke 18. 13 } 10. 22), Q. 18. 20	repeated similarly; cp. Justin, &c.
M. 3. 52, Matt. 11. 28.			
(M.)	†19. 2, Matt. 12. 26, Q.		ἄλλῃ που.
(M. L.)	†19. 7, Matt. 12. 34 (= Luke 6. 45), Q.		
M. 11. 33, Matt. 12. 42.	(addition), Q.		
	11. 33, Matt. 12. 41 (= Luke 11. 32), Q.		
(M. L.)	M. 53, Matt. 13. 16 (= Luke 10. 24), †Q.		
M. 18. 15, Matt. 13. 35†.			
Mk.	19. 20, Mark 4. 34.		
M.	19. 2, Matt. 13. 39, Q.		
M. 3. 52, Matt. 15. 15 (om. μου), Q.			
		11. 19 { Matt. 15. 21–28 (= Mark 7. 24–30).	narrative. Ἰούστα Συροφοινίκισσα.
(M.)	17. 18, Matt. 16. 16 (par.)		
M.		Ep. Clem. 2, Matt. 16. 19.	allusive merely.
M.	Ep. Clem. 6, Matt. 16. 19.		ditto.
(M.)	3. 53, Matt. 17. 5 (par.), Q.		
M.		12. 29, Matt. 18. 7, Q.	addition (τὰ ἀγαθὰ ἐλθεῖν).
M.	17. 7, Matt. 18. 10 (v. l.)		

Exact.	Slightly variant.	Variant.	Remarks.
(L.) 3. 71, Luke 10. 7 (order) (=Matt.10.10).			
L.	†19. 2, Luke 10. 18.		
L.		9. 22, Luke 10. 20.	allusive merely.
L.		17. 5, Luke 18. 6-8, Q. (?)	
		19. 2, μὴ δότε πρόφασιν τῷ πονηρῷ, Q.	Cp. Eph. 4. 27.
		3. 53, Prophet like Moses, Q.	Cp. Acts 3. 22.
(M.)	3. 54, Matt. 19. 8, 4 (=Mark 10. 5, 6), Q.		sense more divergent than words.
		17. 4 ⎧ Matt. 19. 16, 17. ⎫ 18. 1 ⎨ Mark 10. 17, 18. ⎬ 18. 3 ⎨ Luke 18. ⎬ 18. 17 ⎩ 18, 19. ⎭ 3. 57	repeated similarly; cp. Justin.
L.		3. 63, Luke 19.5,9.	not quotation.
M. 8. 4, Matt. 22. 14, Q.			
(M.)		8. 22, Matt. 22. 9. 11.	allusive merely.
		3. 50 ⎧ Matt. 22. 2. 51 ⎨ 29 (=Mark 18. 20 ⎩ 12. 24), Q.	repeated similarly.
		3. 50, διὰ τί οὐ νοεῖτε τὸ εὔλογον τῶν γραφῶν;	
(Mk.) 3. 55, Mark 12. 27 (par.), Q.			
Mk. 3. 57, Mark 12. 29 (ἡμῶν), Q.			
		17. 7, Mark 12. 30 (=Matt. 22. 37).	allusive.
M.	⎧ 3. 18, Matt. 23. 2, 3, Q.		
		3. 18, Matt. 23. 13 (=Luke 11.52). 18. 15.	repeated similarly.
(M.)	11. 29, Matt. 23. 25, 26, Q.		
(Mk.)	⎧ 3. 15, Mark 13. 2 (par.), Q.		
		3. 15, Matt. 24. 3 (par.), Q.	
L.	⎩	Luke 19. 43, Q.	

Exact.	Slightly variant.	Variant.	Remarks.
		16. 21, ἔσονται ψευδαπόστολοι.	
(M.)	3. 60 (3. 64), Matt. 24. 45-51 (= Luke 12. 42-46).		part repeated similarly.
(M.) 3. 65, Matt. 25. 21 (= Luke 19. 17).			
(M. L.)		3. 61, Matt. 25. 26, 27 (= Luke 19. 22, 23).	? mixed peculiarities.
		2. 51) γίνεσθε 3. 50 (τραπεζίται 18. 20) δόκιμοι.	
M.		19. 2, Matt. 25. 41, Q.	ἄλλῃ που. Justin similarly.
L.	11. 20. Luke 23. 34 (v. l.), Q.		
		17. 7, Matt. 28. 19.	allusive.

By far the greater part of the quotations in the Clementine Homilies are taken from the discourses, but some few have reference to the narrative. There can hardly be said to be any material difference from our Gospels, though several apocryphal sayings and some apocryphal details are added. Thus the Clementine writer calls John a 'Hemerobaptist,' i.e. member of a sect which practised daily baptism[1]. He talks about a rumour which became current in the reign of Tiberius about the 'vernal equinox,' that at the same season a king should arise in Judaea who should work miracles, making the blind to see, the lame to walk, healing every disease, including leprosy, and raising the dead; in the incident of the Canaanite woman (whom, with Mark, he calls a Syrophoenician) he adds her name, 'Justa,' and that of her daughter 'Bernice;' he also limits

---

[1] Or rather perhaps 'morning baptism.' (Cf. Lightfoot, *Colossians*, p. 162 sqq., where the meaning of the name and the character and relations of the sect are fully discussed).

the ministry of our Lord to one year[1]. Otherwise, with the exception of the sayings marked as without parallel, all of the Clementine quotations have a more or less close resemblance to our Gospels.

We are struck at once by the small amount of exact coincidence, which is considerably less than that which is found in the quotations from the Old Testament. The proportion seems lower than it is, because many of the passages that have been entered in the above list do not profess to be quotations. Another phenomenon equally remarkable is the extent to which the writer of the Homilies has reproduced the peculiarities of particular extant Gospels. So far from being a colourless text, as it is in some few places which present a parallel to our Synoptic Gospels, the Clementine version both frequently includes passages that are found only in some one of the canonical Gospels, and also, we may say usually, repeats the characteristic phrases by which one Gospel is distinguished from another. Thus we find that as many as eighteen passages reappear in the Homilies that are found only in St. Matthew; one of the extremely few that are found only in St. Mark; and six of those that are peculiar to St. Luke. Taking the first Gospel, we find that the Clementine Homilies contain (in an allusive form) the promises to the pure in heart; as a quotation, with close resemblance, the peculiar precepts in regard to oaths; the special admonition to moderation of language which, as we have seen, seems proved to be Matthaean by the clause τὸ γὰρ περισσὸν τούτων κ. τ. λ.; with close resemblance, again, the directions for secret prayer; identically, the somewhat re-

---

[1] *Hom.* i. 6; ii. 19, 23; iii. 73; iv. 1; xiii. 7; xvii. 19.

markable phrase, δεῦτε πρός με πάντες οἱ κοπιῶντες ; all but identically another phrase, also noteworthy, πᾶσα φυτεία ἣν οὐκ ἐφύτευσεν ὁ πατήρ [μου] ὁ οὐράνιος ἐκριζωθήσεται ; with a resemblance that is closer in the text of B (ἐν τῷ οὐρανῷ for ἐν οὐρανοῖς), the saying respecting the angels who behold the face of the Father; identically again, the text πολλοὶ κλητοί, ὀλίγοι δὲ ἐκλεκτοί : in the shape of an allusion only, the wedding garment ; with near agreement, 'the Scribes and Pharisees sit in Moses' seat.' All these are passages found only in the first Gospel, and in regard to which there is just so much presumption that they had no large circulation among non-extant Gospels, as they did not find their way into the two other Gospels that have come down to us.

There is, however, a passage that I have not mentioned here which contains (if the canonical reading is correct) a strong indication of the use of our actual St. Matthew. The whole history of this passage is highly curious. In the chapter which contains so many parables the Evangelist adds, by way of comment, that this form of address was adopted in order 'that it might be fulfilled which was spoken by the prophet, saying, I will open my mouth in parables; I will utter things which have been kept secret from the foundation of the world.' This is according to the received text, which attributes the quotation to 'the prophet' (διὰ τοῦ προφήτου). It is really taken from Ps. lxxvii. 2, which is ascribed in the heading to Asaph, who, according to the usage of writers at this date, might be called a prophet, as he is in the Septuagint version of 2 Chron. xxix. 30. The phrase ὁ προφήτης λέγει in quotations from the Psalms is not uncommon. The received reading is that of by far the majority of the MSS. and versions: the first hand of the Sinaitic, however, and the valuable cursives 1 and 33 with the Aethiopic (a version on which not much reliance can be placed) and m. of the Old Latin (Mai's 'Speculum,' presenting a mixed African text [1]), insert Ἡσαίου before τοῦ προφήτου. It also appears that Porphyry alleged this as an instance of false ascription. Eusebius admits that it was found in some, though not in the most accurate MSS., and Jerome says that in his day it was still the reading of 'many.'

All this is very fully and fairly stated in 'Supernatural Religion [2],' where it is maintained that Ἡσαίου is the original reading. The critical question is one of great difficulty; because, though the evidence of the Fathers is naturally suspected on account of their desire to explain away the mistake, and though we can easily imagine that the correction would be made very early and would rapidly gain ground, still the very great preponderance of critical authority is hard to get over, and as a rule Eusebius seems to be trustworthy in his estimate of MSS. Tischendorf (in his texts of 1864 and 1869) is, I believe, the only critic of late who has admitted Ἡσαίου into the text.

The false ascription may be easily paralleled; as in Mark i. 2, Matt. xxvii. 9, Justin, Dial. c. Tryph. 28 (where a passage of Jeremiah is quoted as Isaiah), &c.

---

[1] So Tregelles expressly (*Introduction*, p. 240), after Wiseman; Scrivener (*Introd.*, p. 308) adds (?); M·Clellan classes with 'Italic Family' (p. lxxiii). [On returning to this passage I incline rather more definitely to regard the reading Ἡσαίου, from the group in which it is found, as an early Alexandrine corruption. Still the Clementine writer may have had it before him.]

[2] ii. p. 10 sqq.

The relation of the Clementine and of the canonical quotations to each other and to the Septuagint will be represented thus:—

Clem. Hom. xviii. 15.

Καὶ τὸν Ἡσαίαν εἰπεῖν· Ἀνοίξω τὸ στόμα μου ἐν παραβολαῖς καὶ ἐξερεύξομαι κεκρυμμένα ἀπὸ καταβολῆς κόσμου.

Matt. xiii. 35.

Ὅπως πληρωθῇ τὸ ῥηθὲν διὰ ['Ησαίου?] τοῦ προφήτου λέγοντος· Ἀνοίξω ἐν παραβολαῖς τὸ στόμα μου, ἐρεύξομαι κεκρυμμένα ἀπὸ καταβολῆς κόσμου [om. κόσμου a few of the best MSS.]

LXX. *Ps.* lxxvii. 2.

Ἀνοίξω ἐν παραβολαῖς τὸ στόμα μου, φθέγξομαι προβλήματα ἀπ' ἀρχῆς.

The author of 'Supernatural Religion' contends for the reading Ἡσαίου, and yet does not see in the Clementine passage a quotation from St. Matthew. He argues, with a strange domination by modern ideas, that the quotation cannot be from St. Matthew because of the difference of context, and declares it to be 'very probable that the passage with its erroneous reference was derived by both from another and common source.' Surely it is not necessary to go back to the second century to find parallels for the use of 'proof texts' without reference to the context; but, as we have seen, context counts for little or nothing in these early quotations,—verbal resemblance is much more important. The supposition of a common earlier source for both the Canonical and the Clementine text seems to me quite out of the question. There can be little doubt that the reference to the Psalm is due to the first Evangelist himself. Precisely up to this point he goes hand in hand with St. Mark, and the quotation is introduced in his own peculiar style and with his own peculiar formula, ὅπως πληρωθῇ τὸ ῥηθέν.

I must, however, again repeat that the surest criterion of the use of a Gospel is to be sought in the presence of phrases or turns of expression which are shown to be characteristic and distinctive of that Gospel by a comparison with the synopsis of the other Gospels. This criterion can be abundantly applied in the case of the Clementine Homilies and St. Matthew. I will notice a little more at length some of the instances that have been marked in the above table. Let us first take the passage which has a parallel in Matt. v. 18 and in Luke xvi. 17. The three versions will stand thus :—

Matt. v. 18.	*Clem. Hom.* iii. 51. *Ep. Pet.* c. 2.	*Luke* xvi. 17.
Ἀμὴν γὰρ λέγω ὑμῖν· ἕως ἂν παρέλθῃ ὁ οὐρανὸς καὶ ἡ γῆ ἰῶτα ἓν ἢ μία κεραία οὐ μὴ παρέλθῃ ἀπὸ τοῦ νόμου, ἕως ἂν πάντα γένηται.	Ὁ οὐρανὸς καὶ ἡ γῆ παρελεύσονται, ἰῶτα ἓν ἢ μία κεραία οὐ μὴ παρέλθῃ ἀπὸ τοῦ νόμου [Ep. Pet. adds τοῦτο δὲ εἴρηκεν, ἵνα τὰ πάντα γένηται].	Εὐκοπώτερον δέ ἐστι, τὸν οὐρανὸν καὶ τὴν γῆν παρελθεῖν, ἢ τοῦ νόμου μίαν κεραίαν πεσεῖν.

It will be seen that in the Clementines the passage is quoted twice over, and each time with the variation παρελεύσονται for ἕως ἂν παρέλθῃ. The author of 'Supernatural Religion' argues from this that he is quoting from another Gospel[1]. No doubt the fact does tell, so far as it goes, in that direction, but it is easy to attach too much weight to it. The phenomenon of repeated variation may be even said to be a common one in some writers. Dr. Westcott[2] has adduced examples from Chrysostom, and they would be as easy to find in Epiphanius or Clement of Alexandria, where

---

[1] ii. p. 21.   [2] Preface to the fourth edition of *Canon*, p. xxxii.

we can have no doubt that the canonical Gospels are being quoted. A slight and natural turn of expression such as this easily fixes itself in the memory. The author also insists that the passage in the Gospel quoted in the Clementines ended with the word νόμου; but I think it may be left to any impartial person to say whether the addition in the Epistle of Peter does not naturally point to a termination such as is found in the first canonical Gospel. Our critic seems unable to free himself from the standpoint (which he represents ably enough) of the modern Englishman, or else is little familiar with the fantastic trains and connections of reasoning which are characteristic of the Clementines.

Turning from these objections and comparing the Clementine quotation first with the text of St. Matthew and then with that of St. Luke, we cannot but be struck with its very close resemblance to the former and with the wide divergence of the latter. The passage is one where almost every word and syllable might easily and naturally be altered — as the third Gospel shows that they have been altered — and yet in the Clementines almost every peculiarity of the Matthaean version has been retained.

Another quotation which shows the delicacy of these verbal relations is that which corresponds to Matt. vi. 32 (= Luke xii. 30) :—

Matt. vi. 32.	*Clem. Hom.* iii. 55.	*Luke* xii. 30.
Οἶδε γὰρ ὁ πατὴρ ὑμῶν ὁ οὐράνιος, ὅτι χρῄζετε τούτων ἀπάντων.	[ἔφη] Οἶδεν γὰρ ὁ πατὴρ ὑμῶν ὁ οὐράνιος ὅτι χρῄζετε τούτων ἁπάντων, πρὶν αὐτὸν ἀξιώσητε (cp. Matt. vi. 8).	Ὑμῶν δὲ ὁ πατὴρ οἶδεν ὅτι χρῄζετε τούτων.

The natural inference from the exactness of this coincidence with the language of Matthew as compared with Luke, is not neutralised by the paraphrastic addition from Matt. vi. 8, because such additions and combinations, as will have been seen from our table of quotations from the Old Testament, are of frequent occurrence.

The quotation of Matt. v. 45 (= Luke vi. 35) is a good example of the way in which the pseudo-Clement deals with quotations. The passage is quoted as often as four times, with wide difference and indeed complete confusion of text. It is impossible to determine what text he really had before him; but through all this confusion there is traceable a leaning to the Matthaean type rather than the Lucan, ([ὁ] πατ[ὴρ ὁ] ἐν [τοῖς] οὐρανοῖς ... τὸν ἥλιον αὐτοῦ ἀνατέλλει ἐπὶ ἀγαθοὺς καὶ πονηρούς). It does, however, appear that he had some such phrase as ὑετὸν φέρει or παρέχει for βρέχει, and in one of his quotations he has the γίνεσθε ἀγαθοί (for χρηστοί) καὶ οἰκτίρμονες of Justin. Justin, on the other hand, certainly had βρέχει.

The, in any case, paraphrastic quotation or quotations which find a parallel in Matt. vii. 13, 14 and Luke xiii. 24 are important as seeming to indicate that, if not taken from our Gospel, they are taken from another in a later stage of formation. The characteristic Matthaean expressions στενή and τεθλιμμένη are retained, but the distinction between πύλη and ὁδός has been lost, and both the epithets are applied indiscriminately to ὁδός.

In the narrative of the confession of Peter, which belongs to the triple synopsis, and is assigned by Ewald to the 'Collection of Discourses[1],' by Weiss[2] and

---

[1] *Evangelien*, p 31.   [2] *Das Marcus-evangelium*, p. 282.

Holtzmann[1] to the original Gospel of St. Mark, the Clementine writer follows Matthew alone in the phrase Σὺ εἶ ὁ υἱὸς τοῦ ζῶντος Θεοῦ. The synoptic parallels are—

Matt. xvi. 16.	*Mark* viii. 29.	*Luke* ix. 20.
Σὺ εἶ ὁ Χριστός, ὁ υἱὸς τοῦ Θεοῦ τοῦ ζῶντος.	Σὺ εἶ ὁ Χριστός.	τὸν Χριστὸν τοῦ Θεοῦ.

Holtzmann and Weiss seem to agree (the one explicitly, the other implicitly) in taking the words ὁ υἱὸς τοῦ Θεοῦ τοῦ ζῶντος as an addition by the first Evangelist and as not a part of the text of the original document. In that case there would be the strongest reason to think that the pseudo-Clement had made use of the canonical Gospel. Ewald, however, we may infer, from his assigning the passage to the 'Collection of Discourses,' regards it as presented by St. Matthew most nearly in its original form, of which the other two synoptic versions would be abbreviations. If this were so, it would then be *possible* that the Clementine quotation was made directly from the original document or from a secondary document parallel to our first Gospel. The question that is opened out as to the composition of the Synoptics is one of great difficulty and complexity. In any case there is a balance of probability, more or less decided, in favour of the reference to our present Gospel.

Another very similar instance occurs in the next section of the synoptic narrative, the Transfiguration. Here again the Clementine Homilies insert a phrase

---
[1] *Synopt. Ev* p. 193.

which is only found in St. Matthew, [Οὗτός ἐστίν μου ὁ υἱὸς ὁ ἀγαπητός], εἰς ὃν (ἐν ᾧ Matt.) ηὐδόκησα. Ewald and Holtzmann say nothing about the origin of this phrase; Weiss[1] thinks it is probably due to the first Evangelist. In that case there would be an all but conclusive proof—in any case there will be a presumption—that our first Gospel has been followed.

But one of the most interesting, as well as the clearest, indications of the use of the first Synoptic is derived from the discourse directed against the Pharisees. It will be well to give the parallel passages in full :—

Matt. xxiii. 25, 26.	*Clem. Hom.* xi. 29.	*Luke* xi. 39.
Οὐαὶ ὑμῖν γραμματεῖς καὶ Φαρισαῖοι, ὑποκριταί, ὅτι καθαρίζετε τὸ ἔξωθεν τοῦ ποτηρίου καὶ τῆς παροψίδος, ἔσωθεν δὲ γέμουσιν ἐξ ἁρπαγῆς καὶ ἀδικίας. Φαρισαῖε τυφλέ, καθάρισον πρῶτον τὸ ἐντὸς τοῦ ποτηρίου καὶ τῆς παροψίδος, ἵνα γένηται καὶ τὸ ἐκτὸς αὐτῶν καθαρόν.	Οὐαὶ ὑμῖν γραμματεῖς καὶ Φαρισαῖοι, ὑποκριταί, ὅτι καθαρίζετε τοῦ ποτηρίου καὶ τῆς παροψίδος τὸ ἔξωθεν, ἔσωθεν δὲ γέμει ῥύπους. Φαρισαῖε τυφλέ, καθάρισον πρῶτον τοῦ ποτηρίου καὶ τῆς παροψίδος τὸ ἔσωθεν, ἵνα γένηται καὶ τὰ ἔξω αὐτῶν καθαρά.	Νῦν ὑμεῖς οἱ Φαρισαῖοι τὸ ἔξωθεν τοῦ ποτηρίου καὶ τοῦ πίνακος καθαρίζετε, τὸ δὲ ἔσωθεν ὑμῶν γέμει ἁρπαγῆς καὶ πονηρίας. Ἄφρονες οὐχ ὁ ποιήσας τὸ ἔξωθεν καὶ τὸ ἔσωθεν ἐποίησε;

Here there is a very remarkable transition in the first Gospel from the plural to the singular in the sudden turn of the address, Φαρισαῖε τυφλέ. This derives no countenance from the third Gospel, but is exactly reproduced in the Clementine Homilies, which follow closely the Matthaean version throughout.

We may defer for the present the notice of a few passages which with a more or less close resemblance

---

[1] *Das Marcus-evangelium*, p. 295.

to St. Matthew also contain some of the peculiarities of St. Luke.

Taking into account the whole extent to which the special peculiarities of the first Gospel reappear in the Clementines, I think we shall be left in little doubt that that Gospel has been actually used by the writer.

The peculiar features of our present St. Mark are known to be extremely few, yet several of these are also found in the Clementine Homilies. In the quotation Mark x. 5, 6 (= Matt. xix. 8, 4) the order of Mark is followed, though the words are more nearly those of Matthew. In the divergent quotation Mark xii. 24 (= Matt. xxii. 29) the Clementines, with Mark, introduce διὰ τοῦτο. The concluding clause of the discussion about the Levirate marriage stands (according to the best readings) thus :—

Matt. xxii. 32.	*Mark* xii. 27.	*Luke* xx. 38.
Οὐκ ἔστιν ὁ Θεὸς νεκρῶν, ἀλλὰ ζώντων.	Οὐκ ἔστιν Θεὸς νεκρῶν, ἀλλὰ ζώντων.	Θεὸς δὲ οὐκ ἔστιν νεκρῶν, ἀλλὰ ζώντων.

Clem. Hom. iii. 55.
Οὐκ ἔστιν Θεὸς νεκρῶν, ἀλλὰ ζώντων.

Here Θεός is in Mark and the Clementines a predicate, in Matthew the subject. In the introduction to the Eschatological discourse the Clementines approach more nearly to St. Mark than to any other Gospel: Ὁρᾶτε (βλέπεις, Mark) τὰς (μεγάλας, Mark) οἰκοδομὰς ταύτας; ἀμὴν ὑμῖν λέγω (as Matt.) λίθος ἐπὶ λίθον οὐ μὴ ἀφεθῇ ὧδε, ὃς οὐ μὴ (as Mark) καθαιρεθῇ (καταλυθῇ, Mark; other Gospels, future). Instead of τὰς οἰκοδομὰς ταύτας the other Gospels have ταῦτα—ταῦτα πάντα.

But there are two stronger cases than these. The Clementines and Mark alone have the opening clause of the quotation from Deut. vi. 4, Ἄκουε, Ἰσραήλ, Κύριος ὁ Θεὸς ἡμῶν κύριος εἶς ἐστίν. In the synopsis of the first Gospel this is omitted (Matt. xxii. 37). There is a variation in the Clementine text, which for ἡμῶν, has, according to Dressel, σου, and according to Cotelier, ὑμῶν. Both these readings however are represented among the authorities for the canonical text: σου is found in c (Codex Colbertinus, one of the best copies of the Old Latin), in the Memphitic and Aethiopic versions, and in the Latin Fathers Cyprian and Hilary; ὑμῶν (vester) has the authority of the Viennese fragment i, another representative of the primitive African form of the Old Latin [1].

The objection to the inference that the quotation is made from St. Mark, derived from the context in which it appears in the Clementines, is really quite nugatory. It is true that the quotation is addressed to those 'who were beguiled to imagine many gods,' and that 'there is no hint of the assertion of many gods in the Gospel [2];' but just as little hint is there of the assertion 'that God is evil' in the quotation μή με λέγετε ἀγαθόν just before. There is not the slightest reason to suppose that the Gospel from which the Clementines quote would contain any such assertion. In this particular case the mode of quotation cannot be said to be very unscrupulous; but even if it were more so we need not go back to antiquity for parallels: they are to be found in abundance in any

---

[1] A friend has kindly extracted for me, from Holmes and Parsons, the authorities for the Septuagint text of Deut. vi. 4. For σου there are 'Const. App. 219, 354, 355; Ignat. Epp. 104, 112; Clem. Al. 68, 718; Chrys. i. 482 et saepe, al.' For *tuus*, 'Iren. (int.), Tert., Cypr., Ambr., Anonym. ap. Aug., Gaud., Brix., Alii Latini.' No authorities for ὑμῶν. Was the change first introduced into the text of the New Testament?

[2] *S. R.* ii. p. 25.

ordinary collection of proof texts of the Church Catechism or of the Thirty-nine Articles, or in most works of popular controversy. I must confess to my surprise that such an objection could be made by an experienced critic.

Credner[1] gives the last as the one decided approximation to our second Gospel, apparently overlooking the minor points mentioned above; but, at the time when he wrote, the concluding portion of the Homilies, which contains the other most striking instance, had not yet been published. With regard to this second instance, I must express my agreement with Canon Westcott[2] against the author of 'Supernatural Religion.' The passage stands thus in the Clementines and the Gospel:—

Clem. Hom. xix. 20.	Mark iv. 34.
Διὸ καὶ τοῖς αὐτοῦ μαθηταῖς κατ' ἰδίαν ἐπέλυε τῆς τῶν οὐρανῶν βασιλείας τὰ μυστήρια.	... κατ' ἰδίαν δὲ τοῖς μαθηταῖς αὐτοῦ ἐπέλυεν πάντα (compare iv. 11, ὑμῖν τὸ μυστήριον δέδοται τῆς βασιλείας τοῦ Θεοῦ).

The canonical reading, τοῖς μαθηταῖς αὐτοῦ, rests chiefly upon Western authority (D, b, c, e, f, Vulg.) with A, 1, 33, &c. and is adopted by Tregelles—it should be noted before the discovery of the Codex Sinaiticus. The true reading is probably that which appears in this MS. along with B, C, L, Δ, τοῖς ἰδίοις μαθηταῖς. We have however already seen the leaning of the Clementines for Western readings.

When we compare the synopsis of St. Mark and St. Matthew together we should be inclined to set this down as a very decided instance of quotation from the former. The only circumstance that detracts

[1] *Beiträge*, i. p. 326. [2] *On the Canon*, p. 261, n. 2.

from the certainty of this conclusion is that a quotation had been made just before which is certainly not from our canonical Gospels, τὰ μυστήρια ἐμοὶ καὶ τοῖς υἱοῖς τοῦ οἴκου μου φυλάξατε. This is rightly noted in 'Supernatural Religion.' All that we can say is that it is a drawback—it is just a makeweight in the opposite scale, as suggesting that the second quotation may be also from an apocryphal Gospel; but it does not by any means serve to counterbalance the presumption that the quotation is canonical. The coincidence of language is very marked. The peculiar compound ἐπιλύω occurs only once besides (ἐπίλυσις also once) in the whole of the New Testament, and not at all in the Gospels.

With the third Gospel also there are coincidences. Of the passages peculiar to this Gospel the Clementine writer has the fall of Satan (τὸν πονηρόν, Clem.) like lightning from heaven, 'rejoice that your names are written in the book of life' (expanded with evident freedom), the unjust judge, Zacchaeus, the circumvallation of Jerusalem, and the prayer, for the forgiveness of the Jews, upon the cross. It is unlikely that these passages, which are wanting in all our extant Gospels, should have had any other source than our third Synoptic. The 'circumvallation' (περιχαρακώσουσιν Clem., περιβαλοῦσιν χάρακα Luke) is especially important, as it is probable, and believed by many critics, that this particular detail was added by the Evangelist after the event. The parable of the unjust judge, though reproduced with something of the freedom to which we are accustomed in patristic narrative quotations both from the Old and New Testament, has yet remarkable similarities of style and diction (ὁ κριτὴς τῆς ἀδικίας, ποιήσει τὴν ἐκδίκησιν τῶν βοώντων πρὸς αὐτὸν ἡμέρας καὶ νυκτός, Λέγω ὑμῖν, ποιήσει . . ἐν τάχει).

We have to add to these another class of peculiarities which occur in places where the synoptic parallel has been preserved. Thus in the Sermon on the Mount we find the following :—

Matt. vii. 21.	*Clem. Hom.* viii. 7.	*Luke* vi. 46.
Οὐ πᾶς ὁ λέγων μοι, Κύριε, Κύριε, εἰσελεύσεται εἰς τὴν βασιλείαν τῶν οὐρανῶν, ἀλλ' ὁ ποιῶν τὸ θέλημα τοῦ πατρός μου τοῦ ἐν οὐρανοῖς.	Τί με λέγεις· Κύριε, Κύριε, καὶ οὐ ποιεῖς ἃ λέγω;	Τί δέ με καλεῖτε Κύριε, Κύριε, καὶ οὐ ποιεῖτε ἃ λέγω;

This is one of a class of passages which form the *cruces* of Synoptic criticism. It is almost equally difficult to think and not to think that both the canonical parallels are drawn from the same original. The great majority of German critics maintain that they are, and most of these would seek that original in the 'Spruchsammlung' or 'Collection of Discourses' by the Apostle St. Matthew. This is usually (though not quite unanimously) held to have been preserved most intact in the first Gospel. But if so, the Lucan version represents a wide deviation from the original, and precisely in proportion to the extent of that deviation is the probability that the Clementine quotation is based upon it. The more the individuality of the Evangelist has entered into the form given to the saying the stronger is the presumption that his work lay before the writer of the Clementines. In any case the difference between the Matthaean and Lucan versions shows what various shapes the synoptic tradition naturally assumed, and makes it so much the less likely that the coincidence between St. Luke and the Clementines is merely accidental.

Another similar case, in which the issue is presented very clearly, is afforded by the quotation, 'The labourer is worthy of his hire.'

Matt. x. 11.	*Clem. Hom.* iii. 71.	*Luke* x. 7.
Ἄξιος γὰρ ὁ ἐργάτης τῆς τροφῆς αὐτοῦ ἐστίν.	[λογισάμενοι ὅτι] ἄξιός ἐστιν ὁ ἐργάτης τοῦ μισθοῦ αὐτοῦ;	Ἄξιος γὰρ ὁ ἐργάτης τῆς τοῦ μισθοῦ αὐτοῦ ἐστί.

Here, if the Clementine writer had been following the first Gospel, he would have had τροφῆς and not μισθοῦ; and the assumption that there was here a non-extant Gospel coincident with St. Luke is entirely gratuitous and, to an extent, improbable.

Besides these, it will be seen, by the tables given above, that there are as many as eight passages in which the peculiarities not only of one but of both Gospels (the first and third) appear simultaneously. Perhaps it may be well to give examples of these before we make any comment upon them. We may thus take—

Matt. vii. 9–11.	*Clem. Hom.* iii. 56.	*Luke* xi. 11–13.
Ἢ τίς ἐστιν ἐξ ὑμῶν ἄνθρωπος, ὃν ἐὰν αἰτήσῃ ὁ υἱὸς αὐτοῦ ἄρτον, μὴ λίθον ἐπιδώσει αὐτῷ; καὶ ἐὰν ἰχθὺν αἰτήσῃ μὴ ὄφιν ἐπιδώσει αὐτῷ; εἰ οὖν ὑμεῖς πονηροὶ ὄντες οἴδατε δόματα ἀγαθὰ διδόναι τοῖς τέκνοις ὑμῶν, πόσῳ μᾶλλον ὁ πατὴρ ὑμῶν	Τίνα αἰτήσει υἱὸς ἄρτον, μὴ λίθον ἐπιδώσει αὐτῷ; ἢ καὶ ἰχθὺν αἰτήσει, μὴ ὄφιν ἐπιδώσει αὐτῷ; εἰ οὖν ὑμεῖς, πονηροὶ ὄντες, οἴδατε δόματα ἀγαθὰ διδόναι τοῖς τέκνοις ὑμῶν, πόσῳ μᾶλλον ὁ πατὴρ ὑμῶν ὁ οὐράνιος δώσει ἀγαθὰ τοῖς αἰτουμένοις αὐ-	Τίνα δὲ ἐξ ὑμῶν τὸν πατέρα αἰτήσει ὁ υἱὸς ἄρτον, μὴ λίθον ἐπιδώσει αὐτῷ; ἢ καὶ ἰχθύν, μὴ ἀντὶ ἰχθύος ὄφιν ἐπιδώσει αὐτῷ, ἢ καὶ ἐὰν αἰτήσῃ ᾠόν, μὴ ἐπιδώσει αὐτῷ σκορπίον; εἰ οὖν ὑμεῖς, πονηροὶ ὑπάρχοντες, οἴδατε δόματα ἀγαθὰ δι-

Matt. vii. 9–11.	*Clem. Hom.* iii. 56.	*Luke* xi. 11–13.
ὁ ἐν τοῖς οὐρανοῖς δώσει ἀγαθὰ τοῖς αἰτοῦσιν αὐτόν;	τὸν καὶ τοῖς ποιοῦσιν τὸ θέλημα αὐτοῦ;	δόναι τοῖς τέκνοις ὑμῶν, πόσῳ μᾶλλον ὁ πατὴρ ὁ ἐξ οὐρανοῦ δώσει πνεῦμα ἅγιον τοῖς αἰτοῦσιν αὐτόν;

In the earlier part of this quotation the Clementine writer seems to follow the third Gospel (τίνα αἰτήσει, ἢ καί); in the later part the first (omission of the antithesis between the egg and the scorpion, ὄντες, δώσει ἀγαθά). The two Gospels are combined against the Clementines in ἐξ ὑμῶν and the simpler τοῖς αἰτοῦσιν αὐτόν.

The second example shall be—

Matt. x. 28.	*Clem. Hom.* xviii. 5.	*Luke* xii. 4, 5.
Καὶ μὴ φοβεῖσθε ἀπὸ τῶν ἀποκτεινόντων τὸ σῶμα, τὴν δὲ ψυχὴν μὴ δυναμένων ἀποκτεῖναι· φοβεῖσθε δὲ μᾶλλον τὸν δυνάμενον καὶ ψυχὴν καὶ σῶμα ἀπολέσαι ἐν γεέννῃ.	Μὴ φοβηθῆτε ἀπὸ τοῦ ἀποκτείνοντος τὸ σῶμα, τῇ δὲ ψυχῇ μὴ δυναμένου τι ποιῆσαι· φοβήθητε τὸν δυνάμενον καὶ σῶμα καὶ ψυχὴν εἰς τὴν γέενναν τοῦ πυρὸς βαλεῖν. Ναί, λέγω ὑμῖν, τοῦτον φοβήθητε.	Μὴ φοβηθῆτε ἀπὸ τῶν ἀποκτεινόντων τὸ σῶμα καὶ μετὰ ταῦτα μὴ ἐχόντων περισσότερόν τι ποιῆσαι. ὑποδείξω δὲ ὑμῖν τίνα φοβηθῆτε· φοβήθητε τὸν μετὰ τὸ ἀποκτεῖναι ἔχοντα ἐξουσίαν ἐμβαλεῖν εἰς τὴν γέενναν· ναί, λέγω ὑμῖν, τοῦτον φοβήθητε.

In common with Matthew the Clementines have τῇ δὲ ψυχῇ (acc. Matt.) .. δυναμένου (-ων Matt.), and δυνάμενον καὶ σῶμα καὶ ψυχήν (in inverted order, Matt.); in common with Luke μὴ φοβηθῆτε, τι ποιῆσαι, [ἐμ]βαλεῖν εἰς, and the clause ναί κ. τ. λ. The two Gospels agree against the Clementines in the plural τῶν ἀποκτεινόντων.

One more longer quotation :—

Matt. xxiv. 45–51.	*Clem. Hom.* iii. 60.	*Luke* xii. 42–45.
Τίς ἄρα ἐστὶν ὁ πιστὸς δοῦλος καὶ φρόνιμος, ὃν κατέστησεν ὁ κύριος αὐτοῦ ἐπὶ τῆς θεραπείας αὐτοῦ τοῦ δοῦναι αὐτοῖς τὴν τροφὴν ἐν καιρῷ; μακάριος ὁ δοῦλος ἐκεῖνος ὃν ἐλθὼν ὁ κύριος αὐτοῦ εὑρήσει οὕτω ποιοῦντα ... Ἐὰν δὲ εἴπῃ ὁ κακὸς δοῦλος ἐκεῖνος ἐν τῇ καρδίᾳ αὐτοῦ· χρονίζει μου ὁ κύριος, καὶ ἄρξηται τύπτειν τοὺς συνδούλους αὐτοῦ ἐσθίῃ δὲ καὶ πίνῃ μετὰ τῶν μεθυόντων, ἥξει ὁ κύριος τοῦ δούλου ἐκείνου ἐν ἡμέρᾳ ᾗ οὐ προσδοκᾷ καὶ ἐν ὥρᾳ ᾗ οὐ γινώσκει, καὶ διχοτομήσει αὐτὸν καὶ τὸ μέρος αὐτοῦ μετὰ τῶν ὑποκριτῶν θήσει.	Θεοῦ γὰρ βουλῇ ἀναδείκνυται μακάριος ὁ ἄνθρωπος ἐκεῖνος ὃν καταστήσει ὁ κύριος αὐτοῦ ἐπὶ τῆς θεραπείας τῶν συνδούλων αὐτοῦ, τοῦ διδόναι αὐτοῖς τὰς τροφὰς ἐν καιρῷ αὐτῶν, μὴ ἐννοούμενον καὶ λέγοντα ἐν τῇ καρδίᾳ αὐτοῦ· χρονίζει ὁ κύριός μου ἐλθεῖν· καὶ ἄρξηται τύπτειν τοὺς συνδούλους αὐτοῦ, ἐσθίων καὶ πίνων μετά τε πορνῶν καὶ μεθυόντων· καὶ ἥξει ὁ κύριος τοῦ δούλου ἐκείνου ἐν ὥρᾳ ᾗ οὐ προσδοκᾷ καὶ ἐν ἡμέρᾳ ᾗ οὐ γινώσκει, καὶ διχοτομήσει αὐτόν, καὶ τὸ ἀπιστοῦν αὐτοῦ μέρος μετὰ τῶν ὑποκριτῶν θήσει.	Τίς ἄρα ἐστὶν ὁ πιστὸς οἰκονόμος καὶ φρόνιμος, ὃν καταστήσει ὁ κύριος ἐπὶ τῆς θεραπείας αὐτοῦ, τοῦ διδόναι ἐν καιρῷ τὸ σιτομέτριον; μακάριος ὁ δοῦλος ἐκεῖνος, ὃν ἐλθὼν ὁ κύριος αὐτοῦ εὑρήσει ποιοῦντα οὕτως ... Ἐὰν δὲ εἴπῃ ὁ δοῦλος ἐκεῖνος ἐν τῇ καρδίᾳ αὐτοῦ· χρονίζει ὁ κύριός μου ἔρχεσθαι· καὶ ἄρξηται τύπτειν τοὺς παῖδας καὶ τὰς παιδίσκας, ἐσθίειν τε καὶ πίνειν καὶ μεθύσκεσθαι· ἥξει ὁ κύριος τοῦ δούλου ἐκείνου ἐν ἡμέρᾳ ᾗ οὐ προσδοκᾷ, καὶ ἐν ὥρᾳ ᾗ οὐ γινώσκει, καὶ διχοτομήσει αὐτὸν καὶ τὸ μέρος αὐτοῦ μετὰ τῶν ἀπίστων θήσει.

I have given this passage in full, in spite of its length, because it is interesting and characteristic; it might indeed almost be said to be typical of the passages, not only in the Clementine Homilies, but also in other writers like Justin, which present this relation of double similarity to two of the Synoptics. It should be noticed that the passage in the Homilies is not introduced strictly as a quotation but is interwoven with the text. On the other hand, it should be mentioned that the opening clause, Μακάριος ... συνδούλους αὐτοῦ, recurs identically about thirty lines lower down. We observe that of the peculiarities of the first Synoptic the Clementines have δοῦλος (οἰκονόμος, Luke), [ὁ κύριος] αὐτοῦ, τὴν τροφήν (τὰς τροφάς, Clem.; Luke, characteristically, τὸ σιτομέτριον), the order of ἐν καιρῷ, τοὺς συνδούλους αὐτοῦ (τοὺς παῖδας καὶ τὰς παιδίσκας, Luke), μετὰ ... μεθυόντων, and ὑποκριτῶν for ἀπίστων. Of the peculiarities of the third Synoptic the Clementines reproduce the future καταστήσει, the present διδόναι, the insertion of ἐλθεῖν (ἔρχεσθαι, Luke) after χρονίζει, the order of the words in this clause, and a trace of the word ἀπίστων in τὸ ἀπιστοῦν αὐτοῦ μέρος. The two Gospels support each other in most of the places where the Clementines depart from them, and especially in the two verses, one of which is paraphrased and the other omitted.

Now the question arises, What is the origin of this phenomenon of double resemblance? It may be caused in three ways: either it may proceed from alternate quoting of our two present Gospels; or it may proceed from the quoting of a later harmony of those Gospels; or, lastly, it may proceed from the quotation of a document earlier than our two Synoptics, and containing both classes of peculiarities, those which have been dropped in the first Gospel as well as those which have been dropped in the third, as we find to be frequently the case with St. Mark.

Either of the first two of these hypotheses will clearly suit the phenomena; but they will hardly admit of the third. It does indeed derive a very slight countenance from the repetition of the language of the last quotation:

this repetition, however, occurs at too short an interval to be of importance. But the theory that the Clementine writer is quoting from a document older than the two Synoptics, and indeed their common original, is excluded by the amount of matter that is common to the two Synoptics and either not found at all or found variantly in the Clementines. The coincidence between the Synoptics, we may assume, is derived from the fact that they both drew from a common original. The phraseology in which they agree is in all probability that of the original document itself. If therefore this phraseology is wanting in the Clementine quotations they are not likely to have been drawn directly from the document which underlies the Synoptics. This conclusion too is confirmed by particulars. In the first quotation we cannot set down quite positively the Clementine expansion of τοῖς αἰτοῦσιν αὐτόν as a later form, though it most probably is so. But the strange and fantastic phrase in the last quotation, τὸ ἀπιστοῦν αὐτοῦ μέρος μετὰ τῶν ὑποκριτῶν θήσει, is almost certainly a combination of the ὑποκριτῶν of Matthew with a distorted reminiscence of the ἀπίστων of Luke.

We have then the same kind of choice set before us as in the case of Justin. Either the Clementine writer quotes our present Gospels, or else he quotes some other composition later than them, and which implies them. In other words, if he does not bear witness to our Gospels at first hand, he does so at second hand, and by the interposition of a further intermediate stage. It is quite possible that he may have had access to such a tertiary document, and that it may be the same which is the source of his apocryphal quotations: that he did draw from apocryphal sources, partly perhaps oral, but probably in the main written, there can, I think, be little doubt. Neither is it easy to draw the line and say exactly what quotations shall be referred to such sources and what shall not. The facts do not permit us to claim the exclusive use of the canonical Gospels. But that they were used, mediately or immediately and to a greater or less degree, is, I believe, beyond question.

CHAPTER VII.

BASILIDES AND VALENTINUS.

STILL following the order of 'Supernatural Religion,' we pass with the critic to another group of heretical writers in the earlier part of the second century. In Basilides the Gnostic we have the first of a chain of writers who, though not holding the orthodox tradition of doctrine, yet called themselves Christians (except under the stress of persecution) and used the Christian books—whether or to what extent the extant documents of Christianity we must now endeavour to determine.

Basilides carries us back to an early date in point of time. He taught at Alexandria in the reign of Hadrian (117–137 A.D.). Hippolytus expounds at some length, and very much in their own words, the doctrines of Basilides and his school. There is a somewhat similar account by Epiphanius, and more incidental allusions in Clement of Alexandria and Origen.

The notices that have come down to us of the writings of Basilides are confusing. Origen says that 'he had the effrontery to compose a Gospel and call it by his own name [1].' Eusebius quotes from Agrippa Castor, a contemporary and opponent from the orthodox side, a state-

---

[1] *Hom.* 1. *in Lucam.*

ment that 'he wrote four and twenty books (presumably of commentary) upon the Gospel[1].' Clement of Alexandria gives rather copious extracts from the twenty-third of these books, to which he gave the name of 'Exegetics[2].'

Tischendorf assumes, in a manner that is not quite so 'arbitrary and erroneous[3]' as his critic seems to suppose, that this Commentary was upon our four Gospels. It is not altogether clear how far Eusebius is using the words of Agrippa Castor and how far his own. If the latter, there can be no doubt that he understood the statement of Agrippa Castor as Tischendorf understands his, i.e. as referring to our present Gospels; but supposing his words to be those of the earlier writer, it is possible that, coming from the orthodox side, they may have been used in the sense which Tischendorf attributes to them. There can be no question that Irenaeus used τὸ εὐαγγέλιον for the canonical Gospels collectively, and Justin Martyr may *perhaps* have done so. Tischendorf himself does not maintain that it refers to our Gospels *exclusively*. Practically the statements in regard to the Commentary of Basilides lead to nothing.

Neither does it appear any more clearly what was the nature of the Gospel that Basilides wrote. The term εὐαγγέλιον had a technical metaphysical sense in the Basilidian sect and was used to designate a part of the transcendental Gnostic revelations. The Gospel of Basilides may therefore, as Dr. Westcott suggests, reasonably enough, have had a philosophical rather than a historical character. The author of 'Supernatural Religion' censures Dr. Westcott for this suggestion[4], but a

---

[1] *H. E.* iv. 7.
[2] *Strom.* iv. 12.
[3] *S. R.* ii. p. 42.
[4] *Ibid.* n. 2; cp. p. 47.

few pages further on he seems to adopt it himself, though he applies it strangely to the language of Eusebius or Agrippa Castor and not to Basilides' own work.

In any case Hippolytus expressly says that, after the generation of Jesus, the Basilidians held 'the other events in the life of the Saviour followed as they are written in the Gospels[1].' There is no reason at all to suppose that there was a breach of continuity in this respect between Basilides and his school. And if his Gospel really contained substantially the same events as ours, it is a question of comparatively secondary importance whether he actually made use of those Gospels or no.

It is rather remarkable that Hippolytus and Epiphanius, who furnish the fullest accounts of the tenets of Basilides (and his followers), say nothing about his Gospel: neither does Irenaeus or Clement of Alexandria; the first mention of it is in Origen's Homily on St. Luke. This shows how unwarranted is the assumption made in 'Supernatural Religion[2]' that because Hippolytus says that Basilides appealed to a secret tradition he professed to have received from Matthias, and Eusebius that he set up certain imaginary prophets, 'Barcabbas and Barcoph,' he therefore had no other authorities. The statement that he 'absolutely ignores the canonical Gospels altogether' and does not 'recognise any such works as of authority,' is much in excess of the evidence. All that this really amounts to is that neither Hippolytus nor Eusebius say in so many words that Basilides did use our Gospels. It would be a fairer inference to argue from their silence,

---

[1] *Ref. Omn. Haer.* vii. 27.   [2] ii. p. 45.

and still more from that of the 'malleus haereticorum' Epiphanius, that he did not in this depart from the orthodox custom; otherwise the Fathers would have been sure to charge him with it, as they did Marcion. It is really I believe a not very unsafe conclusion, for heretical as well as orthodox writers, that where the Fathers do not say to the contrary, they accepted the same documents as themselves.

The main questions that arise in regard to Basilides are two: (1) Are the quotations supposed to be made by him really his? (2) Are they quotations from our Gospels?

The doubt as to the authorship of the quotations applies chiefly to those which occur in the 'Refutation of the Heresies' by Hippolytus. This writer begins his account of the Basilidian tenets by saying, 'Let us see here how Basilides along with Isidore and his crew belie Matthias[1],' &c. He goes on using for the most part the singular φησίν, but sometimes inserting the plural κατ' αὐτούς. Accordingly, it has been urged that quotations which are referred to the head of the school really belong to his later followers, and the attempt has further been made to prove that the doctrines described in this section of the work of Hippolytus are later in their general character than those attributed to Basilides himself. This latter argument is very fine drawn, and will not bear any substantial weight. It is, however, probably true that a confusion is sometimes found between the 'eponymus,' as it were, of a school and his followers. Whether that has been the case here is a question that we have not sufficient data for deciding

---

[1] *Ref. Omn. Haer.* vii. 20.

positively. The presumption is against it, but it must be admitted to be possible. It seems a forced and unnatural position to suppose that the disciples would go to one set of authorities and the master to another, and equally unnatural to think that a later critic, like Hippolytus, would confine himself to the works of these disciples and that in none of the passages in which quotations are introduced he has gone to the fountain head. We may decline to dogmatise; but probability is in favour of the supposition that some at least of the quotations given by Hippolytus come directly from Basilides.

Some of the quotations discussed in 'Supernatural Religion' are expressly assigned to the school of Basilides. Thus Clement of Alexandria, in stating the opinion which this school held on the subject of marriage, says that they referred to our Lord's saying, 'All men cannot receive this,' &c.

Strom. iii. 1. 1.	*Matt.* xix. 11, 12.
Οὐ πάντες χωροῦσι τὸν λόγον τοῦτον, εἰσὶ γὰρ εὐνοῦχοι οἱ μὲν ἐκ γενετῆς οἱ δὲ ἐξ ἀνάγκης.	Οὐ πάντες χωροῦσι τὸν λόγον τοῦτον, ἀλλ' οἷς δέδοται· εἰσὶν γὰρ εὐνοῦχοι οἵτινες ἐκ κοιλίας μητρὸς ἐγεννήθησαν οὕτως, καὶ εἰσὶν εὐνοῦχοι οἵτινες εὐνουχίσθησαν ὑπὸ τῶν ἀνθρώπων, κ.τ.λ.

The reference of this to St. Matthew is far from being so 'preposterous[1]' as the critic imagines. The use of the word χωρεῖν in this sense is striking and peculiar: it has no parallel in the New Testament, and but slight and few parallels, as it appears from the lexicons and commentators, in previous literature. The whole phrase is

[1] S. R. ii. p. 49.

a remarkable one and the verbal coincidence exact, while the words that follow are an easy and natural abridgment. On the same principles on which it is denied that this is a quotation from St. Matthew it would be easy to prove à *priori* that many of the quotations in Clement of Alexandria could not be taken from the canonical Gospels which, we know, *are* so taken.

The fact that this passage is found among the Synoptics only in St. Matthew must not count for nothing. The very small number of additional facts and sayings that we are able to glean from the writers who, according to 'Supernatural Religion,' have used apocryphal Gospels so freely, seems to be proof that our present Gospels were (as we should expect) the fullest and most comprehensive of their kind. If, then, a passage is found only in one of them, it is fair to conclude, not positively, but probably, that it is drawn from some special source of information that was not widely diffused.

The same remarks hold good respecting another quotation found in Epiphanius, which also comes under the general head of Βασιλειδιανοί, though it is introduced not only by the singular φησίν but by the definite φησὶν ὁ ἀγύρτης. Here the Basilidian quotation has a parallel also peculiar to St. Matthew, from the Sermon on the Mount.

Epiph. Haer. 72 A.	*Matt.* vii. 6.
Μὴ βάλητε τοὺς μαργαρίτας ἔμπροσθεν τῶν χοίρων, μηδὲ δότε τὸ ἅγιον τοῖς κυσί.	Μὴ δῶτε τὸ ἅγιον τοῖς κυσίν, μηδὲ βάλητε τοὺς μαργαρίτας ὑμῶν ἔμπροσθεν τῶν χοίρων. The excellent Alexandrine cursive 1, with some others, has δότε for δῶτε.

The transposition of clauses, such as we see here, is by no means an infrequent phenomenon. There is a remarkable instance of it—to go no further—in the text of the benedictions with which the Sermon on the Mount begins. In respect to the order of the two clauses, 'Blessed are they that mourn' and 'Blessed are the meek,' there is a broad division in the MSS. and other authorities. For the received order we find ℵ, B, C, 1, the mass of uncials and cursives, b, f, Syrr. Pst. and Hcl., Memph., Arm., Aeth.; for the reversed order, 'Blessed are the meek' and 'Blessed are they that mourn,' are ranged D, 33, Vulg., a, c, f^1, g^1, h, k, l, Syr. Crt., Clem., Orig., Eus., Bas. (?), Hil. The balance is probably on the side of the received reading, as the opposing authorities are mostly Western, but they too make a formidable array. The confusion in the text of St. Luke as to the early clauses of the Lord's Prayer is well known. But if such things are done in the green tree, if we find these variations in MSS. which profess to be exact transcripts of the same original copy, how much more may we expect to find them enter into mere quotations that are often evidently made from memory, and for the sake of the sense, not the words. In this instance however the verbal resemblance is very close. As I have frequently said, to speak of certainties in regard to any isolated passage that does not present exceptional phenomena is inadmissible, but I have little moral doubt that the quotation was really derived from St. Matthew, and there is quite a fair probability that it was made by Basilides himself.

The Hippolytean quotations, the ascription of which to Basilides or to his school we have left an open question, will assume a considerable importance when we come to treat of the external evidence for the fourth Gospel. Bearing upon the Synoptic Gospels, we find an allusion to the star of the Magi and an exact verbal quotation (introduced with τὸ εἰρημένον) of Luke i. 35, Πνεῦμα ἅγιον ἐπελεύσεται ἐπὶ σέ, καὶ δύναμις ὑψίστου ἐπισκιάσει σοι. Both these have been already discussed with reference to Justin. All the other Gospels in which the star of the Magi is mentioned belong to a later stage of formation than St. Matthew. The very parallelism between St. Matthew and St. Luke shows that both Gospels were composed at a date when various traditions as to the early portions of the history were current. No doubt secondary, or rather tertiary, works, like the Protevangelium of James, came to be composed later; but it is not begging the question to say that if the allusion is made by Basilides, it is not likely that at that date he should quote any other Gospel than St. Matthew, simply because that is the earliest form in which the story of the Magi has come down to us.

The case is stronger in regard to the quotation from St. Luke. In Justin's account of the Annunciation to Mary there was a coincidence with the Protevangelium and a variation from the canonical text in the phrase πνεῦμα κυρίου for πνεῦμα ἅγιον; but in the Basilidian quotation the canonical text is reproduced syllable for syllable and letter for letter, which, when we consider how sensitive and delicate these verbal relations are, must be taken as a strong proof of identity. The reader may be reminded that the word ἐπισκιάζειν, the phrase δύναμις ὑψίστου, and the construction ἐπέρχεσθαι ἐπί, are all characteristic of St. Luke : ἐπισκιάζειν occurs once in the triple synopsis and besides only here and in Acts v. 15 : ὕψιστος occurs nine times in St. Luke's writings and only four times besides; it is used by the Evangelist especially in phrases like υἱός, δύναμις, προφήτης, δοῦλος ὑψίστου, to which the only parallel is ἱερεὺς τοῦ Θεοῦ τοῦ ὑψίστου in Heb. vii. 1. The construction of ἐπέρχεσθαι with ἐπί and the accusative is found five times in the third Gospel and the Acts and not at all besides in the New Testament; indeed the participial form, ἐπερχόμενος (in the sense of 'future'), is the only shape in which the word appears (twice) outside the eight times that it occurs in St. Luke's writings. This is a body of evidence that makes it extremely difficult to deny that the Basilidian quotation has its original in the third Synoptic.

2.

The case in regard to Valentinus, the next great Gnostic leader, who came forward about the year 140 A.D., is very similar to that of Basilides, though the balance of the argument is slightly altered. It is, on the one hand, still clearer that the greater part of the evangelical references usually quoted are really from our present actual Gospels, but, on the other hand, there is a more distinct probability that these are to be assigned rather to the School of Valentinus than to Valentinus himself.

The supposed allusion to St. John we shall pass over for the present.

There is a string of allusions in the first book of Irenaeus, 'Adv. Haereses,' to the visit of Jesus as a child to the Passover (Luke ii. 42), the jot or tittle of Matt. v. 18, the healing of the issue of blood, the bearing of the cross (Lu. xiv: 27 par.), the sending of a sword and not peace, 'his fan is in his hand,' the salt and light of the world, the healing of the centurion's servant, of Jairus' daughter, the exclamations upon the cross, the call of the unwilling disciples, Zacchaeus, Simon, &c. We may take it, I believe, as admitted, and it is indeed quite indisputable, that these are references to our present Gospels; but there is the further question whether they are to be attributed directly to Valentinus or to his followers, and I am quite prepared to admit that there are no sufficient grounds for direct attribution to the founder of the system. Irenaeus begins by saying that his authorities are certain 'commentaries of the disciples of Valentinus' and his own intercourse with some of them[1]. He proceeds to announce his intention to give a 'brief and clear account of the opinions of those who were then teaching their false doctrines ($νῦν\ παραδιδασκόντων$), that is, of Ptolemaeus and his followers, a branch of the school of Valentinus.' It is fair to infer that the description of the Valentinian system which follows is drawn chiefly from these sources. This need not, however, quite necessarily exclude works by Valentinus himself. It is at any rate clear that Irenaeus had some means of referring to the opinions of Valentinus as distinct from his school; because, after giving a sketch of the system, he proceeds to point out certain contradictions within the school itself, quoting first Valentinus expressly, then a disciple called Secundus, then 'another of their more distinguished and ambitious teachers,' then 'others,' then a further subdivision, finally returning to Ptolemaeus and his party

[1] *Adv. Haer.* i. Pref. 2.

again. On the whole, Irenaeus seems to have had a pretty complete knowledge of the writings and teaching of the Valentinians. We conclude therefore, that, while it cannot be alleged positively that any of the quotations or allusions were really made by Valentinus, it would be rash to assert that none of them were made by him, or that he did not use our present Gospels.

However this may be, we cannot do otherwise than demur to the statement implied in 'Supernatural Religion[1],' that the references in Irenaeus can only be employed as evidence for the Gnostic usage between the years 185-195 A.D. This is a specimen of a kind of position that is frequently taken up by critics upon that side, and that I cannot but think quite unreasonable and uncritical. Without going into the question of the date at which Irenaeus wrote at present, and assuming with the author of 'Supernatural Religion' that his first three books were published before the death of Eleutherus in A.D. 190—the latest date possible for them,—it will be seen that the Gnostic teaching to which Irenaeus refers is supposed to begin at a time when his first book may very well have been concluded, and to end actually five years later than the latest date at which this portion of the work can have been published! Not only does the author allow no time at all for Irenaeus to compose his own work, not only does he allow none for him to become acquainted with the Gnostic doctrines, and for those doctrines themselves to become consolidated and expressed in writing, but he goes so far as to make Irenaeus testify to a state of things five years at least, and very probably

[1] ii. p. 59.

ten, in advance of the time at which he was himself writing! No doubt there is an oversight somewhere, but this is the kind of oversight that ought not to be made.

This, however, is an extreme instance of the fault to which I was alluding—the tendency in the negative school to allow no time or very little for processes that in the natural course of things must certainly have required a more or less considerable interval. On a moderate computation, the indirect testimony of Irenaeus may be taken to refer—not to the period 185–195 A.D., which is out of the question—but to that from 160–180 A.D. This is not pressing the possibility, real as it is, that Valentinus himself, who flourished from 140–160 A.D., may have been included. We may agree with the author of 'Supernatural Religion' that Irenaeus probably made the personal acquaintance of the Valentinian leaders, and obtained copies of their books, during his well-known visit to Rome in 178 A.D.[1] The applications of Scripture would be taken chiefly from the books of which some would be recent but others of an earlier date, and it can surely be no exaggeration to place the formation of the body of doctrine which they contained in the period 160–175 A.D. above mentioned. I doubt whether a critic could be blamed who should go back ten years further, but we shall be keeping on the safe side if we take our *terminus a quo* as to which these Gnostic writings can be alleged in evidence at about the year 160.

A genuine fragment of a letter of Valentinus has been preserved by Clement of Alexandria in the second book

---

[1] *S. R.* ii. p. 211 sq.

of the Stromateis [1]. This is thought to contain references to St. Matthew's Gospel by Dr. Westcott, and, strange to say, both to St. Matthew and St. Luke by Volkmar. These references, however, are not sufficiently clear to be pressed.

A much less equivocal case is supplied by Hippolytus —less equivocal at least so far as the reference goes. Among the passages which received a specially Gnostic interpretation is Luke i. 35, 'The Holy Ghost shall come upon thee, and the power of the Most High shall overshadow thee: wherefore also the holy thing which is born (of thee) shall be called the Son of God.' This is quoted thus, 'The Holy Ghost shall come upon thee, and the power of the Most High shall overshadow thee: wherefore that which is born of thee shall be called holy.'

Luke i. 35.	*Ref. Omn. Haes.* vi. 35.
Πνεῦμα ἅγιον ἐπελεύσεται ἐπὶ σέ, καὶ δύναμις ὑψίστου ἐπισκιάσει σοι, διὸ καὶ τὸ γεννώμενον [ἐκ σοῦ] ἅγιον κληθήσεται υἱὸς Θεοῦ.	Πνεῦμα ἅγιον ἐπελεύσεται ἐπὶ σέ . . . καὶ δύναμις ὑψίστου ἐπισκιάσει σοι . . . διὸ τὸ γεννώμενον ἐκ σοῦ ἅγιον κληθήσεται.

That St. Luke has been the original here seems to be beyond a doubt. The omission of υἱὸς Θεοῦ is of very little importance, because from its position ἅγιον would more naturally stand as a predicate, and the sentence would be quite as complete without the υἱὸς Θεοῦ as with it. On the other hand, it would be difficult to compress into so small a space so many words and expressions that are peculiarly characteristic of St. Luke. In addition to those which have just been noticed in connection with Basilides, there is the very remarkable

---

[1] *Strom.* ii. 20; see Westcott, *Canon*, p. 269; Volkmar, *Ursprung*, p. 152.

τὸ γεννώμενον, which alone would be almost enough to stamp the whole passage.

We are still however pursued by the same ambiguity as in the case of Basilides. It is not certain that the quotation is made from the master and not from his scholars. There is no reason, indeed, why it should be made from the latter rather than the former; the point must in any case be left open: but it cannot be referred to the master with so much certainty as to be directly producible under his name.

And yet, from whomsoever the quotation may have been made, if only it has been given rightly by Hippolytus, it is a strong proof of the antiquity of the Gospel. The words ἐκ σοῦ, it will be noticed, are enclosed in brackets in the text of St. Luke as given above. They are a corruption, though an early and well-supported corruption, of the original. The authorities in their favour are C (first hand), the good cursives 1 and 33, one form of the Vulgate, a, c, e, m of the Old Latin, the Peshito Syriac, the Armenian and Aethiopic versions, Irenaeus, Gregory Thaumaturgus, Tertullian, Cyprian, and Epiphanius. On the other hand, for the omission are A, B, C (third hand), D, ℵ, and the rest of the uncials and cursives, another form of the Vulgate, b, f, ff, g², l of the Old Latin, the Harclean and Jerusalem Syriac, the Memphitic, Gothic, and some MSS. of the Armenian versions, Origen, Dionysius and Peter of Alexandria, and Eusebius. A text critic will see at once on which side the balance lies. It is impossible that ἐκ σοῦ could have been the reading of the autograph copy, and it is not, I believe, admitted into the text by any recent editor. But if it was present in the copy made use of by the Gnostic writer, whoever he was, that copy must have been already far enough removed from the original to admit of this corruption; in other words, it has lineage enough to throw the original some way behind it. We shall come to more of such phenomena in the next chapter.

I said just now that the quotation could not with certainty be referred to Valentinus, but it is at least considerably earlier than the contemporaries of Hippolytus. It appears that there was a division in the Valentinian School upon the interpretation of this very passage. Ptolemaeus and Heracleon, representing the Western branch, took one side, while Axionicus and Bardesanes, representing the Eastern, took the other. Ptolemaeus and Heracleon were both, we know, contemporaries of Irenaeus, so that the quotation was used among the Valentinians at least in the time of Irenaeus, and very possibly earlier, for it usually takes a certain time for a subject to be brought into controversy. We must thus take the *terminus ad quem* for the quotation not later than 180 A.D. How much further back it goes we cannot say, but even then (if the Valentinian text is correctly preserved by Hippolytus) it presents features of corruption.

That the Valentinians made use of unwritten sources as well as of written, and that they possessed a Gospel of their own which they called the Gospel of Truth, does not affect the question of their use of the Synoptics. For these very same Valentinians undoubtedly did use the Synoptics, and not only them but also the fourth Gospel. It is immediately after he has spoken of the 'unwritten' tradition of the Valentinians that Irenaeus proceeds to give the numerous quotations from the Synoptics referred to above, while in the very same chapter, and within two sections of the place in which he alludes to the Gospel of Truth, he expressly says that these same Valentinians used the Gospel according to St. John freely (plenissime[1]). It should also be remembered that the alleged acceptance of the four Gospels by the Valentinians rests upon the statement of Irenaeus[2] as well as upon that of the less scrupulous and accurate Tertullian. There is no good reason for doubting it.

[1] *Adv. Haer.* iii. 11. 7, 9.   [2] *Ibid.* iii. 12. 12.

CHAPTER VIII.

MARCION[1].

OF the various chapters in the controversy with which we are dealing, that which relates to the heretic Marcion is one of the most interesting and important; important, because of the comparative fixity of the data on which the question turns; interesting, because of the peculiar nature of the problem to be dealt with.

We may cut down the preliminary disquisitions as to the life and doctrines of Marcion, which have, indeed, a certain bearing upon the point at issue, but will be found given with sufficient fulness in 'Supernatural Religion,' or in any of the authorities. As in most

---

[1] The corresponding chapter to this in 'Supernatural Religion' has been considerably altered, and indeed in part rewritten, in the sixth edition. The author very kindly sent me a copy of this after the appearance of my article in the *Fortnightly Review*, and I at once made use of it for the part of the work on which I was engaged; but I regret that my attention was not directed, as it should have been, to the changes in this chapter until it was too late to take quite sufficient account of them. The argument, however, I think I may say, is not materially affected. Several criticisms which I had been led to make in the *Fortnightly* I now find had been anticipated, and these have been cancelled or a note added in the present work; I have also appended to the volume a supplemental note of greater length on the reconstruction of Marcion's text, the only point on which I believe there is really very much room for doubt.

other points relating to this period, there is some confusion in the chronological data, but these range within a comparatively limited area. The most important evidence is that of Justin, who, writing as a contemporary (about 147 A.D.[1]), says that at that time Marcion had 'in every nation of men caused many to blaspheme[2];' and again speaks of the wide spread of his doctrines (ᾧ πολλοὶ πεισθέντες, κ.τ.λ.[3]). Taking these statements along with others in Irenaeus, Tertullian, and Epiphanius, modern critics seem to be agreed that Marcion settled in Rome and began to teach his peculiar doctrines about 139-142 A.D. This is the date assigned in 'Supernatural Religion[4].' Volkmar gives 138 A.D.[5] Tischendorf, on the apologetic side, would throw back the date as far as 130, but this depends upon the date assigned by him to Justin's 'Apology,' and conflicts too much with the other testimony.

It is also agreed that Marcion himself did actually use a certain Gospel that is attributed to him. The exact contents and character of that Gospel are not quite so clear, and its relation to the Synoptic Gospels, and especially to our third Synoptic, which bears the name of St. Luke, is the point that we have to determine.

The Church writers, Irenaeus, Tertullian, and Epiphanius, without exception, describe Marcion's Gospel as a mutilated or amputated version of St. Luke. They contrast his treatment of the evangelical tradition with that pursued by his fellow-Gnostic, Valentinus[6]. Valentinus sought to prove his tenets by wresting the inter-

---

[1] See above, p. 89.   [2] *Apol.* i. 26.   [3] *Ibid.* i. 58.
[4] ii. p. 80.   [5] *Der Ursprung*, p. 89.
[6] Cf. Tertullian, *De Praescript. Haeret.* c. 38.

pretation of the Apostolic writings; Marcion went more boldly to work, and, having first selected his Gospel, our third Synoptic, cut out the passages both in it and in ten Epistles of St. Paul, admitted by him to be genuine, which seemed to conflict with his own system. He is also said to have made additions, but these were in any case exceedingly slight.

The statement of the Church writers should hardly, perhaps, be put aside quite so summarily as is sometimes done. The life of Irenaeus overlapped that of Marcion considerably, and there seems to have been somewhat frequent communication between the Church at Lyons, where he was first presbyter and afterwards bishop, and that of Rome, where Marcion was settled; but Irenaeus[1], as well as Tertullian and Epiphanius, alludes to the mutilation of St. Luke's Gospel by Marcion as a notorious fact. Too much stress, however, must not be laid upon this, because the Catholic writers were certainly apt to assume that their own view was the only one tenable.

The modern controversy is more important, though it has to go back to the ancient for its data. The question in debate may be stated thus. Did Marcion, as the Church writers say, really mutilate our so-called St. Luke (the name is not of importance, but we may use it as standing for our third Synoptic in its present shape)? Or, is it not possible that the converse may be true, and that Marcion's Gospel was the original and ours an interpolated version? The importance of this may, indeed, be exaggerated, because Marcion's Gospel is at any rate evidence for the existence at his

---

[1] *Adv. Haer.* iv. 27. 2; 12. 12.

date in a collected form of so much of the third Gospel (rather more than two-thirds) as he received. Still the issue is not inconsiderable: for, upon the second hypothesis, if the editor of our present Gospel made use of that which was in the possession of Marcion, his date may be —though it does not follow that it certainly would be— thrown into the middle of the second century, or even beyond, if the other external evidence would permit; whereas, upon the first hypothesis, the Synoptic Gospel would be proved to be current as early as 140 A.D.; and there will be room for considerations which may tend to date it much earlier. There will still be the third possibility that Marcion's Gospel may be altogether independent of our present Synoptic, and that it may represent a parallel recension of the evangelical tradition. This would leave the date of the canonical Gospel undetermined.

It is a fact worth noting that the controversy, at least in its later and more important stages, had been fought, and, to all appearance, fought out, within the Tübingen school itself. Olshausen and Hahn, the two orthodox critics who were most prominently engaged it it, after a time retired and left the field entirely to the Tübingen writers.

The earlier critics who impugned the traditional view appear to have leaned rather to the theory that Marcion's Gospel and the canonical Luke are, more or less, independent offshoots from the common ground-stock of the evangelical narratives. Ritschl, and after him Baur and Schwegler, adopted more decidedly the view that the canonical Gospel was constructed out of Marcion's by interpolations directed against that heretic's teaching. The reaction came from a quarter whence it would not quite naturally have been expected—from one whose name we have already seen associated with some daring theories, Volkmar, Professor of Theology at Zürich. With him was allied the more sober-minded, laborious investigator, Hilgenfeld. Both these writers returned to the charge once and again. Volkmar's original paper was supplemented by an elaborate volume in 1852, and Hilgenfeld, in like manner, has reasserted his conclusions. Baur and Ritschl professed themselves convinced by the arguments brought forward, and retracted or greatly modified their views. So far as I am aware, Schwegler is the only writer whose opinion still stands as it was at first expressed; but for some years before his death, which occurred in 1857, he had left the theological field.

Without at all prejudging the question on this score, it is difficult not to feel a certain presumption in favour of a conclusion which has been reached after such elaborate argument, especially where, as here, there could be no suspicion of a merely apologetic tendency on either side. Are we, then, to think that our English critic has shown cause for reopening the discussion? There is room to doubt whether he would quite maintain as much as this himself. He has gone over the old ground, and reproduced the old arguments; but these arguments already lay before Hilgenfeld and Volkmar in their elaborate researches, and simply as a matter of scale the chapter in 'Supernatural Religion' can hardly profess to compete with these.

Supposing, for the moment, that the author has proved the points that he sets himself to prove, to what will this amount? He will have shown (*a*) that the patristic statement that Marcion mutilated St. Luke is not to be accepted at once without further question; (β) that we cannot depend with perfect accuracy upon the details of his Gospel, as reconstructed from the statements of Tertullian and Epiphanius; (γ) that it is difficult to explain the whole of Marcion's alleged omissions, on purely dogmatic grounds — assuming the consistency of his method.

With the exception of the first, I do not think these points are proved to any important extent; but, even if they were, it would still, I believe, be possible to show that Marcion's Gospel was based upon our third Synoptic by arguments which hardly cross or touch them at all.

But, before we proceed further, it is well that we should have some idea as to the contents of the Marcionitic Gospel. And here we are brought into collision with the second of the propositions just enunciated. Are we able to reconstruct that Gospel from the materials available to us with any tolerable or sufficient approach to accuracy? I believe no one who has gone into the question carefully would deny that we can. Here it is necessary to define and guard our statements, so that they may cover exactly as much ground as they ought and no more.

Our author quotes largely, especially from Volkmar, to show that the evidence of Tertullian and Epiphanius is not to be relied upon. When we refer to the chapter in which Volkmar deals with this subject [1]—a chapter which is an admirable specimen of the closeness and

---

[1] *Das Ev. Marcion's*, pp. 28–54. [Volkmar's view is stated less inadequately in the sixth edition of *S. R.*, but still not quite adequately. Perhaps it could hardly be otherwise where arguments that were originally adduced in favour of one conclusion are employed to support its opposite.]

thoroughness of German research—we do indeed find some such expressions, but to quote them alone would give an entirely erroneous impression of the conclusion to which the writer comes. He does not say that the statements of Tertullian and Epiphanius are untrustworthy, simply and absolutely, but only that they need to be applied with caution *on certain points*. Such a point is especially the silence of these writers as proving, or being supposed to prove, the absence of the corresponding passage in Marcion's Gospel. It is argued, very justly, that such an inference is sometimes precarious. Again, in quoting longer passages, Epiphanius is in the habit of abridging or putting an &c. (καὶ τὰ ἑξῆς—καὶ τὰ λοιπά), instead of quoting the whole. This does not give a complete guarantee for the intermediate portions, and leaves some uncertainty as to where the passage ends. Generally it is true that the object of the Fathers is not critical but dogmatic, to refute Marcion's system out of his own Gospel. But when all deductions have been made on these grounds, there are still ample materials for reconstructing that Gospel with such an amount of accuracy at least as can leave no doubt as to its character. The wonder is that we are able to do so, and that the statements of the Fathers should stand the test so well as they do. Epiphanius especially often shows the most painstaking care and minuteness of detail. He has reproduced the manuscript of Marcion's Gospel that he had before him, even to its clerical errors[1]. He and Tertullian are writing quite independently, and yet they confirm each other in a remarkable manner. 'If we compare the two witnesses,' says Volkmar, 'we find

---

[1] Οἶδα for εἶδας in Luke xiv. 20. Cf. Volkmar. p. 46.

the most satisfactory (sicher-stellendste) coincidence in their statements, entirely independent as they are, as well in regard to that which Marcion has in common with Luke, as in regard to very many of the points in which his text differed from the canonical. And this applies not only to simple omissions which Epiphanius expressly notes and Tertullian confirms by passing over what would otherwise have told against Marcion, but also to the minor variations of the text which Tertullian either happens to name or indicate by his translation, while they are confirmed by the direct statement of [the other] opponent who is equally bent on finding such differences[1].' Out of all the points on which they can be compared, there is a real divergence only in two. Of these, one Volkmar attributes to an oversight on the part of Epiphanius, and the other to a clerical omission in his manuscript[2]. When we consider the cumbrousness of ancient MSS., the absence of divisions in the text, and the consequent difficulty of making exact references, this must needs be taken for a remarkable result. And the very fact that we have two—or, including Irenaeus, even three—independent authorities, makes the text of Marcion's Gospel, so far as those authorities are available, or, in other words, for the greater part of it, instead of being uncertain among quite the most certain of all the achievements of modern criticism[3].

[1] *Das Ev. Marcion's*, p. 45.
[2] *Ibid.* pp. 46-48.
[3] 'We have, in fact, no guarantee of the accuracy or trustworthiness of any of their statements' (*S. R.* ii. p. 100). We have just the remarkable coincidence spoken of above. It does not prove that Tertullian did not faithfully reproduce the text of Marcion to show, which is the real drift of the argument on the preceding page (*S. R.* ii. p. 99), that he had not the

This is seen practically—to apply a simple test—in the large amount of agreement between critics of the most various schools as to the real contents of the Gospel. Our author indeed speaks much of the 'disagreement.' But by what standard does he judge? Or, has he ever estimated its extent? Putting aside merely verbal differences, the total number of whole verses affected will be represented in the following table :—

iv. 16-30: doubt as to exact extent of omissions affecting about half the verses.
  38, 39: omitted according to Hahn; retained according to Hilgenfeld and Volkmar.
vii. 29-35: omitted, Hahn and Ritschl; retained, Hilgenfeld and Volkmar.
x. 12-15: ditto ditto.
xiii. 6-10: omitted, Volkmar; retained, Hilgenfeld and Rettig.
xvii. 5-10: omitted, Ritschl; retained, Volkmar and Hilgenfeld.
  14-19: doubt as to exact omissions.
xix. 47, 48: omitted, Hilgenfeld and Volkmar; retained, Hahn and Anger.
xxii. 17, 18: doubtful.
  23-27: omitted, Ritschl; retained, Hilgenfeld and Volkmar.
  43, 44: ditto ditto.
xxiii. 39-42: ditto ditto.
  47-49: omitted, Hahn; retained, Ritschl, Hilgenfeld, Volkmar.
xxiv. 47-53: uncertain [1].

This would give, as a maximum estimate of variation, some 55 verses out of about 804, or, in other words, about seven per cent. But such an estimate would be in fact much too high, as there can be no doubt that the earlier researches of Hahn and Ritschl ought to be corrected by those of Hilgenfeld and Volkmar; and the difference between these two critics is quite

canonical Gospel before him; rather it removes the suspicion that he might have confused the text of Marcion's Gospel with the canonical.

[1] This table has been constructed from that of De Wette, *Einleitung*, pp. 123-132, compared with the works of Volkmar and Hilgenfeld.

insignificant. Taking the severest view that it is possible to take, no one will maintain that the differences between the critics are such as to affect the main issue, so that upon one hypothesis one theory would hold good, and upon another hypothesis another. It is a mere question of detail.

We may, then, reconstruct the Gospel used by Marcion with very considerable confidence that we have its real contents before us. In order to avoid any suspicion I will take the outline given in 'Supernatural Religion' (ii. p. 127), adding only the passage St. Luke vii. 29–35, which, according to the author's statement (a mistaken one, however [1]), is 'generally agreed' to have been wanting in Marcion's Gospel. In that Gospel, then, the following portions of our present St. Luke were omitted:—

Chaps. i. and ii. including the prologue, the Nativity, and the birth of John the Baptist.
Chap. iii (with the exception of ver. 1), containing the baptism of our Lord, the preaching of St. John, and the genealogy.
    iv. 1-13, 17-20, 24: the Temptation, the reading from Isaiah.
    vii. 29-35: the gluttonous man.
    xi. 29-32, 49-51: the sign of Jonas, and the blood of the prophets.
    xiii. 1-9, 29-35: the slain Galileans, the fig-tree, Herod, Jerusalem.
    xv. 11-32: the prodigal son.
    xvii. 5-10: the servant at meat.
    xviii. 31-34: announcement of the Passion.
    xix. 29-48: the Triumphal Entry, woes of Jerusalem, cleansing of the Temple.
    xx. 9-18, 37, 38: the wicked husbandmen; the God of Abraham.
    xxi. 1-4, 18, 21, 22: the widow's mite; 'a hair of your head;' flight of the Church.
    xxii. 16-18, 28-30, 35-38, 49-51: the fruit of the vine, 'eat at my table,' 'buy a sword,' the high-priest's servant.
    xxiv. 47-53: the last commission, the Ascension.

[1] S. R. ii. p. 110, n. 3. The statement is mistaken in regard to Volkmar and Hilgenfeld. Both these writers would make Marcion retain this passage. It happens rather oddly that this is one of the sections on which

Here we have another remarkable phenomenon. The Gospel stands to our Synoptic entirely in the relation of *defect*. We may say entirely, for the additions are so insignificant—some thirty words in all, and those for the most part supported by other authority—that for practical purposes they need not be reckoned. With the exception of these thirty words inserted, and some, also slight, alterations of phrase, Marcion's Gospel presents simply an *abridgment* of our St. Luke.

Does not this almost at once exclude the idea that they can be independent works? If it does not, then let us compare the two in detail. There is some disturbance and re-arrangement in the first chapter of Marcion's Gospel, though the substance is that of the third Synoptic; but from this point onwards the two move step by step together but for the omissions and a single transposition (iv. 27 to xvii. 18). Out of fifty-three sections peculiar to St. Luke—from iv. 16 onwards—all but eight were found also in Marcion's Gospel. They are found, too, in precisely the same order. Curious and intricate as is the mosaic work of the third Gospel, all the intricacies of its pattern are reproduced in the Gospel of Marcion. Where Luke makes an insertion in the groundstock of the narrative, there Marcion makes an insertion also; where Luke omits part of the narrative, Marcion does the same. Among the documents peculiar to St. Luke are some of a very marked and individual character, which seem to have come from some private source of information. Such, for instance, would be the document viii. 1–3, which introduces names so entirely unknown to the rest of

the philological evidence for St. Luke's authorship is least abundant (see below).

the evangelical tradition as Joanna and Susanna[1]. A trace of the same, or an allied document, appears in chap. xxiv, where we have again the name Joanna, and afterwards that of the obscure disciple Cleopas. Again, the mention of Martha and Mary is common only to St. Luke and the fourth Gospel. Zacchaeus is peculiar to St. Luke. Yet, not only does each of the sections relating to these personages re-appear in Marcion's Gospel, but it re-appears precisely at the same place. A marked peculiarity in St. Luke's Gospel is the 'great intercalation' of discourses, ix. 51 to xviii. 14, evidently inserted without regard to chronological order. Yet this peculiarity, too, is faithfully reproduced in the Gospel of Marcion with the same disregard of chronology —the only change being the omission of about forty-one verses from a total of three hundred and eighty. When Luke has the other two Synoptics against him, as in the insertions Matt. xiv. 3–12, Mark vi. 17–29, and again Matt. xx. 20–28, Mark x. 35–45, and Matt. xxi. 20–22, Mark xi. 20–26, Marcion has them against him too. Where the third Synoptist breaks off from his companions (Luke ix. 17, 18) and leaves a gap, Marcion leaves one too. It has been noticed as characteristic of St. Luke that, where he has recorded a similar incident before, he omits what might seem to be a repetition of it: this characteristic is exactly reflected in Marcion, and that in regard to the very same incidents. Then, wherever the patristic statements give us the opportunity of comparing Marcion's text with the Synoptic—and this they do very largely

---

[1] There is direct evidence for the presence in Marcion's Gospel of the passages relating to the personages here named, except Martha and Mary; see Tert. Adv. Marc. iv. 19, 37, 43.

indeed—the two are found to coincide with no greater variation than would be found between any two not directly related manuscripts of the same text. It would be easy to multiply these points, and to carry them to any degree of detail; if more precise and particular evidence is needed it shall be forthcoming, but in the meantime I think it may be asserted with confidence that two alternatives only are possible. Either Marcion's Gospel is an abridgment of our present St. Luke, or else our present St. Luke is an expansion by interpolation of Marcion's Gospel, or of a document coextensive with it. No third hypothesis is tenable.

It remains, then, to enquire which of these two Gospels had the priority—Marcion's or Luke's; which is to stand first, both in order of time and of authenticity. This, too, is a point that there are ample data for determining.

(1.) And, first, let us consider what presumption is raised by any other part of Marcion's procedure. Is it likely that he would have cut down a document previously existing? or, have we reason for thinking that he would be scrupulous in keeping such a document intact?

The author of 'Supernatural Religion' himself makes use of this very argument; but I cannot help suspecting that his application of it has slipped in through an oversight or misapprehension. When first I came across the argument as employed by him, I was struck by it at once as important if only it was sound. But, upon examination, not only does it vanish into thin air as an argument in support of the thesis he is maintaining, but there remains in its place a positive argument that tells directly and strongly against that thesis. A passage is quoted from Canon Westcott, in which it is stated that while Tertullian and Epiphanius accuse Marcion of altering the text of the books which he received, so far as his treatment of the Epistles is concerned this is not borne out by the facts, out of seven readings noticed by Epiphanius two only being unsupported by other authority. It is argued from this that Marcion 'equally preserved without alteration the text which he found in his manuscript of the Gospel.' 'We have no reason to believe the accusation of the Fathers in regard to the Gospel—which we cannot fully test— better founded than that in regard to the Epistles, which we can test, and find unfounded[1].' No doubt the premisses of this argument are true, and so also is the conclusion, strictly as it stands. It is true that the Fathers accuse Marcion of tampering with the text in various places, both in the Epistles and in the Gospels where the allegation can be tested, and where it is found that the supposed perversion is simply a difference of reading, proved to be such by its presence in other authorities[2]. But what is this to the point? It is not contended that Marcion altered to any considerable extent (though he did slightly even in the Epistles[3]) the text *which he retained*, but that he mutilated and cut out whole passages from that text. He can be proved to have done this in regard to the Epistles, and therefore it is fair to infer that he dealt in the same

---

[1] *S. R.* ii. 142 sq.

[2] This admission does not damage the credit of Tertullian and Epiphanius as witnesses; because what we want from them is a statement of the facts; the construction which they put upon the facts is a matter of no importance.

[3] The omission in 2 Cor. iv. 13 must be due to Marcion (*Epiph.* 321 c.); so probably an insertion in 1 Cor. ix. 8.

way with the Gospel. This is the amended form in which the argument ought to stand. It is certain that Marcion made a large excision before Rom. xi. 33, and another after Rom. viii. 11; he also cut out the 'mentiones Abrahae' from Gal. iii. 7, 14, 16–18[1]. I say nothing about his excision of the last two chapters of the Epistle to the Romans, because on that point a controversy might be raised. But the genuineness of these other passages is undisputed and indisputable. It cannot be argued here that our text of the Epistle has suffered from later interpolation, and therefore, I repeat, it is so much the more probable that Marcion took from the text of the Gospel than that a later editor added to it.

(2.) In examining the internal evidence from the nature and structure of Marcion's Gospel, it has hitherto been the custom to lay most stress upon its dogmatic character. The controversy in Germany has turned chiefly on this. The critics have set themselves to show that the variations in Marcion's Gospel either could or could not be explained as omissions dictated by the exigencies of his dogmatic system. This was a task which suited well the subtlety and inventiveness of the German mind, and it has been handled with all the usual minuteness and elaboration. The result has been that not only have Volkmar and Hilgenfeld proved their point to their own satisfaction, but they also convinced Ritschl and partially Baur; and generally we

---

[1] Tert. *Adv. Marc.* v. 16: 'Haec si Marcion de industriâ erasit,' &c. V. 14: 'Salio et hic amplissimum abruptum intercisae scripturae.' V. 3: 'Ostenditur quid supra haeretica industria eraserit, mentionem scilicet Abrahae,' &c. Cf. Bleek, *Einleitung*, p. 136; Hilgenfeld, *Evv. Justin's*, &c., p. 473.

may say that in Germany it seems to be agreed at the present time that the hypothesis of a mutilated Luke suits the dogmatic argument better than that of later Judaising interpolations.

I have no wish to disparage the results of these labours, which are carried out with the splendid thoroughness that one so much admires. Looking at the subject as impartially as I can, I am inclined to think that the case is made out in the main. The single instance of the perverted sense assigned to κατῆλθεν in iv. 31 must needs go a long way. Marcion evidently intends the word to be taken in a transcendental sense of the emanation and descent to earth of the Æon Christus[1]. It is impossible to think that this sense is more original than the plain historical use of the word by St. Luke, or to mistake the dogmatic motive in the heretical recension. There is also an evident reason for the omission of the first chapters which relate the human birth of Christ, which Marcion denied, and one somewhat less evident, though highly probable, for the omission of the account of the Baptist's ministry, John being regarded as the finisher of the Old Testament dispensation—the work of the Demiurge. This omission is not quite consistently carried out, as the passage vii. 24–28 is retained—probably because ver. 28 itself seemed to contain a sufficient qualification. The genealogy, as well as viii. 19, was naturally omitted for the same reason as the Nativity. The narrative of the Baptism Marcion could not admit, because it supplied the foundation for that very Ebionism to which

---

[1] 'Anno xv. Tiberii Christus Jesus de coelo manare dignatus est' (Tert. Adv. Marc. i. 19).

his own system was diametrically opposed. The Temptation, x. 21 ('Lord ... of earth'), xxii. 18 ('the fruit of the vine'), xxii. 30 ('eat and drink at my table'), and the Ascension, may have been omitted because they contained matter that seemed too anthropomorphic or derogatory to the Divine Nature. On the other hand, xi. 29-32 (Jonah and Solomon), xi. 49-51 (prophets and apostles), xiii. 1 sqq. (the fig-tree, as the Jewish people?), xiii. 31-35 (the prophet in Jerusalem), the prodigal son (perhaps?), the wicked husbandmen (more probably), the triumphal entry (as the fulfilment of prophecy), the announcement of the Passion (also as such), xxi. 21, 22 (the same), and the frequent allusions to the Old Testament Scriptures, seem to have been expunged as recognising or belonging to the kingdom of the Demiurge[1]. Again, the changes in xiii. 28, xvi. 17, xx. 35, are fully in accordance with Marcion's system[2]. The reading which Marcion had in xi. 22 is expressly stated to have been common to the Gnostic heretics generally. In some of these instances the dogmatic motive is gross and palpable, in most it seems to have been made out, but some (such as especially xiii. 1-9) are still doubtful, and the method of excision does not appear to have been carried out with complete consistency.

[1] I give mainly the explanations of Volkmar, who, it should be remembered, is the very reverse of an apologist, indicating the points where they seem least satisfactory.

[2] It is highly probable that many of the points mentioned by Tertullian and Epiphanius as 'adulterations' were simply various readings in Marcion's Codex; such would be v. 14, x. 25, xvii. 2, and xxiii. 2, which are directly supported by other authority: xi. 2 and xii. 28 would probably belong to this class. So perhaps the insertion of iv. 27 in the history of the Samaritan leper. The phenomenon of a transposition of verses from one part of a Gospel to another is not an infrequent one in early MSS.

This, indeed, was only to be expected. We are constantly reminded that Tertullian, a man, with all his faults, of enormous literary and general power, did not possess the critical faculty, and no more was that faculty likely to be found in Marcion. It is an anachronism to suppose that he would sit down to his work with that regularity of method and with that subtle appreciation of the affinities of dogma which characterise the modern critic. The Septuagint translators betray an evident desire to soften down the anthropomorphism of the Hebrew; but how easy would it be to convict them of inconsistency, and to show that they left standing expressions as strong as any that they changed! If we judge Marcion's procedure by a standard suited to the age in which he lived, our wonder will be, not that he has shown so little, but so much, consistency and insight.

I think, therefore, that the dogmatic argument, so far as it goes, tells distinctly in favour of the 'mutilation' hypothesis. But at the same time it should not be pressed too far. I should be tempted to say that the almost exclusive and certainly excessive use of arguments derived from the history of dogma was the prime fallacy which lies at the root of the Tübingen criticism. How can it be thought that an Englishman, or a German, trained under and surrounded by the circumstances of the nineteenth century, should be able to thread all the mazes in the mind of a Gnostic or an Ebionite in the second? It is difficult enough for us to lay down a law for the actions of our own immediate neighbours and friends; how much more difficult to 'cast the shell of habit,' and place ourselves at the point of view of a civilisation and world of thought wholly different from our own, so as not only to explain its apparent aberrations, but to be able to say, positively, 'this must have been so,' 'that must have been otherwise.' Yet such is the strange and extravagant supposition that we are assumed to make. No doubt the argument from dogma has its place in criticism; but, on the whole, the literary argument is safer, more removed from the influence of subjective impressions, more capable of being cast into a really scientific form.

(3.) I pass over other literary arguments which hardly admit of this form of expression—such as the improbability that the Preface or Prologue was not part of the original Gospel, but a later accretion; or, again, from Marcion's treatment of the Synoptic matter in the third Gospel, both points which might be otherwise worth dilating upon. I pass over these, and come at once, without further delay, to the one point which seems to me really to decide the character of Marcion's Gospel and its relation to the Synoptic. The argument to which I allude is that from style and diction. True the English mind is apt to receive literary arguments of that kind with suspicion, and very justly so long as they rest upon a mere vague subjective *ipse dixit;* but here the question can be reduced to one of definite figures and of weighing and measuring. Bruder's Concordance is a dismal-looking volume—a mere index of words, and nothing more. But it has an eloquence of its own for the scientific investigator. It is strange how clearly many points stand out when this test comes to be applied, which before had been vague and obscure. This is especially the case in regard to the Synoptic Gospels; for, in the first place, the vocabulary of the writers is very limited and similar phrases have a constant tendency to recur, and, in the second place, the critic has the immense advantage of being enabled to compare their treatment of the same common matter, so that he can readily ascertain what are the characteristic modifications introduced by each. Dr. Holtzmann, following Zeller and Lekebusch, has made a full and careful analysis of the style and vocabulary of St. Luke[1], but of course without reference to the particular omissions of Marcion. Let us then, with the help of Bruder, apply Holtzmann's results to these omissions, with a view to see whether there is evidence that they are by the same hand as the rest of the Gospel.

It would be beyond the proportions of the present enquiry to exhibit all the evidence in full. I shall, therefore, not transcribe the whole of my notes, but merely give a few samples of the sort of evidence producible, along with a brief summary of the general results.

Taking first certain points by which the style of the third Evangelist is distinguished from that of the first in their treatment of common matter, Dr. Holtzmann observes, that where Matthew has γραμματεύς, Luke has in six places the word νομικός, which is only found three times besides in the New Testament (once in St. Mark, and twice in the Epistle to Titus). Of the places where it is used by St. Luke, one is the omitted passage, vii. 30. In citations where Matthew has τὸ ῥηθέν (14 times; not at all in Luke), Luke prefers the perfect form τὸ εἰρημένον, so in ii. 24 (Acts twice); compare εἴρηται, iv. 21. Where Matthew has ἄρτι (7 times), Luke has always νῦν, never ἄρτι: νῦν is used in the following

---

[1] *Die Synoptischen Evangelien*, 1863, pp. 302 sqq.

passages, omitted by Marcion: i. 48, ii. 29, xix. 42, xxii. 18, 36. With Matthew the word ἔλεος is masculine, with Luke neuter, so five times in ch. i. and in x. 37, which was retained by Marcion.

Among the peculiarities of style noted by Dr. Holtzmann which recur in the omitted portions the following are perhaps some of the more striking. Peculiar use of τό covering a whole phrase, i. 62 (τὸ τί ἂν θέλοι καλεῖσθαι), xix. 48, xxii. 37, and five other places. Peculiar attraction of the relative with preceding case of πᾶς, iii. 19, xix. 37, and elsewhere. The formula ἔλεγε (εἶπε) δὲ παραβολήν (not found in the other Synoptics), xiii. 6, xx. 9, 19, and ten times besides. Τοῦ pleonastic with the infinitive, once in Mark, six times in Matthew, twenty-five times in Luke, of which three times in chap. i, twice in chap. ii, iv. 10, xxi. 22. Peculiar combinations with κατά, κατὰ τὸ ἔθος, εἰωθός, εἰθισμένον, i. 9, ii. 27, 42, and twice. Καθ' ἡμέραν, once in the other Gospels, thirteen times in Luke and Acts xix. 47; κατ' ἔτος, ii. 41; κατά with peculiar genitive of place, iv. 14 xxiii. 5)[1]. Protasis introduced by καὶ ὅτε, ii. 21, 22, 42, καὶ ὡς, ii. 39, xv. 25, xix. 41. Uses of ἐγένετο, especially with ἐν τῷ and infinitive, twice in Mark, in Luke twenty-two times, i. 8, ii. 6, iii. 21, xxiv. 51; ἐν τῷ with the infinitive, three times in St. Matthew, once in St. Mark, thirty-seven times in St. Luke, including i. 8, 21, ii. 6, 27, 43, iii. 21. Adverbs: ἑξῆς and καθεξῆς, ten times in the third Gospel and the Acts alone in the New Testament, i. 3; ἄχρι, twenty times in the third Gospel and Acts, only once in the other Gospels, i. 20, iv. 13; ἐξαίφνης,

---

[1] Where a reference is given thus in brackets, it is confirmatory, from the part of the Gospel retained by Marcion.

four times in the Gospel and Acts, once besides in the New Testament, ii. 13 ; παραχρῆμα, seventeen times in the Gospel and Acts, twice in the rest of the New Testament, i. 64 ; ἐν μέσῳ, thirteen times in the Gospel and Acts, five times in the other Synoptics, ii. 46, xxi. 21. Fondness for optative in indirect constructions, i. 29, 62, iii. 15, xv. 26. Peculiar combination of participles, ii. 36 (προβεβηκυῖα ζήσασα), iii. 23 (ἀρχόμενος ὤν), iv. 20 (πτύξας ἀποδούς), very frequent. Εἶναι, with participle for finite verb (forty-eight times in all), i. 7, 10, 20, 21, 22, ii. 8, 26, 33, 51, iii. 23, iv. 16 (ἦν τεθραμμένος, omitted by Marcion), iv. 17, 20, xv. 24, 32, xviii. 34, xix. 47, xx. 17, xxiv. 53. Construction of πρός with accusative after εἰπεῖν, λαλεῖν, ἀποκρίνεσθαι, frequent in Luke, rare in the rest of the New Testament, i. 13, 18, 19, 28, 34, 55, 61, 73, ii. 15, 18, 34, 48, 49, iii. 12, 13, 14, iv. 4, xiii. 7, 34, xv. 22, xviii. 31, xix. 33, 39, xx. 9, 14, 19. This is thrown into marked relief by the contrast with the other Synoptics; the only two places where Matthew appears to have the construction are both ambiguous, iii. 15 (doubtful reading, probably αὐτῷ), and xxvii. 14 (ἀπεκρίθη αὐτῷ πρὸς οὐδὲ ἓν ῥῆμα). No other evangelist speaks so much of Πνεῦμα ἅγιον, i. 15, 35, 41, 67, ii. 25, 66, iii. 16, 22, iv. 1 (found also in Marcion's reading of xi. 2). Peculiar use of pronouns: Luke has the combination καὶ αὐτός twenty-eight times, Matthew only twice (one false reading), Mark four or perhaps five times, i. 17, 22, ii. 28, iii. 23, xv. 14; καὶ αὐτοί Mark has not at all, Matthew twice, Luke thirteen times, including ii. 50, xviii. 34, xxiv. 52.

We now come to the test supplied by the vocabulary. The following are some of the words peculiar to St. Luke, or found in his writings with marked and characteristic frequency, which occur in those parts of our present Gospel that were wanting in Marcion's recension: ἀνέστην, ἀναστάς occur three times in St. Matthew, twice in St. John, four times in the writings of St. Paul, twenty-six times in the third Gospel and thirty-five times in the Acts, and are found in i. 39, xv. 18, 20; ἀντιλέγειν appears in ii. 34. five times in the rest of the Gospel and the Acts, and only four times together in the rest of the New Testament; ἅπας occurs twenty times in the Gospel, sixteen times in the Acts, only ten times in the rest of the New Testament, but in ii. 39, iii. 16, 21, iv. 6, xv. 13, xix. 37, 48, xxi. 4 (bis); three of these are, however, doubtful readings. ἄφεσις τῶν ἁμαρτιῶν, ten times in the Gospel and Acts, seven times in the rest of the New Testament, i. 77, iii. 3. δεῖ, Dr. Holtzmann says, 'is found more often in St. Luke than in all the other writers of the New Testament put together.' This does not appear to be strictly true; it is, however, found nineteen times in the Gospel and twenty-five times in the Acts to twenty-four times in the three other Gospels; it occurs in ii. 49, xiii. 33, xv. 32, xxii. 37. δέχεσθαι, twenty-four times in the Gospel and Acts, twenty-six times in the rest of the New Testament, six times in St. Matthew, three in St. Mark, ii. 28, xxii. 17. διατάσσειν, nine times in the Gospel and Acts, seven times in the rest of the New Testament (Matthew once), iii. 13, xvii. 9, 10. διέρχεσθαι occurs thirty-two times in the Gospel and Acts, twice in each of the other Synoptics, and eight times in the rest of the New Testament, and is found in ii. 15, 35. διότι, i. 13, ii. 7 (xxi. 28, and Acts, not besides in the Gospels). ἐάν, xxii. 51 (once besides in the Gospel, eight times in the Acts, and three times in the rest of the New Testament). ἔθος, i. 9, ii. 42, eight times besides in St. Luke's writings and only twice in the rest of the New Testament. ἐναντίον, five times in St. Luke's writings, once besides, i. 8. ἐνώπιον, correcting the readings, twenty times in the Gospel, fourteen times in the Acts, not at all in the other Synoptists, once in St. John, four times in chap. i, iv. 7, xv. 18, 21 (this will be noticed as a very remarkable instance of the extent to which the diction of the third Evangelist impressed itself upon his writings). ἐπιβιβάζειν, xix. 35 (and twice, only by St. Luke). ἐπιπίπτειν, i. 12, xv. 20 (eight times in the Acts and three times in the rest of the New Testament). αἱ ἔρημοι, only in St. Luke, i. 80, and twice. ἔτος (fifteen times in the Gospel, eleven times in the Acts, three times in the other Synoptics and three times in St. John), four times in chap. ii, iii. 1, 23, xiii. 7, 8, xv. 29. θαυμάζειν ἐπί τινι, Gospel and Acts five times (only besides in Mark xii. 17), ii. 33. ἱκανός in the sense of 'much,' 'many,' seven times in the Gospel, eighteen times in the Acts, and only three times besides in the New Testament, iii. 16, xx. 9 (compare xxii. 38). καθότι (like καθεξῆς above), is only found in St. Luke's writings, i. 7, and five times in the rest of the Gospel and the Acts. λατρεύειν, 'in Luke much oftener than in other parts of the New Testament,' i. 74, ii. 37, iv. 8, and five times in the Acts. λιμός, six times in the Gospel and Acts, six times in the rest of the New Testament, xv. 14, 17. μήν (month), i. 24, 26, 36, 56 (iv. 25), alone in the Gospels, in the Acts five times. οἶκος for 'family,' i. 27, 33, 69, ii. 4, and three times besides in the Gospel, nine times in the Acts. πλῆθος (especially in the form πᾶν τὸ πλῆθος), twenty-five times in St. Luke's writings, seven times in the rest of the New Testament, i. 19, ii. 13, xix. 37. πλῆσαι, πλησθῆναι, twenty-two times in St. Luke's writings, only three times besides in the New Testament, i. 15, 23, 41, 57, 67, ii. 6, 21, 22, xxi. 22. προσδοκᾶν, eleven times in the Gospel and Acts, five times in the rest of the New Testament (Matthew twice and 2 Peter), i. 21, iii. 15. σκάπτειν, only in Luke three times, xiii. 8. σπεύδειν, except in 2 Peter iii. 12, only in St. Luke's writings, ii. 16. συλλαμβάνειν, ten times in the Gospel and Acts, five times in the rest of the New Testament, i. 24, 31, 36, ii. 21. συμβάλλειν, only in Lucan writings, six times, ii. 19. συνέχειν, nine times in the Gospel and Acts, three times besides in the New Testament, xix. 43. σωτηρία, in chap. i. three times, in the rest of the Gospel and Acts seven times, not in the other Synoptic Gospels. ὑποστρέφειν, twenty-two times in the Gospel, eleven times in the Acts, and only five times in the rest of the New Testament (three of which are doubtful readings), i. 56, ii. 20, 39, 43, 45, iv. 1, (14), xxiv. 52. ὕψιστος occurs nine times in the Gospel and Acts, four times in the rest of the New Testament, i. 32, 35, 76, ii. 14, xix. 38. ὕψος is also found in i. 78, xxiv. 49. χάρις is found, among the Synoptics, only in St. Luke, eight times in the Gospel, seventeen times in the Acts, i. 30, ii. 40, 52, xvii. 9. ὡσεί occurs nineteen times in the Gospel and Acts (four doubtful readings, of which two are probably false), seventeen times in the rest of the New Testament (ten doubtful readings, of which in the Synoptic Gospels three are probably false), i. 56, iii. 23.

It should be remembered that the above are only samples from the whole body of evidence, which would take up a much larger space if exhibited in full. The total result may be summarised thus. Accepting the scheme of Marcion's Gospel given some pages back. which is substantially that of 'Supernatural Religion,' Marcion will have omitted a total of 309 verses. In those verses there are found 111 distinct peculiarities of St. Luke's style, numbering in all 185 separate instances; there are also found 138 words peculiar to or specially characteristic of the third Evangelist, with 224 instances. In other words, the verified peculiarities of St. Luke's style and diction (and how marked many of these are will have been seen from the examples above) are found in the portions of the Gospel omitted by Marcion in a proportion averaging considerably more than one to each verse [1]! Coming to detail, we find that in the principal omission—that of the first two chapters, containing 132 verses—there are 47 distinct peculiarities of style, with 105 instances; and 82 characteristic words, with 144 instances. In the 23 verses of chap. iii. omitted by Marcion (for the genealogy need not be reckoned), the instances are 18 and 14, making a total of 32. In 18 verses omitted from chap. iv. the instances are 13 and 8 = 21. In another longer passage—the parable of the prodigal son—the instances are 8 of the first class and 20 of the second. In 20

[1] An analysis of the words which are only found in St. Luke, or very rarely found elsewhere, gives the following results.—The number of words found only in the portion of the Gospel retained by Marcion and in the Acts is 231; that of words found in these retained portions and not besides in the Gospels or the two other Synoptics is 58; and both these classes together for the portions omitted in Marcion's Gospel reach a total of 62, which is decidedly under the proportion that might have been expected. The list is diminished by a number of words which are found only in the omitted and retained portions, furnishing evidence, as above, that both proceed from the same hand.

verses omitted from chap. xix. the instances are 11 and 6; and in 11 verses omitted from chap. xx, 9 and 8. Of all the isolated fragments that Marcion had ejected from his Gospel, there are only four—iv. 24, xi. 49–51, xx. 37, 38, xxii. 28–30, nine verses in all—in which no peculiarities have been noticed. And yet even here the traces of authorship are not wanting. It happens strangely enough that in a list of parallel passages given by Dr. Holtzmann to illustrate the affinities of thought between St. Luke and St. Paul, two of these very passages—xi. 49 and xx. 38—occur. I had intended to pursue the investigation through these resemblances, but it seems superfluous to carry it further.

It is difficult to see what appeal can be made against evidence such as this. A certain allowance should indeed be made for possible errors of computation, and some of the points may have been wrongly entered, though care has been taken to put down nothing that was not verified by its preponderating presence in the Lucan writings, and especially by its presence in that portion of the Gospel which Marcion undoubtedly received. But as a rule the method applies itself mechanically, and when every deduction has been made, there will still remain a mass of evidence that it does not seem too much to describe as overwhelming.

(4.) We may assume, then, that there is definite proof that the Gospel used by Marcion presupposes our present St. Luke, in its complete form, as it has been handed down to us. But when once this assumption has been made, another set of considerations comes in, which also carry with them an important inference. If Marcion's Gospel was an extract from a manuscript containing our present St. Luke, then not only is it certain that that

Gospel was already in existence, but there is further evidence to show that it must have been in existence for some time. The argument in this case is drawn from another branch of Biblical science to which we have already had occasion to appeal—text-criticism. Marcion's Gospel, it is known, presents certain readings which differ both from the received and other texts. Some of these are thought by Volkmar and Hilgenfeld to be more original and to have a better right to stand in the text than those which are at present found there. These critics, however, base their opinion for the most part on internal grounds, and the readings defended by them are not as a rule those which are supported by other manuscript authority. It is to this second class rather that I refer as bearing upon the age of the canonical Gospel. The most important various readings of the existence of which we have proof in Marcion's Gospel are as follows [1]:—

> v. 14. The received (and best) text is εἰς μαρτύριον αὐτοῖς. Marcion, according to the express statement of Epiphanius (312 B), read ἵνα ᾖ μαρτύριον τοῦτο ὑμῖν, which is confirmed by Tertullian, who gives (*Marc.* iv. 8) 'Ut sit vobis in testimonium.' The same or a similar reading is found in D, ἵνα εἰς μαρτύριον ᾖ ὑμῖν τοῦτο, 'ut sit in testimonium vobis hoc,' d; 'ut sit in testimonium (—monia, ff) hoc vobis,' a (Codex Vercellensis), b (Codex Veronensis), c (Codex Colbertinus), ff (Codex Corbeiensis), l (Codex Rhedigerianus), of the Old Latin [2].
>
> v. 39 was *probably* omitted by Marcion (this is inferred from the silence

---

[1] This list has been made from the valuable work of Rönsch, *Das Neue Testament Tertullian's*, 1871, and the critical editions, compared with the text of Marcion's Gospel as given by Hilgenfeld and Volkmar.

[2] It might be thought that Tertullian was giving his own text and not that of Marcion's Gospel, but this supposition is excluded both by the confirmation which he receives from Epiphanius, and also by the fact, which is generally admitted (see *S. R.* ii. p. 100), that he had not the canonical Luke, but only Marcion's Gospel before him.

of Tertullian by Hilgenfeld, p. 403, and Rönsch, p. 634). The verse is also omitted in D, a, b, c, d, e, ff.

x. 22. Marcion's reading of this verse corresponded with that of other Gnostics, but has no extant manuscript authority. We have touched upon it elsewhere.

x. 25. ζωὴν αἰώνιον, Marcion omitted αἰώνιον (Tert. *Adv. Marc.* iv. 25); so also the Old Latin Codex g² (San Germanensis).

xi. 2. Marcion read ἐλθέτω τὸ ἅγιον πνεῦμά σου ἐφ' ἡμᾶς (or an equivalent; see Rönsch, p. 640) either for the clause ἁγιασθήτω τὸ ὄνομά σου or for γενηθήτω τὸ θέλημά σου, which is omitted in B, L, 1, Vulg., ff, Syr. Crt. There is a curious stray ἐφ' ἡμᾶς in D which may conceivably be a trace of Marcion's reading.

xii. 14. Marcion (and probably Tertullian) read κριτήν (or δικαστήν) only for κριτὴν ἢ μεριστήν; so D, a ('ut videtur,' Tregelles), c, Syr. Crt.

xii. 38. Marcion had τῇ ἑσπερινῇ φυλακῇ for ἐν τῇ δευτέρᾳ φυλακῇ καὶ ἐν τῇ τρίτῃ φυλακῇ. So b: D, c, e, ff, i, Iren. 334, Syr. Crt., combine the two readings in various ways.

xvi. 12. Marcion read ἐμόν for ὑμέτερον. So e (Palatinus), i (Vindobonensis), l (Rhedigerianus). ἡμέτερον B, L, Origen.

xvii. 2. Marcion inserted the words οὐκ ἐγεννήθη ἤ (Tert. iv. 35), 'ne nasceretur aut,' a, b, c, ff, i, l.

xviii. 19. Here again Marcion had a variation which is unsupported by manuscript authority, but has to some extent a parallel in the Clementine Homilies, Justin, &c.

xxi. 18 was omitted by Marcion (Epiph. 316 B), and is also omitted in the Curetonian Syriac.

xxi. 27. Tertullian (iv. 39) gives the reading of Marcion as 'cum plurima virtute' = μετὰ δυνάμεως πολλῆς [καὶ δόξης], for μετὰ δυν. κ. δοξ. πολλῆς; so D (ἐν δυν. πολ.), and approximately Vulg., a, c, e, f, ff, Syr. Crt., Syr. Pst.

xxiii. 2. Marcion read διαστρέφοντα τὸ ἔθνος καὶ καταλύοντα τὸν νόμον καὶ τοὺς προφήτας καὶ κελεύοντα φόρους μὴ δοῦναι καὶ ἀναστρέφοντα τὰς γυναῖκας καὶ τὰ τέκνα (Epiph., 316 D), where καταλύοντα τὸν νόμον καὶ τοὺς προφήτας and ἀναστρέφοντα τὰς γυναῖκας καὶ τὰ τέκνα are additions to the text, and κελεύοντα φόρους μὴ δοῦναι is a variation. Of the two additions the first finds support in b, (c), e, (ff), i, l; the second is inserted, with some variation, by c and e in verse 5.

We may thus tabulate the relation of Marcion to these various authorities. The brackets indicate that the agreement is only approximate. Marcion agrees with—

D, d, v. 14, v. 39; xii. 14, (xii. 28), (xxi. 27).
a (Verc.), v. 14, v. 39, xii. 14 (apparently), xvii. 2, (xxi. 27).
b (Ver.), v. 14, v. 39, xii. 38, xvii. 2, (xxiii. 2).
c (Colb.), v. 14, v. 39, xii. 14, (xii. 38), xvii. 2, (xxi. 27), (xxiii. 2), (xxiii. 2).
e (Pal.), v. 39, (xii. 38), xvi. 12, (xxi. 27), xxiii. 2, (xxiii. 2).
ff (Corb.), v. 14, v. 39, (xii. 38), xvii. 2, (xxi. 27), (xxiii. 2).
g² (Germ.), x. 25.
i (Vind.), (xii. 38), xvi. 12, xvii. 2, xxiii. 2.
l (Rhed.), v. 14, xvi. 12, xvii. 2, xiii. 2.
Syr. Crt., xii. 14, (xii. 38), xxi. 18, (xxi. 27).

It is worth noticing that xxii. 19 b, 20 (which is omitted in D, a, b, e, ff, i, l) appears to have been found in Marcion's Gospel, as in the Vulgate, c, and f (see Rönsch, p. 239). ἀπὸ τοῦ μνημείου in xxiv. 9 is also found (Rönsch, p. 246), though omitted by D, a, b, c, e, ff, l. There is no evidence to show whether the additions in ix. 55, xxiii. 34, and xxii. 43, 44 were present in Marcion's Gospel or not.

It will be observed that the readings given above have all what is called a 'Western' character. The Curetonian Syriac is well known to have Western affinities[1]. Codd. a, b, c, and the fragment of i which extends from Luke x. 6 to xxiii. 10, represent the most primitive type of the Old Latin version; e, ff, and l give a more mixed text. As we should expect, the revised Latin text of Cod. f has no representation in Marcion's Gospel[2].

These textual phenomena are highly interesting, but at the same time an exact analysis of them is difficult.

---

[1] See Crowfoot, *Observations on the Collation in Greek of Cureton's Syriac Fragments of the Gospels,* 1872, p. 5; Scrivener, *Introduction to the Criticism of the New Testament,* 2nd edition, 1874, p. 452.

[2] See Scrivener, *Introduction,* p. 307 sq.; and Dr. Westcott's article on the 'Vulgate' in Smith's Dictionary. It should be noticed that Dr. Westcott's literation differs from that of Dr. Scrivener and Tregelles, which has been adopted here.

No simple hypothesis will account for them. There can be no doubt that Marcion's readings are, in the technical sense, false: they are a deviation from the type of the pure and unadulterated text. At a certain point, evidently of the remotest antiquity, in the history of transcription, there was a branching off which gave rise to those varieties of reading which, though they are not confined to Western manuscripts, still, from their preponderance in these, are called by the general name of 'Western.' But when we come to consider the relations among those Western documents themselves, no regular descent or filiation seems traceable. Certain broad lines indeed we can mark off as between the earlier and later forms of the Old Latin, though even here the outline is in places confused; but at what point are we to insert that most remarkable document of antiquity, the Curetonian Syriac? For instance, there are cases (e.g. xvii. 2, xxiii. 2) where Marcion and the Old Latin are opposed to the Old Syriac, where the latter has undoubtedly preserved the correct reading. To judge from these alone, we should naturally conclude that the Syriac was simply an older and purer type than Marcion's Gospel and the Latin. But then again, on the other hand, there are cases (such as the omission of xxi. 18) where Marcion and the Syriac are combined, and the Old Latin adheres to the truer type. This will tend to show that, even at that early period, there must have been some comparison and correction—a *con*vergence as well as a *di*vergence—of manuscripts, and not always a mere reproduction of the particular copy which the scribe had before him; at the same time it will also show that Marcion's Gospel, so far from being an original document, has behind it a deep historical background, and stands at the head of a series of copies which have already passed through a number of hands and been exposed to a proportionate amount of corruption. Our author is inclined to lay stress upon the 'slow multiplication and dissemination of MSS.' Perhaps he may somewhat exaggerate this, as antiquarians give us a surprising account of the ease and rapidity with which books were produced by the aid of slave-labour[1]. But even at Rome the publishing trade upon this large scale was a novelty dating back no further than to Atticus, the friend of Cicero, and we should naturally expect that among the Christians—a poor and widely scattered body, whose tenets would cut them off from the use of such public machinery—the multiplication of MSS. would be slower and more attended with difficulty. But the slower it was the more certainly do such phenomena as these of Marcion's text throw back the origin of the prototype from which that text was derived. In the year 140 A.D. Marcion possesses a Gospel which is already in an advanced stage of transcription—which has not only undergone those changes which in some regions the text underwent before it was translated into Latin, but has undergone other changes besides. Some of its peculiarities are not those of the earliest form of the Latin version, but of that version in what may be called its second stage (e.g. xvi. 12). It has also affinities to another version kindred to the Latin and occupying a similar place to the Old Latin among the Churches of Syria. These circumstances together point to an antiquity fully as great as any that an orthodox critic would claim.

[1] Cf. Friedländer, *Sittengeschichte Roms*, iii. p. 315.

It should not be thought that because such indications are indirect they are therefore any the less certain. There is perhaps hardly a single uncanonical Christian document that is admittedly and indubitably older than Marcion; so that direct evidence there is naturally none. But neither is there any direct evidence for the antiquity of man or of the earth. The geologist judges by the fossils which he finds embedded in the strata as relics of an extinct age; so here, in the Gospel of Marcion, do we find relics which to the initiated eye carry with them their own story.

Nor, on the other hand, can it rightly be argued that because the history of these remains is not wholly to be recovered, therefore no inference from them is possible. In the earlier stages of a science like palaeontology it might have been argued in just the same way that the difficulties and confusion in the classification invalidated the science along with its one main inference altogether. Yet we can see that such an argument would have been mistaken. There will probably be some points in every science which will never be cleared up to the end of time. The affirmation of the antiquity of Marcion's Gospel rests upon the simple axiom that every event must have a cause, and that in order to produce complicated phenomena the interaction of complicated causes is necessary. Such an assumption involves time, and I think it is a safe proposition to assert that, in order to bring the text of Marcion's Gospel into the state in which we find it, there must have been a long previous history, and the manuscripts through which it was conveyed must have parted far from the parent stem.

The only way in which the inference drawn from the

text of Marcion's Gospel can be really met would be by showing that the text of the Latin and Syriac translations is older and more original than that which is universally adopted by text-critics. I should hardly suppose that the author of 'Supernatural Religion' will be prepared to maintain this. If he does, the subject can then be argued. In the meantime, these two arguments, the literary and the textual—for the others are but subsidiary—must, I think, be held to prove the high antiquity of our present Gospel.

CHAPTER IX.

TATIAN—DIONYSIUS OF CORINTH.

TATIAN was a teacher of rhetoric, an Assyrian by birth, who was converted to Christianity by Justin Martyr, but after his death fell into heresy, leaning towards the Valentinian Gnosticism, and combining with this an extreme asceticism.

The death of Justin is clearly the pivot on which his date will hinge. If we are to accept the conclusions of Mr. Hort this will have occurred in the year 148 A.D.; according to Volkmar it would fall not before 155 A.D., and in the ordinary view as late as 163-165 A.D.[1] The beginning of Tatian's literary activity will follow accordingly.

Tatian's first work of importance, an 'Address to Greeks,' which is still extant, was written soon after the death of Justin. It contains no references to the Synoptic Gospels upon which stress can be laid.

An allusion to Matth. vi. 19 in the Stromateis of Clement[2] has been attributed to Tatian, but I hardly know for what reason. It is introduced simply by

---

[1] See p. 89, above.
[2] *Strom.* iii. 12; compare *S. R.* ii. p. 151.

τις (βιάζεταί τις λέγων), but there were other Encratites besides Tatian, and the very fact that he has been mentioned by name twice before in the chapter makes it the less likely that he should be introduced so vaguely.

The chief interest however in regard to Tatian centres in his so-called 'Diatessaron,' which is usually supposed to have been a harmony of the four Gospels.

Eusebius mentions this in the following terms: 'Tatian however, their former leader, put together, I know not how, a sort of patchwork or combination of the Gospels and called it the "Diatessaron," which is still current with some[1].'

I am rather surprised to see that Credner, who is followed by the author of 'Supernatural Religion,' argues from this that Eusebius had not seen the work in question[2]. This inference is not by any means conveyed by the Greek. Οὐκ οἶδ' ὅπως (thus introduced) is an idiomatic phrase referring to the principle on which the harmony was constructed, and might well be paraphrased 'a curious sort of patchwork or dovetailing,' 'a not very intelligible dovetailing,' &c. Standing in the position it does, the phrase can hardly mean anything else. Besides it is not likely that Eusebius, an eager collector and reader of books, with the run of Pamphilus' library, should not have been acquainted with a work that he says himself was current in more quarters than one. Eusebius, it will be observed, is quite explicit in his statement. He says that the Diatessaron was a

---

[1] Ὁ μέντοι γε πρότερος αὐτῶν ἀρχηγὸς ὁ Τατιανὸς συνάφειάν τινα καὶ συναγωγὴν οὐκ οἶδ' ὅπως τῶν εὐαγγελίων συνθεὶς τὸ διὰ τεσσάρων τοῦτο προσωνόμασεν, ὃ καὶ παρά τισιν εἰσέτι νῦν φέρεται. H. E. iv. 29.

[2] *Beiträge*, i. p. 441.

harmony of the Gospels, i. e. (in his sense) of our present Gospels, and that Tatian gave the name of Diatessaron to his work himself. We do not know upon what these statements rest, but there ought to be some valid reason before we dismiss them entirely.

Epiphanius writes that 'Tatian is said to have composed the Diatessaron Gospel which some call the "Gospel according to the Hebrews[1]."' And Theodoret tells us that 'Tatian also composed the Gospel which is called the Diatessaron, cutting out the genealogies and all that shows the Lord to have been born of the seed of David according to the flesh.' 'This,' he adds, 'was used not only by his own party, but also by those who followed the teaching of the Apostles, as they had not perceived the mischievous design of the composition, but in their simplicity made use of the book on account of its conciseness.' Theodoret found more than two hundred copies in the churches of his diocese (Cyrrhus in Syria), which he removed and replaced with the works of the four Evangelists[2].

Victor of Capua in the sixth century speaks of Tatian's work as a 'Diapente' rather than a 'Diatessaron[3].' If we are to believe the Syrian writer Bar-Salibi in the twelfth century, Ephrem Syrus commented on Tatian's

---

[1] *Haer.* 391 D (xlvi. 1).

[2] Οὗτος καὶ τὸ διὰ τεσσάρων καλούμενον συντέθεικεν εὐαγγέλιον, τάς τε γενεαλογίας περικύψας, καὶ τὰ ἄλλα, ὅσα ἐκ σπέρματος Δαβὶδ κατὰ σάρκα γεγεννημένον τὸν Κύριον δείκνυσιν. Ἐχρήσαντο δὲ τούτῳ οὐ μόνον οἱ τῆς ἐκείνου συμμορίας, ἀλλὰ καὶ οἱ τοῖς ἀποστολικοῖς ἑπόμενοι δόγμασι, τὴν τῆς συνθήκης κακουργίαν οὐκ ἐγνωκότες, ἀλλ' ἁπλούστερον ὡς συντόμῳ τῷ βιβλίῳ χρησάμενοι. Εὗρον δὲ κἀγὼ πλείους ἢ διακοσίας βίβλους τοιαύτας ἐν ταῖς παρ' ἡμῖν ἐκκλησίαις τετιμημένας, καὶ πάσας συναγαγὼν ἀπεθέμην, καὶ τὰ τῶν τεττόρων εὐαγγελιστῶν ἀντεισήγαγον εὐαγγέλια (*Haeret. Fab.* i. 20, quoted by Credner, *Beiträge*, i. p. 442).

[3] See *S. R.* ii. p. 15.

Diatessaron, and it began with the opening words of St. John. This statement however is referred by Gregory Bar-Hebraeus not to the Harmony of Tatian, but to one by Ammonius made in the third century[1].

Here there is clearly a good deal of confusion.'

But now we come to the question, was Tatian's work really a Harmony of our four Gospels? The strongest presumption that it was is derived from Irenaeus. Irenaeus, it is well known, speaks of the four Gospels with absolute decision, as if it were a law of nature that their number must be four, neither more nor less[2], and his four Gospels were certainly the same as our own. But Tatian wrote within a comparatively short interval of Irenaeus. It is sufficiently clear that Irenaeus held his opinion at the very time that Tatian wrote, though it was not published until later. Here then we have a coincidence which makes it difficult to think that Tatian's four Gospels were different from ours.

The theory that finds favour with Credner[3] and his followers, including the author of 'Supernatural Religion,' is that Tatian's Gospel was the same as that used by Justin. I am myself not inclined to think this theory improbable; it would have been still less so, if Tatian had been the master and Justin the pupil[4]. We have seen that the phenomena of Justin's evangelical quotations are as well met by the hypothesis that he made use of a Harmony as by any other. But that Harmony,

---

[1] *S. R.* ii. p. 162; compare Credner, *Beiträge*, i. p. 446 sqq.
[2] *Adv. Haer.* iii. 11. 8.
[3] *Beit.* i. p. 443.
[4] May not Tatian have given his name to a collection of materials begun, used, and left in a more or less advanced stage of compilation, by Justin? However, we can really do little more than note the resemblance: any theory we may form must be purely conjectural.

as we have also seen, included at least our three Synoptics. The evidence (which we shall consider presently) for the use of the fourth Gospel by Tatian is so strong as to make it improbable that that work was not included in the Diatessaron. The fifth work, alluded to by Victor of Capua, may possibly have been the Gospel according to the Hebrews.

2.

Just as the interest of Tatian turns upon the interpretation to be put upon a single term 'Diatessaron,' so the interest of Dionysius of Corinth depends upon what we are to understand by his phrase 'the Scriptures of the Lord.'

In a fragment, preserved by Eusebius, of an epistle addressed to Soter Bishop of Rome (168–176 A.D.) and the Roman Church, Dionysius complains that his letters had been tampered with. 'As brethren pressed me to write letters I wrote them. And these the apostles of the devil have filled with tares, taking away some things and adding others, for whom the woe is prepared. It is not wonderful, then, if some have ventured to tamper with the Scriptures of the Lord when they have laid their plots against writings that have no such claims as they[1].' It must needs be a straining of language to make the Scriptures here refer, as the author of 'Supernatural Religion' seems to do, to the Old Testament. It

---

[1] Ἐπιστολὰς γὰρ ἀδελφῶν ἀξιωσάντων με γράψαι ἔγραψα. Καὶ ταύτας οἱ τοῦ διαβόλου ἀπόστολοι ζιζανίων γεγέμικαν, ἃ μὲν ἐξαιροῦντες, ἃ δὲ προστιθέντες. Οἷς τὸ οὐαὶ κεῖται. Οὐ θαυμαστὸν ἄρα, εἰ καὶ τῶν κυριακῶν ῥᾳδιουργῆσαί τινες ἐπιβέβληνται γραφῶν, ὁπότε ταῖς οὐ τοιαύταις ἐπιβεβουλεύκασι. H. E. iv. 23 (Routh, Rel. Sac. i. p. 181).

is true that Justin lays great stress upon type and prophecy as pointing to Christ, but there is a considerable step between this and calling the whole of the Old Testament 'Scriptures of the Lord.' On the other hand, we can hardly think that Dionysius refers to a complete collection of writings like the New Testament. It seems most natural to suppose that he is speaking of Gospels—possibly not the canonical alone, and yet, with Irenaeus in our mind's eye, we shall say probably to them. There is the further reason for this application of the words that Dionysius is known to have written against Marcion—'he defended the canon of the truth[1],' Eusebius says—and such 'tampering' as he describes was precisely what Marcion had been guilty of.

The reader will judge for himself what is the weight of the kind of evidence produced in this chapter. I give a chapter to it because the author of 'Supernatural Religion' has done the same. Doubtless it is not the sort of evidence that would bear pressing in a court of English law, but in a question of balanced probabilities it has I think a decided leaning to one side, and that the side opposed to the conclusions of 'Supernatural Religion.'

---

[1] Ἄλλη δ' ἐπιστολή τις αὐτοῦ πρὸς Νικομηδέας φέρεται· ἐν ᾗ τὴν Μαρκίωνος αἵρεσιν πολεμῶν τῷ τῆς ἀληθείας παρίσταται κανόνι. *H. E.* iv. 23.

CHAPTER X.

MELITO—APOLLINARIS—ATHENAGORAS—THE EPISTLE OF VIENNE AND LYONS.

We pass on, still in a region of fragments—'waifs and strays' of the literature of the second century—and of partial and indirect (though on that account not necessarily less important) indications.

In Melito of Sardis (c. 176 A.D) it is interesting to notice the first appearance of a phrase that was destined later to occupy a conspicuous position. Writing to his friend Onesimus, who had frequently asked for selections from the Law and the Prophets bearing upon the Saviour, and generally for information respecting the number and order of 'the Old Books,' Melito says 'that he had gone to the East and reached the spot where the preaching had been delivered and the acts done, and that having learnt accurately the books of the Old Covenant (or Testament) he had sent a list of them'— which is subjoined[1]. Melito uses the word which became established as the title used to distinguish the elder Scriptures from the younger—the Old Covenant or Testament (ἡ παλαιὰ διαθήκη); and it is argued from this that he implies the existence of a 'definite New Testa-

---

[1] Ἀκριβῶς μαθὼν τὰ τῆς παλαιᾶς διαθήκης βιβλία, ὑποτάξας ἔπεμψά σοι. Euseb. *H. E.* iv. 26 (Routh, *Rel. Sac.* i. p. 119).

ment, a written antitype to the Old[1].' The inference however seems to be somewhat in excess of what can be legitimately drawn. By παλαιὰ διαθήκη is meant rather the subject or contents of the books than the books themselves. It is the system of things, the dispensation accomplished 'in heavenly places,' to which the books belong, not the actual collected volume. The parallel of 2 Cor. iii. 14 (ἐπὶ τῇ ἀναγνώσει τῆς παλαιᾶς διαθήκης), which is ably pointed to in 'Supernatural Religion[2],' is too close to allow the inference of a written New Testament. And yet, though the word has not actually acquired this meaning, it was in process of acquiring it, and had already gone some way to acquire it. The books were already there, and, as we see from Irenaeus, critical collections of them had already begun to be made. Within thirty years of the time when Melito is writing Tertullian uses the phrase Novum Testamentum precisely in our modern sense, intimating that it had then become the current designation[3]. This being the case we cannot wonder that there should be a certain reflex hint of such a sense in the words of Melito.

The tract 'On Faith,' published in Syriac by Dr. Cureton and attributed to Melito, is not sufficiently authenticated to have value as evidence.

It should be noted that Melito's fragments contain nothing especially on the Gospels.

---

[1] Westcott, *On the Canon*, p. 201.

[2] ii. p. 177.

[3] *Adv. Marc.* iv. 1 (cf. Rönsch, *Das neue Testament Tertullian's*, p. 48), 'duo deos dividens, proinde diversos, alterum alterius instrumenti—vel quod magis usui est dicere, testamenti.'

2.

Some time between 176-180 A.D. Claudius Apollinaris, Bishop of Hierapolis, addressed to the Emperor Marcus Aurelius an apology of which rather more than three lines have come down to us. A more important fragment however is assigned to this writer in the Paschal Chronicle, a work of the seventh century. Here it is said that 'Apollinaris, the most holy bishop of Hierapolis in Asia, who lived near the times of the Apostles, in his book about Easter, taught much the same, saying thus: "There are some who through ignorance wrangle about these matters, in a pardonable manner; for ignorance does not admit of blame but rather needs instruction. And they say that on the 14th the Lord ate the lamb with His disciples, and that on the great day of unleavened bread He himself suffered; and they relate that this is in their view the statement of Matthew. Whence their opinion is in conflict with the law, and according to them the Gospels are made to be at variance[1]."' This variance or disagreement in the Gospels evidently has reference to the apparent discrepancy between the Synoptics, especially St. Matthew and St. John, the former treating the Last Supper as the Paschal meal, the latter placing it before the Feast of the Passover and making the Crucifixion coincide with the slaughter of the Paschal lamb. Apollinaris would thus seem to

---

[1] Εἰσὶ τοίνυν οἱ δι' ἄγνοιαν φιλονεικοῦσι περὶ τούτων, συγγνωστὸν πρᾶγμα πεπονθότες· ἄγνοια γὰρ οὐ κατηγορίαν ἀναδέχεται, ἀλλὰ διδαχῆς προσδεῖται. Καὶ λέγουσιν ὅτι τῇ ιδ' τὸ πρόβατον μετὰ τῶν μαθητῶν ἔφαγεν ὁ Κύριος· τῇ δὲ μεγάλῃ ἡμέρᾳ τῶν ἀζύμων αὐτὸς ἔπαθεν· καὶ διηγοῦνται Ματθαῖον οὕτω λέγειν ὡς νενοήκασιν· ὅθεν ἀσύμφωνός τε νόμῳ ἡ νόησις αὐτῶν, καὶ στασιάζειν δοκεῖ κατ' αὐτοὺς τὰ εὐαγγέλια. *Chron. Pasch.* in Routh, *Rel. Sac.* i. p. 160.

recognise both the first and the fourth Gospels as authoritative.

Is this fragment of Apollinaris genuine? It is alleged against it[1] (1) that Eusebius was ignorant of any such work on Easter, and that there is no mention of it in such notices of Apollinaris and his writings as have come down to us from Theodoret, Jerome, and Photius. There are some good remarks on this point by Routh (who is quoted in 'Supernatural Religion' *apparently* as adverse to the genuineness of the fragments). He says: 'There seems to me to be nothing in these extracts to compel us to deny the authorship of Apollinaris. Nor must we refuse credit to the author of the Preface [to the Paschal Chronicle] any more than to other writers of the same times on whose testimony many books of the ancients have been received, although not mentioned by Eusebius or any other of his contemporaries; especially as Eusebius declares below that it was only some select books that had come to his hands out of many that Apollinaris had written[2].' It is objected (2) that Apollinaris is not likely to have spoken of a controversy in which the whole Asiatic Church was engaged as the opinion of a 'few ignorant wranglers.' A fair objection, if he was really speaking of such a controversy. But the great issue between the Churches of Asia and that of Rome was whether the Paschal festival should be kept, according to the Jewish custom, always on the fourteenth day of the month Nisan, or whether it should be kept on the Friday after the

---

[1] *S. R.* ii. p. 188 sqq. The reference to Routh is given on p. 188, n. 1; that to Lardner in the same note should, I believe, be ii. p. 316, not p. 296.

[2] *Rel. Sac.* i. p. 167.

Paschal full moon, on whatever day of the month it might fall. The fragment appears rather to allude to some local dispute as to the day on which the Lord suffered. To go thoroughly into this question would involve us in all the mazes of the so-called Paschal controversy, and in the end a precise and certain conclusion would probably be impossible. So far as I am aware, all the writers who have entered into the discussion start with assuming the genuineness of the Apollinarian fragment.

There remains however the fact that it rests only upon the attestation of a writer of the seventh century, who may possibly be wrong, but, if so, has been led into his error not wilfully but by accident. No reason can be alleged for the forging or purposely false ascription of a fragment like this, and it bears the stamp of good faith in that it asks indulgence for opponents instead of censure. We may perhaps safely accept the fragment with some, not large, deduction from its weight.

3.

An instance of the precariousness of the argument from silence would be supplied by the writer who comes next under review—Athenagoras. No mention whatever is made of Athenagoras either by Eusebius or Jerome, though he appears to have been an author of a certain importance, two of whose works, an Apology addressed to Marcus Aurelius and Commodus and a treatise on the Resurrection, are still extant. The genuineness of neither of these works is doubted.

The Apology, which may be dated about 177 A.D., contains a few references to our Lord's discourses, but not such as can have any great weight as evidence. The first that is usually given, a parallel to Matt. v. 39, 40 (good for evil), is introduced in such a way as to show that the author intends only to give the sense and not the words. The same may be said of another sentence that is compared with Mark x. 6[1]:—

Athenagoras,
Leg. pro Christ. 33.
Ὅτι ἐν ἀρχῇ ὁ Θεὸς ἕνα ἄνδρα ἔπλασε καὶ μίαν γυναῖκα.

Mark x. 6.
Ἀπὸ δὲ ἀρχῆς κτίσεως ἄρσεν καὶ θῆλυ ἐποίησεν αὐτοὺς ὁ Θεός.

All that can be said is that the thought here appears to have been suggested by the Gospel—and that not quite immediately.

A much closer—and indeed, we can hardly doubt, a real—parallel is presented by a longer passage:—

Athenagoras,
Leg. pro Christ. 11.
What then are the precepts in which we are instructed? I say unto you: Love your enemies, bless them that curse, pray for them that persecute you; that ye may become the sons of your Father which is in heaven: who maketh his sun to rise on the evil and the good, and sendeth rain on the just and the unjust.

Matt. v. 44, 45.
I say unto you: Love your enemies [bless them that curse you, do good to them that hate you], and pray for them that persecute you; that ye may become the sons of your Father which is in heaven: for he maketh his sun to rise on the evil and the good, and sendeth rain on the just and the unjust.

---

[1] The quotations from Athenagoras are transcribed from 'Supernatural Religion' and Lardner (*Credibility* &c., ii. p. 195 sq.). I have not access to the original work.

Τίνες οὖν ἡμῶν οἱ λόγοι, οἷς ἐντρεφύμεθα; λέγω ὑμῖν, ἀγαπᾶτε τοὺς ἐχθροὺς ὑμῶν, εὐλογεῖτε τοὺς καταρωμένους, προσεύχεσθε ὑπὲρ τῶν διωκόντων ὑμᾶς, ὅπως γένησθε υἱοὶ τοῦ πατρὸς ὑμῶν τοῦ ἐν οὐρανοῖς, ὃς τὸν ἥλιον αὐτοῦ ἀνατέλλει ἐπὶ πονηροὺς καὶ ἀγαθοὺς καὶ βρέχει ἐπὶ δικαίους καὶ ἀδίκους.

ἐγὼ δὲ λέγω ὑμῖν, ἀγαπᾶτε τοὺς ἐχθροὺς ὑμῶν [εὐλογεῖτε τοὺς καταρωμένους ὑμᾶς, καλῶς ποιεῖτε τοὺς μισοῦντας ὑμᾶς], προσεύχεσθε ὑπὲρ τῶν διωκόντων ὑμᾶς ὅπως γένησθε υἱοὶ τοῦ πατρὸς ὑμῶν τοῦ ἐν οὐρανοῖς, ὅτι τὸν ἥλιον αὐτοῦ ἀνατέλλει ἐπὶ πονηροὺς καὶ ἀγαθοὺς καὶ βρέχει ἐπὶ δικαίους καὶ ἀδίκους.

The bracketed clauses in the text of St. Matthew are both omitted and inserted by a large body of authorities, but, as it is rightly remarked in 'Supernatural Religion,' they are always either both omitted or both inserted; we must therefore believe that the omission and insertion of one only by Athenagoras is without manuscript precedent. Otherwise the exactness of the parallel is great; and it is thrown the more into relief when we compare the corresponding passage in St. Luke.

The quotation is completed in the next chapter of Athenagoras' work:—

Athenagoras,
Leg. pro Christ. 12.

Matt. v. 46.

For if ye love, he says, them which love and lend to them which lend to you, what reward shall ye have?

For if ye shall love them which love you, what reward have ye?

Ἐὰν γὰρ ἀγαπᾶτε, φησὶν, τοὺς ἀγαπῶντας, καὶ δανείζετε τοῖς δανείζουσιν ὑμῖν, τίνα μισθὸν ἕξετε;

Ἐὰν γὰρ ἀγαπήσητε τοὺς ἀγαπῶντας ὑμᾶς τίνα μισθὸν ἔχετε;

Here the middle clause in the quotation appears to be a reminiscence of St. Luke vi. 34 (ἐὰν δανίσητε παρ' ὧν ἐλπίζετε λαβεῖν). Justin also, it should be noted, has ἀγαπᾶτε (but εἰ ἀγαπᾶτε) for ἀγαπήσητε. If this passage had stood alone, taking into account the variations and the even run and balance of the language we might have thought perhaps that Athenagoras had had before him a different version. Yet the τίνα μισθόν, compared with the ποία χάρις of St. Luke and τί καινὸν ποιεῖτε of Justin, would cause misgivings, and greater run and balance is precisely what would result from 'unconscious cerebration.'

Two more references are pointed out to Matt. v. 28 and Matt. v. 32, one with slight, the other with medium, variation, which leave the question very much in the same position.

We ought not to omit to notice that Athenagoras quotes one uncanonical saying, introducing it with the phrase πάλιν ἡμῖν λέγοντος τοῦ λόγου. I am not at all clear that this is not merely one of the 'precepts' (οἱ λόγοι) alluded to above. At any rate it is exceedingly doubtful that the Logos is here personified. It seems rather parallel to the ὁ λόγος ἐδήλου of Justin (Dial. c. Tryph. 129).

Considering the date at which he wrote I have little doubt that Athenagoras is actually quoting from the Synoptics, but he cannot, on the whole, be regarded as a very powerful witness for them.

4.

After the cruel persecution from which the Churches of Vienne and Lyons had suffered in the year 177 A.D., a letter was written in their name, containing an account of what had happened, which Lardner describes as 'the finest thing of the kind in all antiquity[1].' This letter,

[1] *Credibility &c.*, ii. p. 161.

which was addressed to the Churches of Asia and Phrygia, contained several quotations from the New Testament, and among them one that is evidently from St. Luke's Gospel.

It is said of one of the martyrs, Vettius Epagathus, that his manner of life was so strict that, young as he was, he could claim a share in the testimony borne to the more aged Zacharias. Indeed he had *walked in all the commandments and ordinances of the Lord blameless*, and in the service of his neighbour untiring, &c.[1] The italicised words are a verbatim reproduction of Luke i. 6.

There is an ambiguity in the words συνεξισοῦσθαι τῇ τοῦ πρεσβυτέρου Ζαχαρίου μαρτυρίᾳ. The genitive after μαρτυρίᾳ may be either subjective or objective—'the testimony borne *by*' or 'the testimony borne *to* or *of*' the aged Zacharias. I have little doubt that the translation given above is the right one. It has the authority of Lardner ('equalled the character of') and Routh ('Zachariae senioris elogio aequaretur'), and seems to be imperatively required by the context. The eulogy passed upon Vettius Epagathus is justified by the uniform strictness of his daily life (he has walked in *all* the commandments &c.), not by the single act of his constancy in death.

The author of 'Supernatural Religion,' apparently following Hilgenfeld[2], adopts the other translation, and bases on it an argument that the allusion is to the *martyrdom* of Zacharias, and therefore not to our third Gospel in which no mention of that martyrdom is contained. On the other hand, we are reminded that the narrative of the martyrdom of Zacharias enters into

---

[1] *Ep. Vien. et Lugd.* § 3 (in Routh, *Rel. Sac.* i. p. 297).
[2] *S. R.* ii. p. 203; *Evv. Justin's u. s. w.* p. 155.

the Protevangelium of James. That apocryphal Gospel however contains nothing approaching to the words which coincide exactly with the text of St. Luke.

Even if there had been a greater doubt than there is as to the application of μαρτυρία, it would be difficult to resist the conclusion that the Synoptic Gospel is being quoted. The words occur in the most peculiar and distinctive portion of the Gospel; and the correspondence is so exact and the phrase itself so striking as not to admit of any other source. The order, the choice of words, the construction, even to the use of the nominative ἄμεμπτος where we might very well have had the adverb ἀμέμπτως, all point the same way. These fine edges of the quotation, so to speak, must needs have been rubbed off in the course of transmission through several documents. But there is not a trace of any other document that contained such a remark upon the character of Zacharias.

This instance of a Synoptic quotation may, I think, safely be depended upon.

Another allusion, a little lower down in the Epistle, which speaks of the same Vettius Epagathus as 'having in himself the Paraclete [there is a play on the use of the word παράκλητος just before], the Spirit, more abundantly than Zacharias,' though in exaggerated and bad taste, probably has reference to Luke i. 67, 'And Zacharias his father was filled with the Holy Ghost,' &c.

[Mr. Mason calls my attention to ἔνδυμα νυμφικόν in § 13, and also to the misleading statement in *S. R.* ii. p. 201 that 'no writing of the New Testament is directly referred to.' I should perhaps have more fault to find with the sentence on p. 204, 'It follows clearly and few venture to doubt,' &c. I have assumed however for some time that the reader will be on his guard against expressions such as these.]

CHAPTER XI.

PTOLEMAEUS AND HERACLEON—CELSUS—THE MURATORIAN FRAGMENT.

WE are now very near emerging into open daylight: but there are three items in the evidence which lie upon the border of the debateable ground, and as questions have been raised about these it may be well for us to discuss them.

We have already had occasion to speak of the two Gnostics Ptolemaeus and Heracleon. It is necessary, in the first place, to define the date of their evidence with greater precision, and, in the second, to consider its bearing.

Let us then, in attempting to do this, dismiss all secondary and precarious matter; such as (1) the argument drawn by Tischendorf[1] from the order in which the names of the disciples of Valentinus are mentioned and from an impossible statement of Epiphanius which seems to make Heracleon older than Cerdon, and (2) the argument that we find in Volkmar and 'Supernatural Religion[2]' from the use of the present tense by Hippolytus, as if the two writers, Ptolemaeus and

---

[1] *Wann wurden u. s. w.* p. 48 sq.
[2] *Ursprung*, p. 130; *S. R* ii. p. 222.

Heracleon, were contemporaries of his own in 225–235 A.D. Hippolytus does indeed say, speaking of a division in the school of Valentinus, 'Those who are of Italy, of whom is Heracleon and Ptolemaeus, say' &c. But there is no reason why there should not be a kind of historic present, just as we might say, 'The Atomists, of whom are Leucippus and Democritus, hold' &c., or 'St. Peter says this, St. Paul says that.' The account of such presents would seem to be that the writer speaks as if quoting from a book that he has actually before him. It is not impossible that Heracleon and Ptolemaeus may have been still living at the time when Hippolytus wrote, but this cannot be inferred simply from the tense of the verb. Surer data are supplied by Irenaeus.

Irenaeus mentions Ptolemaeus several times in his first and second books, and on one occasion he couples with his the name of Heracleon. But to what date does this evidence of Irenaeus refer? At what time was Irenaeus himself writing. We have seen that the *terminus ad quem*, at least for the first three books, is supplied by the death of Eleutherus (c. A.D. 190). On the other hand, the third book at least was written after the publication of the Greek version of the Old Testament by Theodotion, which Epiphanius tells us appeared in the reign of Commodus (180–190 A.D.). A still more precise date is given to Theodotion's work in the Paschal Chronicle, which places it under the Consuls Marcellus (Massuet would read 'Marullus') and Ælian in the year 184 A.D.[1] This last statement is worth very little, and it is indeed disputed whether

---

[1] Cf. Credner, *Beiträge*, ii. p. 254.

Theodotion's version can have appeared so late as this. At any rate we must assume that it was in the hands of Irenaeus about 185 A.D., and it will be not before this that the third book of the work 'Against Heresies' was written. It will perhaps sufficiently satisfy all parties if we suppose that Irenaeus was engaged in writing his first three books between the years 182–188 A.D. But the name of Ptolemaeus is mentioned very near the beginning of the Preface; so that Irenaeus would be committing to paper the statement of his acquaintance with Ptolemaeus as early as 182 A.D.

This is however the last link in the chain. Let us trace it a little further backwards. Irenaeus' acquaintance with Ptolemaeus can hardly have been a fact of yesterday at the time when he wrote. Ptolemaeus represented the 'Italian' branch of the Valentinian school, and therefore it seems a fair supposition that Irenaeus would come in contact with him during his visit to Rome in 178 A.D.; and the four years from that date to 182 A.D. can hardly be otherwise than a short period to allow for the necessary intimacy with his teaching to have been formed.

But we are carried back one step further still. It is not only Ptolemaeus but Ptolemaeus *and his party* (οἱ περὶ Πτολεμαῖον[1]). There has been time for Ptolemaeus to found a school within a school of his own; and his school has already begun to express its opinions, either collectively or through its individual members.

In this way the real date of Ptolemaeus seems still to recede, but I will not endeavour any further to put a numerical value upon it which might be thought to be

---

[1] *Adv. Haer.* i. Praef. 2.

prejudiced. It will be best for the reader to fill up the blank according to his own judgment.

Heracleon will to a certain extent go with Ptolemaeus, with whom he is persistently coupled, though, as he is only mentioned once by Irenaeus, the data concerning him are less precise. They are however supplemented by an allusion in the fourth book of the Stromateis of Clement of Alexandria (which appears to have been written in the last decade of the century) to Heracleon as one of the chief of the school of Valentinus[1], and perhaps also by a statement of Origen to the effect that Heracleon was said to be a γνώριμος of Valentinus himself[2]. The meaning of the latter term is questioned, and it is certainly true that it may stand for pupil or scholar, as Elisha was to Elijah or as the Apostles were to their Master; but that it could possibly be applied to two persons who never came into personal contact must be, I cannot but think, very doubtful. This then, if true, would throw back Heracleon some little way even beyond 160 A.D.

From the passage in the Stromateis we gather that Heracleon, if he did not (as is usually inferred) write a commentary, yet wrote an isolated exposition of a portion of St. Luke's Gospel. In the same way we learn from Origen that he wrote a commentary upon St. John.

We shall probably not be wrong in referring many of the Valentinian quotations given by Irenaeus to Ptolemaeus and Heracleon. By the first writer we also have extant an Epistle to a disciple called Flora, which

---

[1] *Strom.* iv. 9.
[2] Τὸν Οὐαλεντίνου λεγόμενον εἶναι γνώριμον Ἡρακλέωνα ... Origen, *Comm. in Joh.* ii. p. 60 (quoted by Volkmar, *Ursprung*, p. 127).

has been preserved by Epiphanius. This Epistle, which there is no reason to doubt, contains unequivocal references to our first Gospel.

Epistle to Flora.
Epiph. Hær. 217 A.
οἰκία γὰρ ἢ πόλις μερισθεῖσα ἐφ᾽ ἑαυτὴν ὅτι μὴ δύναται στῆναι [ὁ σωτὴρ ἡμῶν ἀπεφήνατο].

Matt. xii. 25 (*Mark* iii. 25, *Luke* xi. 17).
πᾶσα πόλις ἢ οἰκία μερισθεῖσα καθ᾽ ἑαυτῆς οὐ σταθήσεται.

Ibid. 217 D.
[ἔφη αὐτοῖς ὅτι] Μωυσῆς πρὸς τὴν σκληροκαρδίαν ὑμῶν ἐπέτρεψε τὸ ἀπολύειν τὴν γυναῖκα αὐτοῦ. ἀπ᾽ ἀρχῆς γὰρ οὐ γέγονεν οὕτως. Θεὸς γὰρ (φησὶ) συνέζευξε ταύτην τὴν συζυγίαν καὶ ὃ συνέζευξεν ὁ κύριος, ἄνθρωπος (ἔφη) μὴ χωριζέτω.

Matt. xix. 8, 6 (*Mark* x. 5, 6, 9).
λέγει αὐτοῖς· Ὅτι Μωυσῆς πρὸς τὴν σκληροκαρδίαν ὑμῶν ἐπέτρεψεν ὑμῖν ἀπολῦσαι τὰς γυναῖκας ὑμῶν· ἀπ᾽ ἀρχῆς δὲ οὐ γέγονεν οὕτως. . . . ὃ οὖν ὁ Θεὸς συνέζευξεν ἄνθρωπος μὴ χωριζέτω.

Ibid. 218 D.
ὁ γὰρ Θεὸς (φησὶν) εἶπε τίμα τὸν πατέρα σου καὶ τὴν μητέρα σου, ἵνα εὖ σοι γένηται· ὑμεῖς δὲ (φησὶν) εἰρήκατε (τοῖς πρεσβυτέροις λέγων), δῶρον τῷ θεῷ ὃ ἐὰν ὠφεληθῇς ἐξ ἐμοῦ, καὶ ἠκυρώσατε τὸν νόμον τοῦ Θεοῦ, διὰ τὴν παράδοσιν ὑμῶν τῶν πρεσβυτέρων. τοῦτο δὲ Ἡσαΐας ἐξεφώνησεν εἰπών· ὁ λαὸς οὗτος τοῖς χείλεσί με τιμᾷ ἡ δὲ καρδία αὐτῶν πόρρω ἀπέχει ἀπ᾽ ἐμοῦ. μάτην δὲ σέβονταί με, διδάσκοντες διδασκαλίας, ἐντάλματα ἀνθρώπων.

Matt. xv. 4-8 (*Mark* vii. 10, 11, 6, 9).
ὁ γὰρ Θεὸς ἐνετείλατο λέγων, Τίμα τὸν πατέρα καὶ τὴν μητέρα . . ὑμεῖς δὲ λέγετε· ὃς ἂν εἴπῃ τῷ πατρὶ ἢ τῇ μητρί· Δῶρον ὃ ἐὰν ἐξ ἐμοῦ ὠφεληθῇς, . . καὶ ἠκυρώσατε τὸν νόμον τοῦ Θεοῦ διὰ τὴν παράδοσιν ὑμῶν. ὑποκριταί, καλῶς ἐπροφήτευσεν περὶ ὑμῶν Ἡσαΐας λέγων· Ὁ λαὸς οὗτος τοῖς χείλεσίν με τιμᾷ, ἡ δὲ καρδία αὐτῶν πόρρω ἀπέχει ἀπ᾽ ἐμοῦ· μάτην δὲ σέβονταί με διδάσκοντες διδασκαλίας ἐντάλματα ἀνθρώπων.

Ibid. 220 D, 221 A.	*Matt.* v. 38, 39 (*Luke* vi. 29).
τὸ γάρ, 'Οφθαλμὸν ἀντὶ ὀφθαλ- μοῦ καὶ ὀδόντα ἀντὶ ὀδόντος ... ἐγὼ γὰρ λέγω ὑμῖν μὴ ἀντιστῆναι ὅλως τῷ πονηρῷ ἀλλὰ ἐάν τίς σε ῥαπίσῃ στρέψον αὐτῷ καὶ τὴν ἄλλην σιαγόνα.	ἠκούσατε ὅτι ἐρρήθη, 'Οφθαλμὸν ἀντὶ ὀφθαλμοῦ καὶ ὀδόντα ἀντὶ ὀδόντος· ἐγὼ δὲ λέγω ὑμῖν μὴ ἀντι- στῆναι τῷ πονηρῷ· ἀλλ' ὅστις σε ῥαπίζει εἰς τὴν δεξίαν σιαγόνα σου, στρέψον αὐτῷ καὶ τὴν ἄλλην.

Some doubt indeed appears to be entertained by the author of 'Supernatural Religion[1]' as to whether these quotations are really taken from the first Synoptic; but it would hardly have arisen if he had made a more special study of the phenomena of patristic quotation. If he had done this, I do not think there would have been any question on the subject. A comparison of the other Synoptic parallels, and of the Septuagint in the case of the quotation from Isaiah, will make the agreement with the Matthaean text still more conspicuous. It is instructive to notice the reproduction of the most characteristic features of this text—πόλις, μερισθεῖσα (ἐὰν μερισθῇ Mark, διαμερισθεῖσα Luke), ὅτι Μωυσῆς, ἐπέτρεψεν ἀπολῦ- [σαι] τ[ὰς] γυναῖκ[as], οὐ γέγονεν οὕτως, ἠκυρώσατε .. διὰ τὴν π., ὀφθαλμόν ... ὀδόντος, ἀντιστῆναι τῷ πονηρῷ, στρέψον, and the order and cast of sentence in all the quotations. The first quotation, with ἐφ' ἑαυτήν and δύναται στῆναι, which may be compared (though, from the context, somewhat doubtfully) with Mark, presents, I believe, the only trace of the influence of any other text.

To what period in the life of Ptolemaeus this Epistle to Flora may have belonged we have no means of knowing; but it is unlikely that the writer should have

---

[1] 'In affirming that [these quotations] are taken from the Gospel according to St. Matthew apologists exhibit their usual arbitrary haste,' &c. *S. R.* ii. p. 224.

used one set of documents at one part of his life and another set at another. Viewed along with so much confirmatory matter in the account of the Valentinians by Irenaeus, the evidence may be taken as that of Ptolemaeus himself rather than of this single letter.

2.

The question in regard to Celsus, whose attacks upon Christianity called forth such an elaborate reply from Origen, is chiefly one of date. To go into this at once adequately and independently would need a much longer investigation than can be admitted into the present work. The subject has quite recently been treated in a monograph by the well-known writer Dr. Keim[1], and, as there will be in this case no suspicion of partiality, I shall content myself with stating Dr. Keim's conclusions.

Origen himself, Dr. Keim thinks, was writing under the Emperor Philip about A.D. 248. But he regards his opponent Celsus, not as a contemporary, but as belonging to a past age (Contra Celsum, i. 8, vii. 11), and his work as nothing recent, but rather as having obtained a certain celebrity in heathen literature (v. 3). For all this it had to be disinterred, as it were, and that not without difficulty, by a Christian (viii. 76).

Exact and certain knowledge however about Celsus Origen did not possess. He leans to the opinion that his opponent was an Epicurean of that name who lived 'under Hadrian and later' (i. 8). This Epicurean had

---

[1] *Celsus' Wahres Wort*, Zurich, 1873. For what follows, see especially p. 261 sqq.

also written several books against Magic (i. 68). Now it is known that there was a Celsus, a friend of Lucian, who had also written against Magic, and to whom Lucian dedicated his 'Pseudomantis, or Alexander of Abonoteichos.'

It was clearly obvious to identify the two persons, and there was much to be said in favour of the identification. But there was this difficulty. Origen indeed speaks of the Celsus to whom he is replying as an Epicurean, and here and there Epicurean opinions are expressed in the fragments of the original work that Origen has preserved. But Origen himself was somewhat puzzled to find that the main principles of the author were rather Platonic or Neo-platonic than Epicurean, and this observation has been confirmed by modern enquiry. The Celsus of Origen is in reality a Platonist.

It still being acknowledged that the friend of Lucian was an Epicurean, this discovery seemed fatal to the supposition that he was the author of the work against the Christians. Accordingly there was a tendency among critics, though not quite a unanimous tendency, to separate again the two personalities which had been united. At this point Dr. Keim comes upon the scene, and he asks the question, Was Lucian's friend really an Epicurean? Lucian nowhere says so in plain words, but it was taken as a *primâ facie* inference from some of the language used by him. For instance, he describes the Platonists as being on good terms with this very Alexander of Abonoteichos whom he is ridiculing and exposing. He appeals to Celsus to say whether a certain work of Epicurus is not his finest. He says that his friend will be pleased to know that one of his objects in writing is to see justice done to Epicurus. All these expressions Dr. Keim thinks may be explained as the quiet playful irony that was natural to Lucian, and from other indications in the work he concludes that Lucian's Celsus may well have been a Platonist, though not a bigoted one, just as Lucian himself was not in any strict and narrow sense an Epicurean.

When once the possibility of the identification is conceded, there are, as Dr. Keim urges, strong reasons for its adoption. The characters of the two owners of the name Celsus, so far as they can be judged from the work of Origen on the one hand and Lucian on the other, are the same. Both are distinguished for their opposition to magical arts. The Celsus of the Pseudomantis is a friend of Lucian, and it is precisely from a friend of Lucian that the 'Word of Truth' replied to by Origen might be supposed to have come. Lastly, time and place both support the identification. The Celsus of Lucian lived under Marcus Aurelius and Commodus, and Dr. Keim decides, after an elaborate examination of the internal evidence, that the Celsus of Origen wrote his work in the year 178 A.D., towards the close of the reign of Marcus Aurelius.

Such is Dr. Keim's view. In the date assigned to the Λόγος ἀληθής it does not differ materially from that of the large majority of critics. Grätz alone goes as far back as to the time of Hadrian. Hagenbach, Hasse, Tischendorf, and Friedländer fix upon the middle, Mosheim, Gieseler, Baur, and Engelhardt upon the second half, of the second century; while the following writers assume either generally the reign of Marcus Aurelius, or specially with Dr. Keim one of the two great persecutions— Spencer, Tillemont, Neander, Tzschirner, Jachmann,

Bindemann, Lommatzsch, Hase, Redepenning, Zeller. The only two writers mentioned by Dr. Keim as contending for a later date are Ueberweg and Volkmar, 'who strangely misunderstands both Origen and Baur[1].' Volkmar is followed by the author of 'Supernatural Religion.'

At whatever date Celsus wrote, it appears to be sufficiently clear that he knew and used all the four canonical Gospels[2].

3.

The last document that need be discussed by us at present is the remarkable fragment which, from its discoverer and from its contents, bears the name of the Canon of Muratori[3].

Whatever was the original title and whatever may have been the extent of the work from which it is taken, the portion of it that has come down to us is by far the most important of all the direct evidence for the Canon both of the Gospels and of the New Testament in general with which we have yet had to deal. It is indeed the first in which the conception of a Canon is quite unequivocally put forward. We have for the first time a definite list of the books received by the Church and a distinct separation made between these and those that are rejected.

The fragment begins abruptly with the end of a

---

[1] Keim, *Celsus' Wahres Wort*, p. 262.

[2] Ibid. p. 228 sq.; Volkmar, *Ursprung*, p. 80.

[3] The text of this document is printed in full by Routh, *Rel. Sac.* i. pp. 394-396; Westcott, *On the Canon*, p. 487 sqq.; Hilgenfeld, *Der Kanon und die Kritik des N. T.* ad p. 40, n.; Credner, *Geschichte des Neutestamentlichen Kanon*, ed. Volkmar, p. 153 sqq., &c.

sentence apparently relating to the composition of the Gospel according to St. Mark. Then follows 'in the third place the Gospel according to St. Luke,' of which some account is given. 'The fourth of the Gospels' is that of John, 'one of the disciples of the Lord.' A legend is related as to the origin of this Gospel. Then mention is made of the Acts, which are attributed to Luke. Then follow thirteen Epistles of St. Paul by name. Two Epistles professing to be addressed to the Laodiceans and Alexandrines are dismissed as forged in the interests of the heresy of Marcion. The Epistle of Jude and two that bear the superscription of John are admitted. Likewise the two Apocalypses of John and Peter. [No mention is made, it will be seen, of the Epistle to the Hebrews, of that of James, of I and II Peter, and of III John[1].]

The Pastor of Hermas, a work of recent date, may be read but not published in the Church before the people, and cannot be included either in the number of the prophets or apostles.

On the other hand nothing at all can be received of Arsinous, Valentinus, or Miltiades; neither the new Marcionite book of Psalms, which with Basilides and the Asian founder of the Cataphryges (or the founder of the Asian Cataphryges, i.e. Montanus) is rejected.

The importance of this will be seen at a glance. The chief question is here again in regard to the date, which must be determined from the document itself. A sufficiently clear indication seems to be given in the language used respecting the Pastor of Hermas. This work is said to have been composed 'very lately in our times,

---

[1] See however Dr. Lightfoot in *Cont. Rev.*, Oct. 1875, p. 837.

Pius the brother of the writer occupying the episcopal chair of the Roman Church.' The episcopate of Pius is dated from 142–157 A.D., so that 157 A.D. may be taken as the starting-point from which we have to reckon the interval implied by the words 'very recently in our times' (nuperrime temporibus nostris). Taking these words in their natural sense, I should think that the furthest limit they would fairly admit of would be a generation, or say thirty years, after the death of Pius (for even in taking a date such as this we are obliged to assume that the Pastor was published only just before the death of that bishop). The most probable construction seems to be that the unknown author meant that the Pastor of Hermas was composed within his own memory. Volkmar is doubtless right in saying[1] that he meant to distinguish the work in question from the writings of the Prophets and Apostles, but still the double use of the words 'nuperrime' and 'temporibus nostris' plainly indicate something more definite than merely 'our post-apostolic time.' If this had been the sense we should have had some such word as 'recentius' instead of 'nuperrime.' The argument of 'Supernatural Religion[2],' that 'in supposing that the writer may have appropriately used the phrase thirty or forty years after the time of Pius so much licence is taken that there is absolutely no reason why a still greater interval may not be allowed,' is clearly playing fast and loose with language, and doing so for no good reason; for the only ground for assigning a later date is that the earlier one is inconvenient for the critic's theory. The other indications tally quite sufficiently with the date 170–190 A.D.

[1] *Ursprung*, p. 28. [2] ii. p. 245.

Basilides, Valentinus, Marcion, the Marcionites, we know were active long before this period. The Montanists (who appear under the name by which they were generally known in the earlier writings, 'Cataphryges') were beginning to be notorious, and are mentioned in the letter of the Churches of Vienne and Lyons. Miltiades was a contemporary of Claudius Apollinaris who wrote against him[1]. All the circumstances point to such a date as that of Irenaeus, and the conception of the Canon is very similar to that which we should gather from the great work 'Against Heresies.' If this does not agree with preconceived opinions as to what the state of the Canon ought to have been, it is the opinion that ought to be rectified accordingly, and not plain words explained away.

I can see no sound objection to the date 170–180 A.D., but by adding ten years to this we shall reach the extreme limit admissible.

I do not know whether it is necessary to refer to the objection from the absence of any mention of the first two Synoptic Gospels, through the mutilated state of the document. It is true that the inference that they were originally mentioned rests only 'upon conjecture[2],' but it is the kind of conjecture that, taking all things into consideration—the extent to which the evidence of the fragment in other respects corresponds with the Catholic tradition, the state of the Canon in Irenæus, the relation of the evidence for the first Gospel in particular to that for the others—can be reckoned at very little less than ninety-nine chances out of a hundred.

---

[1] Cf. Credner, *Gesch. des Kanon*, p. 167.
[2] *S. R.* ii. p. 241.

To the same class belongs Dr. Donaldson's suggestion[1] that the passage which contains the indication of date may be an interpolation. It is always possible that the particular passage that happens to be important in any document of this date may be an interpolation, but the chances that it really is so must be in any case very slight, and here there is no valid reason for suspecting interpolation. It does not at all follow, as Dr. Donaldson seems to think, that because a document is mutilated therefore it is more likely to be interpolated; for interpolation is the result of quite a different series of accidents. The interpolation, if it were such, could not well be accidental because it has no appearance of being a gloss; on the other hand, only far-fetched and improbable motives can be alleged for it as intentional.

The full statement of the fragment in regard to St. Luke's Gospel is as follows. 'Luke the physician after the Ascension of Christ, having been taken into his company by Paul, wrote in his own name to the best of his judgment (ex opinione), and, though he had not himself seen the Lord in the flesh, so far as he could ascertain; accordingly he begins his narrative with the birth of John.' The greater part of this account appears to be taken simply from the Preface to the Gospel, which is supplemented by the tradition that St. Luke was a physician and also the author of the Acts. As evidence to those facts a document dating some hundred years after the composition of the Gospel is not of course very weighty; its real importance is as showing the authority which the Gospel at this date possessed in the Church. That authority cannot have been acquired in a day, but represents the culmination of a long and

[1] Quoted in *S. R.* ii. p. 247.

gradual movement. What we have to note is that the movement, some of the stages of which we have been tracing, has now definitely reached its culmination.

In regard to the fourth Gospel the Muratorian fragment has a longer story to tell, but before we touch upon this, and before we proceed to draw together the threads of the previous enquiry, it will be well for us first to bring up the evidence for the fourth Gospel to the same date and position as that for the other three. This then will be the subject of the next chapter.

CHAPTER XII.

THE EXTERNAL EVIDENCE FOR THE FOURTH GOSPEL.

THE fourth Gospel was, upon any theory, written later than the others, and it is not clear that it was published as soon as it was written. Both tradition and the internal evidence of the concluding chapter seem to point to the existence of somewhat peculiar relations between the Evangelist and the presbyters of the Asian Church, which would make it not improbable that the Gospel was retained for some time by the latter within their own private circle before it was given to the Church at large.

We have the express statement of Irenaeus[1], who, if he was born as is commonly supposed at Smyrna about 140 A.D., must be a good authority, that the Apostle St. John lived on till the times of Trajan (98–117 A.D.). If so, it is very possible that the Gospel was not yet published, or barely published, when Clement of Rome wrote his Epistle to the Corinthians. Neither, considering its almost esoteric character and the slow rate at which such a work would travel at first, should we

[1] *Adv. Haer.* ii. 22. 5, iii. 3. 4.

be very much surprised if it was not in the hands of Barnabas (probably in Alexandria) and Hermas (at Rome). In no case indeed could the silence of these two writers be of much moment, as in the Epistle of Barnabas the allusions to the New Testament literature are extremely few and slight, while in the Shepherd of Hermas there are no clear and certain references either to the Old Testament or the New Testament at all.

And yet there is a lively controversy round these two names as to whether or not they contain evidence for the fourth Gospel, and that they do is maintained not only by apologists, but also by writers of quite unquestionable impartiality like Dr. Keim. Dr. Keim, it will be remembered, argues against the Johannean authorship of the Gospel, and yet on this particular point he seems to be almost an advocate for the side to which he is opposed.

'Volkmar,' he says[1], 'has recently spoken of Barnabas as undeniably ignorant of the Logos-Gospel, and explained the early date assigned to his Epistle by Ewald and Weizsäcker and now also by Riggenbach as due to their perplexity at finding in it no trace of St. John. There is room for another opinion. However much it may be shown that Barnabas gives neither an incident nor a single sentence from the Gospel, that he is unacquainted with the conception of the Logos, that expressions like 'water and blood,' or the Old Testament types of Christ, and especially the serpent reared in the wilderness as an object of faith, are employed by him independently—for all this the deeper order of conceptions in the Epistle coincides in the gross or in detail so repeatedly with the Gospel that science must either assume a connection between them, or, if it leaves the problem unsolved, renounces its own calling. "The Son of God" was to be manifested in the flesh, manifested through suffering, to go to his glory through death and the Cross, to bring life and the immanent presence of the Godhead, such is here and there the leading idea. Existing before the foundation of the world, the Lord of the world, the sender of the prophets, the object of their prophecies, beheld even by Abraham, in the person of Moses himself typified as the only centre of Israel's hopes, and

[1] *Geschichte Jesu von Nazara*, i. pp. 141-143.

in so far already revealed and glorified in type before his incarnation, he was at last to appear, to dwell among us, to be seen, not as son of David but as Son of God, in the garment of the flesh, by those who could not even endure the light of this world's sun. So did he come; nay, so did he die to fulfil the promise, in the very act of his apparent defeat to dispense purification, pardon, life, to destroy death, to overcome the devil, to show forth the Resurrection, and with the Resurrection his right to future judgment; at the same time, it is true, to fill up the measure of the sins of Israel, whom he had loved exceedingly and for whom he had done such great wonders and signs, and to prepare for himself again a new people who should keep his commandments, his new law. The mission that his Father gave him he has accomplished, of his own free will and for our sake—the true explanation of his death—did he suffer. "The Jews" have not hoped upon him, clearly as the typical design of the Old Testament and Moses himself pointed to him, and, in opposition to the spiritual teaching of Moses, they have been seduced into the carnal and sensual by the devil; they have set their trust and their hopes, not upon God, but upon the fleshly circumcision and upon the visible house of God, worshipping the Lord in the temple almost like the heathen. But the Christian raises himself above the flesh and its lusts, which disturb the faculties of knowledge as well as those of will, to the Spirit and the spiritual service of God, above the ways of darkness to the ways of light; he presses on to faith, and with faith to perfect knowledge, as one born again, who is full of the Spirit of God, in whom God dwells and prophesies, interpreting past and future without being seen or heard; as taught of God and fulfilling the commandments of the new law of the Lord, a lover of the brethren, and in himself the child of peace, of joy, and of love. For this class of ideas there is no analogy in St. Paul, or even in the Epistle to the Hebrews, but only in this Gospel, much as the connection has hitherto been overlooked. Indeed, though it may still in places be questioned on which side the relation of dependence lies (it might be thought that Barnabas supplied the ideas, John the application of them, and the conception of the Logos crowning all), in any case the Gospel appeared at a date near to that of the Epistle of Barnabas. With more reason may it be said that it is not until we come to the Epistle of Barnabas that we find stiff scholastic theory a more predominant typology, an artificialised view of Judaism; besides the points of view always appear as something received and not originated—water and blood, new law, new people—and in the solemn manifestation of the Son of God immediately after the selection of the Apostles, in the great but fruitless exhibition of miracle and love for Israel, there is evidently allusion to history, that is, to John ii and xii.'

'The Epistle of Barnabas,' Dr. Keim adds, 'after the lucid demonstration of Volkmar—in spite of Hilgenfeld and Weizsäcker, and now also of Riggenbach—was undoubtedly written at the time of the re-building of the temple under the Emperor Hadrian, about the year 120 A.D. (according to Volkmar, at the earliest, 118-119), at latest 130.'

It is not to be expected that this full and able statement should carry conviction to every reader. And yet I believe that it has some solid foundation. The single instances are not perhaps such as could be pressed very far, but they derive a certain weight when taken together and as parts of a wider circle of ideas. The application of the type of the brazen serpent to Jesus in c. xii. may have been suggested by John iii. 14 sqq., but we cannot say that it was so with certainty. The same application is made by Justin in a place where there is perhaps less reason to assume a connection with the fourth Gospel; and we know that types and prophecies were eagerly sought out by the early Christians, and were soon collected in a kind of common stock from which every one drew at his pleasure. A stronger case, and one that I incline to think of some importance, is supplied by the peculiar combination of 'the water and the cross' in Barn. c. xi; not that here there is a direct and immediate, but more probably a mediate, connection with the fourth Gospel. The phrase ὁ υἱὸς τοῦ θεοῦ is not peculiar to, though it is more frequent in, and to some degree characteristic of, the Gospel and First Epistle of St. John. Φανεροῦσθαι may be claimed more decidedly, especially by comparison with the other Gospels, though it occurs with similar reference to the Incarnation in the later Pauline Epistles. Ἐλθεῖν ἐν σαρκί is again rightly classed as a Johannean phrase, though the exact counterpart is found rather in the Epistles than the Gospel. The doctrine of pre-existence is certainly taught in such passages as the application of the text, 'Let us make man in our image,' which is said to have been addressed to the Son 'from the foundation of the world' (c. v). Generally I think it may be said that the doctrine of the Incarnation, the typology, and the use of the Old Testament prophecies, approximate most distinctly to the Johannean type, though under the latter heads there is of course much debased exaggeration. The soteriology we might be perhaps tempted to connect rather on the one hand with the Epistle to the Hebrews, and on the other with those of St. Paul. There may be something of an echo of the fourth Gospel in the allusions to the unbelief and carnalised religion of the Jews. But the whole question of the speculative affinities of a writing like this requires subtle and delicate handling, and should be rather a subject for special treatment than an episode in an enquiry like the present. The opinion of Dr. Keim must be of weight, but on the whole I think it will be safest and fairest to say that, while the round assertion that the author of the Epistle was ignorant of our Gospel is not justified, the positive evidence that he made use of it is not sufficiently clear to be pressed controversially.

A similar condition of things may be predicated of the Shepherd of Hermas, though with a more decided leaning to the negative side. Here again Dr. Keim[1], as well as Canon Westcott[2], thinks that we can trace an acquaintance with the Gospel, but the indications are too general and uncertain to be relied upon. The imagery of the shepherd and the flock, as perhaps of the tower and the gate, may be as well taken from the scenes of the Roman Campagna as from any previous

---

[1] *Geschichte Jesu von Nazara*, i. pp. 143, 144.
[2] *On the Canon*, p. 182 sqq.

writing. The keeping of the commandments is a commonplace of Christianity, not to say of religion. And the Divine immanence in the soul is conceived rather in the spirit of the elder Gospels than of the fourth.

There is a nearer approach perhaps in the identification of 'the gate' with the 'Son of God,' and in the explanation with which it is accompanied. 'The rock is old because the Son of God is older than the whole of His creation; so that He was assessor to His Father in the creation of the world; the gate is new, because He was made manifest at the consummation of the last days, and they who are to be saved enter by it into the kingdom of God' (Sim. ix. 12). Here too we have the doctrine of pre-existence; and considering the juxtaposition of these three points, the pre-existence, the gate (which is the only access to the Lord), the identification of the gate with the incarnation of Jesus, we may say perhaps a *possible* reference to the fourth Gospel; *probable* it might be somewhat too much to call it. We must leave the reader to form his own estimate.

A somewhat greater force, but not as yet complete cogency, attaches to the evidence of the Ignatian letters. A parallel is alleged to a passage in the Epistle to the Romans which is found both in the Syriac and in the shorter Greek or Vossian version. 'I take no relish in corruptible food or in the pleasures of this life. I desire bread of God, heavenly bread, bread of life, which is the flesh of Jesus Christ, the Son of God, who was born in the latter days of the seed of David and Abraham; and I desire drink of God, His blood, which is love imperishable and ever-abiding life¹' (Ep. ad Rom. c. vii). This is compared with the discourse in the synagogue at Capernaum in the sixth chapter of St. John. It should be said that there is a difference of reading, though not one that materially influences the question, in the Syriac. If the parallel holds good, the peculiar diction of the author must be seen in the substitution of πόμα for πόσις of John vi. 55, and ἀένναος ζωή for ζωὴ αἰώνιος of John vi. 54. [The Ignatian phrase is perhaps more than doubtful, as it does not appear either in the Syriac, the Armenian, or the Latin version.] Still this need not stand in the way of referring the original of the passage ultimately to the Gospel. The ideas are so remarkable that it seems difficult to suppose either are accidental coincidence or quotation from another writer. .I suspect that Ignatius or the author of the Epistle really had the fourth Gospel in his mind, though not quite vividly, and by a train of comparatively remote suggestions.

The next supposed allusion is from the Epistle to the Philadelphians: 'The Spirit, coming from God, is not to be deceived; for it knoweth whence it cometh and whither it goeth, and it searcheth that which is hidden².' This is obviously *the converse* of John iii. 5, where it is said that we *do not know* the way of the Spirit, which is like the wind, &c. And yet the exact verbal similarity of the phrase οἶδεν πόθεν ἔρχεται καὶ ποῦ ὑπάγει, and its appearance in the same connection, spoken

---

[1] Οὐχ ἥδομαι τροφῇ φθορᾶς, οὐδὲ ἡδοναῖς τοῦ βίου τούτου. Ἄρτον Θεοῦ θέλω, ἄρτον οὐράνιον, ἄρτον ζωῆς, ὅς ἐστιν σὰρξ Ἰησοῦ Χριστοῦ τοῦ Υἱοῦ τοῦ Θεοῦ τοῦ γενομένου ἐν ὑστέρῳ ἐκ σπέρματος Δαβὶδ καὶ Ἀβραάμ· καὶ πόμα Θεοῦ θέλω τὸ αἷμα αὐτοῦ, ὅ ἐστιν ἀγάπη ἄφθαρτος καὶ ἀέννaos ζωή. Ep. ad Rom. c. vii.

[2] Ἀλλὰ τὸ Πνεῦμα οὐ πλανᾶται, ἀπὸ Θεοῦ ὄν· οἶδεν γὰρ πόθεν ἔρχεται καὶ ποῦ ὑπάγει, καὶ τὰ κρυπτὰ ἐλέγχει. Ep. ad Philad. c. vii.

of the Spirit, leads us to think that there was—as there may very well have been—an association of ideas. This particular phrase πόθεν ἔρχεται καὶ ποῦ ὑπάγει is very characteristically Johannean. It occurs three times over in the fourth Gospel, and not at all in the rest of the New Testament. The combination of ἔρχεσθαι and ὑπάγειν also occurs twice, and ποῦ [ὅπου] ὑπάγω [-γει, -γεις] in all twelve times in the Gospel and once in the Epistle (οὐκ οἶδε ποῦ ὑπάγει); this too, it is striking to observe, not at all elsewhere. The very word ὑπάγω is not found at all in St. Paul, St. Peter, or the Epistle to the Hebrews. Taken together with the special application to the Spirit, this must be regarded as a strong case.

Neither do the arguments of 'Supernatural Religion' succeed in proving that there is no connection with St. John in such sentences as, 'There is one God who manifested Himself through Jesus Christ His Son, who is His eternal Word' (Ad Magn. c. viii), or who is Himself the door of the Father (Ad Philad. c. ix). In regard to the first of these especially, it is doubtless true that Philo also has 'the eternal Word,' which is even the 'Son' of God; but the idea is much more consciously metaphorical, and not only did the incarnation of the Logos in a historical person never enter into Philo's mind, but 'there is no room for it in his system[1].'

It should be said that these latter passages are all found only in the Vossian recension of the Epistles, and therefore, as we saw above, are in any case evidence for the first half of the second century, while they *may* be the genuine works of Ignatius.

The Epistle of Polycarp to the Philippians, which goes

---

[1] Cf. Lipsius in Schenkel's *Bibel-Lexicon*, i. p. 98.

very much with the Ignatian Epistles and the external evidence for which it is so hard to resist, testifies to the fourth Gospel through the so-called first Epistle. That this Epistle is really by the same author as the Gospel is not indeed absolutely undoubted, but I imagine that it is as certain as any fact of literature can be. The evidence of style and diction is overwhelming [1].

We may set side by side the two passages which are thought to be parallel.

Ep. ad Phil. c. vii.

Πᾶς γὰρ ὃς ἂν μὴ ὁμολογῇ Ἰησοῦν Χριστὸν ἐν σαρκὶ ἐληλυθέναι ἀντίχριστός ἐστι· καὶ ὃς ἂν μὴ ὁμολογῇ τὸ μαρτύριον τοῦ σταυροῦ ἐκ τοῦ διαβόλου ἐστί· καὶ ὃς ἂν μεθοδεύῃ τὰ λόγια τοῦ Κυρίου πρὸς τὰς ἰδίας ἐπιθυμίας, καὶ λέγῃ μήτε ἀνάστασιν μήτε κρίσιν εἶναι, οὗτος πρωτότοκός ἐστι τοῦ Σατανᾶ.

1 *John* iv. 2, 3.

Πᾶν πνεῦμα ὃ ὁμολογεῖ Ἰησοῦν Χριστὸν ἐν σαρκὶ ἐληλυθότα ἐκ τοῦ Θεοῦ ἐστίν. καὶ πᾶν πνεῦμα ὃ μὴ ὁμολογεῖ τὸν Ἰησοῦν ἐκ τοῦ Θεοῦ οὐκ ἔστιν, καὶ τοῦτό ἐστιν τὸ τοῦ ἀντιχρίστου, κ.τ.λ.

This is precisely one of those passages where at a superficial glance we are inclined to think that there is no parallel, but where a deeper consideration tends to convince us of the opposite. The suggestion of Dr. Scholten cannot indeed be quite excluded, that both writers 'have adopted a formula in use in the early Church against various heretics [2].' But if such a formula existed it is highly probable that it took its rise from St. John's Epistle. This passage of the Epistle of Polycarp is the earliest instance of the use of the word 'Antichrist' outside the Johannean writings in which,

---

[1] The second and third Epistles stand upon a somewhat different footing.
[2] Cf. *S. R.* ii. p. 269.

alone of the New Testament, it occurs five times. Here too it occurs in conjunction with other characteristic phrases, ὁμολογεῖν, ἐν σαρκὶ ἐληλυθέναι, ἐκ τοῦ διαβόλου. The phraseology and turns of expression in these two verses accord so entirely with those of the rest of the Epistle and of the Gospel that we must needs take them to be the original work of the writer and not a quotation, and we can hardly do otherwise than see an echo of them in the words of Polycarp.

There is naturally a certain hesitation in using evidence for the Epistle as available also for the Gospel, but I have little doubt that it may justly so be used and with no real diminution of its force. The chance that the Epistle had a separate author is too small to be practically worth considering.

This then will apply to the case of Papias, of whose relations to the fourth Gospel we have no record, but of whom Eusebius expressly says, that 'he made use of testimonies from the first Epistle of John.' There is the less reason to doubt this statement, as in *every* instance in which a similar assertion of Eusebius can be verified it is found to hold good. It is much more probable that he would overlook real analogies than be led astray by merely imaginary ones—which is rather a modern form of error. In textual matters the ancients were not apt to go wrong through over-subtlety, and Eusebius himself does not, I believe, deserve the charge of 'inaccuracy and haste' that is made against him [1].

In regard to the much disputed question of the use of the fourth Gospel by Justin, those who maintain the affirmative have again emphatic support from Dr. Keim [2].

---

[1] *S. R.* ii. p. 323.   [2] *Geschichte Jesu von Nazara*, i. p. 138 sq.

We will examine some of the instances which are adduced on this side.

And first, in his account of John the Baptist, Justin has two particulars which are found in the fourth Gospel and in no other. That Gospel alone makes the Baptist himself declare, 'I am not the Christ;' and it alone puts into his mouth the application of the prophecy of Isaiah, 'I am the voice of one crying in the wilderness.' Justin combines these two sayings, treating them as an answer made by John to some who supposed that he was the Christ.

Justin, Dial. c. 88.	*John* i. 19, 20, 23.
To whom he himself also cried: 'I am not the Christ, but the voice of one crying [οὐκ εἰμὶ ὁ Χριστὸς, ἀλλὰ φωνὴ βοῶντος]; for there shall come one stronger than I,' &c.	And this is the record of John, when the Jews sent priests and Levites from Jerusalem to ask him, Who art thou? And he confessed, and denied not: but confessed, I am not the Christ [ὅτι οὐκ εἰμὶ ἐγὼ ὁ Χριστός] ... I am the voice of one crying [ἐγὼ φωνὴ βοῶντος] in the wilderness,' &c.

The passage in Justin does not profess to be a direct quotation; it is merely a historical reproduction, and, as such, it has quite as much accuracy as we should expect to find. The circumstantial coincidences are too close to be the result of accident. And Dr. Keim is doubtless right in ridiculing Volkmar's notion that Justin has merely developed Acts xiii. 25, which contains neither of the two phrases (ὁ Χριστός, φωνὴ βοῶντος) in question. To refer the passage to an unknown source such as the Gospel according to the Hebrews—all we know of which shows its affinities to have been rather on the side of the Synoptics—when we have a known source in the fourth Gospel ready to hand, is quite unreasonable [1].

No great weight, though perhaps some fractional quantity, can be ascribed to the statement that Jesus healed those who were maimed from their birth (τοὺς ἐκ γενετῆς πηρούς [2]). The word πηρός is used specially for the blind, and the fourth Evangelist is the only one who mentions the healing of congenital infirmity, which he does under this same phrase ἐκ γενετῆς, and that of a case of blindness (John ix. 1). The possibility urged in 'Supernatural Religion,' that Justin may be merely drawing from tradition, may detract from the force of this but cannot altogether remove it, especially as we have no other trace of a tradition containing this particular.

Tischendorf [3] lays stress on a somewhat remarkable phenomenon in connection with the quotation of Zech. xvi. 10, 'They shall look on him whom they pierced.' Justin gives the text of this in precisely the same form as St. John, and with the same variation from the Septuagint, ὄψονται εἰς ὃν ἐξεκέντησαν for ἐπιβλέψονται πρός με ἀνθ' ὧν κατωρχήσαντο—a variation which is also found in Rev. i. 7. Those who believe that the Apocalypse had the same author as the Gospel, naturally see in this a confirmation of their view, and it would seem to follow that Justin had had either one or both writings before him. But the assumption of an identity of authorship between the Apocalypse and the Gospel, though I believe less unreasonable than is

[1] Cf. *S. R.* ii. p. 302.
[2] So *Dial. c. Tryph.* 69; in *Apol.* i. 22 the MSS. of Justin read πονηρούς, which might stand, though some editors substitute or prefer πηρούς. In both quotations ἐκ γενετῆς is added. The nearest parallel in the Synoptics is Mark ix. 21, ἐκ παιδιόθεν (of the paralytic boy).
[3] *Wann wurden u. s. w.* p. 34.

generally supposed, still is too much disputed to build anything upon in argument. We must not ignore the other theory, that all three writers had before them and may have used independently a divergent text of the Septuagint. Some countenance is given to this by the fact that ten MSS. of the Septuagint present the same reading [1]. There can be little doubt however that it was in its origin a Christian correction, which had the double advantage of at once bringing the Greek into closer conformity to the Hebrew, and of also furnishing support to the Christian application of the prophecy. Whether this correction was made before either the Apocalypse or the Gospel were written, or whether it appeared in these works for the first time and from them was copied into other Christian writings, must remain an open question.

The saying in Apol. i. 63, 'so that they are rightly convicted both by the prophetic Spirit and by Christ Himself, that they knew neither the Father nor the Son' (οὔτε τὸν πατέρα οὔτε τὸν υἱὸν ἔγνωσαν), certainly presents a close resemblance to John xvi. 3, οὐκ ἔγνωσαν τὸν πατέρα οὐδὲ ἐμέ. But a study of the context seems to make it clear that the only passage consciously present to Justin's mind was Matt. xi. 27. Dr. Keim thinks that St. John supplied him with a commentary on the Matthaean text; but the coincidence may be after all accidental.

But the most important isolated case of literary parallelism is the well-known passage in Apol. i. 61 [2].

---

[1] Cf. Credner, *Beiträge*, ii. p. 296.

[2] [I have much pleasure in referring to a paper by Mr. James Drummond in the *Theological Review*, Oct. 1875, p. 471 sqq., dealing specially with this quotation, and maintaining much the same conclusion as my own. Compare also p. 391 sq. below.]

Apol. i. 61.	*John* iii. 3–5.
For Christ said: Except ye be born again, ye shall not enter into the kingdom of heaven. Now that it is impossible for those who have once been born to return into the wombs of those who bare them is evident to all.	Jesus answered and said unto him, Verily, verily, I say unto thee, Except any one be born over again (or possibly 'from above'), he cannot see the kingdom of God. Nicodemus saith unto him, How can a man be born when he is old? can he enter a second time into his mother's womb, and be born? Jesus answered, Verily, verily, I say unto thee, Except any one be born of Water and Spirit, he cannot enter into the kingdom of God.
Καὶ γὰρ ὁ Χριστὸς εἶπεν· Ἂν μὴ ἀναγεννηθῆτε, οὐ μὴ εἰσέλθητε εἰς τὴν βασιλείαν τῶν οὐρανῶν. Ὅτι δὲ καὶ ἀδύνατον εἰς τὰς μήτρας τῶν τεκουσῶν τοὺς ἅπαξ γεννωμένους ἐμβῆναι, φανερὸν πᾶσίν ἐστι.	Ἀπεκρίθη Ἰησοῦς καὶ εἶπεν αὐτῷ· Ἀμὴν ἀμὴν λέγω σοί, ἐὰν μή τις γεννηθῇ ἄνωθεν οὐ δύναται ἰδεῖν τὴν βασιλείαν τοῦ Θεοῦ. Λέγει πρὸς αὐτὸν ὁ Νικόδημος· Πῶς δύναται ἄνθρωπος γεννηθῆναι γέρων ὤν; μὴ δύναται εἰς τὴν κοιλίαν τῆς μητρὸς αὐτοῦ δεύτερον εἰσελθεῖν καὶ γεννηθῆναι; κ.τ.λ.

Here we have first to determine the meaning of the word ἄνωθεν in the phrase γεννηθῇ ἄνωθεν of John iii. 3 on which the extent of the parallelism to some degree turns. Does it mean 'be born *over again*,' like Justin's ἀναγεννηθῆτε? Or does it mean 'be born *from above*,' i. e. by a heavenly, divine, regeneration? To express an opinion in favour of the first of these views would naturally be to incur the charge of taking it up merely to suit the occasion. It is not however necessary; for it is sufficient to know that whether or not this meaning was originally intended by the Evangelist, it is a meaning that Justin might certainly put upon the words. That this is the case is sufficiently proved by the fact that the Syriac version (which is quoted in 'Supernatural Religion,' by a pardonable mistake, on the other side [1]) actually translates the words thus. So also does the Vulgate; with Tertullian ('renatus'), Augustine, Chrysostom (partly), Luther, Calvin, Maldonatus, &c. For the sense 'from above' are the Gothic version, Origen, Cyril, Theophylact, Bengel, &c.; on the whole a fairly equal division of opinion. The question has been of late elaborately re-argued by Mr. McClellan [2], who decides in favour of 'again.' But, without taking sides either way, it is clear that Justin would have had abundant support, in particular that of his own national version, if he intended ἀναγεννηθῆτε to be a paraphrase of γεννηθῇ ἄνωθεν.

It is obvious that if he is quoting St. John the quotation is throughout paraphrastic. And yet it is equally noticeable that he does not use the exact Johannean phrase, he uses others that are in each case almost precisely equivalent. He does not say οὐ δύναται ἰδεῖν—τὴν βασιλείαν τοῦ Θεοῦ, but he says οὐ μὴ εἰσέλθητε εἰς—τὴν βασιλείαν τῶν οὐρανῶν, the latter pair phrases which the Synoptics have already taught us to regard as convertible. He does not say μὴ δύναται εἰς τὴν κοιλίαν τῆς μητρὸς αὐτοῦ δεύτερον εἰσελθεῖν καὶ γεννηθῆναι, but he says ἀδύνατον εἰς τὰς μήτρας τῶν τεκουσῶν τοὺς ἅπαξ γεννωμένους ἐμβῆναι. And the scale seems decisively turned by

---

[1] ii. p. 308. [Has the author perhaps misunderstood Credner (*Beit.* i. p. 253), whose argument on this head is not indeed quite clear?]
[2] *The New Testament &c.*, i. p. 709.

the very remarkable combination in Justin and St. John of the saying respecting spiritual regeneration with the same strangely gross physical misconception. It is all but impossible that two minds without concert or connection should have thought of introducing anything of the kind. Nicodemus makes an objection, and Justin by repeating the same objection, and in a form that savours so strongly of platitude, has shown, I think we must say, conclusively, that he was aware that the objection had been made.

Such are some of the chief literary coincidences between Justin and the fourth Gospel; but there are others more profound. Justin undoubtedly has the one cardinal doctrine of the fourth Gospel—the doctrine of the Logos.

Thus he writes: 'Jesus Christ is in the proper sense (ἰδίως) the only Son begotten of God, being His Word (λόγος) and Firstborn Power[1].' Again, 'But His Son who alone is rightly (κυρίως) called Son, who before all created things was with Him and begotten of Him as His Word, when in the beginning He created and ordered all things through Him,' &c. Again, 'Now the next Power to God the Father and Lord of all, and Son[2], is the Word, of whom we shall relate in what follows how He was made flesh and became Man.' Again, 'The Word of God is His Son.' Again, speaking of the Gentile philosophers and lawgivers, 'Since they did not know all things respecting the Word, who is Christ, they have also frequently contradicted each

---

[1] See *Apol.* i. 23, 32, 63; ii. 10.

[2] Ἡ δὲ πρώτη δύναμις μετὰ τὸν πατέρα πάντων καὶ δεσπότην Θεὸν καὶ υἱὸς ὁ Λόγος ἐστίν. This is not quite rightly translated by Tischendorf and in 'Supernatural Religion:' υἱός, like δύναμις, is a predicate; 'the next Power who also stands in the relation of Son.'

other.' These passages are given by Tischendorf, and they might be added to without difficulty; but it is not questioned that the term Logos is found frequently in Justin's writings, and in the same sense in which it is used in the Prologue of the fourth Gospel of the eternal Son of God, who is at the same time the historical person Jesus Christ.

The natural inference that Justin was acquainted with the fourth Gospel is met by suggesting other sources for the doctrine. These sources are of two kinds, Jewish or Alexandrine.

It is no doubt true that a vivid personification of the Wisdom of God is found both in the Old Testament and in the Apocrypha. Thus in the book of Proverbs we have an elaborate ode upon Wisdom as the eternal assessor in the counsels of God: 'The Lord possessed me in the beginning of His way, before His works of old. I was set up from everlasting, from the beginning, or ever the earth was. When there were no depths, I was brought forth; when there were no fountains of water... When He prepared the heavens, I was there: when He set a compass upon the face of the deep... Then I was by Him, as one brought up with Him: and I was daily His delight, rejoicing always before Him [1].' The ideas of which this is perhaps the clearest expression are found more vaguely in other parts of the same book, in the Psalms, and in the book of Job, but they are further expanded and developed in the two Apocryphal books of Wisdom. There [2] Wisdom is represented as the 'breath of the power of God, and a pure influence flowing from the glory of the Almighty,' as 'the bright-

---

[1] Prov. viii. 22–24, 27, 30. [2] Wisd. vii. 25, 26; viii. 1, 4.

ness (ἀπαύγασμα) of the everlasting light, the unspotted mirror of the power of God, and the image of His goodness.' Wisdom 'sitteth by the throne' of God. She 'reacheth from one end to another mightily: and sweetly doth she order all things.' 'She is privy to the mysteries of the knowledge of God and a lover of His works.' God ' created her before the world[1].' We also get by the side of this, but in quite a subordinate place and in a much less advanced stage of personification, the idea of the Word or Logos: 'O God of my fathers ... who hast made all things with thy word, and ordained man through thy wisdom[2].' 'It was neither herb nor mollifying plaister that restored them to health: but thy word, O Lord, which healeth all things.' It was 'the Almighty word' (ὁ παντοδύναμος λόγος) 'that leaped down from heaven' to slay the Egyptians.

But still it will be seen that there is a distinct gap between these conceptions and that which we find in Justin. The leading idea is that of Wisdom, not of the Word. The Word is not even personified separately; it is merely the emitted power or energy of God. And the personification of Wisdom is still to a large extent poetical, it does not attain to separate metaphysical hypostasis; it is not thought of as being really personal.

The Philonian conception, on the other hand, is metaphysical, but it contains many elements that are quite discordant and inconsistent with that which we find in Justin. That it must have been so will be seen at once when we think of the sources from which Philo's doctrine was derived. It included in itself the Platonic theory of Ideas, the diffused Logos or *anima mundi* of the Stoics, and the Oriental angelology or doctrine of

---

[1] Ecclus. xxiv. 9.   [2] Wisd. ix. 1, 2; xvi. 12; xviii. 15.

intermediate beings between God and man. On its Platonic side the Logos is the Idea of Ideas summing up the world of high abstractions which themselves are also regarded as possessing a separate individuality; they are Logoi by the side of the Logos. On its Stoic side it becomes a Pantheistic Essence pervading the life of things; it is 'the law,' 'the bond' which holds the world together; the world is its 'garment.' On its Eastern side, the Logos is the 'Archangel,' the 'Captain of the hosts of heaven,' the 'Mother-city' from which they issue as colonists, the 'Vice-gerent' of the Great King [1].

It needed a more powerful mind than Justin's to reduce all this to its simple Christian expression, to take the poetry of Judaea and the philosophy of Alexandria and to interpret and realise both in the light of the historical events of the birth and life of Christ. 'The Word became flesh' is the key by which Justin is made intelligible, and that key is supplied by the fourth Gospel. No other Christian writer had combined these two ideas before—the divine Logos, with the historical personality of Jesus. When therefore we find the ideas combined as in Justin, we are necessarily referred to the fourth Gospel for them; for the strangely inverted suggestion of Volkmar, that the author of the fourth Gospel borrowed from Justin, is on chronological, if not on other grounds, certainly untenable. We shall see that the fourth Gospel was without doubt in existence at the date which Volkmar assigns to Justin's Apology, 150 A.D.

The history of the discussion as to the relation of the Clementine Homilies to the fourth Gospel is highly

[1] Cf. Lipsius in *S. B. L.* i. p. 95 sqq.

instructive, not only in itself, but also for the light which it throws upon the general character of our enquiry and the documents with which it is concerned. It has been already mentioned that up to the year 1853 the Clementine Homilies were only extant in a mutilated form, ending abruptly in the middle of Hom. xix. 14. In that year a complete edition was at last published by Dressel from a manuscript in the Vatican containing the rest of the nineteenth and the twentieth Homily. The older portion occupies in all, with the translation and critical apparatus, 381 large octavo pages in Dressel's edition; the portion added by Dressel occupies 34. And yet up to 1853, though the Clementine Homilies had been carefully studied with reference to the use of the fourth Gospel, only a few indications had been found, and those were disputed. In fact, the controversy was very much at such a point as others with which we have been dealing; there was a certain probability in favour of the conclusion that the Gospel had been used, but still considerably short of the highest. Since the publication of the conclusion of the Homilies the question has been set at rest. Hilgenfeld, who had hitherto been a determined advocate of the negative theory, at once gave up his ground[1]; and Volkmar, who had somewhat less to retract, admitted and admits[2] that the fact of the use of the Gospel must be considered as proved. The author of 'Supernatural Religion' stands alone in still resisting this conviction[3], but the result I suspect will be only to show in stronger relief the one-sidedness of his critical method.

---

[1] *Der Kanon und die Kritik des N. T.* (Halle, 1863), p. 29; *Einleitung*, p. 43, n.
[2] *Der Ursprung unserer Evangelien*, p. 63.   [3] ii. p. 346.

We will follow the example that is set us in presenting the whole of the passages alleged to contain allusions to the fourth Gospel; and it is the more interesting to do so with the key that the recent discovery has put into our hands. The first runs thus:—

Hom. iii. 52.	*John* x. 9.
Therefore he, being a true prophet, said: I am the gate of life; he that entereth in through me entereth into life: for the teaching that can save is none other [than mine].	I am the door: by me if any one enter in, he shall be saved, and shall come in and go out, and shall find pasture.
Διὰ τοῦτο αὐτὸς ἀληθὴς ὢν προφήτης ἔλεγεν· Ἐγώ εἰμι ἡ πύλη τῆς ζωῆς· ὁ δι' ἐμοῦ εἰσερχόμενος εἰσέρχεται εἰς τὴν ζωήν· ὡς οὐκ οὔσης ἑτέρας τῆς σώζειν δυναμένης διδασκαλίας.	Ἐγώ εἰμι ἡ θύρα· δι' ἐμοῦ ἐάν τις εἰσέλθῃ σωθήσεται καὶ εἰσελεύσεται καὶ ἐξελεύσεται καὶ νομὴν εὑρήσει.

Apart from other evidence it would have been somewhat precarious to allege this as proof of the use of the fourth Gospel, and yet I believe there would have been a distinct probability that it was taken from that work. The parallel is much closer—in spite of θύρα for πύλη—than is Matt. vii. 13, 14 (the 'narrow gate') which is adduced in 'Supernatural Religion,' and the interval is very insufficiently bridged over by Ps. cxviii. 19, 20 ('This is the gate of the Lord'). The key-note of the passage is given in the identification of the gate with the person of the Saviour ('*I* am the door') and in the remarkable expression 'he that entereth in *through me*,' which is retained in the Homily. It is curious to notice the way in which the σωθήσεται of the Gospel has been expanded exegetically.

U

Less doubtful—and indeed we should have thought almost beyond a doubt—is the next reference; 'My sheep hear my voice.'

Hom. iii. 52.	*John* x. 27.
Τὰ ἐμὰ πρόβατα ἀκούει τῆς ἐμῆς φωνῆς.	Τὰ πρόβατα τὰ ἐμὰ τῆς φωνῆς μου ἀκούει.

'There was no more common representation amongst the Jews of the relation of God and his people than that of Shepherd and his sheep[1].' That is to say, it occurs of Jehovah or of the Messiah some twelve or fifteen times in the Old and New Testament together, but never with anything at all closely approaching to the precise and particular feature given here. Let the reader try to estimate the chances that another source than the fourth Gospel is being quoted. Criticism is made null and void when such seemingly plain indications as this are discarded in favour of entirely unknown quantities like the 'Gospel according to the Hebrews.' If the author of 'Supernatural Religion' were to turn his own powers of derisive statement against his own hypotheses they would present a very strange appearance.

The reference that follows has in some respects a rather marked resemblance to that which we were discussing in Justin, and for the relation between them to be fully appreciated should be given along with it:—

Justin, Apol. i. 61.	*Clem. Hom.* xi. 26.	*John* iii. 3, 5.
Except ye be born again ye shall not enter into the kingdom of heaven.	Verily I say unto you, Except ye be born again with living water, in the	Verily, verily, I say unto thee, Except any one be born over again (or 'from

[1] S. R. ii. p. 340.

name of Father, Son and Holy Ghost, ye shall not enter into the kingdom of heaven.		above'), he cannot see the kingdom of God ... Except any one be born of water and Spirit, he cannot enter into the kingdom of God.
Ἂν μὴ ἀναγεννηθῆτε οὐ μὴ εἰσέλθητε εἰς τὴν βασιλείαν τῶν οὐρανῶν.	Ἀμὴν ὑμῖν λέγω, ἐὰν μὴ ἀναγεννηθῆτε ὕδατι ζῶντι εἰς ὄνομα πατρός, υἱοῦ, ἁγίου πνεύματος, οὐ μὴ εἰσέλθητε εἰς τὴν βασιλείαν τῶν οὐρανῶν.	Ἀμὴν ἀμὴν λέγω σοι, ἐὰν μή τις γεννηθῇ ἄνωθεν, οὐ δύναται ἰδεῖν τὴν βασιλείαν τοῦ Θεοῦ ... ἐὰν μή τις γεννηθῇ ἐξ ὕδατος καὶ πνεύματος, οὐ δύναται εἰσελθεῖν εἰς τὴν βασιλείαν τοῦ Θεοῦ.
		πνεύμ. add. ἁγίου Vulg. (Clementine edition), a, ff, m, Æth., Orig. (Latin translator).

Here it will be noticed that Justin and the Clementines have four points in common, ἀναγεννηθῆτε for γεννηθῇ ἄνωθεν, the second person plural (twice over) for τις and the singular, οὐ μὴ and the subjunctive for οὐ δύναται and infinitive, and τὴν βασιλείαν τῶν οὐρανῶν for τὴν βασιλείαν τοῦ Θεοῦ. To the last of these points much importance could not be attached in itself, as it represents a persistent difference between the first and the other Synoptists even where they had the same original. As both the Clementines and Justin used the first Gospel more than the others, it is only natural that they should fall into the habit of using its characteristic phrase. Neither would the other points have had very much importance taken separately, but their importance increases considerably when they come to be taken together.

On the other hand, we observe in the Clementines (where it is however connected with Matt. xxviii. 19) the sufficiently near equivalent for the striking Johannean phrase ἐξ ὕδατος καὶ πνεύματος which is omitted entirely by Justin.

The most probable view of the case seems to be that both the Clementines and Justin are quoting from memory. Both have in their memory the passage of St. John, but both have also distinctly before them (so much the more distinctly as it is the Gospel which they habitually used) the parallel passage in Matt. xviii. 3,—where *all the last three* out of the four common variations are found, besides, along with the Clementines, the omission of the second ἀμήν,—'Verily I say unto you, Except ye be converted, and become as little children, ye shall not enter into the kingdom of heaven' (οὐ μὴ εἰσέλθητε εἰς τὴν βασιλείαν τῶν οὐρανῶν). It is out of the question that this *only* should have been present to the mind of the writers; and, in view of the repetition of Nicodemus' misunderstanding by Justin and of the baptism by water and Spirit in the Clementine Homilies, it seems equally difficult to exclude the reference to St. John. It is in fact a Johannean saying in a Matthaean framework.

There is the more reason to accept this solution, that neither Justin nor the Clementines can in any case represent the original form of the passages quoted. If Justin's version were correct, whence did the Clementines get the ὕδατι ζῶντι κ.τ.λ.? if the Clementine, then whence did Justin get the misconception of Nicodemus? But the Clementine version is in any case too eccentric to stand.

The last passage is the one that is usually considered to be decisive as to the use of the fourth Gospel.

Hom. xix. 22.	*John* ix. 1–3.
Hence too our Teacher, when explaining to those who asked of him respecting the man who was blind from his birth and recovered his sight, whether this man sinned or his parents that he should be born blind, replied: Neither this man sinned, nor his parents; but that through him the power of God might be manifested healing the sins of ignorance.	And as he passed by, he saw a man blind from his birth. And his disciples asked him, saying, Rabbi, who sinned, this man or his parents, that he should be born blind? Jesus answered, Neither hath this man sinned, nor his parents: but that the works of God should be manifested in him.
Ὅθεν καὶ διδάσκαλος ἡμῶν περὶ τοῦ[1] ἐκ γενετῆς πηροῦ καὶ ἀναβλέψαντος παρ' αὐτοῦ ἐξετάζων ἐρωτήσασιν, εἰ οὗτος ἥμαρτεν ἢ οἱ γονεῖς αὐτοῦ, ἵνα τυφλὸς γεννηθῇ[1] ἀπεκρίνατο οὔτε οὗτός τι ἥμαρτεν, οὔτε οἱ γονεῖς αὐτοῦ, ἀλλ' ἵνα δι' αὐτοῦ φανερωθῇ ἡ δύναμις τοῦ Θεοῦ τῆς ἀγνοίας ἰωμένη τὰ ἁμαρτήματα.	Καὶ παράγων εἶδεν ἄνθρωπον τυφλὸν ἐκ γενετῆς. καὶ ἠρώτησαν αὐτὸν οἱ μαθηταὶ αὐτοῦ λέγοντες, Ῥαββεί, τίς ἥμαρτεν, οὗτος ἢ οἱ γονεῖς αὐτοῦ, ἵνα τυφλὸς γεννηθῇ; ἀπεκρίθη Ἰησοῦς, Οὔτε οὗτος ἥμαρτεν οὔτε οἱ γονεῖς αὐτοῦ, ἀλλ' ἵνα φανερωθῇ τὰ ἔργα τοῦ Θεοῦ ἐν αὐτῷ.

The author of 'Supernatural Religion' undertakes to show 'that the context of this passage in the Homily bears positive characteristics which render it impossible that it can have been taken from the fourth Gospel[2].' I think we may venture to say that he does indeed show

---

[1] The force of the article (τοῦ πηροῦ) should be noticed, as showing that the incident (and therefore the Gospel) is assumed to be well known.

[2] *S. R.* ii. p. 341.

somewhat conspicuously the way in which he uses the word 'impossible' and the kind of grounds on which that and such like terms are employed throughout his work.

It is a notorious fact, abundantly established by certain quotations from the Old Testament and elsewhere, that the last thing regarded by the early patristic writers was context. But in this case the context is perfectly in keeping, and to a clear and unprejudiced eye it presents no difficulty. The Clementine writer is speaking of the origin of physical infirmities, and he says that these are frequently due, not to moral error, but to mere ignorance on the part of parents. As an instance of this he gives the case of the man who was born blind, of whom our Lord expressly said that neither he nor his parents had sinned—morally or in such a way as to deserve punishment. On the contrary they had erred simply through ignorance, and the object of the miracle was to make a display of the Divine mercy removing the consequences of such error. 'And in reality,' he proceeds, 'things of this kind are the result of ignorance. The misfortunes of which you spoke, proceed from ignorance and not from any wicked action.' This is perfectly compatible with every word of the Johannean narrative. The concluding clause of the quotation is merely a paraphrase of the original (no part of the quotation professes to be exact), bringing out a little more prominently the special point of the argument. There is ample room for this. The predetermined object of the miracle, says St. John, was to display the works of God, and the Clementine writer specifies the particular work of God displayed—the mercy which heals the evil consequences of ignorance.

If there is anything here at all inconsistent with the Gospel it would be interesting to know (and we are not told) what was the kind of original that the author of the Homily really had before him.

A further discussion of this passage I should hardly suppose to be necessary. Nothing could be more wanton than to assign this passage to an imaginary Gospel merely on the ground alleged. The hypothesis was less violent in regard to the Synoptic Gospels, which clearly contain a large amount of common matter that might also have found its way into other hands. We have evidence of the existence of other Gospels presenting a certain amount of affinity to the first Gospel, but the fourth is stamped with an idiosyncracy which makes it unique in its kind. If there is to be this freedom in inventing unknown documents, reproducing almost verbatim the features of known ones, sober criticism is at an end.

That the Clementine Homilies imply the use of the fourth Gospel may be considered to be, not indeed certain in a strict sense of the word, but as probable as most human affairs can be. The real element of doubt is in regard to their date, and their evidence must be taken subject to this uncertainty.

It is perhaps hardly worth while to delay over the Epistle to Diognetus: not that I do not believe the instances alleged by Tischendorf and Dr. Westcott[1] to be in themselves sound, but because there exists too little evidence to determine the date of the Epistle, and because it may be doubted whether the argument for

---

[1] Tischendorf, *Wann wurden*, p. 40; Westcott, *Canon*, p. 80.

the use of the fourth Gospel in the Epistle can be expressed strongly in an objective form. The allusions in question are not direct quotations, but are rather reminiscences of language. The author of 'Supernatural Religion' has treated them as if they were the former[1]; he has enquired into the context &c., not very successfully. But such enquiry is really out of place. When the writer of the Epistle says, 'Christians dwell in the world but are not of the world' (οὐκ εἰσὶ δὲ ἐκ τοῦ κόσμου, = exactly John xvii. 14; note peculiar use of the preposition); 'For God loved men for whose sakes He made the world ... unto whom He sent His only-begotten Son' (= John iii. 16, 'God so loved the world that He gave His only-begotten Son'); 'How will you love Him who so beforehand loved you' (προαγαπήσαντα; cf. 1 John iv. 19, πρῶτος ἠγάπησεν); 'He sent His Son as wishing to save ... and not to condemn' (σώζων ... κρίνων, cf. John iii. 16),—the probability is about as great that he had in his mind St. John's language as it would be if the same phrases were to occur in a modern sermon. It is a real probability; but not one that can be urged very strongly.

Of more importance—indeed of high importance—is the evidence drawn from the remains of earlier writers preserved by Irenaeus and Hippolytus. There is a clear reference to the fourth Gospel in a passage for which Irenaeus alleges the authority of certain 'Presbyters,' who at the least belonged to an elder generation than his own. There can be little doubt indeed that they are the same as those whom he describes three sentences later and with only a momentary break in the

[1] ii. p. 357 sqq.

oblique narration into which the passage is thrown, as 'the Presbyters, disciples of the Apostles.' It may be well to give the language of Irenaeus in full as it has been the subject of some controversy. Speaking of the rewards of the just in the next world, he says [1]:—

'For Esaias says, "Like as the new heaven and new earth which I create remain before me, saith the Lord, so your seed and your name shall stand." And as the Presbyters say, then too those who are thought worthy to have their abode in Heaven shall go thither, and some shall enjoy the delights of Paradise, while others shall possess the splendour of the City; for everywhere the Saviour shall be seen according as they shall be worthy who look upon Him. [So far the sentence has been in oratio recta, but here it becomes oblique.] And [they say] that there is this distinction in dwelling between those who bear fruit an hundred fold and those who bear sixty and those who bear thirty, some of whom shall be carried off into the Heavens, some shall stay in Paradise, and some shall dwell in the City. And for this reason, [they say that] the Lord declared (εἰρηκέναι) that *in my Father's* [realm] *are many mansions;* for all things [are] of God, who gives to all the fitting habitation: even as His Word saith (*ait*), that to all is allotted by the Father as each is or shall be worthy. And this is (*est*) the couch upon which they shall recline who are bidden to His marriage supper. That this is (*esse*) the order and disposition of the saved, the Presbyters, disciples of the Apostles, say,' etc.

That Irenaeus is here merely giving the 'exegesis of his own day,' as the author of 'Supernatural Religion' suggests[2], is not for a moment tenable. Irenaeus does indeed interpose for two sentences (Omnia enim ... ad nuptias) to give his own comment on the saying of the Presbyters; but these are sharply cut off from the rest by the use of the present indicative instead of the infinitive. There can be no question at all that the quotation 'in My Father's realm are many mansions' (ἐν τοῖς τοῦ Πατρός μου μονὰς εἶναι πολλάς) belongs to the Presbyters, and there can be but little doubt that these Presbyters are the same as those spoken of as 'disciples of the Apostles.'

[1] *Adv. Haer.* v. 36. 1, 2.   [2] *S. R.* ii. p. 329.

Whether they were also 'the Presbyters' referred to as his authority by Papias is quite a secondary and subordinate question. Considering the Chiliastic character of the passage, the conjecture[1] that they were does not seem to me unreasonable. This however we cannot determine positively. It is quite enough that Irenaeus evidently attributes to them an antiquity considerably beyond his own; that, in fact, he looks upon them as supplying the intermediate link between his age and that of the Apostles.

Two quotations from the fourth Gospel are attributed to Basilides, both of them quite indisputable as quotations. The first is found in the twenty-second chapter of the seventh book of the 'Refutation,' 'That was the true light which lighteth every man that cometh into the world[2]' ($\tilde{\eta}\nu$ τὸ φῶς τὸ ἀληθινόν, ὃ φωτίζει πάντα ἄνθρωπον ἐρχόμενον εἰς τὸν κόσμον$=$John i. 9), and the second in the twenty-seventh chapter, 'My hour is not yet come' (οὔπω ἥκει ἡ ὥρα μου$=$John ii. 4). Both of these passages are instances of the exegesis by which the Basilidian doctrines were defended.

The real question is here, as in regard to the Synoptics, whether the quotations were made by Basilides himself or by his disciples, 'Isidore and his crew.' The second instance I am disposed to think may possibly

---

[1] Advanced by Routh (or rather Feuardentius in his notes on Irenaeus; cf. *Rel. Sac.* i. p. 31), and adopted by Tischendorf and Dr. Westcott. [The identification has since been ably and elaborately maintained by Dr. Lightfoot; see *Cont. Rev.* Oct. 1875, p. 841 sqq.]

[2] It is not necessary here to determine the sense in which these words are to be taken. I had elsewhere given my reasons for taking ἐρχόμενον with ἄνθρωπον, as A. V. (*Fourth Gospel*, p. 6, n.). Mr. M'Clellan is now to be added to the number of those who prefer to take it with φῶς, and argues ably in favour of his opinion.

be due to the later representatives of this school, because, though the quotation is introduced by φησί in the singular, and though Basilides himself can in no case be excluded, still there is nothing in the chapter to identify the subject of φησί specially with him, and in the next sentence Hippolytus writes, 'This is that which they understand (ὁ κατ' αὐτοὺς νενοημένος) by the inner spiritual man,' &c. But the earlier instance is different. There Basilides himself does seem to be specially singled out.

He is mentioned by name only two sentences above that in which the quotation occurs. Hippolytus is referring to the Basilidian doctrine of the origin of things. He says, 'Now since it was not allowable to say that something non-existent had come into being as a projection from a non-existent Deity — for Basilides avoids and shuns the existences of things brought into being by projection'—for what need is there of projection, or why should matter be presupposed in order that God should make a world, just as a spider its web or as mortal man in making things takes brass or wood or any other portion of matter? But He spake—so he says—and it was done, and this is, as these men say, that which is said by Moses: "Let there be light, and there was light." Whence, he says, came the light? Out of nothing; for we are not told—he says—whence it came, but only that it was at the voice of Him that spake. Now He that spake—he says—was not, and that which was made, was not. Out of that which was not—he

---

[1] The translation of this difficult passage has been left on purpose somewhat baldly literal. The idea seems to be that Basilides refused to accept projection or emanation as a hypothesis to account for the existence of created things. Compare Mansel, *Gnost. Her.* p. 148.

says—was made the seed of the world, the word which was spoken, "Let there be light;" and this—he says—is that which is spoken in the Gospels; "That was the true light which lighteth every man that cometh into the world."' We must not indeed overlook the fact that the plural occurs once in the middle of this passage as introducing the words of Moses; 'as these men say.' And yet, though this decidedly modifies, I do not think that it removes the probability that Basilides himself is being quoted. It seems a fair inference that at the beginning of the passage Hippolytus had the work of Basilides actually before him; and the single digression in λέγουσιν οὗτοι does not seem enough to show that it was laid aside. This is confirmed when we look back two chapters at the terms in which the whole account of the Basilidian system is introduced. 'Let us see,' Hippolytus says, 'how flagrantly Basilides as well as (B. ὁμοῦ καὶ) Isidore and all their crew contradict not only Matthias but the Saviour himself.' Stress is laid upon the name of Basilides, as if to say, 'It is not merely a new-fangled heresy, but dates back to the head and founder of the school.' When in the very next sentence Hippolytus begins with φησί, the natural construction certainly seems to be that he is quoting some work of Basilides which he takes as typical of the doctrine of the whole school. A later work would not suit his purpose or prove his point. Basilides includes Isidore, but Isidore does not include Basilides.

We conclude then that there is a probability—not an overwhelming, but quite a substantial, probability—that Basilides himself used the fourth Gospel, and used it as an authoritative record of the life of Christ. But

Basilides began to teach in 125 A.D., so that his evidence, supposing it to be valid, dates from a very early period indeed: and it should be remembered that this is the only uncertainty to which it is subject. That the quotation is really from St. John cannot be doubted.

The account which Hippolytus gives of the Valentinians also contains an allusion to the fourth Gospel; 'All who came before Me are thieves and robbers' (cf. John x. 8). But here the master and the disciples are more confused. Less equivocal evidence is afforded by the statements of Irenaeus respecting the Valentinians. He says that the Valentinians used the fourth Gospel very freely (plenissime[1]). This applies to a date that cannot be in any case later than 180 A.D., and that may extend almost indefinitely backwards. There is no reason to say that it does not include Valentinus himself. Positive evidence is wanting, but negative evidence still more. Apart from evidence to the contrary, there must be a presumption against the introduction of a new work which becomes at once a frequently quoted authority midway in the history of a school.

But to keep to facts apart from presumptions. Irenaeus represents Ptolemaeus as quoting largely from the Prologue to the Gospel. But Ptolemaeus, as we have seen, had already gathered a school about him when Irenaeus became acquainted with him. His evidence therefore may fairly be said to cover the period from 165–175 A.D. The author of 'Supernatural Religion' seems to be somewhat beside the mark when he says that 'in regard to Ptolemaeus all that is affirmed is that in the Epistle to Flora ascribed to him expressions

---

[1] *Adv. Haer.* iii. 11. 7.

found in John i. 3 are used.' True it is that such expressions are found, and before we accept the theory in 'Supernatural Religion' that the parenthesis in which they occur is due to Epiphanius who quotes the letter in full himself[1], it is only right that some other instance should be given of such parenthetic interruption. The form in which the letter is quoted, not in fragments interspersed with comments but complete and at full length, with a formal heading and close, really excludes such a hypothesis. But, a century and a half before Epiphanius, Irenaeus had given a string of Valentinian comments on the Prologue, ending with the words, 'Et Ptolemaeus quidem ita[2].' Heracleon, too, is coupled with Ptolemaeus by Irenaeus[3], and according to the view of the author of 'Supernatural Religion,' had a school around him at the time of Irenaeus' visit to Rome in 178 A.D. But this Heracleon was the author of a Commentary on St. John's Gospel to which Origen in his own parallel work frequently alludes. These are indeed dismissed in 'Supernatural Religion' as 'unsupported references.' But we may well ask, what support they need. The references are made in evident good faith. He says, for instance[4], that Heracleon's exegesis

---

[1] *Haer.* 216-222.

[2] It should however be noticed that these words are given only in the old Latin translation of Irenaeus and are wanting in the Greek as preserved by Epiphanius. Whether the words were accidentally omitted, or whether they were inserted inferentially, for greater clearness, by the translator, it is hard to say. In any case the bearing of the quotations must be very much the same. If not made by Ptolemaeus himself, they were made by a contemporary of Ptolemaeus, i. e. at least by a writer anterior to Irenaeus.

[3] *Adv. Haer.* ii. 4. 1 ; cf. *S. R.* ii. p. 211 sq.

[4] The somewhat copious fragments of Heracleon's Commentary are given in Stieren's edition of Irenaeus, p. 938 sqq. Origen says that Heracleon read 'Bethany' in John i. 28 (M'Clellan, i. p. 708).

of John i. 3, 'All things were made by Him,' excluding from this the world and its contents, is very forced and without authority. Again, he has misinterpreted John i. 4, making 'in Him was life' mean not 'in Him' but 'in spiritual men.' Again, he wrongly attributes John i. 18, not to the Evangelist, but to the Baptist. And so on.' The allusions are all made in this incidental manner; and the life of Origen, if he was born, as is supposed, about 185 A.D., would overlap that of Heracleon. What evidence could be more sufficient? or if such evidence is to be discarded, what evidence are we to accept? Is it to be of the kind that is relied upon for referring quotations to the Gospel according to the Hebrews, or the Gospel according to Peter, or the Γέννα Μαρίας? There are sometimes no doubt reasonable grounds for scepticism as to the patristic statements, but none such are visible here. On the contrary, that Heracleon should have written a commentary on the fourth Gospel falls in entirely with what Irenaeus says as to the large use that was made of that Gospel by the Valentinians.

As we approach the end of the third and beginning of the fourth quarter of the second century the evidence for the fourth Gospel becomes widespread and abundant. At this date we have attention called to the discrepancy between the Gospels as to the date of the Crucifixion by Claudius Apollinaris. We have also Tatian, the Epistle of the Churches of Vienne and Lyons, the heathen Celsus and the Muratorian Canon, and then a very few years later Theophilus of Antioch and Irenaeus.

I imagine that there can be really no doubt about

Tatian. Whatever may have been the nature of the Diatessaron, the 'Address to the Greeks' contains references which it is mere paradox to dispute. I will not press the first of these which is given by Dr. Westcott, not because I do not believe that it is ultimately based upon the fourth Gospel, still less that there is the slightest contradiction to St. John's doctrine, but because Tatian's is a philosophical comment perhaps a degree too far removed from the original to be quite producible as evidence. It is one of the earliest speculations as to the ontological relation between the Father and the Son. In the beginning God was alone—though all things were with Him potentially. By the mere act of volition He gave birth to the Logos, who was the real originative cause of things. Yet the existence of the Logos was not such as to involve a separation of identity in the Godhead; it involved no diminution in Him from whom the Logos issued. Having been thus first begotten, the Logos in turn begat our creation, &c. The Logos is thus represented as being at once prior to creation (the Johannean ἐν ἀρχῇ) and the efficient cause of it—which is precisely the doctrine of the Prologue.

The other two passages are however quite unequivocal.

Orat. ad Graecos, c. xiii.	*John* i. 5.
And this is therefore that saying:	
The darkness comprehends not the light.	And the light shineth in the darkness; and the darkness comprehended it not.
Καὶ τοῦτο ἔστιν ἄρα τὸ εἰρημένον· Ἡ σκοτία τὸ φῶς οὐ καταλαμβάνει.	Καὶ τὸ φῶς ἐν τῇ σκοτίᾳ φαίνει, κ ὶ ἡ σκοτία αὐτὸ οὐ κατέλαβεν.

On this there is the following comment in 'Supernatural Religion [1]:' '"The saying" is distinctly different in language from the parallel in the Gospel, and it may be from a different Gospel. We have already remarked that Philo called the Logos "the Light," and quoting in a peculiar form, Ps. xxvi. 1: 'For the Lord is my light (φῶς) and my Saviour,' he goes on to say that as the sun divides day and night, so Moses says, 'God divides light and darkness' (τὸν Θεὸν φῶς καὶ σκότος διατειχίσαι), when we turn away to things of sense we use 'another light' which is in no way different from 'darkness.' The constant use of the same similitude of light and darkness in the Canonical Epistles shows how current it was in the Church; and nothing is more certain than the fact that it was neither originated by, nor confined to, the fourth Gospel.' Such criticism refutes itself, and it is far too characteristic of the whole book. Nothing is adduced that even remotely corresponds to the very remarkable phrase ἡ σκοτία τὸ φῶς καταλαμβάνει, and yet for these imaginary parallels one that is perfectly plain and direct is rejected.

The use of the phrase τὸ εἰρημένον should be noticed. It is the formula used, especially by St. Luke, in quotation from the Old Testament Scriptures.

The other passage is:—

Orat. ad Graecos, c. xix.	*John* i. 3.
All things were by him, and without him hath been made nothing.	All things were made through him; and without him was nothing made [that hath been made].

[1] ii. p. 378.

Πάντα ὑπ' αὐτοῦ καὶ χωρὶς αὐτοῦ γέγονεν οὐδὲ ἕν.	Πάντα δι' αὐτοῦ ἐγένετο, καὶ χωρὶς αὐτοῦ ἐγένετο οὐδὲ ἕν [ὃ γέγονεν]. 'The early Fathers, no less than the early heretics,' placed the full stop at οὐδὲ ἕν, connecting the words that follow with the next sentence. See M'Clellan and Tregelles *ad loc.*

'Tatian here speaks of God and not of the Logos, and in this respect, as well as language and context, the passage differs from the fourth Gospel[1],' &c. Nevertheless it may safely be left to the reader to say whether or not it was taken from it.

The Epistle of the Churches of Vienne and Lyons contains the following :—

Ep. Vienn. et Lugd. § iv.	*John* xvi. 2.
Thus too was fulfilled that which was spoken by our Lord; that a time shall come in which every one that killeth you shall think that he offereth God service.	Yea, the hour cometh, that every one that killeth you will think he offereth God service.
Ἐλεύσεται καιρὸς ἐν ᾧ πᾶς ὁ ἀποκτείνας ὑμᾶς δόξει λατρείαν προσφέρειν τῷ Θεῷ.	Ἀλλ' ἔρχεται ὥρα ἵνα πᾶς ὁ ἀποκτείνας ὑμᾶς, δόξῃ λατρείαν προσφέρειν τῷ Θεῷ.

It is true that there are 'indications of similar discourses' in the Synoptics, but of none containing a trait at all closely resembling this. The chances that precisely the same combination of words (ὁ ἀποκτείνας ὑμᾶς δόξει λατρείαν προσφέρειν τῷ Θεῷ) occurred in a lost Gospel must be necessarily very small indeed, especially

---

[1] *S. R.* ii. p. 379.

when we remember that the original saying was probably spoken in Aramaic and not in Greek[1].

Dr. Keim, in the elaborate monograph mentioned above, decides that Celsus made use of the fourth Gospel. He remarks upon it as curious, that more traces should indeed be found 'both in Celsus and his contemporary Tatian of John than of his two nearest predecessors[2].' Of the instances given by Dr. Keim, the first (i. 41, the sign seen by the Baptist) depends on a somewhat doubtful reading (παρὰ τῷ Ἰωάννῃ, which should be perhaps παρὰ τῷ Ἰορδάνῃ); the second, the demand for a sign localised specially in the temple (i. 67; cf. John x. 23, 24), seems fairly to hold good. 'The destination of Jesus alike for good and evil' (iv. 7, 'that those who received it, having been good, should be saved; while those who received it not, having been shown to be bad, should be punished') is indeed an idea peculiarly Johannean and creates a *presumption* of the use of the Gospel; we ought not perhaps to say more. I can hardly consider the simple allusions to 'flight' (φεύγειν, ii. 9; τῇδε κἀκεῖσε ἀποδεδρακέναι, i. 62) as necessarily references to the retreat to phraim in John xi. 54. So too the expression 'bound' in ii. 9, and the 'conflict with Satan' in vi. 42, ii. 47, seem too vague to be used as proof. Still Volkmar too declares it to be 'notorious' that Celsus was acquainted with the fourth Gospel, alleging i. 67 (as above), ii. 31 (an allusion to the Logos), ii. 36 (a satirical allusion to the issue of blood and water), which passages really seem on the

---

[1] There is also perhaps a probable reference to St. John in § 6, τῆς αἰωνίου πηγῆς τοῦ ὕδατος τῆς ζωῆς τοῦ ἐξιόντος ἐκ τῆς νηδύος τοῦ Χριστοῦ.

[2] *Celsus' Wahres Wort*, p. 229.

whole to justify the assertion, though not in a quite unqualified form.

We ought not to omit to mention that there is a second fragment by Apollinaris, bishop of Hierapolis, besides that to which we have already alluded, and preserved like it in the Paschal Chronicle, which confirms unequivocally the conclusion that he knew and used the fourth Gospel. Amongst other titles that are applied to the crucified Saviour, he is spoken of as 'having been pierced in His sacred side,' as 'having poured out of His side those two cleansing streams, water and blood, word and spirit [1].' This incident is recorded only in the fourth Gospel.

In like manner when Athenagoras says 'The Father and the Son being one' (ἑνὸς ὄντος τοῦ Πατρὸς καὶ τοῦ Υἱοῦ), it is probable that he is alluding to John x. 30, 'I and my Father are one,' not to mention an alleged, but perhaps somewhat more doubtful, reference to John xvii. 3 [2].

But the most decisive witness before we come to Irenaeus is the Muratorian Canon. Here we have the fourth Gospel definitely assigned to its author, and finally established in its place amongst the canonical or authoritative books. It is true that the account of the way in which the Gospel came to be composed is mixed up with legendary matter. According to it the Gospel was written in obedience to a dream sent to Andrew the Apostle, after he and his fellow disciples and bishops had fasted for three days at the request of John. In

---

[1] ὁ τὴν ἁγίαν πλευρὰν ἐκκεντηθείς, ὁ ἐκχέας ἐκ τῆς πλευρᾶς αὐτοῦ τὰ δύο πάλιν καθάρσια, ὕδωρ καὶ αἷμα, λόγον καὶ πνεῦμα. See Routh, *Rel. Sac.* i. p. 161.

[2] Lardner, *Credibility*, &c., ii. p. 196.

this dream it was revealed that John should write the narrative subject to the revision of the rest. So the Gospel is the work of an eyewitness, and, though it and the other Gospels differ in the objects of their teaching, all are inspired by the same Spirit.

There may perhaps in this be some kernel of historical fact, as the sort of joint authorship or revision to which it points seems to find some support in the concluding verses of the Gospel ('we know that his witness is true'). However this may be, the evidence of the fragment is of more real importance and value, as showing the estimation in which at this date the Gospel was held. It corresponds very much to what is now implied in the word 'canonical,' and indeed the Muratorian fragment presents us with a tentative or provisional Canon, which was later to be amended, completed, and ratified. So far as the Gospels were concerned, it had already reached its final shape. It included the same four which now stand in our Bibles, and the opposition that they met with was so slight, and so little serious, that Eusebius could class them all among the Homologoumena or books that were universally acknowledged.

CHAPTER XIII.

ON THE STATE OF THE CANON IN THE LAST QUARTER OF THE SECOND CENTURY.

I SHOULD not be very much surprised if the general reader who may have followed our enquiry so far should experience at this point a certain feeling of disappointment. If he did not know beforehand something of the subject-matter that was to be enquired into, he might not unnaturally be led to expect round assertions, and plain, pointblank, decisive evidence. Such evidence has not been offered to him for the simple reason that it does not exist. In its stead we have collected a great number of inferences of very various degrees of cogency, from the possible and hypothetical, up to strong and very strong probability. Most of our time has been taken up in weighing and testing these details, and in the endeavour to assign to each as nearly as possible its just value. It could not be thought strange if some minds were impatient of such minutiae; and where this objection was not felt, it would still be very pardonable to complain that the evidence was at best inferential and probable.

An inference in which there are two or three steps

may be often quite as strong as that in which there is only one, and probabilities may mount up to a high degree of what is called moral or practical certainty. I cannot but think that many of those which have been already obtained are of this character. I cannot but regard it as morally or practically certain that Marcion used our third Gospel; as morally or practically certain that all four Gospels were used in the Clementine Homilies; as morally or practically certain that the existence of three at least out of our four Gospels is implied in the writings of Justin; as probable in a lower degree that the four were used by Basilides; as not really disputable (apart from the presumption afforded by earlier writers) that they were widely used in the interval which separates the writings of Justin from those of Irenaeus.

All of these seem to me to be tolerably clear propositions. But outside these there seems to be a considerable amount of convergent evidence, the separate items of which are less convincing, but which yet derive a certain force from the mere fact that they are convergent. In the Apostolic Fathers, for example, there are instances of various kinds, some stronger and some weaker; but the important point to notice is that they confirm each other. Every new case adds to the total weight of the evidence, and helps to determine the bearing of those which seem ambiguous.

It cannot be too much borne in mind that the evidence with which we have been dealing is cumulative; and as in all other cases of cumulative evidence the subtraction of any single item is of less importance than the addition of a new one. Supposing it to be shown that some of the allusions which are thought to be taken from our Gospels were merely accidental coincidences of language, this would not materially affect the part of the evidence which could not be so explained. Supposing even that some of these allusions could be definitely referred to an apocryphal source, the possibility would be somewhat, but not so very much, increased that other instances which bear resemblance to our Gospels were also in their origin apocryphal. But on the other hand, if a single instance of the use of a canonical Gospel really holds good, it is proof of the existence of that Gospel, and every new instance renders the conclusion more probable, and makes it more and more difficult to account for the phenomena in any other way.

The author of 'Supernatural Religion' seems to have overlooked this. He does not seem to have considered the mutual support which the different instances taken together lend to each other. He summons them up one by one, and if any sort of possibility can be shown of accounting for them in any other way than by the use of our Gospels he dismisses them altogether. He makes no allowance for any residual weight they may have. He does not ask which is the more probable hypothesis. If the authentication of a document is incomplete, if the reference of a passage is not certain, he treats it as if it did not exist. He forgets the old story of the faggots, which, weak singly, become strong when combined. His scales will not admit of any evidence short of the highest. Fractional quantities find no place in his reckoning. If there is any flaw, if there is any possible loophole for escape, he does not make the due deduction and accept the evidence with that deduction, but he ignores it entirely, and goes on to the next item just as if he were leaving nothing behind him.

This is really part and parcel of what was pointed out at the outset as the fundamental mistake of his method. It is much too forensic. It takes as its model, not the proper canons of historical enquiry, but the procedure of English law. Yet the inappropriateness of such a method is seen as soon as we consider its object and origin. The rules of evidence current in our law courts were constructed specially with a view to the protection of the accused, and upon the assumption that it is better nine guilty persons should escape, than that one innocent person should be condemned. Clearly such rules will be inapplicable to the historical question which of two hypotheses is most likely to be true. The author forgets that the negative hypothesis is just as much a hypothesis as the positive, and needs to be defended in precisely the same manner. Either the Gospels were used, or they were not used. In order to prove the second side of this alternative, it is necessary to show not merely that it is *possible* that they were not used, but that the theory is the *more probable* of the two, and accounts better for the facts. But the author of 'Supernatural Religion' hardly professes or attempts to do this. If he comes across a quotation apparently taken from our Gospels he is at once ready with his reply, 'But it may be taken from a lost Gospel.' Granted; it may. But the extant Gospel is there, and the quotation referable to it; the lost Gospel is an unknown entity which may contain anything or nothing. If we admit that the possibility of quotation from a lost Gospel impairs the certainty of the reference to an extant Gospel, it is still quite another thing to argue that it is the more probable explanation and an explanation that the critic ought to accept. In very few cases, I believe, has the author so much as attempted to do this.

We might then take a stand here, and on the strength of what can be satisfactorily proved, as well as of what can be probably inferred, claim to have sufficiently established the use and antiquity of the Gospels. This is, I think, quite a necessary conclusion from the data hitherto collected.

But there is a further objection to be made to the procedure in 'Supernatural Religion.' If the object were to obtain clear and simple and universally appreciable evidence, I do not hesitate to say that the enquiry ends just where it ought to have begun. Through the faulty method that he has employed the author forgets that he has a hypothesis to make good and to carry through. He forgets that he has to account on the negative theory, just as we account on the positive, for a definite state of things. It may sound paradoxical, but there is really no great boldness in the paradox, when we affirm that at least the high antiquity of the Gospels could be proved, even if not one jot or tittle of the evidence that we have been discussing had existed. Supposing that all those fragmentary remains of the primitive Christian literature that we have been ransacking so minutely had been swept away, supposing that the causes that have handed it down to us in such a mutilated and impaired condition had done their work still more effectually, and that for the first eighty years of the second century there was no Christian literature extant at all; still I maintain that, in order to explain the phenomena that we find after that date, we should have to recur to the same assumptions that our previous enquiry would seem to have established for us.

Hitherto we have had to grope our way with difficulty and care; but from this date onwards all ambiguity and uncertainty disappears. It is like emerging out of twilight into the broad blaze of day. There is really a greater disproportion than we might expect between the evidence of the end of the century and that which leads up to it. From Justin to Irenaeus the Christian writings are fragmentary and few, but with Irenaeus a whole body of literature seems suddenly to start into being. Irenaeus is succeeded closely by Clement of Alexandria, Clement by Tertullian, Tertullian by Hippolytus and Origen, and the testimony which these writers bear to the Gospel is marvellously abundant and unanimous. I calculate roughly that Irenaeus quotes directly 193 verses of the first Gospel and 73 of the fourth. Clement of Alexandria and Tertullian must have quoted considerably more, while in the extant writings of Origen the greater part of the New Testament is actually quoted [1].

But more than this; by the time of Irenaeus the canon of the four Gospels, as we understand the word now, was practically formed. We have already seen that this was the case in the fragment of Muratori. Irenaeus is still more explicit. In the famous passage [2] which is so often quoted as an instance of the weakmindedness of the Fathers, he lays it down as a necessity of things that the Gospels should be four in number, neither less nor more:—

'For as there are four quarters of the world in which we live, as there are also four universal winds, and as the Church is scattered over all the earth, and the Gospel is the pillar and base of the Church and the breath

---

[1] Tregelles in Horne's *Introduction*, p. 334. [2] *Adv. Haer.* iii. 11. 8.

(or spirit) of life, it is likely that it should have four pillars breathing immortality on every side and kindling afresh the life of men. Whence it is evident that the Word, the architect of all things, who sitteth upon the cherubim and holdeth all things together, having been made manifest unto men, gave to us the Gospel in a fourfold shape, but held together by one Spirit. As David, entreating for His presence, saith: Thou that sittest upon the Cherubim show thyself. For the Cherubim are of fourfold visage, and their visages are symbols of the economy of the Son of man . . . . And the Gospels therefore agree with them over which presideth Jesus Christ. That which is according to John declares His generation from the Father sovereign and glorious, saying thus: In the beginning was the Word, and the Word was with God, and the Word was God. And, All things were made by Him, and without Him was not anything made . . . . But the Gospel according to Luke, as having a sacerdotal character, begins with Zacharias the priest offering incense unto God . . . . But Matthew records His human generation, saying, The book of the generation of Jesus Christ, the Son of David, the Son of Abraham . . . . Mark took his beginning from the prophetic Spirit coming down as it were from on high among men. The beginning, he says, of the Gospel according as it is written in Esaias the prophet, &c.'

Irenaeus also makes mention of the origin of the Gospels, claiming for their authors the gift of Divine inspiration [1]:—

'For after that our Lord rose from the dead and they were endowed with the power of the Holy Ghost coming upon them from on high, they were fully informed concerning all things, and had a perfect knowledge: they went out to the ends of the earth, preaching the Gospel of those good things that God hath given to us and proclaiming heavenly peace to men, having indeed both all in equal measure and each one singly the Gospel of God. So then Matthew among the Jews put forth a written Gospel in their own tongue while Peter and Paul were preaching the Gospel in Rome and founding the Church. After their decease (or 'departure'), Mark, the disciple and interpreter of Peter, himself too has handed down to us in writing the subjects of Peter's preaching. And Luke, the companion of Paul, put down in a book the Gospel preached by him. Afterwards, John, the disciple of the Lord, who also leaned upon His breast, likewise published his Gospel while he dwelt at Ephesus in Asia.'

We have not now to determine the exact value of these traditions; what we have rather to notice is the

---

[1] *Adv. Haer.* iii. 1. 1.

fact that the Gospels are at this time definitely assigned to their reputed authors, and that they are already regarded as containing a special knowledge divinely imparted. It is evident that Irenaeus would not for a moment think of classing any other Gospel by the side of the now strictly canonical four.

Clement of Alexandria, who, Eusebius says, 'was illustrious for his writings,' in the year 194 gives a somewhat similar, but not quite identical, account of the composition of the second Gospel[1]. He differs from Irenaeus in making St. Peter cognisant of the work of his follower. Neither is he quite consistent with himself; in one place he makes St. Peter 'authorise the Gospel to be read in the churches;' in another he says that the Apostle 'neither forbade nor encouraged it[2].' These statements have both of them been preserved for us by Eusebius, who also alleges, upon the authority of Clement, that the 'Gospels containing the genealogies were written first.' 'John,' he says, 'who came last, observing that the natural details had been set forth clearly in the Gospels, at the instance of his friends and with the inspiration of the Spirit ($\pi\nu\epsilon\acute{v}\mu\alpha\tau\iota\ \theta\epsilon o\phi o\rho\eta\theta\acute{\epsilon}\nu\tau\alpha$), wrote a spiritual Gospel[3].'

Clement draws a distinct line between the canonical and uncanonical Gospels. In quoting an apocryphal saying supposed to have been given in answer to Salome, he says, expressly: 'We do not find this saying in the four Gospels that have been handed down to us, but in that according to the Egyptians[4].'

---

[1] See Lardner, *Credibility*, &c., ii. pp. 223, 224, and Eus. *H. E.* ii. 15 (14 Lardner).
[2] Compare *H. E.* ii. 15 and vi. 14.
[3] *H. E.* vi. 14.
[4] *Strom.* iii. 13.

Tertullian is still more exclusive. He not only regards the four Gospels as inspired and authoritative, but he makes no use of any extra-canonical Gospel. The Gospels indeed held for him precisely the same position that they do with orthodox Christians now. He says respecting the Gospels: 'In the first place we lay it down that the evangelical document (evangelicum instrumentum[1]) has for its authors the Apostles, to whom this office of preaching the Gospel was committed by the Lord Himself. If it has also Apostolic men, yet not these alone but in company with Apostles and after Apostles. For the preaching of disciples might have been suspected of a desire for notoriety if it were not supported by the authority of Masters, nay of Christ, who made the Apostles Masters. In fine, of the Apostles, John and Matthew first implant in us faith, Luke and Mark renew it, starting from the same principles, so far as relates to the one God the Creator and His Christ born of the virgin, to fulfil the law and the prophets[2].' He grounds the authority of the Gospels upon the fact that they proceed either from Apostles or from those who held close relation to Apostles, like Mark, 'the interpreter of Peter,' and Luke, the companion of Paul[3]. In another passage he expressly asserts their authenticity[4], and he claimed to use them and them alone as his weapons in the conflict with heresy[5].

No less decided is the assertion of Origen, who writes:

---

[1] For the meaning of this word ('schriftliche Beweisurkunde') see Rönsch, *Das N. T. Tertullian's*, p. 48.
[2] *Adv. Marc.* iv. 2.
[3] *Ibid.* iv. 5.
[4] *Ibid.* v. 9.
[5] *Ibid.* iv. 2–5; compare v. 9, and Rönsch, pp. 53, 54.

'As I have learnt from tradition concerning the four Gospels, which alone are undisputed in the Church of God under heaven, that the first in order of the scripture is that according to Matthew, who was once a publican but afterwards an Apostle of Jesus Christ ... The second is that according to Mark, who wrote as Peter suggested to him ... The third is that according to Luke, the Gospel commended by Paul ... Last of all that according to John[1].' And again in his commentary upon the Preface to St. Luke's Gospel he expressly guards against the possibility that it might be thought to have reference to the other (Canonical) Gospels: 'In this word of Luke's "*have taken in hand*" there is a latent accusation of those who without the grace of the Holy Spirit have rushed to the composing of Gospels. Matthew, indeed, and Mark, and John, and Luke, have not "*taken in hand*" to write, but *have written* Gospels, being full of the Holy Spirit ... The Church has four Gospels; the Heresies have many[2].'

But besides the Fathers, and without going beyond the bounds of the second century, there is other evidence of the most distinct and important kind for the existence of a canon of the Gospels. Among the various translations of the New Testament one certainly, two very probably, and three perhaps probably, were made in the course of the second century.

The old Latin (as distinct from Jerome's revised) version of the Gospels and with them of a considerable portion of the New Testament was, I think it may be said, undoubtedly used by Tertullian and by the Latin

---

[1] Eus. *H. E.* vi. 25.
[2] See M'Clellan on Luke i. 1-4. On the general position of Origen in regard to the Canon, compare Hilgenfeld, *Kanon*, p. 49.

translator of Irenaeus, who appears to be quoted by Tertullian, and in that case could not be placed later than 200 A.D.[1] On this point I shall quote authorities that will hardly be questioned. And first that of a writer who is accustomed to weigh, with the accuracy of true science, every word that he puts down, and who upon this subject is giving the result of a most minute and careful investigation. Speaking of the Latin translation of the New Testament as found in Tertullian he says: 'Although single portions of this, especially passages which are translated in several different ways, may be due to Tertullian himself, still it cannot be doubted that in by far the majority of cases he has followed the text of a version received in his time by the Africans and specially the Carthaginian Christians, and made perhaps long before his time, and that consequently his quotations represent the form of the earliest Latinized Scriptures accepted in those regions[2].' Again: 'In the first place we may conclude from the writings of Tertullian, that remarkable Carthaginian presbyter at the close of the second century, that in his time there existed several, perhaps many, Latin translations of the Bible . . . . . Tertullian himself frequently quotes in his writings one and the same passage of Scripture in entirely different forms, which indeed in many cases may be explained by his quoting freely from memory, but certainly not seldom has its ground in the diversity of the translations

---

[1] So Westcott in *S. D.* iii. 1692, n. Tregelles, in Horne's *Introduction*, p. 333, speaks of this translation as 'coeval, apparently, with Irenaeus himself.' We must not, however, omit to notice that Rönsch (p. 43, n.) is more reserved in his verdict on the ground that the translation of Irenaeus 'in its peculiarities and in its relation to Tertullian has not yet received a thorough investigation;' compare Hilgenfeld, *Einleitung*, p. 797.

[2] Rönsch, *Das N. T. Tertullian's*, p. 43.

used at the time¹.' On this last point, the unity of the Old Latin version, there is a difference of opinion among scholars, but none as to its date. Thus Dr. Tregelles writes: 'The expressions of Tertullian have been rightly rested on as showing that he knew and recognised *one translation*, and that this version was in several places (in his opinion) opposed to what was found "in Graeco authentico." This version must have been made a sufficiently long time before the age when Tertullian wrote, and before the Latin translator of Irenaeus, for it to have got into general circulation. This leads us back *towards* the middle of the second century at the latest: how much *earlier* the version may have been we have no proof; for we are already led back into the time when no records tell us anything respecting the North African Church².' Dr. Tregelles, it should be remembered, is speaking as a text critic, of which branch of science his works are one of the noblest monuments, and not directly of the history of the Canon. His usual opponent in text critical matters, but an equally exact and trustworthy writer, Dr. Scrivener, agrees with him here both as to the unity of the version and as to its date from the middle of the century³. Dr. Westcott too writes in his well-known and valuable article on the Vulgate in Smith's Dictionary⁴: 'Tertullian distinctly recognises the general currency of a Latin Version of the New Testament, though not necessarily of every book at present included in the Canon, which even in his time had been able to mould the popular language. This was characterised by a "rudeness" and "simplicity," which seems to point to the nature of its origin.' I do

---

[1] Rönsch, *Itala und Vulgata*, pp. 2, 3.   [2] Horne's *Introduction*, p. 233.
[3] *Introduction* (2nd ed.), pp. 300, 302, 450, 452.   [4] iii. p. 1690 b.

not suppose that the currency at the end of the second century of a Latin version, containing the four Gospels and no others, will be questioned[1].

With regard to the Syriac version there is perhaps a somewhat greater room to doubt, though Dr. Tregelles begins his account of this version by saying: 'It may stand as an admitted fact that a version of the New Testament in Syriac existed in the second century[2].' Dr. Scrivener also says[3]: 'The universal belief of later ages, and the very nature of the case, seem to render it unquestionable that the Syrian Church was possessed of a translation both of the Old and New Testament, which it used habitually, and for public worship exclusively, from the second century of our era downwards: as early as A.D. 170 ὁ Σύρος is cited by Melito on Genesis xxii. 13.' The external evidence, however, does not seem to be quite strong enough to bear out any very positive assertion. The appeal to the Syriac by Melito[4] is pretty conclusive as to the existence of a Syriac Old Testament, which, being of Christian origin, would probably be accompanied by a translation of the New. But on the other hand, the language of Eusebius respecting Hegesippus (ἔκ τε τοῦ καθ' Ἑβραίους εὐαγγελίου καὶ τοῦ Συριακοῦ ... τινα τίθησιν) seems to be rightly interpreted by Routh as having reference not to any '*version* of the Gospel, but to a separate Syro-Hebraic (?)

---

[1] Hilgenfeld, in his recent *Einleitung*, says expressly (p. 797) that 'the New Testament had already in the second century been translated into Latin.' This admission is not affected by the argument which follows, which goes to prove that the version used by Tertullian was not the 'Itala' properly so called.

[2] See Smith's Dictionary, iii. p. 1630 b.

[3] *Introduction*, p. 274.

[4] See Routh, *Rel. Sac.* i. pp. 124 and 152.

Gospel' like that according to the Hebrews. In any case the Syriac Scriptures 'were familiarly used and claimed as his national version by Ephraem of Edessa' (299-378 A.D.) as well as by Aphraates in writings dating A.D. 337 and 344 [1].

A nearer approximation of date would be obtained by determining the age of the version represented by the celebrated Curetonian fragments. There is a strong tendency among critics, which seems rapidly approaching to a consensus, to regard this as bearing the same relation to the Peshito that the Old Latin does to Jerome's Vulgate, that of an older unrevised to a later revised version. The strength of the tendency in this direction may be seen by the very cautious and qualified opinion expressed in the second edition of his Introduction by Dr. Scrivener, who had previously taken a decidedly antagonistic view, and also by the fact that Mr. M'Clellan, who is usually an ally of Dr. Scrivener, here appears on the side of his opponents [2]. All the writers who have hitherto been mentioned place either the Curetonian Syriac or the Peshito in the second century, and the majority, as we have seen, the Curetonian. Dr. Tregelles, on a comparative examination of the text, affirms that 'the Curetonian Syriac presents such a text as we might have concluded would be current in the second century [3].' English text criticism is probably on the whole in advance of Continental; but it may be noted that Bleek (who however was imperfectly acquainted with the Curetonian form of the text) yet asserts that the Syriac version

---

[1] See Scrivener, *loc. cit.*
[2] See *New Testament*, &c., i. p. 635.
[3] *S. D.* iii. p. 1634 b.

'belongs without doubt to the second century A.D.[1]' Reuss[2] places it at the beginning, Hilgenfeld towards the end[3], of the third century.

The question as to the age of the version is not necessarily identical with that as to the age of the particular form of it preserved in Cureton's fragments. This would hold the same sort of relation to the original text of the version that (e. g.) a, or b, or c—any primitive codex of the version—holds to the original text of the Old Latin. It also appears that the translation into Syriac of the different Gospels, conspicuously of St. Matthew's, was made by different hands and at different times[4]. Bearing these considerations in mind, we should still be glad to know what answer those who assign the Curetonian text to the second century make to the observation that it contains the reading Βηθαβαρᾷ in John i. 28 which is generally assumed to be not older than Origen[5]. On the other hand, the Curetonian, like the Old Latin, still has in John vii. 8 οὐκ for οὔπω—a change which, according to Dr. Scrivener[6], 'from the end of the third century downwards was very generally and widely diffused.' This whole set of questions needs perhaps a more exhaustive discussion than it has obtained hitherto[7].

---

[1] *Einleitung in das Neue Testament*, p. 724.
[2] *Geschichte der heiligen Schriften Neuen Testaments*, p. 302.
[3] *Einleitung*, p. 804.   [4] See Tregelles, *loc. cit.*
[5] Cf. Hilgenfeld, *Einleitung*, p. 805. It hardly seems clear that Origen had *no* MS. authority for his reading.
[6] *Introduction*, p. 530. But οὔπω is admitted into the text by Westcott and Hort.
[7] 'The text of the Curetonian Gospels is in itself a sufficient proof of the extreme antiquity of the Syriac Version. This, as has been already remarked, offers a striking resemblance to that of the Old Latin, and cannot be later than the middle or close of the second century. It would

The third version that may be mentioned is the Egyptian. In regard to this Dr. Lightfoot says [1], that 'we should probably not be exaggerating if we placed one or both of the principal Egyptian versions, the Memphitic and the Thebaic, or at least parts of them, before the close of the second century.' In support of this statement he quotes Schwartz, the principal authority on the subject, 'who will not be suspected of any theological bias.' The historical notices on which the conclusion is founded are given in Scrivener's 'Introduction.' If we are to put a separate estimate upon these, it would be perhaps that the version was made in the second century somewhat more probably than not; it was certainly not made later than the first half of the third [2].

Putting this version however on one side, the facts that have to be explained are these. Towards the end of the second century we find the four Gospels in general circulation and invested with full canonical authority, in Gaul, at Rome, in the province of Africa, at Alexandria, and in Syria. Now if we think merely of the time that would be taken in the transcription and dissemination of MSS., and of the struggle that works such as the Gospels would have to go through before they could obtain recognition, and still more an exclusive recognition, this alone would tend to overthrow any such theory as that one of the Gospels, the fourth, was not composed before 150 A.D., or indeed anywhere near that date.

But this is not by any means all. It is merely the

be difficult to point out a more interesting subject for criticism than the respective relations of the Old Latin and Syriac Versions to the Latin and Syriac Vulgates. But at present it is almost untouched.' Westcott, *On the Canon* (3rd ed.), p. 218, n. 3.

[1] See Scrivener's *Introduction*, p. 324.
[2] Cf. Bleek, *Einleitung*, p. 735; Reuss, *Gesch. N. T.* p. 447.

first step in a process that, quite independently of the other external evidence, thrusts the composition of the Gospels backwards and backwards to a date certainly as early as that which is claimed for them.

Let us define a little more closely the chronological bearings of the subject. There is a decidedly preponderant probability that the Muratorian fragment was not written much later than 170 A.D. Irenaeus, as we have seen, was writing in the decade 180–190 A.D. But his evidence is surely valid for an earlier date than this. He is usually supposed to have been born about the year 140 A.D.[1], and the way in which he describes his relations to Polycarp will not admit of a date many years later. But his strong sense of the continuity of Church doctrine and the exceptional veneration that he accords to the Gospels seem alone to exclude the supposition that any of them should have been composed in his own lifetime. He is fond of quoting the 'Presbyters,' who connected his own age with that, if not of the Apostles, yet of Apostolic men. Pothinus, bishop of Lyons, whom he succeeded, was more than ninety years old at the time of his martyrdom in the persecution of A.D. 177[2], and would thus in his boyhood be contemporary with the closing years of the last Evangelist. Irenaeus also had before him a number of writings—some, e.g. the works of the Marcosians, in addition to those that have been discussed in the course of this work—in which our Gospels are largely quoted, and which, to say the least, were earlier than his own time of writing.

---

[1] This is the date commonly accepted since Massuet, *Diss. in Irenaeum*, ii. 1. 2. Grabe had previously placed the date in A.D. 108, Dodwell as early as A.D. 97 (cf. Stieren, *Irenaeus*, ii. pp. 32, 34, 182).

[2] Routh, *Rel. Sac.* i. p. 306.

Clement of Alexandria began to flourish (ἐγνωρίζετο [1]), in the reign of Commodus (180-190 A. D.), and had obtained a still wider celebrity as head of the Catechetical School of Alexandria in the time of Severus [2] 193–211). The opinions therefore to which he gives expression in his works of this date were no doubt formed at an earlier period. He too appeals to the tradition of which he had been himself a recipient. He speaks of his teachers, 'those blessed and truly memorable men,' one in Greece, another in Magna Graecia, a third in Coele-Syria, a fourth in Egypt, a fifth in Assyria, a sixth in Palestine, to whom the doctrine of the Apostles had been handed down from father to son [3].

Tertullian is still bolder. In his controversy with Marcion he confidently claims as on his side the tradition of the Apostolic Churches. By it is guaranteed the Gospel of St. Luke which he is defending, and not only that, but the other Gospels [4]. In one passage Tertullian even goes so far as to send his readers to the Churches of Corinth, Philippi, &c. for the very autographs ('authenticae literae') of St. Paul's Epistles [5]. But this is merely a characteristic flourish of rhetoric. All for which the statements of Tertullian may safely be said to vouch is, that the Gospels had held their 'prerogative' position within his memory and that of most members of the Church to which he belonged.

But the evidence of the Fathers is most decisive when

---

[1] Eus. H. E. v. 11, vi. 6. Eusebius, in his 'Chronicle,' speaks of Clement as eminent for his writings 'συντάττων διέλαμπεν' in A.D. 194.

[2] The books called 'Stromateis' or 'Miscellanies' date from this reign. H. E. vi. 6.

[3] *Stromateis*, i. 1.

[4] *Adv. Marc.* iv. 5.

[5] *De Praescript. Haeret.* c. 36; see Scrivener, *Introduction*, p. 446.

it is unconscious. That the Gospels as used by the Christian writers at the end of the first century, so far from being of recent composition, had already a long history behind them, is nothing less than certain. At this date they exhibit a text which bears the marks of frequent transcription and advanced corruption. 'Origen's,' says Dr. Scrivener[1], 'is the highest name among the critics and expositors of the early Church; he is perpetually engaged in the discussion of various readings of the New Testament, and employs language in describing the then state of the text, which would be deemed strong if applied even to its present condition with the changes which sixteen more centuries must needs have produced. . . . Respecting the sacred autographs, their fate or their continued existence, he seems to have had no information, and to have entertained no curiosity: they had simply passed by and were out of his reach. Had it not been for the diversities of copies in all the Gospels on other points (he writes) he should not have ventured to object to the authenticity of a certain passage (Matt. xix. 19) on internal grounds: "But now," saith he, "great in truth has become the diversity of copies, be it from the negligence of certain scribes, or from the evil daring of some who correct what is written, or from those who in correcting add or take away what they think fit."' This is respecting the MSS. of one region only, and now for another[2]: 'It is no less true to fact than paradoxical in sound, that the worst corruptions to which the New Testament has ever been subjected, originated within a hundred years after

---

[1] pp. 450, 451.

[2] p. 452. These facts may be held to show that the books were not regarded with the same veneration as now.

it was composed; that Irenaeus and the African Fathers and the whole Western, with a portion of the Syrian Church, used far inferior manuscripts to those employed by Stunica, or Erasmus, or Stephens thirteen centuries later, when moulding the Textus Receptus.' Possibly this is an exaggeration, but no one will maintain that it is a very large exaggeration of the facts.

I proceed to give a few examples which serve to bring out the antiquity of the text. And first from Irenaeus.

There is a very remarkable passage in the work Against Heresies[1], bearing not indeed directly upon the Gospels, but upon another book of the New Testament, and yet throwing so much light upon the condition of the text in Irenaeus' time that it may be well to refer to it here. In discussing the signification of the number of the beast in Rev. xiii. 18, Irenaeus already found himself confronted by a variety of reading: some MSS. with which he was acquainted read 616 ($\chi\iota\varsigma'$) for 666 ($\chi\xi\varsigma'$). Irenaeus himself was not in doubt that the latter was the true reading. He says that it was found in all the 'good and ancient copies,' and that it was further attested by 'those who had seen John face to face.' He thinks that the error was due to the copyists, who had substituted by mistake the letter ι for ξ. He adds his belief that God would pardon those who had done this without any evil motive.

Here we have opened out a kind of vista extending back almost to the person of St. John himself. There is already a multiplicity of MSS., and of these some are set apart 'as good and ancient' ($\dot{\epsilon}\nu$ πᾶσι τοῖς σπουδαίοις καὶ ἀρχαίοις ἀντιγράφοις). The method by which the

---

[1] v. 30. 1.

correct reading had to be determined was as much historical as it is with us at the present day.

A not dissimilar state of things is indicated somewhat less explicitly in regard to the first Gospel. In the text of Matt. i. 18 all the Greek MSS., with one exception, read, τοῦ δὲ Ἰησοῦ Χριστοῦ ἡ γένεσις οὕτως ἦν. B alone has τοῦ δὲ Χριστοῦ Ἰησοῦ. The Greek of D is wanting at this point, but the Latin, d, reads with the best codices of the Old Latin, the Vulgate, and the Curetonian Syriac, 'Christi autem generatio sic erat' (or an equivalent). Now Irenaeus quotes this passage three times. In the first passage[1] the original Greek text of Irenaeus has been preserved in a quotation of Germanus, Patriarch of Constantinople (the context also by Anastasius Sinaita, but these words appear to be omitted); and the reading of Germanus corresponds to that of the great mass of MSS. This however is almost certainly false, as the ancient Latin translation of Irenaeus has 'Christi autem generatio,' and it was extremely natural for a copyist to substitute the generally received text, especially in a combination of words that was so familiar. Irenaeus leaves no doubt as to his own reading on the next occasion when he quotes the passage, as he does twice over. Here he says expressly: 'Ceterum potuerat dicere Matthaeus: *Jesu vero generatio sic erat;* sed praevidens Spiritus sanctus depravatores, et praemuniens contra fraudulentiam eorum, per Matthaeum ait: *Christi autem generatio sic erat*[2].' Irenaeus founds an argument upon this directed against the heretics who supposed that the Christus and Jesus were not identical, but that Jesus was the son of Mary, upon

---

[1] *Adv. Haer.* iii. 11. 8.   [2] *Ib.* iii. 14. 2.

whom the aeon Christus afterwards descended. In opposition to these Irenaeus maintains that the Christus and Jesus are one and the same person.

There is a division of opinion among modern critics as to which of the two readings is to be admitted into the text; Griesbach, Lachmann, Tischendorf (eighth edition), and Scrivener support the reading of the MSS.; Tregelles, Westcott and Hort, and M'Clellan prefer that of Irenaeus. The presence of this reading in the Old Latin and Curetonian Syriac proves its wide diffusion. At the same time it is clear that Irenaeus himself was aware of the presence of the other reading in some copies which he regarded as bearing the marks of heretical depravation.

It is unfortunate that fuller illustration cannot be given from Irenaeus, but the number of the quotations from the Gospels of which the Greek text still remains is not large, and where we have only the Latin interpretation we cannot be sure that the actual text of Irenaeus is before us. Much uncertainty is thus raised. For instance, a doubt is expressed by the editors of Irenaeus whether the words 'without a cause' ($\epsilon i \kappa \hat{\eta}$—sine caussa) in the quotation of Matt. v. 22 [1] belong to the original text or not. Probably they did so, as they are found in the Old Latin and Curetonian Syriac and in Western authorities generally. They are wanting however in B, in Origen, and 'in the true copies' according to Jerome, &c. The words are expunged from the sacred text by Lachmann, Tischendorf, Westcott and Hort, and M'Clellan. There is a less weight of authority for their retention. In any case the double reading was certainly

---

[1] Cf. *Adv. Haer.* iv. 13. 1.

current at the end of the second century, as the words are found in Irenaeus and omitted by Tertullian.

The elaborately varied readings of Matt. xi. 25-27 and Matt. xix. 16, 17 there can be little doubt are taken from the canonical text. They are both indeed found in a passage (Adv. Haer. i. 20. 2, 3) where Irenaeus is quoting the heretical Marcosians; and various approximations are met with, as we have seen, under ambiguous circumstances in Justin, the Clementine Homilies, and Marcion. But similar approximations are also found in Irenaeus himself (speaking in his own person), in Clement of Alexandria, Origen, and Epiphanius, who are undoubtedly quoting from our Gospels; so that the presence of the variations at that early date is proved, though in the first case they receive none, and in the second very limited, support from the extant MSS.[1] A variety of reading that was in the first instance accidental seemed to afford a handle either to the orthodox or to heretical parties, and each for a time maintained its own; but with the victory of the orthodox cause the heretical reading gave way, and was finally suppressed before the time at which the extant MSS. were written.

These are really conspicuous instances of the confusion of text already existing, but I forbear to press them because, though I do not doubt myself the correctness of the account that has been given of them, still there is just the ambiguity alluded to, and I do not wish to seem to assume the truth of any particular view.

For minor variations the text of Irenaeus cannot be used satisfactorily, because it is always doubtful whether the Latin version has correctly reproduced the original.

---

[1] The varieties of reading in this verse are exhibited in full by Dr. Westcott, *On the Canon*, p. 120, notes 4 and 5.

And even in those comparatively small portions where the Greek is still preserved, it has come down to us through the medium of other writers, and we have just had an instance how easily the distinctive features of the text might be obliterated.

Neither of these elements of uncertainty exists in the case of Tertullian; and therefore, as the text of his New Testament quotations has been edited in a very exact and careful form, I shall illustrate what has been said respecting the corruptions introduced in the second century chiefly from him. The following may be taken as a few of the instances in which the existence of a variety of reading can be verified by a comparison of Tertullian's text with that of the MSS. The brackets (as before) indicate partial support.

Matt. iii. 8. Dignos poenitentiae fructus (*Pudic.* 10). Καρποὺς ἀξίους τῆς μετανοίας Textus Receptus, L, U, 33, a, g², m, Syrr. Crt. and Pst., etc. Καρπὸν ἄξιον τ.'μετ. B, C (D), Δ, 1, etc.; Vulg., b, c, d, f, ff¹, Syr. Hcl., Memph., Theb., Iren., Orig., etc. [Tertullian himself has the singular in *Hermog.* 12, so that he seems to have had both readings in his copies.]

Matt. v. 4, 5. The received order 'beati lugentes' and 'beati mites' is followed in *Pat.* 11 [Rönsch p. 589 and Tisch., correcting Treg.]. So ℵ, B, C, rel., b, f, Syrr. Pst. and Hcl., Memph., Arm., Aeth. Order inverted in D, 33, Vulg., a, c, ff¹, g¹·², h, k, l, Syr. Crt., Clem., Orig., Eus., Hil.

Matt. v. 16. 'Luceant opera vestra' for 'luceat lux vestra,' Tert. (bis). So Hil., Ambr., Aug., Celest. [see above, p. 134] against all MSS. and versions.

Matt. v. 28. Qui viderit ad concupiscentiam, etc. This verse is cited six times by Tertullian, and Rönsch says (p. 590) that 'in these six citations almost every variant of the Greek text is represented.'

Matt. v. 48. Qui est in caelis: ὁ ἐν τοῖς οὐρανοῖς, Textus Receptus, with Δ, E², rel., b, c, d, g¹, h, Syrr. Crt. and Pst., Clem., ὁ οὐράνιος, ℵ, B, D², Z, and i, 33, Vulg., a, f, etc.

Matt. vi. 10. Fiat voluntas tua in caelis et in terra, omitting 'sicut.' So D, a, b, c, Aug. (expressly, 'some codices').

Matt. xi. 11. Nemo major inter natos feminarum Joanne baptizatore.

'The form of this citation, which neither corresponds with Matt. xi. 11 nor with Luke vii. 28, coincides almost exactly with the words which in both the Greek and Latin text of the Codex Bezae form the conclusion of Luke vii. 26, [ὅτι] οὐδεὶς μείζων ἐν γεννητοῖς γυναικῶν [προφήτης] Ἰωάννου τοῦ βαπτιστοῦ' (Rönsch, p. 608).

Matt. xiii. 15. Sanem: ἰάσωμαι, K, U, X, Δ, 1; Latt. (exc. d), Syr. Crt.; ἰάσομαι, B, C, D, ℵ, rel.

Matt. xv. 26. Non est (only), so Eus. in Ps. 83; ἔξεστιν, D, a, b, c, ff, g¹, l, Syr. Crt., Orig., Hil.; οὐκ ἔστιν καλόν, B, C, ℵ, rel., Vulg., e, f, g², k, Orig.

There are of course few quotations that can be distinctly identified as taken from St. Mark, but among these may be noticed:—

Mark i. 24. Scimus: οἴδαμέν σε, ℵ, L, Δ, Memph., Iren., Orig., Eus.; οἶδά σε τίς εἶ, A, B, C, D, rel., Latt., Syrr.

Mark ix. 7. Hunc audite: αὐτοῦ ἀκούετε, A, X, rel., b, f, Syrr.; ἀκούετε αὐτοῦ, ℵ, B, C, D, L, a, c, ff¹, etc. [This may be however from Matt. xvii. 5, where Tertullian's reading has somewhat stronger support.]

The variations in quotations from St. Luke have been perhaps sufficiently illustrated in the chapter on Marcion. We may therefore omit this Gospel and pass to St. John. A very remarkable reading meets us at the outset.

John i. 13. Non ex sanguine nec ex voluntate carnis nec ex voluntate viri, sed ex deo natus est. The Greek of all the MSS. and Versions, with the single exception of b of the Old Latin, is οἱ ἐγεννήθησαν. A sentence is thus applied to Christ that was originally intended to be applied to the Christian. Tertullian (*De Carne Christ.* 19, 24), though he also had the right reading before him, boldly accuses the Valentinians of a falsification, and lays stress upon the reading which he adopts as proof of the veritable birth of Christ from a virgin. The same text is found in b (Codex Veronensis) of the Old Latin, Pseudo-Athanasius, the Latin translator of Origen's commentary on St. Matthew, in Augustine, and three times in Irenaeus. The same codex has, like Tertullian, the singular ex sanguine for the plural ἐξ αἱμάτων; so Eusebius and Hilary.

John iii. 36. Manebit (=μενεῖ, for μένει). So b, e, g, Syr. Pst., Memph., Aeth., Iren., Cypr.; against a, c, d, f, ff, Syrr. Crt. and Hcl., etc.

John v. 3, 4. The famous paragraph which describes the moving of the waters of the pool of Bethesda was found in Tertullian's MS. It is also found in the mass of MSS., in the Old Latin and Vulgate, in Syrr. Pst. and Jer., and in some MSS. of Memph. It is omitted in ℵ, B, C, D (v. 4), f, l, Syr. Crt., Theb., Memph. (most MSS.). Tertullian gives the name of the pool as Bethsaida with B, Vulg., c, Syr. Hcl., Memph. Most of the authorities read Βηθεσδά. Βηθζαθά, Βηζαθά, Berzeta, Belzatha, and Betzeta are also found.

John v. 43. Recepistis, perf. for pres. (λαμβάνετε). So a, b, Iren., Vigil., Ambr., Jer.

John vi. 39. Non perdam ex eo quicquam. Here 'quicquam' is an addition (= μηδέν), found in D, a, b, ff, Syr. Crt.

John vi. 51. Et panis quem ego dedero pro salute mundi, caro mea est. This almost exactly corresponds with the reading of ℵ, ὁ ἄρτος ὃν ἐγὼ δώσω ὑπὲρ τῆς τοῦ κόσμου ζωῆς, ἡ σάρξ μου ἐστίν. Similarly, but with inversion of the last two clauses (ἡ σάρξ μου ἐστὶν ὑπὲρ τῆς τοῦ κόσμου ζωῆς), B, C, D and T, 33, Vulg., a, b, c, e, m, Syr. Crt., Theb., Aeth., Orig., Cypr. The received text is καὶ ὁ ἄρτος [δὲ] ὃν ἐγὼ δώσω, ἡ σάρξ μου ἐστὶν ἣν ἐγὼ δώσω ὑπὲρ τῆς τοῦ κόσμου ζωῆς, after E, G, H, K, M, S, etc.

John xii. 30. Venit (= ἦλθεν for γέγονεν), with D (Tregelles), [also a, b, l, n (?), Vulg. (*fuld.*), Hil., Victorin.; Rönsch].

The instances that have been here given are all, or nearly all, false readings on the part of Tertullian. It is, of course, only as such that they are in point for the present enquiry. Some few of those mentioned have been admitted into the text by certain modern editors. Thus, on Matt. v. 4, 5 Tertullian's reading finds support in Westcott and Hort and M'Clellan, against Tischendorf and Tregelles. [This instance perhaps should not be pressed. I leave it standing, because it shows interesting relations between Tertullian and the various forms of the Old Latin.] The passage omitted in John v. 3, 4 is argued for strenuously by Mr. M'Clellan, with more hesitation by Dr. Scrivener, and in 'Supernatural Religion' (sixth edition), against Tregelles, Tischendorf, Milligan, Lightfoot, Westcott and Hort. In the same passage Bethsaida is read by Lachmann (margin) and by

Westcott and Hort. In John vi. 51 the reading of Tertullian and the Sinaitic Codex is defended by Tischendorf; the approximate reading of B, C, D, &c. is admitted by Lachmann, Tregelles, Milligan, Westcott and Hort, and the received text has an apologist in Mr. M'Clellan (with Tholuck and Wordsworth). On these points then it should be borne in mind that Tertullian *may* present the true reading; on all the others he is pretty certainly wrong.

Let us now proceed to analyse roughly these erroneous (in three cases *doubtfully* erroneous) readings. We shall find [1] that Tertullian—

Agrees with	*Differs from*
ℵ (Codex Sinaiticus) in Mark i. 24, John vi. 51.	ℵ in Matt. iii. 18, v. 16, v. 48, vi. 10, xi. 11, xiii. 15, xv. 26, Mark ix. 7, John i. 13, v. 3, 4, v. 43, vi. 39, xii. 30.
A (Codex Alexandrinus [2]) in Mark ix. 7, John v. 3, 4.	A in Mark i. 24, John i. 13, v. 43, vi. 39, xii. 30.
B (Codex Vaticanus) in John v. 2, (vi. 51).	B in Matt. iii. 8, v. 16, v. 48, vi. 10, xi. 11, xiii. 15, xv. 26, Mark i. 24, ix. 7, John i. 13, v. 3, 4, v. 43, vi. 39, xii. 30.
C (Codex Ephraemi — somewhat fragmentary) in John (vi. 51).	C in Matt. iii. 8, xi. 11, xiii. 15, xv. 26, Mark i. 24, ix. 7, John i. 13, v. 3, 4, vi. 39.
D (Codex Bezae — in some places wanting) in Matt. vi. 10, xi. 11, (xv. 26), John (vi. 51), xii. 30.	D in Matt. (iii. 8), v. 16, v. 48, xiii. 15, Mark i. 24, ix. 7, John i. 13, iii. 36, v. 4, v. 43.

[1] Matt. v. 28 is omitted as too ambiguous and confusing, though it is especially important for the point in question as showing that Tertullian himself had a variety of MSS. before him.

[2] St. Matthew's Gospel is wanting in this MS. to xxv. 6; two leaves are also lost, from John vi. 50 to viii. 52.

Agrees with.	Differs from.
GREEK FATHERS.	
Clement of Alexandria, in Matt. v. 16, v. 48.	
Origen, in Matt. (xv. 26), Mark i. 24, John i. 13 (Latin translator), (vi. 51).	Origen, in Matt. iii. 8, xv. 26.
Eusebius, in Matt. xv. 26, Mark i. 24, John i. 13 (partially).	
LATIN FATHERS.	
Irenaeus, in Mark i. 24, John i. 13 (ter), iii. 36, v. 43.	Irenaeus, in Matt. iii. 8.
Cyprian, in John iii. 36, (vi. 51).	
Augustine, in Matt. v. 16, vi. 10.	
Ambrose, in Matt. v. 16, John v. 43.	
Hilary, in Matt. v. 16, (xv. 26), John xii. 30.	
Others, in Matt. v. 16, v. 48, John i. 13, v. 43, xii. 30.	
VERSIONS.	
Old Latin—	
a (Codex Vercellensis), in Matt. (iii. 8), vi. 10, xiii. 15, (xv. 26), John v. 3, 4, v. 43, (vi. 51), xii. 30.	a, in Matt. v. 16, v. 48, xi. 11, Mark i. 24, ix. 7, John i. 13, iii. 36.
b (Codex Veronensis), in Matt. v. 48, vi. 10, xiii. 15, (xv. 36), Mark ix. 7, John i. 13, iii. 36, v. 3, 4, v. 43, (vi. 51), xii. 30.	b, in Matt. iii. 8, v. 16, xi. 11, Mark i. 24.
c (Codex Colbertinus), in Matt. v. 48, vi. 10, xiii. 15, (xv. 26), John v. 3, 4, (vi. 51).	c, in Matt. iii. 8, v. 16, xi. 11, Mark i. 24, ix. 7, John i. 13, iii. 36, v. 43, vi. 39, xii. 30.

Agrees with.	*Differs from.*
f (Codex Brixianus), in Matt. xiii. 15, Mark ix. 7.	f, in Matt. iii. 8, v. 16, v. 48, vi. 10, xi. 10, xv. 26, Mark i. 24, John i. 13, iii. 36, v. 3, 4, v. 43, vi. 39, vi. 51, xii. 30.
Other codices, in Matt. iii. 8, vi. 10, xiii. 5, (xv. 26), John iii. 36, v. 3, 4, vi. 39, (vi. 51), xii. 30.	Other codices, in Matt. iii. 8, v. 16, v. 48, vi. 10, xi. 11, Mark i. 24, ix. 7, John i. 13, iii. 36, v. 3, 4, v. 43, vi. 39, vi. 51, xii. 30.
Vulgate, in Matt. xiii. 15, John v. 3, 4, (vi. 51), xii. 30 (*fuld.*).	Vulgate, in Matt. iii. 8, v. 16, v. 48, vi. 10, xi. 11, xv. 26, Mark i. 24, ix. 7, John i. 13, iii. 36, v. 43, vi. 39.
Syriac—	
Syr. Crt. (fragmentary), in Matt. iii. 8, v. 48, xiii. 15, (xv. 26), John (i. 13, ? Crowfoot), vi. 39, (vi. 51).	Syr. Crt., in Matt. v. 16, vi. 10, xi. 11, John (i. 13, ? Tregelles), iii. 36, v. 3, 4, v. 43.
Syr. Pst., in Matt. iii. 8, v. 48, Mark ix. 7, John iii. 36, v. 3, 4.	Syr. Pst., in Matt. vi. 10, Mark i. 24, John i. 13, (vi. 51), xii. 30.

[The evidence of this and the following versions is only given where it is either expressly stated or left to be clearly inferred by the editors.]

Egyptian—	
Thebaic, in John (vi. 51).	Thebaic, in Matt. iii. 8, v. 16, Mark ix. 7, John v. 3, 4.
Memphitic, in Mark i. 24, John iii. 36.	Memphitic, in Matt. iii. 8, v. 16, (v. 48), Mark ix. 7, John v. 3, 4, vi. 51.

Summing up the results numerically they would be something of this kind :—

Uncial MSS.

	ℵ	A	B	C	D
Agreement	2	2	2	1	5
Difference	13	5	14	9	10

Greek Fathers.

	Clement of Alexandria.	Origen.	Eusebius.
Agreement	1	4	3
Difference	0	2	0

Latin Fathers.

	Irenaeus.	Cyprian.	Augustine.	Ambrose.	Hilary.	Others.
Agreement	4	2	2	2	3	5
Difference	1	0	0	0	0	0

Versions.

Old Latin.

	a	b	c	f	rel.	Vulgate.
Agreement	8	11	6	2	9	4
Difference	7	4	10	14	14	12

Syriac. Egyptian.

	Crt.	Pst.	Theb.	Memph.
Agreement	7	5	1	2
Difference	7	5	4	6

Now the phenomena here, as on other occasions when we have had to touch upon text criticism, are not quite simple and straightforward. It must be remembered too that our observations extend only over a very narrow area. Within that area they are confined to the cases where Tertullian has *gone wrong;* whereas, in order to anything like a complete induction, all the cases of various reading ought to be considered. Some results, however, of a rough and approximate kind may be said to be reached; and I think that these will be perhaps best exhibited if, premising that they are thus rough and approximate, we throw them into the shape of a genealogical tree.

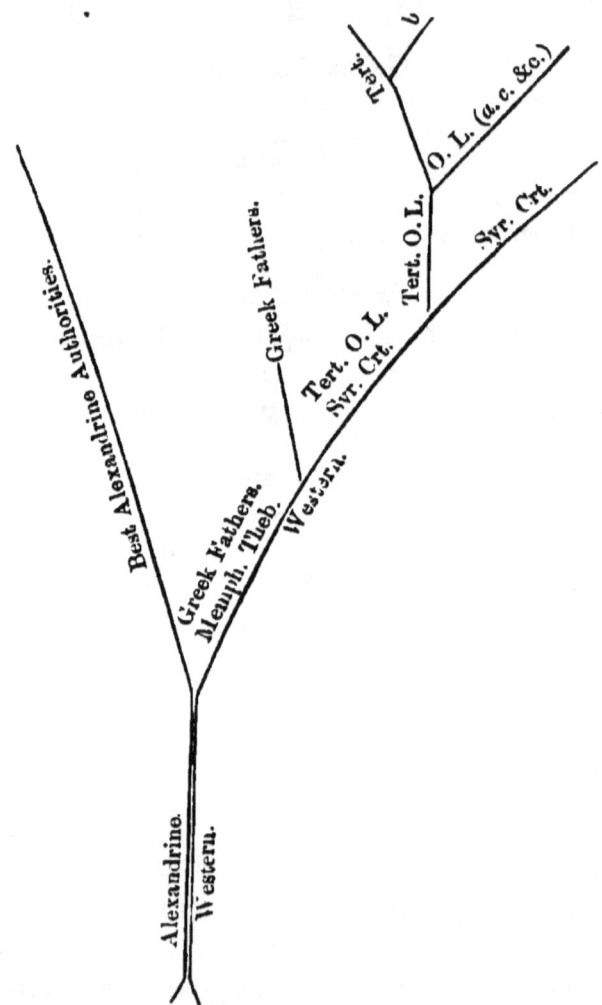

The Sacred Autographs.

In accordance with the sketch here given we may present the history of the text, up to the time when it reached Tertullian, thus. First we have the sacred autographs, which are copied for some time, we need not say immaculately, but without change on the points included in the above analysis. Gradually a few errors slip in, which are found especially in the Egyptian versions and in the works of some Alexandrine and Palestinian Fathers. But in time a wider breach is made. The process of corruption becomes more rapid. We reach at last that strange document which, through more or less remote descent, became the parent of the Curetonian Syriac on the one hand and of the Old Latin on the other. These two lines severally branch off. The Old Latin itself divides. One of its copies in particular (b) seems to represent a text that has a close affinity to that of Tertullian, and among the group of manuscripts to which it belongs is that which Tertullian himself most frequently and habitually used.

Strictly speaking indeed there can be no true genealogical tree. The course of descent is not clear and direct all the way. There is some confusion and some crossing and recrossing of the lines. Thus, for instance, there is the curious coincidence of Tertullian with ℵ, a member of a group that had long seemed to be left behind, in John vi. 51. This however, as it is only on a point of order and that in a translation, may very possibly be accidental; I should incline to think that the reading of the Greek Codex from which Tertullian's Latin was derived agreed rather with that of B, C, D, &c., and these phenomena would increase the probability that these manuscripts and Tertullian had really preserved the original text. If that were the case—and it is the conclusion arrived at by a decided majority of the best editors—there would then be no considerable difficulty in regard to the relation between Tertullian and the five great Uncials, for the reading of Mark ix. 7 is of much less importance. Somewhat more difficult to adjust would be Tertullian's relations to the different forms of the Old Latin and Curetonian Syriac. In one instance, Matt. xi. 11 (or Luke vii. 26), Tertullian seems to derive his text from the Dd branch rather than the b branch of the Old Latin. In another (Matt. iii. 8) he seems to overleap b and most copies of the Old Latin altogether and go to the Curetonian Syriac. How, too, did he come to have the paraphrastic reading of Matt. v. 16 which is found in no MSS. or versions but in Justin (approximately), Clement of Alexandria, and several Latin Fathers? The paraphrase might naturally enough occur to a single writer here or there, but the extent of the coincidence is remarkable. Perhaps we are to see here another sign of the study bestowed by the Fathers upon the writings of their predecessors leading to an unconscious or semi-conscious reproduction of their deviations. It is a noticeable fact that in regard to the order of the clauses in Matt. v. 4, 5, Tertullian has preserved what is probably the right reading along with b alone, the other copies of the Old Latin (all except the revised f) with the Curetonian Syriac having gone wrong. On the whole the complexities and cross relations are less, and the genealogical tree holds good to a greater extent, than we might have been prepared for. The hypothesis that Tertullian used a manuscript in the main resembling b of the Old Latin satisfies most elements of the problem.

But the merest glance at these phenomena must be enough to show that the Tübingen theory, or any theory which attributes a late origin to our Gospels, is out of the question. To bring the text into the state in which it is found in the writings of Tertullian, a century is not at all too long a period to allow. In fact I doubt whether any subsequent century saw changes so great, though we should naturally suppose that corruption would proceed at an advancing rate for every fresh copy that was made. The phenomena that have to be accounted for are not, be it remembered, such as might be caused by the carelessness of a single scribe. They are spread over whole groups of MSS. together. We can trace the gradual accessions of corruption at each step as we advance in the history of the text. A certain false reading comes in at such a point and spreads over all the manuscripts that start from that; another comes in at a further stage and vitiates succeeding copies there; until at last a process of correction and revision sets in; recourse is had to the best standard manuscripts, and a purer text is recovered by comparison with these. It is precisely such a text that is presented by the Old Latin Codex f, which, we find accordingly, shows a maximum of difference from Tertullian. A still more systematic revision, though executed—if we are to judge from the instances brought to our notice—with somewhat more reserve, is seen in Jerome's Vulgate.

It seems unnecessary to dilate upon this point. I will only venture to repeat the statement which I made at starting; that if the whole of the Christian literature for the first three quarters of the second century could be blotted out, and Irenaeus and Tertullian alone remained, as well as the later manuscripts with which to compare them, there would still be ample proof that the latest of our Gospels cannot overstep the bounds of the first century. The abundant indications of internal evidence are thus confirmed, and the age and date of the Synoptic

Gospels, I think we may say, within approximate limits, established.

But we must not forget that there is a double challenge to be met. The first part of it—that which relates to the evidence for the existence of the Gospels—has been answered. It remains to consider how far the external evidence for the Gospels goes to prove their authenticity. It may indeed well be asked how the external evidence can be expected to prove the authenticity of these records. It does so, to a considerable extent, indirectly by throwing them back into closer contact with the facts. It also tends to establish the authority in which they were held, certainly in the last quarter of the second century, and very probably before. By this time the Gospels were acknowledged to be all that is now understood by the word 'canonical.' They were placed upon the same footing as the Old Testament Scriptures. They were looked up to with the same reverence and regarded as possessing the same Divine inspiration. We may trace indeed some of the steps by which this position was attained. The γέγραπται of the Epistle of Barnabas, the public reading of the Gospels in the churches mentioned by Justin, the τὸ εἰρημένον of Tatian, the κυριακαὶ γραφαί of Dionysius of Corinth, all prepare the way for the final culmination in the Muratorian Canon and Irenaeus. So complete had the process been that Irenaeus does not seem to know of a time when the authority of the Gospels had been less than it was to him. Yet the process had been, of course, gradual. The canonical Gospels had to compete with several others before they became canonical. They had to make good their own claims and to displace rival documents; and they succeeded. It is a striking instance of the 'survival of the fittest.' That they were really the fittest is confirmed by nearly every fragment of the lost Gospels that remains, but it would be almost sufficiently proved by the very fact that they survived.

In this indirect manner I think that the external evidence bears out the position assigned to the canonical Gospels. It has preserved to us the judgment of the men of that time, and there is a certain relative sense in which the maxim, 'Securus judicat orbis terrarum,' is true. The decisions of an age, especially decisions such as this where quite as much depended upon pious feeling as upon logical reasoning, are usually sounder than the arguments that are put forward to defend them. We should hardly endorse the arguments by which Irenaeus proves *a priori* the necessity of a 'fourfold Gospel,' but there is real weight in the fact that four Gospels and no more were accepted by him and others like him. It is difficult to read without impatience the rough words that are applied to the early Christian writers and to contrast the self-complacency in which our own superior knowledge is surveyed. If there is something in which they are behind us, there is much also in which we are behind them. Among the many things for which Mr. Arnold deserves our gratitude he deserves it not least for the way in which he has singled out two sentences, one from St. Augustine and the other from the Imitation, 'Domine fecisti nos ad te et irrequietum est cor nostrum donec requiescat in te,' and, 'Esto humilis et pacificus et erit tecum Jesus.' The men who could write thus are not to be despised.

But beyond their more general testimony it is not clear what else the early Fathers could be expected to do. They could not prove—at least their written remains that have come down to us could not prove—that the Gospels were really written by the authors traditionally assigned to them. When we say that the very names of the first two Evangelists are not mentioned before a date that may be from 120-166 (or 155) A.D. and the third and fourth not before 170-175 A.D., this alone is enough, without introducing other elements of doubt, to show that the evidence must needs be inconclusive. If the author of 'Supernatural Religion' undertook to show this, he undertook a superfluous task. So much at least, Mr. Arnold was right in saying, 'might be stated in a sentence and proved in a page.' There is a presumption in favour of the tradition, and perhaps, considering the relation of Irenaeus to Polycarp and of Polycarp to St. John, we may say, a fairly strong one; but we need now-a-days, to authenticate a document, closer evidence than this. The cases are not quite parallel, and the difference between them is decidedly in favour of Irenaeus, but if Clement of Alexandria could speak of an Epistle written about 125 A.D. as the work of the apostolic Barnabas the companion of St. Paul[1], we must not lay too much stress upon the direct testimony of Irenaeus when he attributes the fourth Gospel to the Apostle St. John.

These are points for a different set of arguments to determine. The Gospel itself affords sufficient indications as to the position of its author. For the conclusion that he was a Palestinian Jew, who had lived in Palestine before the destruction of Jerusalem, familiar with the hopes and expectations of his people, and himself mixed up with the events which he describes, there is evidence of such

---

[1] *Strom.* ii. 20.

volume and variety as seems exceedingly difficult to resist. As I have gone into this subject at length elsewhere [1], and as, so far as I can see, no new element has been introduced into the question by 'Supernatural Religion,' I shall not break the unity of the present work by considering the objections brought in detail. I am very ready to recognise the ability with which many of these are stated, but it is the ability of the advocate rather than of the impartial critic. There is a constant tendency to draw conclusions much in excess of the premisses. An observation, true in itself with a certain qualification and restriction, is made in an unqualified form, and the truth that it contains is exaggerated. Above all, wherever there is a margin of ignorance, wherever a statement of the Evangelist is not capable of direct and exact verification, the doubt is invariably given against him and he is brought in guilty either of ignorance or deception. I have no hesitation in saying that if the principles of criticism applied to the fourth Gospel—not only by the author of 'Supernatural Religion,' but by some other writers of repute, such as Dr. Scholten—were applied to ordinary history or to the affairs of every-day life, much that is known actually to have happened could be shown on *a priori* grounds to be impossible. It is time that the extreme negative school should justify more completely

---

[1] In a volume entitled *The Authorship and Historical Character of the Fourth Gospel*, Macmillan, 1872. I may say with reference to this book—a 'firstling' of theological study—that I am inclined now to think that I exaggerated somewhat the importance of minute details as an evidence of the work of an eye-witness. The whole of the arguments, however, summarised on pp. 287-293 seem to me to be still perfectly valid and sound, and the greater part of them—notably that which relates to the Messianic expectations—is quite untouched by 'Supernatural Religion.'

their canons of criticism. As it is, the laxity of these repels many a thoughtful mind quite as firmly convinced as they can be of the necessity of free enquiry and quite as anxious to reconcile the different sides of knowledge. The question is not one merely of freedom or tradition, but of reason and logic; and until there is more agreement as to what is reasonable and what the laws of logic demand, the arguments are apt to run in parallel lines that never meet[1].

But, it is said, 'Miracles require exceptional evidence.' True: exceptional evidence they both require and possess; but that evidence is not external. Incomparably the strongest attestation to the Gospel narratives is that which they bear to themselves. Miracles have exceptional evidence because the non-miraculous portions of the narrative with which they are bound up are exceptional. These carry their truth stamped upon their face, and that truth is reflected back upon the miracles. It is on the internal investigation of the Gospels that the real issue lies. And this is one main reason why the belief of mankind so little depends upon formal apologetics. We can all feel the self-evidential force of the Gospel story; but who shall present it adequately in words? We are reminded of the fate of him who thought the ark of God was falling and put out his hand to steady it— and, for his profanity, died. It can hardly be said that good intentions would be a sufficient justification, because that a man should think himself fit for the task would be in itself almost a sufficient sign that he was mistaken.

---

[1] It is instructive to compare the canons elaborately drawn up by Mr. M'Clellan (*N. T.* i. 375-389) with those tacitly assumed in 'Supernatural Religion.' The inference in the one case seems to be 'possible, therefore true,' in the other, 'not probable, or not confirmed, therefore false.' Surely neither of these tallies with experience.

It is not indeed quite incredible that the qualifications should one day be found. We seem almost to see that, with a slight alteration of circumstances, a little different training in early life, such an one has almost been among us. There are passages that make us think that the author of 'Parochial and Plain Sermons' might have touched even the Gospels with cogency that yet was not profane. But the combination of qualities required is such as would hardly be found for centuries together. The most fine and sensitive tact of piety would be essential. With it must go absolute sincerity and singleness of purpose. Any dash of mere conventionalism or self-seeking would spoil the whole. There must be that clear illuminated insight that is only given to those who are in a more than ordinary sense 'pure in heart.' And on the other hand, along with these unique spiritual qualities must go a sound and exact scientific training, a just perception of logical force and method, and a wide range of knowledge. One of the great dangers and drawbacks to the exercise of the critical faculty is that it tends to destroy the spiritual intuition. And just in like manner the too great reliance upon this intuition benumbs and impoverishes the critical faculty. Yet, in a mind that should present at all adequately the internal evidence of the Gospels, both should co-exist in equal balance and proportion. We cannot say that there will never be such a mind, but the asceticism of a life would be a necessary discipline for it to go through, and that such a life as the world has seldom seen.

In the meantime the private Christian may well be content with what he has. 'If any man will do His will, he shall know of the doctrine whether it be of God.'

CHAPTER XIV.

CONCLUSION.

AND now that we have come to the end of the purely critical portion of this enquiry, I may perhaps be allowed to say a few words on its general tendency and bearing. As critics we have only the critical question to deal with. Certain evidence is presented to us which it is our duty to weigh and test by reference to logical and critical laws. It must stand or fall on its own merits, and any considerations brought in from without will be irrelevant to the question at issue. But after this is done we may fairly look round and consider how our conclusion affects other conclusions and in what direction it is leading us. If we look at 'Supernatural Religion' in this way we shall see that its tendency is distinctly marked. Its attack will fall chiefly upon the middle party in opinion. And it will play into the hands of the two extreme parties on either side. There can be little doubt that indirectly it will help the movement that is carrying so many into Ultramontanism, and directly it is of course intended to win converts to what may perhaps be called comprehensively Secularism.

Now it is certainly true that the argument from consequences is one that ought to be applied with great caution. Yet I am not at all sure that it has not a real basis in philosophy as well as in nature. The very existence of these two great parties, the Ultramontane and the Secularist, over against each other, seems to be a kind of standing protest against either of them. If Ultramontanism is true, how is it that so many wise and good men openly avow Secularism? If Secularism is true, how is it that so many of the finest and highest minds take refuge from it—a treacherous refuge, I allow—in Ultramontanism? There is something in this more than a mere defective syllogism—more than an insufficient presentation of the evidence. Truth, in the widest sense, is that which is in accordance with the laws and conditions of human nature. But where beliefs are so directly antithetical as they are here, the repugnance and resistance which each is found to cause in so large a number of minds is in itself a proof that those laws and conditions are insufficiently complied with. To the spectator, standing outside of both, this will seem to be easily explained: the one sacrifices reason to faith; the other sacrifices faith to reason. But there is abundant evidence to show that both faith (meaning thereby the religious emotions) and reason are ineradicable elements in the human mind. That which seriously and permanently offends against either cannot be true. For creatures differently constituted from man—either all reason or all pure disembodied emotion—it might be otherwise; but, for man, as he is, the epithet 'true' seems to be excluded from any set of propositions that has such results.

Even in the more limited sense, and confining the term to propositions purely intellectual, there is, I think we must say, a presumption against the truth of that which involves so deep and wide a chasm in human nature. Without importing teleology, we should naturally expect that the intellect and the emotions should be capable of working harmoniously together. They do so in most things: why should they not in the highest matters of all? If the one set of opinions is anti-rational and the other anti-emotional, as we see practically that they are, is not this in itself an antecedent presumption against either of them? It may not be enough to prove at once that the syllogism is defective: still less is it a sufficient warrant for establishing an opposite syllogism. But it does seem to be enough to give the scientific reasoner pause, and to make him go over the line of his argument again and again and yet again, with the suspicion that there is (as how well there may be!) a flaw somewhere.

It would not, I think, be difficult to point out such flaws [1]—some of them, as it appears, of considerable

---

[1] This, perhaps, is one that is apt to be overlooked. In order to be quite sure that the process of analysis is complete it must be supplemented and verified by the reversed process of synthesis. If a compound has been resolved into its elements, we cannot be sure that it has been resolved into *all* its elements until the original compound has been produced by their recombination. Where this second reverse process fails, the inference is that some unknown element which was originally present has escaped in the analysis. The analysis may be true as far as it goes, but it is incomplete. The causes are 'verae causae,' but they are not *all* the causes in operation. So it seems to be with the analysis of the vital organism. We may be said to know entirely what air and water are because the chemist can produce them, but we only know very imperfectly the nature of life and will and conscience, because when the physiological analysis has been carried as far as it will go there still remains a large unknown element. Within this element may very well reside those distinctive properties which make man (as the moralist is *obliged* to assume that he is) a responsible and religious being. The hypotheses which lie at the root of morals and religion are derived from another source than physiology, but physiology does not exclude them, and will not do so until it gives a far more verifiably complete account of human nature than it does at present.

magnitude. But the subject is one that would take us far away out of our present course, and for its proper development would require a technical knowledge of the processes of physical science which I do not possess. Leaving this on one side, and regarding them only in the abstract, the considerations stated above seem to point to the necessity of something of the nature of a compromise. And yet there is, strictly speaking, no such thing as compromise in opinions. Compromise belongs to the world of practice; it is only admitted by an illicit process into the world of thought. The author of 'Supernatural Religion' is doubtless right in deprecating that 'illogical zeal which flings to the pursuing wolves of doubt and unbelief, scrap by scrap,' all the distinctive doctrines of Christianity. Belief, it is true, must be ultimately logical to stand. It must have an inner cohesion and inter-dependence. It must start from a fixed principle. This has been, and still is, the besetting weakness of the theology of mediation. It is apt to form itself merely by stripping off what seem to be excrescences from the outside, and not by radically reconstructing itself, on a firmly established basis, from within. The difficulty in such a process is to draw the line. There is a delusive appearance of roundness and completeness in the creeds of those who either accept everything or deny everything: though, even here, there is, I think we may say, always, some little loophole left of belief or of denial, which will inevitably expand until it splits and destroys the whole structure. But the moment we begin to meet both parties half way, there comes in that crucial question: Why do you accept just so much and no more? Why do you deny just so much and no more[1]?

It must, in candour, be confessed that the synthetic formula for the middle party in opinion has not yet been found. Other parties have their formulae, but none that will really bear examination. *Quod semper, quod ubique, quod ab omnibus*, would do excellently if there was any belief that had been held 'always, everywhere, and by all,' if no discoveries had been made as to the facts, and if there had been no advance in the methods of knowledge. The ultimate universality and the absolute uniformity of physical antecedents has a plausible appearance until it is seen that logically carried out it reduces men to machines, annihilates responsibility,

[1] Mr. Browning has expressed this with his usual incisiveness and penetration:—

'I hear you recommend, I might at least
Eliminate, decrassify my faith . . . .
Still, when you bid me purify the same,
To such a process I discern no end,
Clearing off one excrescence to see two;
There's ever a next in size, now grown as big,
That meets the knife: I cut and cut again!
First cut the liquefaction, what comes last
But Fichte's clever cut at God himself?'

But also, on the other hand:—

'Where's
The gain? how can we guard our unbelief?
Just when we are safest, there's a sunset-touch,
A fancy from a flower-bell, some one's death,
A chorus ending from Euripides,—
And that's enough for fifty hopes and fears,
As old and new at once as Nature's self,
To rap and knock and enter in our soul . . . .
All we have gained then by our unbelief
Is a life of doubt diversified by faith,
For one of faith diversified by doubt:
We called the chess-board white,—we call it black.'

Bishop Blongram's Apology.

and involves conclusions on the assumption of the truth of which society could not hold together for a single day. If we abandon these Macedonian methods for unloosing the Gordian knot of things and keep to the slow and laborious way of gradual induction, then I think it will be clear that all opinions must be held on the most provisional tenure. A vast number of problems will need to be worked out before any can be said to be established with a pretence to finality. And the course which the inductive process is taking supplies one of the chief 'grounds of hope' to those who wish to hold that middle position of which I have been speaking. The extreme theories which from time to time have been advanced have not been able to hold their ground. No doubt they may have done the good that extreme theories usually do, in bringing out either positively or negatively one side or another of the truth; but in themselves they have been rejected as at once inadequate and unreal solutions of the facts. First we had the Rationalism (properly so called) of Paulus, then the Mythical hypothesis of Strauss, and after that the 'Tendenz-kritik' of Baur. But what candid person does not feel that each and all of these contained exaggerations more incredible than the difficulties which they sought to remove? There has been on each of the points raised a more or less definite ebb in the tide. The moderate conclusion is seen to be also the reasonable conclusion. And not least is this the case with the enquiry on which we have been just engaged. The author of 'Supernatural Religion' has overshot the mark very much indeed. There is, as we have seen, a certain truth in some things that he has said, but the whole sum of truth is very far from bearing out his conclusions.

When we look up from these detailed enquiries and lift up our eyes to a wider horizon we shall be able to relegate them to their true place. The really imposing witness to the truth of Christianity is that which is supplied by history on the one hand, and its own internal attractiveness and conformity to human nature on the other. Strictly speaking, perhaps, these are but two sides of the same thing. It is in history that the laws of human nature assume a concrete shape and expression. The fact that Christianity has held its ground in the face of such long-continued and hostile criticism is a proof that it must have some deeply-seated fitness and appropriateness for man. And this goes a long way towards saying that it is true. It is a theory of things that is being constantly tested by experience. But the results of experience are often expressed unconsciously. They include many a subtle indication that the mind has followed but cannot reproduce to itself in set terms. All the reasons that go to form a judge's decision do not appear in his charge. Yet there we have a select and highly-trained mind working upon matter that presents no very great degree of complexity. When we come to a question so wide, so subtle and complex as Christianity, the individual mind ceases to be competent to sit in judgment upon it. It becomes necessary to appeal to a much more extended tribunal, and the verdict of that tribunal will be given rather by acts than in words. Thus there seems to have always been a sort of half-conscious feeling in men's minds that there was more in Christianity than the arguments for it were able to bring out. In looking back over the course that apologetics have taken, we cannot help being struck by a disproportion between the controversial aspect and the practical. It will probably on the whole be admitted that the balance of argument has in the past been usually somewhat on the side of the apologists; but the argumentative victory has seldom if ever been so decisive as quite to account for the comparatively undisturbed continuity of the religious life. It was in the height of the Deist controversy that Wesley and Whitfield began to preach, and they made more converts by appealing to the emotions than probably Butler did by appealing to the reason.

A true philosophy must take account of these phenomena. Beliefs which issue in that peculiarly fine and chastened and tender spirit which is the proper note of Christianity, cannot, under any circumstances, be dismissed as 'delusion.' Surely if any product of humanity is true and genuine, it is to be found here. There are indeed truths which find a response in our hearts without apparently going through any logical process, not because they are illogical, but because the scales of logic are not delicate and sensitive enough to weigh them.

'Except ye be converted and become as little children, ye shall not enter into the kingdom of heaven.' 'I will arise and go to my father, and will say unto him: Father, I have sinned against heaven and before thee, and am no more worthy to be called thy son.' 'Come unto me all ye that labour and are heavy laden, and I will give you rest.' The plummet of science—physical or metaphysical, moral or critical—has never sounded so deep as sayings such as these. We may pass them over unnoticed in our Bibles, or let them slip glibly and thoughtlessly from the tongue; but when they once really come home, there is nothing to do but to bow the head and cover the face and exclaim with the Apostle, 'Depart from me, for I am a sinful man, O Lord.'

And yet there is that other side of the question which is represented in 'Supernatural Religion,' and this too must have justice done to it. There is an intellectual, as well as a moral and spiritual, synthesis of things. Only it should be remembered that this synthesis has to cover an immense number of facts of the most varied and intricate kind, and that at present the nature of the facts themselves is in many cases very far from being accurately ascertained. We are constantly reminded in reading 'Supernatural Religion,' able and vigorous as it is, how much of its force depends rather upon our ignorance than our knowledge. It supplies us with many opportunities of seeing how easily the whole course and tenour of an argument may be changed by the introduction of a new element. For instance, I imagine that if the author had given a little deeper study to the seemingly minute and secondary subject of text-criticism, it would have aroused in him very considerable misgivings as to the results at which he seemed to have arrived. There is a solidarity in all the different departments of human knowledge and research, especially among those that are allied in subject. These are continually sending out offshoots and projections into the neighbouring regions, and the conclusions of one science very often have to depend upon those of another. The course of enquiry that has been taken in 'Supernatural Religion' is peculiarly unfortunate. It starts from the wrong end. It begins with propositions into which *a priori* considerations largely enter, and, from the standpoint given by these, it proceeds to dictate terms in a field that can only be trodden by patient and unprejudiced study. A far more hopeful and scientific process would have been to begin upon ground where dogmatic questions do not enter, or enter only in a remote degree, and where there is a sufficient number of solid ascertainable facts to go upon, and then to work the way steadily and cautiously upwards to higher generalisations.

It will have been seen in the course of the present enquiry how many side questions need to be determined. It would be well if monographs were written upon all the quotations from the Old Testament in the Christian literature of the first two centuries, modelled upon Credner's investigations into the quotations in Justin. Before this is done there should be a new and revised edition of Holmes' and Parsons' Septuagint[1]. Everything short of this would be inadequate, because we need to know not only the best text, but every text that has definite historical attestation. In this way it would be possible to arrive at a tolerably exact, instead of a merely approximate, deduction as to the habit of quotation generally, which would supply a firmer basis for inference

---

[1] As to the defects of the present edition, see Tischendorf, Prolegomena to *Vetus Testamentum Graece juxta LXX Interpretes,* p. liii: 'Eae vero (collationes) quemadmodum in editis habentur non modo universae graviter differunt inter se fide atque accuratione, sed ad ipsos principales testes tam negligenter tamque male factae sunt ut etiam atque etiam dolendum sit tantos numos rara liberalitate per Angliam suppeditatos criticae sacrae parum profuisse.' Similarly Credner, in regard to the use of the Codex Alexandrinus, *Beiträge,* ii. 16: 'Wahrhaft unbegreiflich und unverzeihlich ist es, dass die Herausgeber der kostbaren Kritischen Ausgabe der LXX, welcher zu Oxford vor wenigen Jahren vollendet und von Holmes und Parsons besorgt worden ist, statt eine sorgfältige Vergleichung des in London aufbewahrten Cod. Alex. zu veranstalten, sich lediglich auf die Ausgabe von Grabe beschränkt haben, dessen Kritik vielfach nicht einmal verstanden worden ist.'

in regard to the New Testament than that which has been assumed here. At the same time monographs should be written in English, besides those already existing in German, upon the date or position of the writers whose works come under review. Without any attempt to prove a particular thesis, the reader should be allowed to see precisely what the evidence is and how far it goes. Then if he could not arrive at a positive conclusion, he could at least attain to the most probable. And, lastly, it is highly important that the whole question of the composition and structure of the Synoptic Gospels should be investigated to the very bottom. Much valuable labour has already been expended upon this subject, but the result, though progress has been made, is rather to show its extreme complexity and difficulty than to produce any final settlement. Yet, as the author of 'Supernatural Religion' has rather dimly and inadequately seen, we are constantly thrown back upon assumptions borrowed from this quarter.

Pending such more mature and thorough enquiries, I quite feel that my own present contribution belongs to a transition stage, and cannot profess to be more than provisional. But it will have served its purpose sufficiently if it has helped to mark out more distinctly certain lines of the enquiry and to carry the investigation along these a little way; suggesting at the same time—what the facts themselves really suggest—counsels of sobriety and moderation.

What the end will be, it would be presumptuous to attempt to foretell. It will probably be a long time before even these minor questions—much more the major questions into which they run up—will be solved. Whether they will ever be solved—all of them at least—

in such a way as to compel entire assent is very doubtful. Error and imperfection seem to be permanently, if we may hope diminishingly, a condition of human thought and action. It does not appear to be the will of God that Truth should ever be so presented as to crush out all variety of opinion. The conflict of opinions is like that of Hercules with the Hydra. As fast as one is cut down another arises in its place; and there is no searing-iron to scorch and cicatrize the wound. However much we may labour, we can only arrive at an inner conviction, not at objective certainty. All the glosses and asseverations in the world cannot carry us an inch beyond the due weight of the evidence vouchsafed to us. An honest and brave mind will accept manfully this condition of things, and not seek for infallibility where it can find none. It will adopt as its motto that noble saying of Bishop Butler—noble, because so unflinchingly true, though opposed to a sentimental optimism—'Probability is the very guide of life.'

With probabilities we have to deal, in the intellectual sphere. But, when once this is thoroughly and honestly recognised, even a comparatively small balance of probability comes to have as much moral weight as the most loudly vaunted certainty. And meantime, apart from and beneath the strife of tongues, there is the still small voice which whispers to a man and bids him, in no superstitious sense but with the gravity and humility which befits a Christian, to 'work out his own salvation with fear and trembling.'

APPENDIX.

Supplemental Note on the Reconstruction of Marcion's Gospel.

IF the reader should happen to possess the work of Rönsch, Das Neue Testament Tertullian's, to which allusion has frequently been made above, and will simply glance over the pages, noting the references, from Luke iv. 16 to the end of the Gospel, I do not think he will need any other proof of the sufficiency of the grounds for the reconstruction of Marcion's Gospel, so as at least to admit of a decision as to whether it was our present St. Luke or not.

Failing this, it may be well to give a brief example of the kind of data available, going back straight to the original authorities themselves.

For this purpose we will take the first chapter that Marcion preserved entire, Luke v, and set forth in full such fragments of it as have come down to us.

We take up the argument of Tertullian at the point where he begins to treat of this chapter.

In the fourth book of the treatise against Marcion Tertullian begins by dealing with the Antitheses (a sort of criticism by Marcion on what he regarded as the Judaising portions of the Canonical Gospel), and then, in general terms, with the actual Gospel which Marcion used. From the general he descends to the particular, and in c. 6 Tertullian pledges himself to show in detail, that even in those parts of the Gospel which Marcion retained there was enough to refute his own system.

Marcion's Gospel began with the descent of Jesus upon Capernaum in the fifteenth year of Tiberias. Tertullian makes points out of this, also from the account of His preaching in the synagogue and of the expulsion of the devil. After this incident Marcion's Gospel represented our Lord as retiring into solitude. It did this as it would appear in words very similar to those of the Canonical Gospel. I place side by side the language of Tertullian with that of the Vulgate (Codex Fuldensis, as given by Tregelles). I have also compared the translation in the two codd., Vercellensis and Veronensis, of the Old Latin in Bianchini's edition. It will be remembered however that Tertullian is admitted to have Marcion's (and *not* the Canonical) Gospel before him, and he probably translates directly from that.

In solitudinem procedit. . . . Detentus a turbis: *Oportet me,* inquit, *et aliis civitatibus annuntiare regnum dei.*	Luke v. 42, 43: Ibat in desertum locum . . . et detinebant illum ne discederet ab eis. Quibus ille ait quia, Et aliis civitatibus oportet me evangelizare regnum dei.

His discussion of the fifth chapter Tertullian begins by asking why, out of all possible occupations, Christ should have fixed upon that of fishing, to take from thence His apostles, Simon and the sons of Zebedee. There was a meaning in the act which appears in the reply to Peter, 'Thou shalt catch men,' where there is a reference to a prophecy of Jeremiah (ch. xvi. 16). By this allusion

Jesus sanctioned those very prophecies which Marcion rejected. In the end the fishermen left their boats and followed Him.

De tot generibus operum quid utique ad piscaturam respexit ut ab illa in apostolos sumeret *Simonem et filios Zebedaei* ... dicens Petro *trepidanti de copiosa indagine piscium: ne time abhinc enim homines eris capiens*.... Denique *relictis naviculis secuti sunt ipsum*...

Luke v. 1–11: [1] Factum est autem cum turbae irruerent in eum ... et ipse stabat secus stagnum Gennesareth : [2] et vidit duas naves.... [3] Ascendens in unam navem quae erat Simonis ... [4] dixit ad Simonem, Duc in altum, et laxate retia vestra in capturam. ... [6] Et cum hoc fecissent concluserunt piscium multitudinem copiosam. ... [7] Et impleverunt ambas naviculas ita ut mergerentur. [8] Quod cum videret Simon Petrus, procidit ad genua Jesu. ... [9] Stupor enim circumdederat eum ... [10] similiter autem Jacobum et Johannem filios Zebedaei. ... Et ait ad Simonem Jesus, Noli timere, ex hoc jam homines eris capiens. [11] Et subductis ad terram navibus relictis omnibus secuti sunt illum.

For Noli timere &c., cod. a has, Noli timere, jam amodo eris vivificans homines ; cod. b, Nol. tim., ex hoc jam eris homines vivificans.

In passing to the incident of the leper, Tertullian argues that the prohibition of contact with a leper was figurative, applying really to the contact with sin. But the Godhead is incapable of pollution, and therefore Jesus touched the leper. It would be in vain for Marcion to suggest that this was done in contempt of the law. For, upon his own (Docetic) theory, the body of Jesus was phantasmal, and therefore could not receive pollution: so that there would be no real contact or contempt of the law. Neither, as Marcion maintained, did a comparison with the miracle of Elisha tend to the disparagement of that prophet. True, Christ healed with a word. So also with a word had the Creator made the world. And, after all, the word of Christ produced no greater result than a river which came from the Creator's hands. Further, the command of Jesus to the leper when healed, showed His desire that the law should be fulfilled. Nay, He added an explanation which conveyed that He was not come to destroy the law, but Himself to fulfil it. This He did deliberately, and not from mere indulgence to the man, who, He knew, would wish to do as the law required.

Argumentatur ... *in leprosi purgationem* ... *Tetigit leprosum* ... Et hoc opponit Marcion ... Christum ... verbo solo, et hoc semel functo, curationem statim repraesentasse. Quantam ad gloriae humanae aversionem pertinebat, *vetuit eum divulgare*. Quantum autem ad tutelam legis jussit ordinem impleri. *Vade, ostende te sacerdoti, et offer munus quod praecepit Moyses*. ... Itaque adjecit: *ut sit vobis in testimonium*.

Luke v. 12–14: [12] Ecce vir plenus lepra: et videns Jesum .. rogavit eum dicens, Domine, si vis, potes me mundare. [13] Et extendens manum tetigit illum dicens, Volo, mundare. Et confestim lepra discessit ab illo. [14] Et ipse praecepit illi ut nemini diceret, sed Vade ostende te sacerdoti, et offer pro emundatione tua sicut praecepit Moses, in testimonium illis.

For emundatione in ver. 14, a has purgatione; b as Vulg. Both a and b have the form offers (see Rönsch, It. u. Vulg. p. 294), b the plural sacerdotibus. Both codd. have a variation similar to that of Marcion, ut sit etc.; a inserts hoc.

Next follows the healing of the paralytic, which was done in fulfilment of Is. xxxv. 2. The miracle also itself in its details was a special and exact fulfilment of the prophecy contained in the next verse, Is. xxxv. 3. That the Messiah should forgive sins had been repeatedly prophesied, e. g. in Is. liii. 12, i. 18, Micah vii. 18. Not only were these prophecies thus actually sanctioned by Christ, but, in forgiving the sins of the paralytic, He was only doing what the Creator or Demiurge had done before Him. In proof of this Tertullian appeals to the examples of the Ninevites, of David and Nathan, of Ahab, of Jonathan the son of Saul, and of the chosen people themselves. Thus Marcion was doubly refuted, because the prerogative of forgiveness was asserted of the Messiah in the prophecies which he rejected and attributed to the Creator whom he denied. In like manner, when Jesus called Himself the 'Son of Man,' He did so in a real sense, signifying that He was really born of a virgin. This appellation too had been applied to Him by the prophet Daniel (Dan. vii. 13, iii. 25). But if Jesus claimed to be the Son of Man, if, standing before the Jews as a man, He claimed as man the power of forgiving sins, He thereby showed that He possessed a real human body and not the mere phantasm of which Marcion spoke.

Curatur et *paralyticus*, et quidem in coetu, spectante

Luke v. 17–26: [17]Et factum est in una dierum et ipse sede-

populo... Cum redintegratione membrorum virium quoque repraesentationem pollicebatur: *Exsurge et tolle grabatum tuum;* —simul et animi vigorem ad non timendos qui dicturi erant: *Quis dimittet peccata nisi solus deus?* ... Cum Judaei merito retractarent non posse hominem *delicta dimittere* sed *deum solum,* cur ... *respondit, habere eum potestatem dimittendi delicta,* quando et *filium hominis* nominans hominem nominaret?

bat docens.... [18] Et ecce viri portantes in lecto hominem qui erat paralyticus, et quaerebant eum inferre ... [19] et non invenientes qua parte illum inferrent prae turba, ... per tegulas ... summiserunt illum cum lecto in medium ante Jesum. [20] Quorum fidem ut vidit, dixit, Homo, remittuntur tibi peccata tua. [21] Et coeperunt cogitare Scribae et Pharisaei, dicentes, Quis est hic qui loquitur blasphemias? quis potest dimittere peccata nisi solus deus? [22] Ut cognovit autem Jesus cogitationes eorum, respondens dixit ad illos. ... [23] Quid est facilius dicere, Dimittuntur tibi peccata, an dicere, Surge et ambula? [24] Ut autem sciatis quia filius hominis potestatem habet in terra dimittere peccata, ait paralytico, Tibi dico, surge, tolle lectum tuum et vade in domum tuam. [25] Et confestim surgens .. abiit in domum suam.

Grabatum is the reading of a in ver. 25.

Marcion drew an argument from the calling of the publican (Levi)—one under ban of the law—as if it were done in disparagement of the law. Tertullian reminds him in reply of the calling and confession of Peter, who was a representative of the law. Further, when he said that 'the whole need not a physician' Jesus declared that the Jews were whole, the publicans sick.

Publicanum adlectum a domino . . . dicendo, *medicum sanis non esse necessarium sed male habentibus* . . .	Luke v. 27–32: [27] Et post hoc exiit et vidit publicanum . . . et ait illi, Sequere me. . . . [30] Et murmurabant Pharisaei et Scribae eorum . . . [31] et respondens Jesus dixit ad illos, Non egent qui sani sunt medico sed qui male habent.

The question respecting the disciples of John is turned against Marcion, as a recognition of the Baptist's mission. If John had not prepared the way for Christ, if he had not actually baptized Him, if, in fact, there was that diversity between the two which Marcion assumed, no one would ever have thought of instituting a comparison between them or the conduct of their disciples. In His reply, 'that the children of the bridegroom could not fast,' Jesus virtually allowed the practice of the disciples of John, and excused, as only for a time, that of His own disciples. The very name, 'bridegroom,' was taken from the Old Testament (Ps. xix. 6 sq., Is. lxi. 10, xlix. 18, Cant. iv. 8); and its assumption by Christ was a sanction of marriage, and showed that Marcion did wrong to condemn the married state.

Unde autem et Joannes venit in medium ? . . . Si nihil omnino administrasset Joannes . . . nemo *discipulos Christi manducantes et bibentes* ad formam *discipulorum Joannis assidue jejunantium et orantium*	Luke v. 33–35: [33] At illi dixerunt ad eum, Quare discipuli Johannis jejunant frequenter et obsecrationes faciunt, . . . tui autem edunt et bibunt ? [34] Quibus ipse ait, Numquid potestis filios sponsi dum cum

provocasset.... Nunc humiliter reddens rationem, quod *non possent jejunare filii sponsi quamdiu cum eis esset sponsus, postea vero jejunaturos* promittens, *cum ablatus ab eis sponsus esset.*

illis est sponsus facere jejunare? [35] Venient autem dies cum ablatus fuerit ab illis sponsus, tunc jejunabunt in illis diebus.

In ver. 33, for obsecrationes a has orationes, and for edunt manducant: a and b also have quamdiu (Vulg. cum) in ver. 35.

Equally erroneous was Marcion's interpretation of the concluding verses of the chapter which dealt with the distinction between old and new. He indeed was intoxicated with 'new wine'—though the real 'new wine' had been prophesied as far back as Jer. iv. 4 and Is. xliii. 19—but He to whom belonged the new wine and the new bottles also belonged the old. The difference between the old and new dispensations was of developement and progression, not of diversity or contrariety. Both had one and the same Author.

Errasti in illa etiam domini pronuntiatione qua videtur nova et vetera discernere. Inflatus es *utribus veteribus* et excerebratus es *novo vino:* atque ita *veteri,* i. e. priori evangelio *pannum* haereticae *novitatis adsuisti* ... *Vinum novum* is *non committit in veteres utres* qui et veteres utres non habuerit, et *novum additamentum nemo inicit veteri vestimento* nisi cui non defuerit vetus vestimentum.

Luke v. 36-38: [36] Dicebat autem et similitudinem ad illos quia nemo commissuram a vestimento novo inmittit in vestimentum vetus .... [37] Et nemo mittit vinum novum in utres veteres .... [38] Sed vinum novum in utres novos mittendum est.

Of the phrases peculiar to Tertullian's version of Marcion's text, a has pannum (-no) and adsuisti (-it).

It is observed that Tertullian does not quote verse 39, which is omitted by D, a, b, c, e, ff, l, and perhaps also by Eusebius.

Two of the Scholia of Epiphanius (Adv. Haer. 322 D sqq.), nos. 1 and 2, have reference to this chapter.

Σχόλ. α'. Ἀπελθὼν δεῖξον σεαυτὸν τῷ ἱερεῖ καὶ προσένεγκε περὶ τοῦ καθαρισμοῦ σου, καθὼς προσέταξε Μωυσῆς, ἵνα ᾖ μαρτύριον τοῦτο ὑμῖν.

Luke v. 14. Ἀπελθὼν δεῖξον σεαυτὸν τῷ ἱερεῖ, καὶ προσένεγκε περὶ τοῦ καθαρισμοῦ σου, καθὼς προσέταξεν Μωυσῆς, εἰς μαρτύριον αὐτοῖς.

v. l. ἵνα εἰς μαρτύριον ἦν (D¹, ᾖ D²) ὑμῖν τοῦτο D, (a, b), c, ff, l.

The comment of Epiphanius on this is similar to that of Tertullian. To bid the leper 'do as Moses commanded,' was practically to sanction the law of Moses. Epiphanius expressly accuses Marcion of falsifying the phrase 'for a testimony unto them.' He says that he changed 'them' to 'you,' without however, even in this perverted form, preventing the text from recoiling upon his own head (διέστρεψας δὲ τὸ ῥητόν, ὦ Μαρκίων, ἀντὶ τοῦ εἰπεῖν ' εἰς μαρτύριον αὐτοῖς' μαρτύριον λέγων ' ὑμῖν.' καὶ τοῦτο σαφῶς ἐψεύσω κατὰ τῆς σαυτοῦ κεφαλῆς.

Σχόλ. β'. Ἵνα δὲ εἰδῆτε ὅτι ἐξουσίαν ἔχει ὁ υἱὸς τοῦ ἀνθρώπου ἀφιέναι ἁμαρτίας ἐπὶ τῆς γῆς.

Luke v. 24. Ἵνα δὲ εἰδῆτε ὅτι ἐξουσίαν ἔχει ὁ υἱὸς τοῦ ἀνθρώπου ἐπὶ τῆς γῆς ἀφιέναι ἁμαρτίας.

In this order, ℵ, A, C, D, rel., a, c, e, Syrr. Pst. and Hcl., (Memph.), Goth., Arm., Aeth.; ἐξ. ἐχ. after ὁ ὑ. τ. ἀ., B, L, Ξ, K, Vulg., b, f, g¹, ff, l.

By calling Himself 'Son of Man,' Epiphanius says, our

Lord asserts His proper manhood and repels Docetism, and, by claiming 'power upon earth,' He declares that earth not to belong to an alien creation.

Reverting to Tertullian, we observe, (1) that the narrative of the draught of fishes, with the fear of Peter, and the promise *in this form*, 'Thou shalt catch men' (Μὴ φοβοῦ· ἀπὸ τοῦ νῦν ἀνθρώπους ἔσῃ ζωγρῶν; the other Synoptists have, Δεῦτε ὀπίσω μου, καὶ ποιήσω ὑμᾶς ἁλιεῖς ἀνθρώπων), are found only in St. Luke; (2) that the second section of the chapter, the healing of the leper, is placed by the other Synoptists in a different order, by Mark immediately after our Lord's retirement into solitude (= Luke iv. 42-44), and by Matthew after the Sermon on the Mount; the phrase εἰς μαρτύριον αὐτοῖς is common to all three Gospels, but in the text of St. Luke alone is there the variant Ut sit vobis &c.; (3) that, while the remaining sections follow in the same order in all the Synoptics, still there is much to identify the text from which Tertullian is quoting with that of Luke. Thus, in the account of the case of Levi, the third Evangelist alone has the word τελώνην (= publicanum) and ὑγιαίνοντες (= sani; the other Gospels ἰσχύοντες = valentes); in the question as to the practice of the disciples of John, he alone has the allusion to prayers (δεήσεις ποιοῦνται) and the combination 'eat and drink' (the other Gospels, οὐ νηστεύουσιν): he too has the simple ἐπίβλημα, for ἐπίβλημα ῥάκους ἀγνάφου. It seems quite incredible that these accumulated coincidences should be merely the result of accident.

But this is only the beginning. The same kind of coincidences run uniformly all through the Gospel. From the next chapter, Luke vi, Marcion had, in due order, the plucking of the ears of corn on the sabbath day ('rubbing them with their hands,' Luke and Marcion alone), the precedent of David and his companions and the shewbread, the watching *of the Pharisees* (so Luke only) to see if He would heal on the sabbath day, the healing of the withered hand—with an exact resemblance to the text of Luke and divergence from the other Gospels (licetne animam liberare an perdere? ψυχὴν ἀπολέσαι Luke, ἀποκτεῖναι Mark), in the order and words of Luke alone, the retreat into the mountain for prayer, the selection of the twelve Apostles, and then, in a strictly Lucan form and introduced precisely at the same point, the Sermon on the Mount, the blessing on 'the poor' (not the 'poor in spirit'), on those 'who hunger' (not on those 'who hunger and thirst after righteousness'), on those 'who weep, for they shall laugh' (not on those 'who mourn, for they shall be comforted'), with an exact translation of St. Luke and difference from St. Matthew, the clause relating to those who are persecuted and reviled: then follow the 'woes;' to the rich, 'for ye have received your consolation;' to 'those who are full, for they shall hunger;' to 'those who laugh now, for they shall mourn:' and so on almost verse by verse.

It is surely needless to go further. There are indeed very rarely what seem to be reminiscences of the other Gospels (e.g. 'esurierunt discipuli' in the parallel to Luke vi. 1), but the total amount of resemblance to St. Luke and divergence from St. Matthew and St. Mark is overwhelming. Of course the remainder of the evidence can easily be produced if necessary, but I do not think it will long remain in doubt that our present St. Luke was really the foundation of the Gospel that Marcion used.

INDEX I.

References to the Four Gospels.

The asterisk indicates that the passage in question is discussed in some detail.

St. Matthew.

PAGE.

I. 1 .... 51, 52.
   2-6 ...... 91.
   18 ....: 51, 52, *330.
   18 ff. ...... 103, 110.
   18-25 .... 52, 91.
   21 .... 91, 104.
   23 .... 92.

II. 1 .... 92.
   1-7 ...... 93.
   1-23 ...... 78, 140 ff.
   2 .... 92.
   5, 6 ..... 92.
   6 .... 20, 21, 24, 46.
   11 .... 92.
   12 .... 93.
   13 .... 52.
   13-15 .... 93.
   16 .... 93.
   17, 18 .... 93.
   18 .... 45.
   22 .... 93.

III. 2 ...... 93.
   4 .... 93.
   8 .... 333, 336, 337, 338, 342.
   10 .... 51.
   11, 12 .... 94, 113, 121.
   15 .... *80, *108, 133, 225.
   16 .... 94.
   18 .... 336.

IV. 1 ...... 94.
   8-10 ..... 163.
   9 .... 94.
   10 .... 132.
   11 .... 94.
   17 .... 95.
   18 .... 95.
   23 .... 95.

St. Matthew.

PAGE.

V. 1-48 .... 154.
   3 .... 163.
   4, 5 ..... 194, 333, *342.
   7 .... *62 ff.
   8 .... 163.
   10 .... *85 f.
   11 .... 86.
   13, 14 .... 49.
   14 .... 104.
   16 .... 114, 121, 134, 333, 336, 337, 338, *342.
   17 .... 53.
   17, 18 .... 52, 163.
   18 .... 49, 52, *172 f., 196.
   20 .... 95, 104, 115, 121.
   21-48 .... 163.
   22 .... 114, 121, 134, 331.
   28 .... 95, 104, 113, 133, 251, 333.
   29 .... 113, 133.
   29, 30 .... 154.
   29-32 .... 95.
   32 .... 113, 154, 251.
   34 .... 52, 95, 114, *122.
   37 .... 52, 95, 114, *122, 134, 164.
   38, 39 .... 259.
   39, 40 .... 114, 127, 132, 249.
   41 .... 114, 121.
   42 .... 73, 95, 113.
   44 .... 86, 95, 114.
   44, 45 .... 164, 249.
   45 .... 52, 95, 113, 164, *174.
   46 .... *250.
   48 .... 86, 333, 336, 337, 338.

VI. 1 ...... 104, 113, 121.
   1-34 ..... 154.
   6 .... 164.
   8 .... 132, 164, 174.

St. Matthew.

	PAGE.
10	333, 336, 337, 338.
13	87.
14	62, 86.
19	238.
19, 20	95, 113, 121.
20	113, 133.
21	95, 113, 134.
25–27	113.
25–37	95.
32	*164, *173 f.
32, 33	113.

VII. 1–29	154.
2	62, 164.
6	52, 193.
7	164.
9–11	164, *182.
12	62, 164.
13, 14	164, *174, 289.
15	52, 104, 114, *131, 164.
16	114.
19	114.
21	104, 114, 121, *181.
22	78, 134.
22, 23	95, 114, 121.
28, 29	119.

VIII. 9	49, 51, 164.
11	52, 132.
11, 12	95, 114, 164.
17	24.
26	54.
28–34	52, 53.

IX. 1–8	94.
13	*74, 95, 113, 164.
16	52.
17	52.
22	94.
29–31	94.
33	94.

X. 1	95.
8	49, 78.
10	166.
11	*182.
13	164.
15	164.
16	52, *77 f.

St. Matthew.

	PAGE.
22	114.
26	49, 52.
28	115, 127, 132, 164, *183.
29, 30	165.
33	52, 53.
38, 39	154.
40	80.

XI. 5	44, 78.
7	52.
10	24, 338.
11	165, 333, 336, 337, 338, 342.
12–15	95, 113.
18	52.
25	50, 165.
25–27	54, 332.
27	115, *131, *132, 165, 281.
28	50, 52, 165.

XII. 1–8	*149.
7	164.
9–14	*150.
17–21	44.
18–21	21.
24	78.
25	*258.
26	165.
31, 32	53.
34	165.
41	165.
42	165.
43	50.
48	52.

XIII. 1–58	154.
3	96.
3 ff.	115.
5	338.
11	54.
15	334, 336, 337, 338.
16	165.
24–30	53.
25	51.
26	*144.
34	115, 119.
35	21, 165, *169 ff.

INDEX I.   375

St. Matthew.

	PAGE.
37–39	53.
38	51.
39	165.
42, 43	114.
XIV. 1	150.
3	94.
3–12	215.
6	94.
XV. 4–6	53.
4–8	*258.
4–9	54.
8	27, *69.
13	80.
15	165.
17	51.
20	53.
21–28	165.
26	334, 336, 337, 338.
36	337.
XVI. 1	104.
1–4	121.
4	96, 104, 115.
15–18	96.
16	165, *175.
19	165.
21	96, 127.
24	75.
24, 25	154.
26	113, 121, 133.
XVII. 3	94.
5	165, 334.
11	94.
11–13	113, *118 ff.
12, 13	93.
13	104.
XVIII. 1–35	154.
3	*292.
6	66.
7	165.
8	53.
8, 9	154.
10	50, 165.
19	80.
XIX. 4	177.

St. Matthew.

	PAGE.
6	53, *258.
8	166, 177, *258.
9	154.
10–12	53.
11, 12	*192.
12	*113, *121.
13	74.
16, 17	96, 114, *132, 166, 332.
17	127.
19	328.
22	119.
26	*126.
XX. 8	292.
16	71.
19	292.
20–28	215.
XXI. 1	96.
5	115.
12, 13	115.
16	165.
20–22	215.
23	50.
33	53.
42	31.
XXII. 9	166.
11	96, 166.
14	*71 f., 166.
21	96.
24	23.
29	166, 177.
30	53, 126.
32	177.
37	166, 178.
37, 38	96.
38	114.
39	114.
40	114.
44	*75.
XXIII. 2	96.
2, 3	166.
5	53.
10	50.
13	166.
15	53, 104, 115.
18	53.

INDEX I.

St. Matthew.

	PAGE.
20	53.
23	53, 115.
24	104, 115.
25	53.
25, 26	166, *176.
27	115.
29	53.
35	53.
XXIV. 1-51	154.
3	166.
24	114, 145.
45-51	167, *184 f.
XXV. 1-46	154.
14-30	96.
21	167.
26, 27	167.
34	53, 96.
41	96, 114, 121, *131, 134, 167.
XXVI. 1-75	154.
17, 18	53.
24	53, *66 ff.
30	96.
31	23, 46, *76, 97.
36, 37	96.
38	50, 51.
39	50, 115.
41	87.
43	119.
56	96, 97.
56, 57	148.
57	96.
64	*142.
XXVII. 9	170.
9, 10	*21 f., 25.
11 f.	97.
14	97, 225.
35	97.
39 ff.	97.
42	97.
43	115.
46	50, 51, 97, 116.
57-60	97.
XXVIII. 1 ff.	97.
12-15	98, 104.
19	98, 104, 167.

St. Mark.

	PAGE.
I. 1	53.
2	24, 170.
4	53.
17	225.
22	119, 225.
24	334, 336, 337, 338.
26	25.
II. 23-28	*149.
28	225.
III. 1-6	*150.
17	95.
23	225.
25	258.
29	53.
IV. 1-34	148.
11	54.
12	23.
33, 34	119.
34	165, *179 f.
V. 1-20	53.
31	49.
VI. 3	93, 104.
11	164.
14	150.
17-29	215.
VII. 6	27, *69 f., 258.
6-13	54, 56.
7	258.
10, 11	258.
11-13	53.
13	54.
21, 22	53.
24-30	165.
VIII. 29	175.
31	127.
34	197.
IX. 7	334, 336, 337, 338, 342.
21	104.
43	53.
47	113.
X. 5	166.
5, 6	177, 258.
6	249.

INDEX I.

St. Mark.

	PAGE.
8	166.
9	53, 258.
17	166.
18	50.
19	24.
21	49.
22	119.
27	*126.
37–45	215.

XI. 20–26 .. 215.

XII. 17 .... 227.
    20 .... 126.
    24 .... 166, 177.
    27 .... 166, *177.
    29 .... 166, *178.
    30 .... 166.
    38–44 .... 148.

XIII. 2 .... 166, *177.
    22 .... 114.

XIV. 12, 13 .. 118.
    12–14 .... 53.
    40 .... 119.
    51, 52 .... 54.

XV. 14 .... 225.
    34 .... 116.

XVI. 14–16 .. 148.

St. Luke.

I. 1–4 ...... 54.
   1–80 ...... 213.
   3 .... 56, 123, 224.
   6 .... 252.
   7 .... 227.
   7–10 ...... 225.
   8 .... 224, 227.
   9 .... 224, 227.
   12 .... 227.
   13 .... 225, 226.
   15 .... 225, 228.
   17 .... 54.
   18, 19 .... 225.
   19 .... 228.
   20 .... 224.

St. Luke.

	PAGE.
20–22	225.
21	224, 228.
23	228.
24	227.
26	91, 227.
27	227.
28	225.
29	225.
31	91, 228.
32	228.
33	227.
34	225.
34, 35	54.
35	91, *195, *200, 225, 228.
36	227, 228.
39	226.
41	225, 228.
48	224.
55	225.
56	227, 228.
57	92, 228.
61	225.
62	224, 225.
64	225.
67	225, 228, 253.
69	227.
73	225.
74	227.
76	54, 228.
77	226.
78	228.
80	227.

II. 1, 2 ...... 92, 106.
    1–52 ...... 213.
    4 .... 92, 227.
    6 .... 224.
    7 .... 92, 226.
    8 .... 225.
    11 .... 54.
    13 .... 225, 228.
    14 .... 54, 228.
    15 .... 225, 226.
    16 .... 228.
    18 .... 225.
    19 .... 228.
    20 .... 228.
    21 .... 228.

INDEX I.

St. Luke.

	PAGE.
21, 22	224.
22	228.
24	223.
25	225.
26	225.
27	224.
28	50, 226.
29	224.
33	227.
34	225.
35	226.
36	225.
37	227.
39	224, 226, 228.
40	228.
41	224.
42	196, 224, 227.
43	224, 228.
45	228.
46	225.
48, 49	54, 225.
49	50, 226.
50	225.
51	225.
52	228.
66	225.
III. 1	227.
1–38	213.
3	93, 226.
12–14	224.
13	226.
15	224.
16	127, 225, 226, 227.
16, 17	95.
17	49, 54.
19	224.
20	95.
21	224, 226.
21, 22	95.
22	108, 133, 225.
23	54, 93, 224, 225, 227, 228.
31–34	91.
IV. 1	225, 228.
1–13	213.
4	225.
6	226.
6–8	163.

St. Luke.

	PAGE.
7	227.
8	227.
10	224.
13	94, 224.
14	224.
16	225.
17	225.
17–20	213.
18, 19	33.
19	23.
20	225.
24	213, 230.
25	227.
32	119.
42, 43	363.
42–44	371.
V. 1	371.
1–11	364.
1–39	363.
12–14	365.
14	54, 231, 370, 371.
17–26	94, 367.
24	370.
27–32	368.
32	74, 95.
33–35	368.
36–38	369.
39	231.
VI. 1	372.
1–5	*149.
1–49	371.
6–11	*150.
13	95.
14	*62 ff.
20	*85, *163.
27, 28	113, 163.
29	114, 127, 259.
30	73, 95, 113, 127.
31	62, 164.
32	113.
34	113, 251.
35	163, 174.
36	50, 113, 131, 132.
36, 37	50.
36–38	*85.
37, 38	62.
45	165.
46	164, *181.

St. Luke.

	PAGE.
VII. 2	*62 ff.
8	49, 164.
11–18	95.
12	*62 ff.
24–28	219.
26	334, 342.
27	54.
28	165, 334.
29–35	213.
30	233.
35	50.
36–38	54.
VIII. 1–3	214.
5	96.
10	24, 54.
19	219.
23	54.
26–39	53.
41	95.
IX. 5	164.
7	150.
17, 18	215.
20	175.
22	96, 115, 127.
55	233.
57, 58	50, 51.
60	50.
61	54.
61, 62	50, 51.
62	54.
X. 3	76.
5, 6	164.
7	166, *182.
10–12	164.
16	114, 134.
18	166.
19	95, 105, 115, *125.
20	166.
21	50, 165, 220.
21, 22	54.
22	165, 232.
23	144.
24	165.
25	232.
37	224.
XI. 2	232.

St. Luke.

	PAGE.
9	164.
11–13	164, *182.
14	94.
17	258.
22	220.
29–32	213, 220.
32	164.
39	175.
42	96, 115, 127.
47	53.
49–51	213, 220, 230.
52	96, 105, 115, 132, 166.
XII. 4, 5	115, 127, 164, *183.
6, 7	165.
9	54.
10	53.
14	232.
22–24	95, 113.
30	164, *172 f.
38	232.
42–46	167, *184.
48	115, 126, 134.
50	50, 54.
XIII. 1 sqq.	220.
1–9	213, 220.
6	224.
7	224.
7, 8	227.
8	228.
24	*174.
26, 27	95, 114.
27	134.
28	220.
28, 29	95.
29	164.
29–35	213.
31–35	220.
33	226.
34	225.
XIV. 27	49, 51, 54. 197
XV. 4	50.
8	50.
11–32	213.
13	226.
14	227.
17	227.

St. Luke.

	PAGE.
18	226.
20	226, 227.
22	225.
24	225.
25	224.
26	225.
29	227.

XVI. 12 .... 232, 235.
16 .... 95, 113, 127.
17 .... *172 f., 220.

XVII. 1, 2 .. *66.
2 .... 68, 232, 234.
5-10 ..... 213.
9 .... 228.
9, 10 ..... 226.

XVIII. 6-8 .. 166.
18, 19 .... 96, 114, 132, 166.
19 .... 127, 232.
27 .... *115, 126.
31 .... 225.
31-34 .... 213.
34 .... 225.
35-43 .... 94.

XIX. 5 ...... 50, 166.
9 .... 166.
17 .... 167.
22, 23 .... 167.
29 .... 96.
29-48 .... 213.
33-39 .... 225.
35 .... 227.
37 .... 224, 228.
37-48 .... 226.
38 .... 228.
41 .... 224.
42 .... 50, 51, 224.
43 .... 166, 228.
46 .... 96.
47 .... 225.

XX. 9 ...... 224, 225, 227.
9-18 ..... 213.
14 .... 225.
17 .... 225.
19 .... 224, 225.
21 .... 143.
22 .... 96.

St. Luke.

	PAGE.
22-25	115.
24	134.
25	96.
35, 36	96, 115, 126.
35	220.
37, 38	213, 230.
38	177, 230.

XXI. 1-4 .... 213.
4 .... 226.
18 .... 213, 232, 234.
21 .... 225.
21, 22 .... 213, 220.
22 .... 224, 228.
27 .... 232.
28 .... 226.
34 .... 54.

XXII. 9-11 .. 53.
16-18 .... 213.
17 .... 226.
18 .... 220.
18-36 .... 224.
19 .... 134.
19, 20 .... 96, 115.
28-30 .... 213, 230.
30 .... 220.
35-38 .... 213.
37 .... 224, 226.
38 .... 227.
42-44 .... 96, 115.
43, 44 .... *124 ff., 134, 233.
53, 54 .... 148.
66 .... 96.

XXIII. 1 ff. .. 97.
2 .... 232, 234.
5 .... 224.
7 .... 97.
34 .... 97, 134, 143, 167, 233.
35 .... 97.
46 .... 97, 116.

XXIV. 1 ff. .. 97.
21 .... 97.
26 .... 97.
32 .... 97.
38, 39 .... 54.
39 .... *81.
40 .... 97.
42 .... 54.

INDEX I.

St. Luke.

	PAGE.
46	97.
47-53	213.
49	228.
50	97.
51	224.
52	228.
53	225.

St. John.

	PAGE.
I. 1, 2	50.
1-3	51, 55.
3	50, 301, *305.
4	50, 302.
5	50, 52, *304 f.
9	298.
13	334, 336, 337, 338.
14	50, 52.
18	302.
19	93.
19, 20	*279.
23	55, *279.
28	324.
II. 4	298.
16, 17	55.
III. 3-5	*282, *290.
5	*275.
6	51, 338.
8	336.
12	55.
14	55, 272.
16	296.
36	334, 336, 337, 338.
IV. 6	51.
V. 2	336.
3, 4	335, 336, 337, 338.
4	336.
8	55.
17	55.
18	55.
43	335, 336, 337, 338.
46	55.
VI. 15	55.
39	335, 336, 337, 338.

St. John.

	PAGE.
51	335, 336, 337, 338, 341.
53	55.
54	*275.
55	*275.
70	55.
VII. 8	324.
38	25.
42	25.
VIII. 17	21.
40	55.
44	55.
IX. 1-3	*293.
X. 8	301.
9	*289.
23, 24	307.
27	*290.
30	308.
XI. 54	55, 307.
XII. 14, 15	23.
22	55.
27	50.
30	335, 336, 337, 338.
40	21.
41	55.
XIII. 18	21.
XIV. 2	51, 52.
6	55.
10	55.
XV. 25	23.
XVI. 2	*306.
3	281.
XVII. 3	55, 308.
11, 12	55.
14	*296.
XVIII. 36	55.
XIX. 36	23.
37	46, *280.

INDEX II.

Chronological and Analytical.

Writer.	Works extant.	Date A.D.	Evangelical Documents used.	Page.
Clement of Rome.	One genuine Epistle addressed to the Corinthians.	c. 95–100.	Traces, perhaps probable, of the three Synoptics.	26 ff., 58 ff., 269.
Barnabas.	Pseud-epigraphal Epistle.	c. 100–125.	Probably St. Matthew, perhaps St. Luke, possibly the fourth Gospel.	31 ff., 71 ff., 270 ff.
Ignatius	Three short Epistles, probably genuine. [Spurious, S. R.]	107 or 115.	Probably St. Matthew, and perhaps St. John.	36, 76 ff., 274 ff.
	Seven short Epistles, perhaps genuine. [Spurious, S. R.]	115 or c. 150.	Probably St. Matthew, perhaps also probably St. John.	
Hermas.	Allegorical work, entitled the 'Shepherd.'	c. 135–140.	No distinct traces of any writing of Old or New Testament.	273 f.
Polycarp.	Short Epistle to Philippians, probably genuine. [Spurious, S. R.]	c. 140–155.	Doubtful traces of St. Matthew, probable of 1 John.	36, 82 ff., 277 f.
Presbyters.	Quoted by Irenaeus.	c. 140?	Probably St. John.	296 ff.
Papias.	Short fragments in Eusebius.	†155. [see pp. 145, 82; 164–167, S. R.]	Some account of works written by St. Matthew and St. Mark, but probably not our present Gospels in their present form.	145 ff.
Basilides. Basilidians.	Allusions, not certain, in Hippolytus, Clem. Alex., Epiphanius, &c.	c. 125. ?	Certain use of St. Luke and St. John, perhaps probably by Basilides himself.	188 ff., 298 ff.

INDEX II. 383

Writer.	Works extant.	Date. A.D.	Evangelical Documents used.	Page.
Marcion.	Copious references in Tertullian and Epiphanius.	c. 140.	Certainly the third Gospel, with text already corrupt.	204 ff.
Justin Martyr.	Two Apologies and Dialogue against Tryphon.	† 148. [166-167, S.R.]	Three Synoptic Gospels either separately or in Harmony, probably the fourth Gospel, and also an Apocryphal Gospel or Gospels; text showing marks of corruption.	40 ff., 88 ff., 278 ff.
	Old Latin Translation of N.T.	c. 150.	Four Canonical Gospels, with corrupt text.	319 ff., 333 ff.
Valentinus. Valentinians.	Allusions, not certain, in Hippolytus, &c.	c. 140. before 178.	References to all four Gospels, but not clear by whom made.	196 ff., 301 ff.
Clement.	Nineteen pseud-epigraphal 'Homilies.'	c. 160?	Four Canonical Gospels (possibly in a Harmony), with other Apocryphal sources to some extent.	37 ff., 161 ff., 288 ff.
Hegesippus.	Few fragments, chiefly preserved by Eusebius.	fl. 157-180.	Apparent traces of St. Matthew and St. Luke.	138 ff.
Tatian.	Few allusions, 'Address to Greeks.'	fl. 150-170.	Diatessaron, probably consisting of our four Gospels. Quotations from St. John in Orat. ad Graec.	238 ff., 304 ff.
	Old Syriac Translation of N.T.	c. 160?	Four Canonical Gospels, with corrupt text.	322 ff., 340 ff.
	Muratorian Fragment.	c. 170.	Four Gospels as Canonical.	263 ff., 308.
Ptolemaeus.	Allusions in Irenaeus, &c., fragment in Epiphanius.	before 178.	Clear references to St. Matthew and St. John.	255 ff., 301 f.

Writer.	Works extant.	Date. A.D.	Evangelical Documents used.	Page.
Heracleon.	Allusions in Irenaeus, &c., fragments in Origen.	before 178.	Third and fourth Gospels.	275, 302 f.
Melito.	Few slight fragments.	c. 176.	Doubtful indirect allusion to Canon of N.T.	244 f.
Apollinaris.	Two slight fragments.	176–180.	Allusion to supposed discrepancy between Gospels. Fourth Gospel.	246 ff., 307 f.
Athenagoras.	An Apology and tract on the Resurrection.	c. 177.	One fairly clear quotation from St. Matthew, perhaps others from St. Mark and St. John.	248 ff., 308.
Churches of Vienne and Lyons.	An Epistle.	177.	Clear allusions to St. Luke and St. John, perhaps also to St. Matthew.	251 ff., 306.
Celsus.	Fragments in Origen.	c. 178.	Somewhat vague traces of all four Gospels.	260 ff., 307 f.
Irenaeus.	Treatise 'Against Heresies.'	c. 140–202.	Four Gospels as Canonical, with corrupt text.	49 ff., 315 ff., 326, 329 ff.
Clement of Alexandria.	Several considerable works.	fl. 185–211.	Four Gospels as Canonical, with corrupt text.	56, 317, 327.
Tertullian.	Voluminous works.	fl. 198–210.	Four Gospels as Canonical, with corrupt text.	318 ff., 327, 333 ff.

www.ingramcontent.com/pod-product-compliance
Lightning Source LLC
Chambersburg PA
CBHW030425300426
44112CB00009B/854